Incredibly Delicious

The Vegan Paradigm Cookbook

By

Gentle World

Gentle World Publishing * Kapa'au, Hawaii

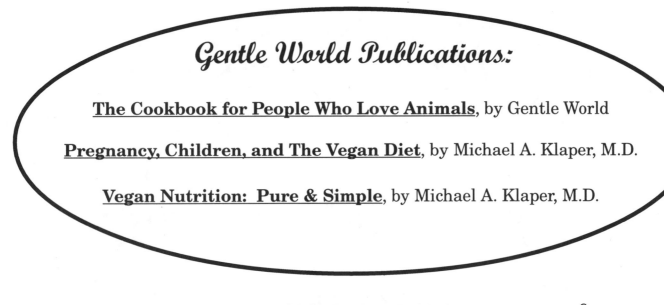

Gentle World Publications:

The Cookbook for People Who Love Animals, by Gentle World

Pregnancy, Children, and The Vegan Diet, by Michael A. Klaper, M.D.

Vegan Nutrition: Pure & Simple, by Michael A. Klaper, M.D.

OTABIND

Bound to stay open

This book is bound with the genuine OTABIND® process, advanced bookbinding technology using a special free-floating cover to provide a high-quality, durable and user-friendly volume.

Open the book at any desired page, press a finger down inside center ("hinge side" of pages) at first, as needed: they will lie flat for easy use.

Cover Design and Illustrations: by Sky Weil, Gentle Art

Text Layout: by Kadar St. John

Published by Gentle World Inc.
P.O. Box 238
Kapa'au, HI 96755

Library of Congress Card Number: 99-069594

ISBN # 0-929274-24-5

Printed on recycled paper with soy ink

"It often happens that
the universal belief of one age,
a belief from which no one was free
or could be free
without an extraordinary effort
of genius or courage,
becomes to a subsequent age,
so palpable an absurdity,
that the only difficulty is
to imagine how such an idea
could ever have appeared credible."

JOHN STUART MILL (1806-1873)
English author and philosopher

Dedication

To the shared vision
of a new world
of gentleness and love,
not in some far-off tomorrow
when the lion lives
in peace with the lamb;
but today, when we do.

Acknowledgments

We are grateful to all those who have contributed their talents which have culminated in this collection of recipes. To those who have been outstanding in their creativity and perseverance, we offer a very special *thank you...*

Light and **Sun Waldbaum** for inspiring and guiding The Vegan Paradigm, from conception to completion.

M. Joy Katz for preparing and testing the recipes, and for her diligence in researching quotes and recording text.

Golden Jennifer Gibson for long hours at the computer, bringing it all together, time and time again.

Justice and **Deer Fields** and **Andy Walker** for their seemingly endless editing.

Freya and **H. Jay Dinshah** for their many helpful suggestions and invaluable expertise.

Vegan, Magic, Miracles and **Beautiful** for proving that dogs can be vegan too!

"The vegetarian ideal as a concept
which embodied a moral imperative-
'thou shalt not kill for food'-
made its first impact on history
in India and Greece
at around the same time, 500 B.C.,
within the lifetimes of both
The Buddha and Pythagoras."

COLIN SPENCER
British Writer and Publisher
The Heretic's Feast: A History of Vegetarianism,
Fourth Estate, London 1994

Table of Contents

Vegan: ('vē-gan) 1. one who chooses a diet and life-style free of consuming animal products, and of supporting business that exploits animals 2. adj. containing no ingredient derived from the animal kingdom.

Paradigm: ('par-å-dime) n. an outstandingly clear example, model or archetype

Foreword

There is no force powerful enough to stem the tide of an idea whose time has come. We can no longer, in good conscience or in good health, continue to use animals for food.

The Vegan Paradigm is not a fad that will pass with time. It is a necessary shift in thinking, that will lead to a heightened empathy and concern for others. It is the expansion of compassion, which is the single most important step in the next evolution of humankind.

When we consider the wolf and the elephant, the shark and the ox, the weasel and the deer, we find that it is not the size or strength of animals, but how they obtain their food, that determines whether their nature is violent or gentle.

We humans are also animals. Therefore, it is how our food is obtained that determines our own nature: violent or gentle. A gentle human nature is essential if we are to evolve; and we must evolve, if we are to survive.

Light
Founder & President
Gentle World

Introduction

You are cordially invited to enjoy a cuisine for the ages - ancient yet modern, simple but elegant, a key to better health, and now - thanks to <u>Incredibly Delicious:</u> <u>The Vegan Paradigm Cookbook</u> - made to taste fabulous! Through many years of innovative cooking (and endless tasting), the people of Gentle World have created this sumptuous collection of vegan (pure vegetarian) recipes. The pages are lovingly filled with ideas for tasty breakfasts, lunches, dinners, soups, salads, side dishes and desserts - and richly seasoned with thoughtful quotes from across the centuries, to feed your heart, mind and spirit.

As a physician, I can attest that if all my patients adopted a diet based on these high-fiber, cholesterol-free foods, we would have a much healthier population. Lower risk of heart disease and colon cancer, as well as actual reduction of elevated blood pressure and cholesterol levels, are predictable benefits from nourishing your body on the ingredients utilized in these recipes. Witnessing the wonderful changes in people as they evolve their diet to this style of eating - becoming more energetic and functional while escaping the plagues of obesity and chronic disease - is always a great joy for this doctor. How wonderful that such powerful medicine can be created in the kitchen!

As a man who loves great-tasting food, I can also attest (after having enjoyed many of these delectable dishes myself) that you are in for a treat with every meal. As a person who wishes to bring peace and healing to my life and to our planet, I appreciate that the recipes in <u>Incredibly Delicious:</u> <u>The Vegan Paradigm Cookbook</u> allow me to remove the products of violence from my dining table, and thus to reduce damage and suffering in the world around me.

One could spend a lifetime eating these foods - in fact, I strongly encourage you to do so. Such a lifetime should be a long and healthy one, and sure to be filled with memorable culinary experiences. This banquet of a book celebrates the best in life and will be your guide to great eating for the next thousand years. I highly recommend it and invite you to enjoy the feast.

Michael A. Klaper, M.D.

Glossary of Ingredients

Agar-Agar - is a gelatin replacement. It is made from sea vegetables and is a gelling agent for cold recipes, such as jelled desserts or fruit pies.

Arrowroot - is powdered root starch that is a replacement for cornstarch. Use one tablespoon of arrowroot per each cup of liquid. It dissolves in liquid and thickens at a simmering temperature. Used in gravies and puddings.

Balanced-Mineral-Bouillon™ - is a formula created by Dr. Bronner and is found in the health food store. It is wonderful for making gravies, and is a flavorful food supplement that adds minerals and vitamins to any dish.

Barley - is one of the oldest cultivated grains. Scotch barley is the whole grain. The more commonly known "pearled barley", which cooks more quickly, is not a whole grain. The whole grain barley contains all nine essential amino acids.

Barley Malt - is a thick, brown syrup, which is about half as sweet as other sweeteners, with a rich, malty flavor. It is a complex carbohydrate made from combining the grain starch with enzymes. It contains B-vitamins and trace minerals.

Bragg™ Liquid Aminos - is an unfermented alternative to tamari or soy sauce. It has a delicious, lighter flavor and less sodium content.

Bran -is the husk of the grain that has been separated from the flour, either oat bran or wheat bran. Used for breading and coating in recipes.

Brown Rice Syrup - is a thick, pale amber, mild syrup made from brown rice and barley enzymes. It is a great honey substitute; sweeter than malt barley, but less sweet than most other sweeteners. Contains trace minerals.

Bulgur - is cracked whole wheat, steamed and dried. To prepare it, pour boiling water over it, cover, and let stand for 1 hour.

Carob - is a cocoa-like powder made from the seed pod of the evergreen carob tree. This chocolate substitute can be purchased raw or roasted. It is naturally sweet, high in fiber, low in fat, and does not contain the caffeine that chocolate does. Carob contains calcium, phosphorus, and iron. There are non-dairy carob chips available in health food stores.

Cold Pressed Oils - are extracted using pressure from a stone or hydraulic press. They are produced by a mechanical batch-pressing process in which heat-producing friction is minimized, so that temperatures remain below 120°. Expeller-pressed oils are produced through a chemical-free, continuous mechanical process in which friction can generate temperatures of up to 185°. Most commercially produced oil is extracted using heat and a volatile solvent, which is flashed off when the oil is heated to 212° and then distilled. The oil is then refined by bleaching, deodorizing, and winterizing.

Cold-pressed or expeller pressed oils are recommended. Safflower is a good all around oil, highest in polyunsaturated fats. Other good vegetable oils are: cold-pressed virgin olive, sunflower, rice bran, sesame and flax. Even cold-pressed oils are exposed to some heat and all processed oil is best used in moderation.

Cous-Cous - is a refined semolina product that has been pre-cooked and needs only to be rehydrated. It conveniently cooks in just minutes, but has less nutritional value than whole wheat cous-cous.

Date Sugar - is ground dehydrated dates. It is a source of vitamins and minerals.

Ener-G® Egg Replacer - is a powdered formula of starches and leavening that when mixed with liquid has an egg-like consistency. Ener-G egg replacer is available in health food stores.

Gluten Flour - is used for making seitan. It is mostly protein, rather than carbohydrate.

Kelp- a powdered form of seaweed with a slightly salty taste, rich in iodine, and a good salt substitute.

Maple Syrup - is produced in a brief yearly season when sugar maple sap is tapped. It comes in different grades of light to dark, but they all contain equal levels of minerals. To make a gallon of maple syrup, about 40 gallons of sap has to be collected and boiled down. During the boiling, the sap tends to foam up, causing the syrup-making process to slow down. To combat this problem a drop of fat or oil is added. (Lard, shortening, vegetable oil). The label does not designate this ingredient. When purchasing maple syrup, look for the kosher symbol, or call the company to see that they use vegetable-based defoamers. Use only 100% pure syrup, and refrigerate after opening. See 'Vegan Alternatives' for a list of companies whose syrup is vegan.

Millet - is a small golden grain which is the staple for nearly 1/3 of the world's population. It is easy to digest and one of the few non-acid forming grains. It is the staple of the Hunzas, renowned for their longevity. This protein-rich grain is high in iron, calcium, magnesium, potassium, vitamins and choline.

Miso - is a salty-flavored fermented paste from soybeans, rice or barley. It is rich in protein, minerals and vitamins. Purchase unpasteurized miso for nutritional benefits. Mix it with water and then add to soups or gravies during the last phase of cooking, in order to keep the nutrients alive. Do not boil it or it loses its nutritional properties. Light or white miso are lower in salt content and sweeter in flavor. Keep refrigerated. Add to salad dressings.

Non-irradiated Spices - The local health food store carries a full line of non-irradiated spices & herbs.

Nori - is a high protein, sun-dried red sea vegetable, pressed into sheets.

Nutritional Yeast - "Cheesy" flavored, yellow powder grown on molasses as a food supplement. A tablespoon of nutritional yeast sprinkled on your food will make vitamin B-12 supplementation convenient and delicious. Nutritional yeast is to be distinguished from "Brewer's Yeast", which may have a bitter taste. Red Star™ Primary Grown Nutritional Yeast 'Vegetarian Support Formula' is a reliable source of Vitamin B-12 that is not from an animal source. Avoid brands that are combined with whey. Nutritional yeast is an excellent source of high quality protein, B vitamins and minerals.

Oat Groats - are oats in a whole grain form. They can be soaked overnight for use in raw recipes. They can be cooked to make healthy whole grain cereals. The more commonly known oats are groats rolled into flakes. Quick-cooking oats are flakes rolled thinner by the application of more pressure. They have the same nutritional value as thicker rolled oats. Steel cut oat groats are easily soaked for raw dishes and breakfast cereals.

Quinoa - (pronounced keen-wa) is a light, fluffy, fast-cooking grain. It is an ancient grain, native to the Andes, now grown organically in Colorado. It has twice the protein found in rice, barley or corn and is high in iron and B-vitamins.

Rice - has been the staple food in most of Asia since 3000 B.C., and is currently the staple food for more than half the world's population. Rice supplies only a small amount of protein. It is a healthy carbohydrate that contains calcium, iron, zinc and most all of the B-vitamins. There are 25,000 varieties of rice! Brown rice retains the bran and the germ; white rice has these layers polished away during refining. Long-grain rice is generally fluffier, while short-grain has a sweeter taste, and is sticky in texture.

Rice Syrup - (also known as "yinny") is a thick syrup, less sweet than other sweeteners. It is a healthy alternative to honey. It is used to complement vinegar in salad dressings.

Sea Salt - is made from evaporated seawater, and retains more than seventy elements commonly found in seawater. Unrefined sea salt is high in trace minerals and contains no chemicals, sugar or added iodine. It is a good idea to regulate all salt intake.

Seitan - or "Wheat-Meat" is an excellent meat substitute. It is a better protein source than beef and it is low in fat. It is sold commercially or you can make it yourself from wheat gluten flour (see seitan recipe in the Entrées section). It is then ready for use as an ingredient in recipes requiring it.

Spike™ Seasoning - is an all purpose seasoning with 35 herbs and spices. The first ingredient is salt, but there is a salt-free Spike Seasoning, as well. The company also makes a seasoning called 'Vegit', which contains kelp.

Sorghum Molasses - is a dark syrup made from the sorghum plant which is related to millet. The stalks of the plant are crushed and the sweet syrup released is cooked and clarified into a dark syrup, rich in minerals such as potassium, iron, calcium and the B-vitamins.

Stock - is water that vegetables have been cooked in. Use it to make gravies and sauces.

Sucanat™ - stands for Sugar Cane Natural. It is a high quality, granulated, evaporated cane juice sweetener. It can replace sugar in recipes. It is the sweetener used most throughout this book.

Tahini - is sesame seed butter. It comes raw or roasted. It is rich in calcium, protein and phosphorus. It needs to be mixed before use as the oil separates from the ground-up seed paste. Storage life is excellent. Combining with water in any measure however, considerably reduces shelf life.

Tamari - is a natural soy sauce made from fermented soybeans. It contains about 1000 mg. of sodium per tablespoon. It often contains wheat.

Tempeh - is a fermented soy product and meat substitute, originally from Indonesia. It is usually sold frozen in health food stores. It is a perishable food, so store frozen or refrigerated. Steaming tempeh before use fluffs it up and allows it to absorb the flavors more easily.

Texturized Vegetable Protein - (known as T.V.P.) is a hearty, high protein food made by processing defatted soy flour to extract most of its soluble sugars. T.V.P. is used in place of meat in chili, lasagna, and casseroles. It is usually fortified with Vitamin B-12.

Tofu - is a truly versatile, easily digested, soy "cheese" made from soybean milk and sold in block form. It is high in protein and rich in vitamins, minerals and polyunsaturated fat, with no cholesterol. It comes in silken, soft and firm textures. The firm is best for slicing into cutlets or cubing into bite size chunks. The soft and silken are for mashing and blending. Tofu barely has any smell at all when it is fresh. Tofu takes on the flavor of whatever seasonings are used, sweet or spicy. Store it in a refrigerator, submerged in cold water and change the water daily. When purchasing packaged tofu, check the expiration date. (If you are using tofu in uncooked dishes, submerge in boiling water to kill any bacteria. Don't leave it in the water more than a few minutes or it changes the texture of the tofu. This does not apply to tofu bought in sealed packaged containers.)

Trocomare™ or **Herbamare™**- herb seasoned sea salt. (Trocomare is spicier.) Both are made with fresh organically grown herbs and found in health food stores.

VeganRella™ Cheese Alternative - is a 100% non-dairy alternative to cheese. It is free of soy as well. It comes in several flavors as well as cream cheese spread. It is firm when cold and melts when heated. It is found in health food stores.

Vanilla - Use pure, non-alcoholic vanilla. For non-baking purposes, try a vanilla powder (no alcohol). Use it in the same proportions as the liquid vanilla extract.

Vinegar - The two recommended vinegars to use are brown rice vinegar or unpasteurized apple cider vinegar. Rice vinegar has half the acidity .

Whole Wheat Flour - is used for baking breads rather than for making pastry.

Whole Wheat Pastry Flour - is a lighter flour, used for pastries and cakes.

> *"I know of no more encouraging fact than the unquestionable ability of man to elevate his life by a conscious endeavor."*
>
> HENRY DAVID THOREAU (1817-1862)
> American essayist and naturalist

Vegan Sources of Minerals and Vitamins

Calcium - broccoli, kale, collard and turnip greens, calcium-precipitated tofu, blackstrap molasses, bok choy, sesame seeds, calcium-fortified soy milk, almonds, corn tortilla.

Magnesium - brown rice, cooked spinach, black/pinto beans, almonds, nuts, legumes, cooked oatmeal, wheat germ/bran, whole grains, green leafy vegetables, broccoli, bananas, peanuts.

Potassium - raisins, raw spinach, potatoes, bananas, raw cauliflower, avocados, kiwi, dried fruits, tomatoes, dried apricots, oranges, grapefruit, strawberries, honeydew, cantaloupe.

Zinc - whole grain products, legumes, soybeans, nuts, sunflower seeds, pumpkin seeds, nuts, wheat germ, yeast, maple syrup, garbanzo beans, raw collard greens, spinach, almonds.

Phosphorus - pinto beans, cereal grains, almonds, nuts, dried beans, peas, lentils, peanuts, bread & baked goods, brown rice, avocados, spinach, many vegetables, yeast.

Iron - green leafy vegetables, legumes & beans, nuts & seeds, blackstrap molasses, dried fruits, watermelon, cream of wheat, prune juice, spinach, cereals & other grain products.

Iodine - iodized salt, sea vegetables, kelp, plants depending on soil iodine content.

Selenium - grain products & kidney beans (depending on soil grown in), brazil nuts, yeast.

Copper- nuts & seeds, whole grains, dried beans, mushrooms.

Manganese - brown rice, whole grains & cereals, cooked oatmeal, wheat germ, nuts, seeds, legumes, cooked spinach and kale, black beans, almonds, avocados, pineapples, strawberries.

Fluoride - fluoridated water, brewed tea, cooked kale & spinach, apples.

Chromium - whole grains, nuts, broccoli, apples, peanut butter, cooked spinach, mushrooms.

Molybdenum - beans, breads, cereals, cooked spinach, strawberries.

Vitamin A - carrots, winter squash, sweet potatoes, apricots, spinach, kale, greens, broccoli.

Vitamin C - bell peppers, broccoli, tomatoes, strawberries, oranges, grapefruits, tomatoes, brussel sprouts, collard greens, potatoes, melon, berries, papayas, turnip greens, orange juice.

Vitamin D - exposure to sunlight, vitamin D-fortified soy milk and other plant milks.

Vitamin E - vegetable/safflower oils, sunflower seeds, raw wheat germ, nuts, peanut butter, green leafy vegetables, whole wheat flour, spinach.

Vitamin K - green leafy vegetables, spinach, turnip greens, kale, parsley, brussel sprouts, broccoli, cauliflower, soybeans, cabbage, green tea, tomatoes.

Vitamin B1-Thiamin - whole grain products, bread, brown rice, pasta, oatmeal, brewer's & nutritional yeast, legumes, cereals, sunflower seeds, nuts, watermelon, raw wheat germ.

Riboflavin - yeast, beans, cereal/grain products, spinach, broccoli, wheat germ, mushrooms.

Niacin B3- legumes, brown rice, green vegetables, potatoes, tomatoes, broccoli.

Vitamin B6 -whole grains, peanuts, nuts/legumes, soybeans, walnuts, bananas, watermelon.

Folic Acid-legumes, green leafy vegetables, nuts, oranges, whole grains, asparagus, spinach.

Vitamin B12 - Vegetarian Support Formula nutritional yeast (Red Star; T6635), meat analogs and soy/rice milks that are vitamin B-12 fortified.

Biotin - cereals & whole grains, breads, yeast, almonds, peanut butter, molasses, legumes.

Panothenic Acid - whole grain cereals, legumes, mushrooms, peanuts, soybeans, avocados, sunflower seeds, banana, raw orange, cooked collard greens, baked potato, broccoli.

"Every nutrient we require - proteins, vitamins, minerals and others - can be obtained (or synthesized by the human body) from plant-based foods."

MICHAEL A. KLAPER, M.D.
author, international lecturer

Preparing to Cook

- **Blender** - is a necessary machine for dressings, milks, gravies and smoothies.

- **Food Processor** - invaluable for many of the recipes in this book. A processor is used for making thicker creams, paté, dips; bean mashes, hummus, frostings and raw treats. Use for all foods that are too thick for a blender.

- **Non-aluminum coated cookware** - stainless steel, ceramic, or glass.

- **Wooden stirring spoons** - use them because it is best not to scratch the surfaces of pots and pans with metal spoons.

- **Wooden cutting boards** - separate ones for fruits and vegetables (especially onions).

- **Vegetable steamer basket** - place in a pot with water. Water level should not exceed the level of food placed in the basket. This will keep vegetables and greens from getting soggy and losing nutrients.

- **Colander** - for draining pasta, beans, potatoes, etc. Washed lettuce can drain in a colander before preparing salad.

- **Grater** - either a hand grater or the grater blade of your food processor is a valuable tool for making raw salads. Many of the recipes call for grated vegetables.

- **Vegetable Peeler**

- **Measuring spoons and cups** - Abbreviations used - cup: C., tablespoon: T., teaspoon: t.

- **Garlic Press**

- **Sifter** - used for sifting flour before using.

- **Citrus Juicer** - for orange or lemon juice in recipes (hand or electric) .

- **Dehydrator** - quite helpful for many of the raw recipes in this book. If you do not own one, set the oven below 101° for dehydrating.

- **Bread Machine, Air Fryer,** and **Juice Extracto**r.

- **Champion Juicer** - A machine that grates, juices and homogenizes.

- **Vita Mix** - A large extra strength blender.

- **Compost bucket** - for your fruit and vegetable peels and all leftover food. The bucket is emptied into outdoor compost piles daily to make your own vegan, vitamin and mineral-rich soil for growing food. See Veganic gardening - page 181.

Metric Conversion Chart

(adjusted slightly for simplicity)

1/4 teaspoon (t.) = 1 1/4 ml (milliliters)
1/2 teaspoon = 2 1/2 ml
1 teaspoon, 1 t. = 5 ml
2 teaspoons, 2 t. = 10 ml
1 Tablespoon, 1 T. = 15 ml
1/4 cup = 60 ml
1/2 cup = 120 ml
1 cup = 235 ml
1 1/4 cup = 300 ml
2 cups = 470 ml
3 cups = 710 ml

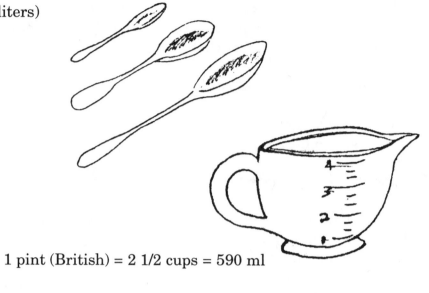

1 fluid oz. = 30 ml
1 pint (U.S.) = 2 cups = 470 ml   1 pint (British) = 2 1/2 cups = 590 ml

Ounces to Grams:

1 oz. = 28 grams
8 oz. = 227 grams
9 oz. = 255 grams

Pounds to Kilograms:

1 lb. (pound) = 0.454 kilograms (approximately)
2 lbs. = 0.907 kilograms (kg) - 2.2 lbs. = 1 kilogram
3 lbs. = 1.36 kilograms   (kg)

Oven temperatures: Oven temperatures in this book are given in Fahrenheit. The Centigrade equivalents are:

300°F. = 150° C.   350°F. = 175° C.
325°F = 160° C.   375°F. = 190° C.
                          400°F. = 200° C.

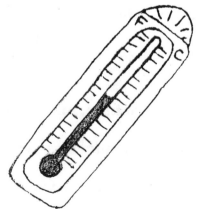

United States Measurement conversions:

3 t. (teaspoons) = 1 T. (Tablespoon)
1 & 1/2 teaspoons = 1/2 Tablespoon
2 Tablespoons = 1/8 cup
4 Tablespoons = 1/4 cup
5 1/3 T. (5 T.+ 1 t.) = 1/3 cup
8 Tablespoons (8 T.) = 1/2 cup

Vegan Baking Guide

You can create incredibly delicious, varied baked goods without eggs, milk or butter. Once you understand the role each plays, you can easily substitute healthier ingredients. The following tips will ease your transition:

1. Replace one egg using any of the following:
   a) Mix 1 T. soy powder with 2 T. water.
   b) Soak 1 1/2 T. ground flax seeds (rich in valuable oils) in 3 T. boiling water for 15 minutes. Pour off excess water and substitute the gelled flax seeds.
   c) Use Ener-G™ Egg Replacer following package instructions.

2. Milk or cream can be replaced with either of the following:
   a) Tofu milk made by blending 8 oz. tofu with 2 C. water
      which makes 2 1/2 cups. Adjust accordingly for each recipe.
   b) A thick, rich rice or soy milk.

3. Pre-heat your oven 15 minutes in advance, then bake food for time given or until done.

4. Always mix wet ingredients such as sweetener, oil, soy/rice/tofu milk, egg substitute and vanilla in a large bowl (some recipes blend in a blender). Sift the dry ingredients such as flours, baking soda, baking powder, salt and dry spices into another bowl. Mix dry ingredients into wet ingredients, unless recipe specifies otherwise.

5. Use oil and flour on baking dishes, or use baking papers or cupcake paper cups.

6. At half time of baking, open oven and rotate trays/pans (move top pan to bottom and bottom pan to top) and rotate front of tray to the back for even baking.

7. To test if a cake, cupcake or muffin is done, insert a wooden toothpick or small knife in the center. If done, it will come out dry and clean.

8. To substitute for processed sugar use date sugar, organic cane sugar, the Ultimate Sweetener™, Sucanat™ or fructose. Instead of honey, use maple syrup, rice syrup, sorghum, malt barley or other liquid sweetener.

> "....every animal that walks the earth, or swims, or flies is precious beyond description, something so rare and wonderful that it equals the stars or the ocean or the mind of man..."
>
> JAMES MICHENER (1902-1997)
> American author and novelist
> "Where Did the Animals Go?" Readers' Digest, June 1976

Cooking Guide for Whole Grains

Use whole grains that still contain all their bran, germ and starch for greater food value.

Instructions: Boil water, add grain, reduce heat to simmer and cook for specified amount of time or until water is gone and grain is fluffy. Leave lid on until finished.

Millet - 1 cup of dry grain to 2 cups of water. 25 minutes cooking time. Yields 3 - 3 1/2 cups of cooked grain. (Some use 3 cups of water to 1 cup of grain.)

Quinoa - 1 cup of dry grain to 2 cups of water. 15-20 minutes cooking time. Yields 3 cups cooked grain. Quinoa is a fluffy and light grain.

Rice - (long grain, brown) 1 cup of dry to 2 cups of water. 40-45 minutes cooking time. Yields 3 cups of cooked grain. Cooks up fluffy with grains remaining separated.

Rice - (short/medium grain brown) 1 cup dry to 2 cups water. 45-50 minutes cooking time. Yields 3 cups cooked grain. Cooks up sticky. Good for loaves and burgers.

Brown Basmati Rice - 1 cup dry grain to 2 cups water. 30-35 minutes cooking time. Cooks up fluffy with grains remaining separated.

Wild Rice - 1 cup dry grain to 2 1/2 to 3 cups water. 40 minutes cooking time.

Cous-Cous - 1 cup dry grain to 1 cup water. Boil water, add Cous-Cous, simmer a few minutes and then shut off heat. Let stand several minutes with lid on and then fluff with a fork. Cover again for another five minutes. (Use whole wheat variety.)

Kasha - (buckwheat groats) - 1 cup dry grain to 2 1/2 cups water. 15 minutes cooking time.

Amaranth - 1 cup dry grain to 2 1/2 - 3 cups of water. 20-25 minutes cooking time. Yields 3 cups of cooked grain. Slightly nutty flavor and soft consistency cooked.

Pearl Barley- 1 cup dry grain to 2 1/2 cups of water. 50-60 minutes cooking time. Yields 3 1/2 cups of cooked grain. A hearty grain good for soups, stews and cold salads.

Kamut - 1 cup dry grain to 3 cups water. 35 minutes cooking time. Yields 3 cups cooked.

Bulgur Wheat - can be reconstituted in boiling water. 1 cup dry grain to 2 cups water. Cover bowl and let sit for 30-45 minutes until water is absorbed by grain. Used to make Tabouli.

"What value has compassion that does not take its object in its arms?"

ANTOINE de SAINT EXUPERY (1900-1944)
French author and aviator

Cooking Guide for Beans

Most dry beans need soaking overnight before cooking. Soak in 4-5 cups of water to 1 cup of beans. Rinse with fresh water before cooking.

1 cup dry bean yields approximately 2 1/2 cups cooked beans.

Lentils - 1 cup dry lentils to 3 cups water. Bring water to boil and simmer for 30 minutes. No pre-soaking necessary. Total cooking time is 45-60 minutes.

Garbanzo Beans (Chick Peas) - 1 cup dry beans to 4 cups water. Soaked overnight, cooking time is 2-3 hours.

Soybeans - 1 cup dry beans to 4 cups water. Soaked overnight, cooking time is 3-4 hours.

Black Beans - 1 cup dry beans to 4 cups water. Soaked, cooking time is 60-90 minutes.

Navy Beans - 1 cup dry beans to 3 cups water. Unsoaked, cooking time is 90 minutes.

Pinto Beans - 1 cup dry beans to 3 cups water. Soaked, cooking time 2 to 2 1/2 hours.

Great Northern Beans - 1 cup dry beans to 3 cups water. Unsoaked, cooking time is 90 minutes. Soaked, cooking time is 60 minutes.

Kidney Beans - 1 cup dry beans to 3 cups water. Soaked, cooking time is 60 + minutes. Unsoaked, cooking time is 90 minutes.

Lima Beans - 1 cup dry beans to 3 cups water. No soaking required. 90 minutes cooking time.

Split Peas - No soaking required. 1 cup dry beans to 3 cups water. 45 minutes cooking time.

Aduki Beans - 1 cup dry beans to 4 cups water. Soaked 1 hour, cooking time is 1 hour. Unsoaked, cooking time is 90 minutes.

"We stopped eating meat many years ago. During the course of a Sunday lunch, we happened to look out of the kitchen window at our young lambs playing happily in the fields. Glancing down at our plates, we suddenly realized that we were eating the leg of an animal who had until recently been playing in a field herself. We looked at each other and said, 'Wait a minute, we love these sheep—they're such gentle creatures. So why are we eating them?' It was the last time we ever did."

PAUL McCARTNEY
English musician, singer, songwriter

Bread
&
Breakfast

"Vegetarianism serves as a criterion by which we know that the pursuit of moral perfection on the part of humanity is genuine and sincere."

COUNT LEO TOLSTOY (1828-1910)
Russian novelist and philosopher

Fresh Fruit Bowl
yields 1 large bowl

1 Mango	1 Papaya or Peach
1 Orange	1 Avocado
1 Banana	1/2 C. Raisins
1/4 C Raspberries or Blueberries	

1. Peel and slice each piece of fruit into a bowl, mix and serve.
   - A fresh fruit bowl is a light way to start the day after a night of fasting.
   - (optional) Squeeze an orange over fruit bowl or top with fruit smoothie sauce.
   - Add sunflower seeds.

Applesauce Homemade
yields 1 quart

20 small Apples, peeled and cored	1 1/2 t. Cinnamon

1. In a saucepan add a little water and then the apples. Steam on medium heat until soft.
2. Add cinnamon half way through. When apples are soft, mash. Chill.
   - (optional) For a raw applesauce, use blender instead of cooking.

Tofu Yogurt
yields 2-4 servings

1 1/2 lb. Tofu (soft)	1/4 C. Fruit Juice
2 T. Sweetener (Maple Syrup, Sucanat)	1 t. Vanilla
1 Banana, peeled, frozen, sliced	1 C. Frozen Berries
1 Banana, ripe (spotted), sliced	Lemon Juice, dash

1. In a blender or food processor, blend all ingredients together until creamy.
2. Chill in the freezer until just before frozen, then serve.
   - For a better consistency use a food processor and omit some liquid if necessary.

> *"There is no question that the combination of a vegan low-fat diet and daily vigorous exercise are keys to radiant good health. And, if one so desires, one can set new limits in the fields of human athletic endeavors, especially as one ages. It is my vegan diet that powers me through triathalons and marathons and 50-60 races per year!"*
>
> RUTH HEIDRICH, Ph.D.
> Ironman Triathlete

Sunflower Milk

yields 1 quart

1 Quart Ice Cold Water   Dash of Vanilla (optional)
2/3 C. Sunflower Seeds   2-3 T. Sweetener

1. Place sunflower seeds in a blender, just covering the blades.
2. Cover seeds with one cup of water and blend to a purée (about 1 minute).
3. Add sweetener and vanilla. Be sure to get the little pieces of seeds off the sides of blender for a non-gritty milk. When the purée becomes difficult to blend, add more water until it becomes smooth.
4. Fill to top with ice cold water while blender is still blending.

   • (optional) Strain milk through a fine strainer or cheese cloth.
   • Use cashews in place of sunflower seeds for a rich, cream-like "milk".
   • Serve with cold cereal, raisins and fruit.

Almond Milk

yields 4-5 cups

1/3-1/2 C. Almonds, blanched   2 1/2 T. Maple Syrup/Sweetener
4 C. Ice Cold Water   Almond Extract, dash

1. To blanch: pour boiling water over almonds and let sit 5-10 minutes. The outer brown layer will come off very easily.
2. Cover the blades of the blender completely with blanched almonds.
3. Pour 3/4 cup of water (a little over the almonds) into the blender and purée until smooth and creamy. Pour a little water down the sides of the blender getting all the little pieces of grit to fall into the purée.
4. When purée is completely smooth add ice cold water to fill the blender nearly to the top. Add maple syrup and a drop of almond extract and blend.

   • Almond milk can be strained for an even smoother texture.

> "A more secret, sweet, and overpowering beauty appears to man when his heart and mind open to the sentiment of virtue. Then he is instructed in what is above him. He learns that his being is without bound; that to the good, to the perfect, he is born."
>
> RALPH WALDO EMERSON (1803-1882)
> American philosopher, poet and essayist

Tofu Cottage Cheese

yields 3 1/2 cups

1 lb. Tofu (firm), drained, mashed
2/3 C. Vegan Mayonnaise
1 t. Sea Salt (optional)

2 t. Onion Powder
1 t. Garlic Powder
1 t. Caraway Seeds

Mix all ingredients together in a bowl. Store in refrigerator.

Baked Granola

yields 7 cups (2 standard baking sheets)

4 C. Rolled Oats
1/2 C. Pecans, chopped
1/2 C. Almonds, chopped
1 C. Walnuts, chopped
1/2 C. Bran
1 C. Shredded Coconut
1 1/2 t. Cinnamon

1/3 C. Maple Syrup
1/2 C. Sunflower Seeds
1 t. Vanilla
1/3 C. Oil
Dash of Cloves, ground
1 C. Raisins (optional)

1. Mix all ingredients together in a bowl.
2. Lightly oil 2 baking sheets and bake in a pre-heated oven at 275°. Bake on one oven rack for 25 minutes and then rotate baking sheets. Bake until golden-browned, another 15-25 minutes. Cool before serving.

   • Stores well in pantry.

Raw Granola

yields 8 cups

4 C. Rolled Oats
1/2 C. Almonds, chopped
1/2 C. Pecans, chopped
1/2 C. Walnuts, chopped
1/2 C. Oat or Wheat Bran
1 C. Shredded Coconut

1 C. Raisins
1/3 C. Figs, chopped
1/3 C. Dates, chopped
1/2 C. Sunflower Seeds
1/2 C. Sucanat™, or to taste
1 t. Cinnamon

1. Mix all ingredients together in a bowl.
2. Store in a sealed container.

   • When serving, pour sunflower or almond milk over it and top with sliced banana.

High Energy Granola

yields 8 cups

4 1/2 C. Rolled Oats	1/2 C. Sweetener (Rice Syrup)
1/2 C. Bran	1/3 C. Apple Juice
1/2 C. Wheat Germ	1/4 C. Safflower Oil (or other)
1/2 C. Nuts and/or Seeds, chopped	1 1/2 C. Assorted Dried Fruit, chopped
1 T. Cinnamon	(Unsulphured Apricots, Apples, Figs)
1/2 t. Nutmeg	

1. Pre-heat oven to 350°. Lightly oil cookie sheet.
2. In a large bowl, mix together all ingredients in first column.
3. Whisk or blend together sweetener, juice and oil.
4. Add oat mixture to sweetened oil mixture and stir until coated.
5. Spread granola onto a baking sheet and bake 25 minutes stirring a few times so it browns evenly. Remove from oven and let cool on a baking sheet for 15 minutes.
6. Add dried fruit when mixture cools. Store in an air tight container.

Hot Cereal

yields 4-5 servings

7 C. Water	1-2 t. Vanilla
1 t. Oil	1-2 t. Cinnamon
1/2 t. Sea Salt	2 C. Rolled Oats
1/2 C. Sweetener	1 1/2 C. Cous-Cous

1. Bring water, oil and sea salt to a boil. Add grains and simmer.
2. When grains start to absorb water, add sweetener and spices. Stir frequently until all water is absorbed.

•Optional: Add raisins to cereal just before it is finished allowing them to soften.

Oatmeal

yields 3-4 bowls

4 - 4 1/2 C. Water	3/4 t. Cinnamon
1 t. Oil (optional)	1 t. Vanilla
Sea Salt, dash	1/3 C. Raisins
1 3/4 C. Rolled Oats	4-5 t. Maple Syrup/Sorghum

1. Bring water, oil and salt to boil and then add rolled oats. Turn heat down to a simmer.
2. Add remaining 4 ingredients. Stir continuously and simmer for approximately 15-20 minutes until water is absorbed and cereal is creamy.

• Serve with sunflower milk.

3 Grain Hot Cereal
Serves 5-6

7 C. Water	1 C. Cous-Cous
1 1/2 t. Oil	5 T. Sucanat™
1/2 t. Sea Salt	5 T. Sorghum
2 C. Rolled Oats	1 t. Cinnamon
2/3 C. Bulgur	1 t. Vanilla

1. Bring water, oil and salt to a boil.
2. Add oats and bulgur and boil until soft.
3. Add cous-cous, sweetener, cinnamon and vanilla. Stir for several minutes and serve.

Tofu Omelette
serves 2

1 1/2 lb. Tofu	2-3 T. Nutritional Yeast
1 T. Tahini	1 t. Turmeric
2 T. Tamari, Bragg's™ or Sea Salt	1 T. Safflower Oil (optional)

1. In a bowl, mash the tofu and mix with all the other ingredients.
2. Place batter in an oiled skillet (or non-stick pan) and press into an omelette shape. Cook on medium heat until brown on one side, then flip and brown the other side.
   •Variation: Add diced bell pepper, mushroom and onion sauté for a Western Omelette.

Low-Oil Omelette
serves 2-3

2 1/2 C. Tofu (mashed)	1 t. Salt-Free Spike™
2 T. Nutritional Yeast	1/2 t. Turmeric
1 T. Bragg™ Liquid Aminos	1/4 t. Sea Salt
	Black Pepper, to taste (optional)

1. In a bowl, mash all ingredients together.
2. Place mix into a lightly oiled fry pan and pat down. Cook on one side, then flip. Batter will get firm and golden colored.

> *"Women should be protected from anyone's exercise of unrighteous power... but then, so should every other living creature."*
>
> GEORGE ELIOT (1819-1880)
> English novelist

Western Omelette

yields 1 large skillet-sized omelette

2 lbs. Tofu, mashed
1/8 C. Nutritional Yeast
1 1/2 T. Tamari or Bragg™ Aminos
1/2 t. Black Pepper
1 t. Sea Salt
1/4 C. Scallions, chopped
1 t. Turmeric

Sauté:
1 C. Onion, diced
3 C. Red Pepper, sliced
1 C. Mushrooms, diced
1 T. Bragg™ Liquid Aminos
1/8 C. Nutritional Yeast

1. In a bowl, mix tofu with seasonings (includes scallions).
2. Sauté in a little oil and/or water, onion, then red pepper, then mushrooms until soft. Season with Bragg's™ and nutritional yeast. Add to tofu batter and mix well.
3. Pan-fry in an oiled skillet. Flip when browned on one side.

•Variation: Baking the batter will use less oil than a fry pan and it will solidify the omelette as well. Place batter in a lightly oiled skillet. Pack the batter into the skillet firmly, pat down and bake in a pre-heated oven for 25 minutes at 350°.

Spanish Omelette Pie

yields 1 large skillet

1 t. Oil (or nonstick pan)
3/4 C. Onion, diced
2 C. Pepper (red & green), diced
3/4 C. Tomato (fresh), diced
1 t. Chile Powder/Mexican Spice
1 T. Bragg™ Liquid Aminos
1/2 C. Tomato Paste
Sea Salt, Paprika, dash of each
2 lbs. Tofu or 4 C. mashed (firm), drained of excess water

1 T. Nutritional Yeast
1/2 t. Turmeric
1/4 t. Paprika
1 t. Sea Salt
1 T. Oil and/or Tahini
1 Potato (Russet) or 1 C. grated
1 T. Oil
2 t. Bragg™ Liquid Aminos
2 t. Nutritional Yeast
Oil (additional) for cooking

1. In a small sauce pot, sauté the onion in oil. When softened, add the peppers; then the diced tomatoes. Add chile/Mexican seasonings and Bragg™ Liquid Aminos with the tomato paste, dash of sea salt and paprika. Cook until vegetables are tender and flavors blend, about 10-15 minutes. Set this sauce aside.
2. Rinse and drain tofu and mash. Add next 5 ingredients: yeast, spices and oil or tahini.
3. Grate 1 C. of potato. Fry the potato in 1 T. oil, the Bragg™ Liquid Aminos and nutritional yeast. Add cooked potato to mashed tofu and mix well. Batter should be a firm.
4. Coat the bottom of a large skillet with enough oil to cover the bottom completely (or use less oil and a nonstick pan). Fry the tofu/potato batter. Flip while cooking (in sections) so it cooks all the way through and then press back together and continue cooking until browned and formed into an omelette shape.
5. Allow to cool somewhat and solidify before flipping onto a serving plate.
6. Warm the sauce (if necessary) and spread on top of the tofu. Serve.

Vegan Cheese Omelette

yields 1 skillet

2 lbs. Tofu, mashed	1/2 t. Turmeric
2 T. Bragg™ Liquid Aminos	1/4 t. Pepper
1 C. VeganRella™ cheese, grated	1/2 t. Sea Salt
(or alternative vegan cheese)	2 T. Nutritional Yeast

1. In a bowl, mash the tofu and mix together with all ingredients.
2. Oil a baking sheet, and place batter on it. Bake in a pre-heated oven at 350° for 25-30 minutes (or lightly fry batter in a skillet).

•Optional: Sprinkle the top with another 1/2 cup of grated VeganRella™ cheese alternative and bake.

Scrambled Tofu

yields 2-3 servings

1 3/4 lb. Tofu	1/8 t. Turmeric
1 T. Bragg™ Liquid Aminos	1 t. Dill
2 T. Oil	1/4 t. Garlic Powder
1/2 t. Sea Salt	1/4 t. Onion Powder
4 T. Nutritional Yeast	1/2 t. Spike™ Seasoning

1. In a bowl, mash the tofu with all the ingredients.
2. Place the batter in a heated, lightly oiled, skillet. Stir fry until browned, approximately 7-10 minutes.

Home-style Hash Browns

serves 4

4 Potatoes (large),	2 T. Soy Powder
peeled & grated	(mixed with 3 1/2 T. Water)
1/3 C. Onions, finely chopped	1/8 t. Crushed Red Pepper (dry)
1/2 t. Sea Salt	2 T. Oil

1. In a medium-sized bowl, mix all ingredients (except oil) into a batter. Using a cast iron skillet, heat oil; then add batter to hot skillet, forming an omelette-shaped circle.
2. Cook until golden brown; then flip to brown the other side.

•Variation: Lightly oil a baking sheet and bake in a pre-heated oven at 350° for 25 minutes.

French Toast
yields 6 slices

3/4 lb. Tofu	1/8 t. Cinnamon
3 T. Sweetener	Nutmeg, dash
1/2 C. Water	1 T. Oil
1 t. Vanilla	6 Slices Whole Wheat Bread

1. In a blender, blend tofu, sweetener, water, vanilla and spices.
2. Pre-heat oil in a skillet. Dip bread slices into mixture and grill on both sides.
3. Serve hot, and top with maple syrup or jam.

Hawaiian Toast
serves 4-6

1 lb. Tofu (firm)	8 (or more) Slices Bread
1 1/2 C. Coconut Milk	Oil for cooking
2 T. Maple Syrup	Pineapple Jam or Preserves
1 t. Vanilla	1/4 C. Coconut, shredded
Sea Salt, pinch	Macadamia Nuts, crushed
	(for garnish)

1. In a blender, combine tofu, coconut milk, maple syrup, vanilla, salt and blend to a smooth consistency.
2. Pour in a bowl and thoroughly dip several pieces of bread in it.
3. In a heated, oiled skillet, place the coated pieces of bread. Cook each side until golden-brown. Repeat until all the batter is used.
4. Cover with pineapple jam, sprinkle with coconut and top with crushed macadamia nuts.

Fluffy Whole Wheat Pancakes
yields 16 pancakes

2 1/2 C. Whole Wheat Pastry Flour	1/2 t. Sea Salt
1/2 t. Cinnamon	4 T. Sucanat™
3 t. Baking Powder (non-aluminum)	2 1/2 C. thin Milk (Soy or Sunflower)
1/2 t. Baking Soda	4 T. Safflower Oil

1. Sift all dry ingredients in a bowl.
2. Add sweetener to the milk and blend.
3. Pour dry mixture into liquid mixture, add oil and mix until smooth. Add more water or sunflower milk if too thick.
4. Drop a spoonful of batter (at first to test grill) onto an oiled hot grill or cast iron skillet. When edges turn brown and bubbles form and remain open in the middle (approximately 1-2 minutes), flip over for another minute or two until done.

Easy Apple-Cinnamon Muffins

yields 18 muffins

1 C. Bran	1 C. Sucanat™
2 C. Whole Wheat Pastry Flour	1 C. Tofu Milk (see Vegan Baking Tips)
1 T. Baking Powder	1/2 C. Oil
1/2 t. Baking Soda	1 C. Apples, grated
1 1/2 t. Cinnamon	1/2 C. Raisins

1. Put bran into a bowl; sift all other dry ingredients and add to bran.
2. In another bowl, blend tofu milk with oil. Add grated apple and raisins. Mix.
3. Add dry batter to the wet and mix.
4. Oil muffin tins. Fill each cup 3/4 full. Bake in a pre-heated oven at 350° for 35 minutes.

Peanut Butter Muffins

yields 12 muffins

2 C. Pastry Flour	1/3 C. Oil
1 T. Baking Powder	1/4 C. Sweetener (Sucanat)
1 1/2 C. Tofu Milk	1/4 C. Peanut Butter

1. Sift flour and baking powder into a bowl.
2. Blend tofu milk, oil and sweetener together. Add peanut butter. Stir with a fork.
   In a bowl, mix dry ingredients into the blended mixture. Mix well but don't beat.
3. Oil a muffin tin. Fill each cup 2/3 full. Bake in a pre-heated oven at 350° for 25 minutes.

Banana-Walnut Muffins

yields 24 muffins

3 C. Mashed Bananas (approx. 6)	3 1/2 C. Pastry Flour
3/4 C. Maple Syrup	2 t. Baking Soda
1/2 C. Oil	1/2 t. Sea Salt (optional)
1/2 T. Vanilla	1/2 C. Walnuts, finely chopped
1 t. Baking Powder (or egg replacer)	1 t. Nutmeg

1. Combine all the wet ingredients. In a separate bowl, sift all the dry ingredients together.
   Add the dry to the wet and mix thoroughly.
2. Oil and flour muffin tins. Fill each cup 3/4 full. Bake in a pre-heated oven at 350° for
   30 minutes, or until a toothpick comes out dry. Muffins will be slightly browned.

"Where mercy, love, and pity dwell, there God is dwelling too."

WILLIAM BLAKE   (1757-1827)
English poet

Sweet Corn Muffins

yields 1 dozen

1/2 C. Sweetener (liquid)	1 1/2 C. Cornmeal, sifted
1/2 C. Sweetener (dry)	1/2 C. Pastry Flour, sifted
1 1/4 C. Tofu Milk, thick	1 t. Baking Soda, sifted
1/4 C. Oil	1/2 t. Sea Salt

1. In a medium-sized bowl, whisk the first four ingredients (see Baking Guide). Into a larger bowl, sift dry ingredients. Add wet to dry ingredients and mix well.
2. Drop batter by the spoonful into an oiled muffin tin or muffin cups, filling each cup 3/4 full. Bake in a pre-heated oven at 400° for 20 minutes or until golden brown.

Carrot Muffins (Party-Sized Recipe)

yields approx. 4 dozen

Wet	Dry
1/2 C. Vegan Margarine	8 C. Whole Wheat Flour
1/2 C. Oil	1 T. Baking Soda
4 1/3 C. Sucanat™	1 T. + 1 t. Cinnamon
2 C. Tofu Milk (8 oz. tofu	1 t. Allspice
blended with 1 1/2 C. water)	1/3 t. Sea Salt
5 C. Carrots, grated	Additional Ingredients
	1 C. Raisins
	1 C. Walnuts, chopped
	1 C. Shredded Coconut (optional)

1. Mix wet ingredients in a very large bowl.
2. Sift dry ingredients in a separate bowl and stir. Mix the dry into the wet.
3. Add raisins, nuts and shredded coconut. Mix well.
4. Pour batter into an oiled muffin tin, filling each cup 3/4 full. Bake in a pre-heated oven at 350° for 20 minutes or until golden brown.

" I care not much for a man's religion
whose dog and cat are not the better for it."

ABRAHAM LINCOLN (1809-1865)
16th President of the United States
-Complete Works

Bran Muffins
yields 1 dozen

1 1/4 C. Pastry Flour, sifted	1/3 C. Oil
1 C. Bran	1/3 C. Sorghum
1 t. Baking Soda, sifted	1 t. Vanilla
1 t. Cinnamon	1 C. Soy Milk (4 T. Soy Powder and Water)

1. In a small bowl, combine the dry ingredients together (all sifted except for the bran).
2. In a separate bowl, whisk the wet ingredients together. Add the dry to the wet and mix.
3. Oil and flour a muffin tin. Spoon batter into each cup 2/3 full. Bake in a pre-heated oven at 400° for 25 minutes or until a toothpick comes out clean.

Blueberry Muffins
yields 1 dozen muffins

2 C. Whole Wheat Pastry Flour	1/4 C. Oil
1/2 t. Baking Powder	1/4 C. Applesauce
1/2 t. Baking Soda	1/3 C. Juice/Water
Sea Salt, pinch	1/2 t. Vanilla
1/2 C. Sweetener	1/2 C. Blueberries

1. In a processor, combine all dry ingredients and blend well.
2. Add all other ingredients except blueberries to the processor. Blend until creamy. Add berries and pulse or mix together, gently.
3. Pour batter into an oiled muffin tin (or baking paper cups), filling each cup 3/4 full. Bake in a pre-heated oven at 350° for 15-20 minutes or until a toothpick comes out dry.

Blueberry Corn Muffins
yields 18 muffins

Wet	Dry
2 C. Sucanat™	3 C. Blue Cornmeal
1/3 C. Oil	2 t. Baking Soda, sifted
2 1/2 C. Soy Milk (thick), (8 oz. tofu blended with 2 C. water)	1/2 t. Sea Salt
1 1/2 C. Blueberries	

1. Mix wet ingredients in a large bowl.
2. Sift dry ingredients together in another bowl. Stir.
3. Add dry to wet and mix. Pour batter into oiled and floured muffin tins.
4. Bake in a pre-heated oven at 350° for 20 minutes or until a toothpick comes out dry.

Whole Wheat English Muffins
yield 1 dozen

1/4 C. Warm Water	1 C. Water
2 T. Baking Yeast	2 T. Oil
1 T. Sucanat™	1/2 T. Sea Salt
	4 C. Whole Wheat Flour

1. Place the first three ingredients in a large bowl and stir. Let rise in a warm (not hot) place. Yeast will bubble up and activate in about 15 minutes, doubling in size.
2. Add remaining ingredients and mix.
3. Knead dough for 10 minutes on a floured board.
4. Roll out dough and cut into a dozen 4 inch rounds.
5. Place muffins on an oiled and floured baking sheet (or use baking paper), cover, and let rise for 1 hour in a warm place.
6. Bake in a pre-heated oven at 350° for 25 minutes or until golden brown.

• Variation: For cinnamon raisin muffins, add 1/2 cup raisins and 1/2 t. cinnamon to the dough.

Wheat-Free Corn Muffins
yields dozen + muffins

Wet	Dry
1 C. Sweetener (dry)	2 C. Cornmeal or
1 1/4 Soy Milk	1 1/2 C. Cornmeal & 1/2 C. Oat Flour
1/4 C. Oil	1 t. Baking Soda
	1/2 t. Baking Powder

1. In a bowl, whisk the wet ingredients.
2. Sift dry ingredients in another bowl and mix.
3. Mix the dry batter into the wet.
4. Oil and flour a muffin tin (or use baking paper cups).
5. Pour batter into muffin tin. Bake in a pre-heated oven at 350° for 15 minutes, or until muffins are golden brown and a toothpick comes out dry.

> *"The moral duty of man consists of imitating the moral goodness and beneficence of God, manifested in the creation, toward all His creatures."*
>
> THOMAS PAINE (1737-1809)
> English born American patriot, author and political thinker
> *The Age of Reason*

Cinnamon Rolls

yields 2 dozen

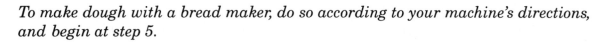

Dough
1 1/2 C. Warm Water
2 t. Dry Active Yeast
1 t. Ener-G® Egg Replacer
1/3 C. Oil
1/2 C. Sweetener
1 1/2 t. Sea Salt
4 1/2 C. Pastry Flour

Filling
1/3 C. Oil (or vegan margarine)
1/3 C. Sucanat™
1/2 C. Walnuts, chopped
1/3 C. Raisins
Glaze
1/4 C. Rice or Soy Milk
1/2 C. Dry Sweetener
1 1/2 t. Vanilla

To make dough with a bread maker, do so according to your machine's directions, and begin at step 5.

1. Combine 1 cup warm water and 1 t. of sweetener, mix in 2 t. of yeast and let rise in a warm (not hot) place. Yeast will bubble up and activate in about 15 minutes, doubling in size.
2. In a separate bowl, whisk the rest of the water (1/2 cup) with egg replacer and mix in oil, sweetener and salt.
3. Sift the flour and slowly add to the wet mixture, mixing thoroughly. Knead for ten minutes. (kneading in more flour if needed to bring to a bread dough texture, not sticky or too dry.)
4. Let stand for one hour in a warm, draft-free place, covered with a clean towel.
5. Punch down and let stand for 1/2 hour. Punch down once more, cut dough in half and roll into two 15 x 12 rectangles.
6. Spread the oil on the dough and sprinkle on the filling.
7. Roll up tight, from the longest side and cut into 1 inch pieces. Lay pieces flat on the baking tray. Let rise for one hour in a draft-free place.
8. Bake in a pre-heated oven at 350° for 25-35 minutes until golden brown.
9. Mix together glaze ingredients and drip over the top of warm rolls.

Many times I am asked why the suffering of animals should call forth more sympathy from me than the suffering of human beings; why I work in this direction of charitable work more than toward any other. My answer is that because I believe that this work includes all the education and lines of reform which are needed to make a perfect circle of peace and goodwill about the earth....."

ELLA WHEELER WILCOX (1850-1919)
American Poet
The Worlds And I

Quick Sweet Rolls
yields 2 dozen

Dry
3 1/2 C. Whole Wheat Pastry Flour
1 T. + 1 t. Baking Powder
1/2 t. Sea Salt
Add
1/2 C. Wheat Bran
Wet
1 1/2 C. Water
3 T. Oil

Filling
1 Orange/Lemon Peel, grated
1/4 C. Sucanat™
1 C. Raisins, chopped
1 C. Nuts, chopped
1 T. Cinnamon

2 T. Oil

1. Sift the dry ingredients in a bowl. Add the wheat bran. Stir.
2. In another bowl, mix the water and oil. Add the dry to the wet and mix.
3. In a separate bowl, mix the Filling ingredients.
4. Roll out half the dough on a floured board into a rectangle. Brush 1 T. of oil on top. Add half of the filling and spread out. Roll up the long way and slice into 1" pieces. Do the same with the other half of dough.
5. Put the pieces on an oiled and floured baking sheet (or baking paper). Bake in a pre-heated oven at 400° for 15-20 minutes, until golden-brown.

Sweet Corn Bread
yields (1) 9 x 9 baking pan or cast iron skillet

2 1/2 C. Tofu Milk (thick)
1/2 C. Oil
2 t. Vanilla
1 1/2 - 2 C. Sweetener (dry)

2 C. Whole Wheat Pastry Flour, sifted
2 C. Cornmeal, sifted
2 t. Baking Soda, sifted
1/2 t. Sea Salt

1. In a blender, blend 1 cup of water with tofu until you reach 2 1/2 cups of thick tofu milk. (Start with small piece of tofu and add as necessary). Add oil, vanilla and sweetener to the tofu milk and blend.
2. In a bowl, sift and combine pastry flour, cornmeal and baking soda. Add sea salt and mix.
3. Pour the blender of liquid into dry ingredients and stir.
4. Fill a lightly oiled baking pan (or cast iron skillet) half way. Bake in a pre-heated oven at 400° for 35-40 minutes, until golden brown. It is done when you stick a toothpick or small knife in the center and it comes out dry. It is important to bake thoroughly. Cool before cutting.

"Universal compassion is the only guarantee of morality."

ARTHUR SCHOPENHAUER (1788-1860)
German author and philosopher

Banana Bread

yields 1 loaf

1/3 C. Sweetener (dry)	2 1/2 C. Pastry Flour, sifted
1/3 C. Maple Syrup	1 1/2 - 2 t. Baking Soda, sifted
1/2 C. Oil	1/2 t. Cinnamon
2 T. Soy Powder & 3 T. Water	1/2 C. Walnuts, chopped
2 C. Ripe Banana, mashed	1/2 C. Raisins, chopped

1. In a large bowl, combine the sweeteners, oil, soy mixture and mashed bananas.
2. In a separate bowl, combine all dry ingredients, then add to liquid mixture. Transfer mixture into an oiled loaf pan.
3. Bake in a pre-heated oven at 350° for 1 hour. Test with a toothpick. If still wet inside, reduce oven to 300° and bake for another 15 minutes.

Foccacia Bread

yields 1 large or 2 small loaves

Bread	Topping
2 t. Active Dry Yeast	4-5 T. Olive Oil
1 1/4 C. Water	1/4 C. Fresh Basil, chopped
2 T. Sweetener	1/2 C. Chives, chopped (or Onion)
3 T. Oil	1/4 C. Garlic, minced
1 1/2 t. Sea Salt	1/4 C. Fresh Rosemary
4 1/2 C. Whole Wheat Pastry Flour	

To make dough with a bread maker, do so according to your machine's directions, and begin at step 3.

1. Dissolve yeast in warm water with sweetener. Let sit in a warm (not hot) place for 15 minutes until doubled in size.
2. Mix with the oil and salt and slowly add the flour until the dough no longer sticks to your fingers but is still elastic and not dry. Knead for 10 more minutes. Let kneaded dough rise for 1 hour in a draft-free, warm place (covered with towel).
3. Punch down dough and coat with 2 T. olive oil. Let dough rise for another 30 minutes.
4. Roll out flat onto one 16" x 20" baking sheet or make 2 smaller loaves.
5. Cover dough with remaining olive oil and sprinkle on the toppings.
6. Bake in a pre-heated oven at 450° for 30 to 35 minutes.

"If a man earnestly seeks a righteous life, his first act of abstinence is from animal food..."

COUNT LEO TOLSTOY (1828-1910)
Russian novelist and philosopher

French Baguettes
yields 2 loaves

2 t. Dry Active Yeast	2 t. Sea Salt
1 3/4 C. Water (warm)	4 1/2 C. Whole Wheat Pastry Flour
2 T. Sweetener	1 T. Oil (optional)

1. Dissolve yeast in warm water with the sweetener. Let sit for 15 minutes until doubled in size.
2. Mix the dissolved yeast with the sea salt. Slowly add the flour until the dough no longer sticks to your fingers, but is still elastic and not dry. Knead for at least 10 minutes. Let dough rise for 1 hour in a warm place (covered with towel).
3. Lightly punch down and let rise again for another 30 minutes or until doubled in size.
4. Roll out dough into a large rectangle, split in half or thirds. Roll up tight from the longer side or make a braided baguette (see recipe below for instructions).
5. Let rise again in a draft-free place for 40 minutes. Brush lightly with oil. Bake in a pre-heated oven at 375° for 20-30 minutes, until golden brown.

Eggless-Challah Bread
yields 1 loaf

2 t. Dry Active Yeast,	2 t. Salt
dissolved in 1/4 C. Warm Water	1/4 C. Oil
2 T. Sweetener	4 1/2 C. Whole Wheat Pastry Flour, sifted
2 1/2 t. Ener-G® Egg Replacer	Topping
mixed with 1 C. Water	2 T. Poppy Seeds

To make dough with a bread maker, do so according to your machine's directions, and begin at step 4.

1. Dissolve yeast with sweetener in warm water (not hot) and let sit at least 15 minutes in a warm place until yeast bubbles and is doubled in size.
2. Mix egg replacer with water in a bowl and add the risen yeast along with the sea salt and oil. Add the flour slowly to the wet mixture, stirring until the dough is not dry, but not sticking to your fingers or the bowl. Knead for 10 minutes, adding flour if needed.
3. Let rise for 1 1/2 hours, then punch down.
4. Divide the dough in thirds making three equal ropes. Pinch together at one end and braid together, pinching at the other end to secure the braid. Let rise until doubled in size about 45 minutes. Brush lightly with oil and sprinkle the poppy seeds on top.
5. Bake in a pre-heated oven at 375° for 25 minutes until golden brown.

> *"It is very significant that some of the most thoughtful and cultured men are partisans of a pure vegetable diet."*
>
> MAHATMA GANDHI (1869-1948)
> Hindu pacifist, spiritual leader

Fluffy Dinner Rolls

yields about 2 1/2 dozen

6 T. Dry Active Yeast
1 1/2 C. Sweetener (dry)
1/2 C. Molasses
4 C. Warm Tofu Milk (Soy Milk)

1 1/2 C. Oil
13 1/2 C. Whole Wheat Pastry Flour, sifted
2 t. Baking Soda, sifted
2 t. Sea Salt

1. Place the yeast in a large bowl, add the sweetener and warm milk, stirring until yeast is dissolved. Add the oil and stir.
2. Add 8 cups of sifted whole wheat pastry flour mixed with 1 teaspoon of baking soda and the sea salt, stir well. Knead for a few minutes and then put dough back in bowl. Cover with towel and allow to rise for 30 minutes.
3. Stir in the remaining flour, salt & baking soda. Cover, allow to rise for 30 minutes more.
4. Lightly oil two cookie sheets. Turn dough onto a floured board and divide into approximately 32 equal parts. Shape either into circles, folded in half or into balls. Place rolls on cookie sheets. They will double in size while baking. Bake in a pre-heated oven at 400° for 20 minutes or until golden brown.

Hope's Crispy Cornbread Recipe

yields 1 skillet (1 loaf)

1 1/2 C. Cornmeal
1/2 C. Pastry Flour
1/2 C. Rice Flour
1/2 C. Semolina Flour
1 T. Sea Salt

4 t. Baking Powder
1/4 C. Oil
3-4 T. Sweetener
1 C. Rice Milk
Mexican Spices (optional)

1. Mix dry ingredients together. Whip wet ingredients and then stir into the dry ingredients. Season with any desired spices, to taste. Place in an oiled cast iron skillet.
2. Bake in a pre-heated oven at 350° for 30-40 minutes, until toothpick comes out dry.

Biscuits

yields 12 or more biscuits

2 C. Pastry Flour, sifted
1 t. Sea Salt
4 t. Baking Powder

2 T. Sweetener
1/4 C. Oil
1 C. Tofu Milk
1 1/2 T. Egg Replacer & 2 T. Water

1. Sift together all dry ingredients, mix well. Combine all the liquid ingredients. Add the liquid mixture to the dry and stir lightly. DO NOT OVER MIX. Oil a muffin tin.
2. Fill each cup half full. Bake in a pre-heated oven at 400° for 20-25 minutes.

Fluffy Dinner Corn Bread

yields 1 large loaf or two small cakes

2 1/2 C. Tofu Milk (thick)	2 t. Baking Soda, sifted
1/2 C. Oil	1/2 t. Garlic Powder
1/4 t. Bragg™ Liquid Aminos	Optional: Chili Powder, to taste
1 C. Sucanat™	1/2 t. Onion Powder
2 C. Cornmeal, sifted	1/2 t. Sea Salt
2 C. Whole Wheat Pastry Flour	1/2 t. Spike™ Seasoning

1. In a blender, make tofu milk. Start with 1 cup water, add 3 to 4 oz. tofu and blend. Keep adding tofu until you reach 2 1/2 cups. Add oil, Bragg's™ and Sucanat™.
2. In a bowl, sift together dry ingredients and spices.
3. Pour wet mixture into dry ingredients. Mix well.
4. Pour batter into a lightly oiled baking pan, filling half way in order to leave room for rising.
5. Bake in pre-heated oven at 400° for 30-40 minutes until toothpick comes out completely dry. Be sure to bake thoroughly. Allow to cool before cutting.

•Variation: Use less wheat and more cornmeal: 3 cups cornmeal & 1 cup pastry flour.

Holiday Pumpkin Bread

yields 1 cake or bread loaf

2 1/4 C. Whole Wheat Pastry Flour, sifted	1/3. C. Oil
1 t. Baking Soda, sifted	1 C. Pumpkin (canned or fresh, cooked)
1/4 t. Sea Salt	1/4. C. Orange Juice
2 1/2 t. Ener-G® Egg Replacer	1 t. Vanilla
2-3 t. Cinnamon	1/2 C. Raisins
1 1/2 C. Sucanat™	1/2 C. Pecans/Walnuts, chopped

1. Sift all the dry ingredients together into a bowl and mix.
2. Add oil, pumpkin, orange juice and vanilla. Mix with a fork.
3. Fold in raisins and nuts. Mix. Pour into an oiled cake or bread pan.
4. Bake in a pre-heated oven at 350° for 45-50 minutes for a cake, 60 minutes for a bread loaf. The bread is done when a toothpick comes out dry.

"I know of no more beautiful prayer than that which the Hindus of old used in closing their public spectacles. It was:
'May all that have life be delivered from suffering.'"

ARTHUR SCHOPENHAUER (1788-1860)
German author and philosopher

Holiday Cranberry Sweet Bread

yields (1) 8" cake pan

2 1/4 C. W. W. Pastry Flour, sifted
1 t. Baking Soda, sifted
1 t. Baking Powder, sifted
1 C. Sweetener (dry)
2 t. Egg Replacer

3/4 C. Orange Juice
1/2 C. Safflower Oil
2-3 t. Orange Rind, grated
1/2 C. Walnuts (optional)
1 C. Cranberries, halved

1. Combine the first 5 ingredients.
2. Whisk the orange juice, oil and orange rinds. Add the dry to the wet batter. Fold in nuts and cranberries.
3. Bake in a pre-heated oven at 350° for 30-40 minutes, until a toothpick comes out dry.

Glazed Rolls

yields 18 rolls

Dough
2 t. Active Dry Yeast
1/3 C. Date Sugar/Dry Sweetener
1 1/2 C. Warm Water
1 1/2 t. Sea Salt
4 1/2 C. W. W. Pastry Flour, sifted
1/3 C. Oil

Topping
1/2 C. Oil (or Vegan Margarine)
1/4 C. Orange Peel, grated
1/2 C. Sweetener

To make dough with a bread maker, do so according to your machine's directions, and begin at step 4.

1. In a bowl, mix the yeast and 1 T. date sugar with the warm water. Set aside for 15 minutes until doubled in size.
2. In another large bowl, sift the salt & flour and mix. Add yeast mixture and oil, mix well.
3. Turn dough onto a well-floured board and knead for approximately 10 minutes until satiny smooth, adding flour as needed. Dough should not be dry or sticky.
4. Place in an oiled bowl. Oil the top of the dough. Cover and allow to rise for about 1 hour, until doubled in bulk.
5. Set dough on a floured surface. Roll into two 12 inch ropes. Cut each rope into 9 pieces.
6. In a bowl, mix topping ingredients Dip the pieces into the topping mixture, covering each piece well.
7. Place on standard baking trays, spaced about 1/2 inch apart. Let rise in a warm draft-free place for 30 minutes, or until doubled in size.
8. Bake in a pre-heated oven at 350° for 20-30 minutes until golden brown.

"Truth above all, even when it upsets us and overwhelms us."

FREDERICK AMIEL (1821-1881)
Swiss philosopher and poet

Sesame Herb Crackers

yields approximately 16 crackers

2 C. W. W. Pastry Flour, sifted	2 T. Bran
1/2 t. Baking Soda, sifted	1/2 t. Oregano, Basil, Garlic and Parsley
1/2 C. Sesame Seeds	3/4 C. Cold Water
2 T. Wheat Germ	4 T. Sesame Oil
1 t. Sea Salt	

1. Sift flour and baking soda into a bowl. Add remaining dry ingredients.
2. Mix water and oil into the dry mixture.
3. Roll dough out onto lightly oiled cookie sheet. Cut into squares before baking.
4. Bake in a pre-heated oven at 400° for 17-20 minutes. Cool and cut into crackers.

   •Variation - substitute 1/4 cup onion flakes for the bran and wheat germ.
   •Variation- eliminate herbs for a simple sesame cracker.

Sesame Flat Bread

yields 20 flat breads

1 2/3 C. Whole Wheat Flour, sifted	1 T. Sweetener
1/2 t. Baking Soda	1/4 C. Oil (or Vegan Margarine)
1/4 t. Sea Salt	1/2 C. Soy Milk
	3 T. Sesame Seeds

1. In a large bowl, sift the dry ingredients and stir. Add Sucanat™ and stir.
2. Cut in vegan margarine or oil. Mixture will form fine crumbs.
3. Stir in soy milk and sesame seeds. Shape dough into a ball.
4. Pinch off pieces of dough and roll into 1" balls. Roll out thin. Lightly oil baking sheet
   and place each flat bread on it. Bake in a pre-heated oven at 400° for 7-10 minutes. Cool.

"The quality of mercy is not strained;
it droppeth as gently as the rain from heaven upon the place beneath;
it is twice blessed:
it blesseth him that gives and him that takes."

WILLIAM SHAKESPEARE (1564-1616)
English poet and playwright
The Merchant of Venice

Sweet Potato Biscuits

yields 2 dozen

<u>Dry</u>	<u>Wet</u>
1 1/2 C. Whole Wheat Flour	3 T. Sweetener
1 T. + 1 t. Baking Powder	1/4 C. Oil or Vegan Margarine
1/2 t. Cinnamon	1 C. Sweet Potatoes (cooked), puréed
1/4 t. Cloves	1/2 C. Soy Milk

1. Sift dry ingredients into a bowl.
2. Mix the wet ingredients in another bowl. Add dry to wet.
3. Drop by tablespoon onto an oiled and floured baking sheet. Bake in a pre-heated oven at 350° for 15-20 minutes.

Whole Wheat Burger Buns

yields 8 buns

1/4 C. Warm Water	1 C. Water
1 T. Dry Active Yeast	1/2 t. Sea Salt
1 t. Sweetener	2 T. Sesame Seeds
3 - 3 1/2 C. Whole Wheat Flour	

1. Place first 3 ingredients into a large bowl and mix. Let rise in a warm (not hot) place. Yeast will bubble up and activate in about 15 minutes, doubling in size.
2. Mix in flour, water and salt. Dough will get stiff. Knead for 10 minutes.
3. Oil a clean bowl. Place dough in bowl, cover bowl with a damp towel and set in a warm place. Let rise for one hour or until doubled in size.
4. Press dough down. Divide into 8 balls and flatten each into 1/2" thick rounds.
5. Press sesame seeds on top.
6. Lay a piece of wax paper, loosely, over top of rolls and let rise until doubled.
7. Bake in a pre-heated oven at 375° for 15-20 minutes. Slice when cooled.

> *"It is my humble assertion that the best way to lower your cholesterol is to stop eating it. Only animals make cholesterol - no plant makes cholesterol in any significant amount."*
>
> MICHAEL A. KLAPER, M.D.
> author, international lecturer
> <u>Vegan Nutrition: Pure and Simple</u>

Scrumptious Salads & Soups

"In a gentle way
you can shake the world."

MAHATMA GANDHI (1869-1948)
Hindu pacifist, spiritual leader

For additional salads, see "Rawesome Recipes"

Tabouli Salad
serves 4-5

2 1/2 C. Bulgur	2 T. Lemon Juice (fresh)
1 Tomato, diced finely	2 T. Bragg's™ or Tamari
1/2 - 1 Cucumber, diced finely	1/4 C. Parsley, chopped finely
1 T. Oil	1/4 Onion (small), diced
1/2 T. Spike™ Seasoning	Lemon Pepper, dash
1/2 t. Onion Powder	1/2 t. Garlic Powder

1. Place the bulgur in a bowl. Pour 5 cups of boiling water over it, cover; let sit for at least an hour. Allow the bulgur to get soft, then drain any excess water.
2. Mix in all the remaining ingredients. Chill and serve.

Festive Carrot Salad
yields 1 medium-sized bowl (1 1/2 - 2 quarts)

6-7 C. Carrots, sliced, steamed	1/4 C. Rice Syrup
1 C. Garbanzo Beans, cooked	1/3 C. Nutritional Yeast
1/2 C. Celery, diced	1/8 C. Water
1/3 C. Onion, diced (or scallion)	1 T. Oregano
1/4 C. Fresh Dill Weed, chopped	1/2 t. Garlic Powder
1/3 C. Oil	1 T. Bragg's™ or Tamari
1/4 C. Apple Cider Vinegar	1 t. Herb Seasoning

1. Steam the sliced carrots. When soft, place 4-5 cups of the carrot slices in a large bowl, saving 1 1/2 cups to remain for the sauce.
2. Add to the bowl, the chic peas (Garbanzo Beans), celery, onion and fresh dill weed.
3. In a blender, blend the remaining 1 1/2 cups of steamed carrots with the oil, vinegar, sweetener, yeast, water and seasonings. Blend well. Pour into the bowl and stir. Allow to marinate and chill before serving, stirring periodically.
- This salad keeps well in the refrigerator.

"A reduction in beef and other meat consumption is the most potent single act you can take to halt the destruction of our environment and preserve our natural resources. Our choices do matter. What's healthiest for each of us personally is also healthiest for the life support system of our precious, but wounded planet."

JEREMY RIFKIN
President of: The Foundation on Economic Trends
Author of: <u>Beyond Beef: The Rise and Fall of the Cattle Culture</u>, Dutton, New York

---

Italian Basil-Bulgur Salad
serves 5

2 C. Bulgur
3 C. Boiling Water
1/4 C. Parsley, chopped
1/4 C. Fresh Basil, chopped
1/2 C. Scallions, chopped
1/3 C. Red Pepper, diced
<u>Blender Mixture</u>
1/8 C. Safflower Oil
1/8 C. Olive Oil
1/8 C. Nutritional Yeast

1 t. Spike™ Seasoning
2 t. Bragg™ Liquid Aminos
1 t. Dill Weed
2 t. Oregano (dried)
1/8 C. Apple Cider Vinegar
1/2 t. Basil (dried)
1 T. Brown Rice Syrup
1 t. Garlic Powder
1/2 C. Water

1. Place the bulgur in a bowl and pour the boiling water over it, cover and allow to sit for 1/2 to 1 hour to absorb the water.
2. Chop the herbs and pepper and set aside until bulgur is soft.
3. Blend the blender ingredients.
4. When bulgur is softened, add all ingredients to it. Mix together and chill before serving. (After several hours of absorbing flavors you may want to add a little lemon juice before serving).

Quinoa Salad
serves 4

3 C. Quinoa (already cooked)
1 Carrot, grated
2 Scallions (small), chopped
1 Celery Stalk
1/2 Bell Pepper, diced
2 T. Lemon Juice

2 T. Bragg™ Liquid Aminos
2 T. Tahini
1 C. Sunflower Seeds
2 T. Sesame Seeds
1 T. Parsley
1/2 Tomato, diced (optional)

1. Boil 2 cups of water & add 1cup quinoa. Simmer for 15-20 minutes. Fluff with fork. Cool.
2. Combine the quinoa, grated carrot, scallions, celery and pepper in a bowl. Add the lemon juice, Bragg's™ and tahini and mix thoroughly.
3. In a skillet, toast the sunflower seeds and sesame seeds. Use a medium flame with a small amount of oil and/or tamari, stir often until seeds are toasted.
4. Mix toasted seeds into the quinoa mixture and then add the parsley and tomato. Refrigerate until serving.

"The greatest revolution of our generation is the discovery that human beings, by changing the inner attitudes of their minds, can change the outer aspects of their lives."

WILLIAM JAMES (1842-1910)
American philosopher, teacher and psychologist

Brook's Caesar Salad
serves 8 or more

1/2 lb. Tofu (firm), crumbled	2 T. Nutritional Yeast
2 t. Tamari	2 Garlic Cloves, crushed
1 t. Turmeric	5-6 T. Lemon Juice
1 T. Sunflower/Safflower Oil	Black Pepper, to taste
2 Romaine Lettuce Heads	1/2 t. Mint (dried)
(washed & torn into small pieces)	1 T. Tahini
4 Green Onions, chopped	3/4 t. Sea Salt
<u>Dressing</u>	1 C. Croutons/toasted bread pieces
1/2 C. Olive Oil	Ground Black Pepper, garnish

1. In a bowl, combine tofu, tamari and turmeric.
2. In a skillet, heat a tablespoon of cooking oil and add tofu mix. Cook several minutes on one side and turn. Allow to lightly brown, then scramble the tofu, remove from heat and allow to cool.
3. Mix lettuce, onion and tofu scramble all together.
4. In a separate bowl, whisk all the dressing ingredients together (total of 8 ingredients). Pour over salad and toss well. Add croutons & pepper garnish, lightly toss and serve.

String Bean Salad
serves 3

1 lb. String Beans, steamed well	1 T. Nutritional Yeast
2 Garlic Cloves, minced	1/2 C. Tahini
1 Onion, diced	2 t. Bragg™ Liquid Aminos
1 T. Oil	1/2 t. Spike™ Seasoning
1 T. Bragg™ Liquid Aminos	1/2 C. Water
1/4 t. Onion Powder	1/4 t. Garlic Powder

1. Steam the green beans until soft.
2. Sauté the minced garlic and the diced onion in a small fry pan with the 1 T. of oil and Bragg's™. Season with onion powder and yeast.
3. In a small jar, mix by shaking vigorously, tahini and remaining ingredients.
4. In a bowl, mash the soft green beans. Add the seasoned onions and tahini dressing and mix. Chill before serving.

"Come, my friends; it is not too late to seek a newer world.
We are one equal temper of heroic hearts."

ALFRED LORD TENNYSON (1809-1892)
English poet
Poet Laureate: 1850

Yellow & Green Bean Salad
serves 8

Vinaigrette Dressing

3 Green Scallions (small), chopped	1/2 t. (each) Salt/Red Pepper/Garlic Powder
2 T. Dijon Mustard	1/4 C. Olive Oil
1/4 C. Vinegar	1 T. Sweetener

In a small bowl, whisk scallions, mustard, vinegar, salt, pepper and garlic powder until mixed. Gradually add oil and sweetener, whisking until all is blended.

Salad

1 lb. Green Beans, trimmed	1/2 lb. Tofu (firm), crumbled
1 lb. Wax Beans (yellow), trimmed	1/2 C. Sunflower Seeds
1 Head Radicchio, shredded	1 Navel Orange, peeled, seeds removed
1 Red Onion (medium), chopped	cut into 1/2" pieces

1. In a large skillet, put 3-4 cups of water. Bring water to a boil over high heat. Add beans and cook 8-10 minutes, until tender and crisp.
2. Rinse with cold water until cool, then drain. Pat dry with paper towels.
3. Place beans in large bowl. Add radicchio, onion, tofu, and sunflower seeds.
4. Add dressing, toss gently to coat. Place in serving dish. Top with orange pieces. Serve at room temperature.

Baba Ghannouj
6 appetizer servings

1 (1lb.) Eggplant	1/2 C. Parsley, diced
2 Garlic Cloves, minced	6 T. Tahini
3/4 C. Lemon Juice	Tamari and/or Spike™, to taste

1. Trim off stem of eggplant. Pierce with fork and bake at 350° until the skin is wrinkled.
2. Let cool and then scoop out inside and place in a bowl with minced garlic. Mash with lemon juice, parsley and tahini. Season to taste with Tamari or Spike™. Refrigerate for 1 hour before serving.

> *"...Dickensian compassion rescued children from sweat shops.*
> *Lincolnian empathy rescued slaves from being 'things'.*
> *Civilization weeps while it awaits one more emancipation."*
>
> PAUL HARVEY
> American syndicated columnist
> from his syndicated column, November 1981

Sweet Beet Salad

yields 3 cups

3 C. Steamed Beets, cubed
2 T. Tahini
4-5 T. Vinegar
1/3 C. Bermuda Onion, diced

2 T. Nutritional Yeast
2 T. Tamari
1/2 t. Garlic Powder

Mix all ingredients together in a bowl. Chill and serve.

Quick & Easy Carrot Salad

serves 3-4

2 C. Carrots, grated finely
  (through a Champion Juicer is best)
4 T. Nayonaise™ (Vegan "Mayonnaise")

Sea Salt, dash
1- 2 Onion Slices, diced
1 t. Tahini (optional)
1/2 t. Mustard (optional)

Mix all ingredients together. Chill and serve.

•This carrot salad is like mock salmon salad. Serve as salad or on a sandwich.

Eggless Salad

serves 2

2 C. Tofu, mashed
1 T. Tamari
1 T. Oil
2 Onion Slices, diced small
5-6 T. Vegan "Mayonnaise"
  (or substitute 2 T. Tahini)

2 Celery Stalks, diced fine
1/2 t. Sea Salt
1 t. Turmeric
4-5 T. Nutritional Yeast
1-2 T. Mustard
1 T. Tahini (optional)

In a bowl, mash the tofu. Add the remaining ingredients and mix. Refrigerate.

•Delicious as a salad or on sandwiches.

"Both breast cancer and colon cancer have been generally associated with the level of consumption of animal fat."

ARTHUR UPTON
Director: National Cancer Institute, Oct. 1979

Heart's Hearty Tofu Salad

serves 2-3

1 lb. Tofu
2 T. Nayonaise™ or Veganaise™
3/4 T. Bragg™ Liquid Aminos
1 1/2 Celery Stalks, diced
1/2 C. Green Pepper, diced
1/2 C. Tomato, diced
1/4 C. Onion, diced

1/2 C. Lettuce, chopped
1/8 C. Nutritional Yeast
1/8 t. Black Pepper
1/4 t. Sea Salt
1/4 t. Kelp
1/2 C. Cilantro (optional), chopped

Mash tofu and then add all ingredients.

Tofuna Salad

serves 2-3

1 lb. Firm Tofu (frozen)
1/2 C. Vegan "Mayonnaise"
1 T. Lemon Juice, (fresh)
2 T. Tamari

1-2 Celery Stalks, diced small
1 Scallion (or onion), diced
1/2 t. Kelp

1. Remove tofu from freezer. Allow to thaw. Squeeze the water out of it.
2. Crumble the tofu, add the remaining ingredients and mix. Chill for a few hours, so tofu can absorb the flavors, before serving.
3. Serve as a salad or on sandwiches.

Mock "Tuna" Salad

serves 3
From: Meatless Meals for Working People by Debra Wasserman and Charles Stahler, published by the Vegetarian Resource Group.

1 C. Chick-peas (canned or precooked and drained)
1 Celery Stalk, diced
1 Onion (small), finely chopped
Vegan "Mayonnaise", to taste
Salt and Pepper, to taste

1. Mash the chick-peas in a small bowl. Add remaining ingredients and mix well.
2. Spread on whole grain bread as a sandwich or serve on a bed of lettuce.

"All truth is a species of revelation."

SAMUEL TAYLOR COLERIDGE (1772-1834)
English poet and author

Thai Tofu Salad

serves 4

4 C. Romaine Lettuce, torn
   into bite-sized pieces
1/2 lb. Tofu (firm),
   cut into 1 1/2" pieces
6 Radishes, sliced thinly
2 Kirby Cucumbers, seeded,
   cut into 1 1/2" strips

1 Red Bell Pepper (large), cored,
   seeded, cut into 1 1/2" strips
1 Red Onion (small), sliced thinly
1/4 C. Basil Leaves, chopped
1/4 C. Cilantro Leaves (fresh), chopped
1/8 C. Mint Leaves (fresh), minced

Dressing
1/4 lb. Tofu (soft)
2 T. Tamari
2 T. Lime Juice
2 T. Fructose

1/4 t. Sea Salt
1/4 t. Crushed Red Pepper Spice
2 T. Safflower Oil
1 t. Roasted Sesame Oil

1. Toss lettuce, tofu, radishes, cucumbers, pepper, onion, basil, cilantro and mint together in a large salad bowl.
2. Place ingredients for dressing in blender or food processor. Process until smooth. Pour over salad and toss. Serve immediately.

Tomato Sesame Salad

serves 6

3 Tomatoes (large), diced
1 C. Mushrooms, sliced
1 Yellow Bell Pepper, diced
1 T. Balsamic Vinegar
1 T. Sweetener
1 T. Sesame Oil

1 t. Tamari or 1/4 t. Sea Salt
1 t. Prepared Mustard
1/2 t. Basil (dried)
Black Pepper and/or Cayenne, to taste
Lettuce for 6, washed/dried/torn (2 sm. heads)
Sesame Seeds, for garnish

1. In a salad bowl, toss first 3 ingredients together.
2. In a mixing bowl, combine the remaining ingredients together, except the lettuce and the garnish, and whisk well. Pour this dressing over the tomato mix. Toss and allow to marinate at least 10 minutes.
3. Arrange the lettuce in 6 salad bowls. Spoon 1/6 of the tomato mix into each bowl. Sprinkle with sesame seeds and serve at room temperature.

*"Our bodies are our gardens, to which our
wills are gardeners."*

WILLIAM SHAKESPEARE (1564-1616)
English poet, playwright

Pasta Salad 1

yields 4 cups (1 small bowl)

4 C. Shells (cooked)=(1) 8 oz. package	1/2 t. Onion Powder
2 T. Oil	1 t. Garlic Powder
1 T. Bragg™ Liquid Aminos	2 T. Nutritional Yeast
1 t. Apple Cider Vinegar	1 t. Spike™ Seasoning
1 t. Oregano (dried)	1/2 t. Black Pepper
1/2 t. Basil	1/2 t. Dill Weed

1. Cook the pasta and drain. Place shells in a small bowl and add all the ingredients. Stir well.
2. Serve right away, as noodles tend to soak up flavorings. If served after letting salad marinate, additional seasonings may be necessary.

Pasta Salad II

serves 4-6

4 C. (cooked) or 8 oz. Pasta Shells	1 T. Dill Weed (fresh), chopped
2-3 T. Olive Oil	1 Tomato, diced
2 T. Bragg™ Liquid Aminos	2 Red Onion Slices, diced
1 T. Apple Cider Vinegar	1/4 Bell Pepper, diced
2 t. Oregano (dried)	1 Cucumber, diced
1 t. Basil (dried)	3/4 t. Black Pepper
4 t. Nutritional Yeast	1 t. Spike™ Seasoning
1/2 t. Onion Powder	1 t. Garlic Powder
1/2 t. Dill Weed (dried)	1/2 C. Chick Peas, (Garbanzos)
	Black Olives, sliced (optional)

Mix all ingredients together in a bowl. Allow to marinate and then serve.

Thai Noodle Salad

serves 6

16 oz. package Rice Noodles (sticks)	2 T. Cilantro (fresh), chopped
2/3 C. Rice Vinegar	1 T. Basil (fresh), chopped
1/4 C. Sweetener	or 1 t. Basil (dried)
2 Cucumbers, peeled, julienne	1/4 C. Bragg's ™ or Soy Sauce
2 Scallions, chopped	1/2 t. Red Pepper Flakes (crushed)
1/2 C. Peanuts, chopped	

1. Cook noodles in boiling water, 5 minutes, until just tender. Drain.
   Combine vinegar and sweetener in a small saucepan.
2. Heat until sweetener dissolves. Cool.
3. In a large bowl, combine noodles, cooled vinegar mixture and remaining ingredients.
   Toss to distribute evenly and coat thoroughly.

Curried Pasta Salad
serves 6-8

<u>Dressing</u>
1 lb. Tofu, (soft, homogenized in
    food processor with "S" blade)
1/2 t. Salt
1/2 t. Curry Powder
1/4 t. Cumin (ground)
1/4 t. Onion Powder

<u>Salad</u>
8 oz. package Elbow Pasta (cooked)
4 C. Assorted Vegetables
    (Pepper, Carrots, Celery), chopped
1/2 Cake Tempeh (or 4 oz.),
    (steamed and crumbled)
2 T. Parsley (for garnish), minced

1. In a large bowl, combine ingredients for tofu dressing. Add drained pasta and stir well.
2. Toss in vegetables and tempeh. Season again, if desired.
3. Chill. To serve, garnish with parsley.

Bean Salsa in Radicchio Leaves
yields approximately 5 cups

3 C. Pinto Beans, cooked
1 Red Onion, chopped
2 Tomatoes, chopped
1 Yellow Bell Pepper, chopped
1 C. Corn Kernels
2 Jalapeño Peppers, thinly sliced

1/3 C. Cilantro, minced
1/2 C. Tomato Sauce
1 T. Vinegar
1 t. Sea Salt (or to taste)
Radicchio Leaves
2 Avocados, cubed

1. In a large bowl, combine all ingredients, except for radicchio and avocados.
   Set aside, at room temperature, for two hours.
2. To serve: place 1/4 cup of bean salsa into each radicchio leaf using a slotted spoon.
   Garnish with avocado.

   •Variation: Toss Bean Salsa with hot or cold pasta.

Navy Beans & Corn Salad
serves 6

5 T. Apple Cider Vinegar
4 T. Dijon Mustard
1 t. Sea Salt
1/2 t. Red Pepper
2 t. Sweetener
2 T. Olive Oil

4 C. Corn Kernels
4 C. Navy Beans (cooked), drained, rinsed
1 Red Onion (small), chopped
1 Head of Romaine Lettuce, washed,
    drained and finely chopped

1. Combine vinegar, mustard, salt, pepper and sweetener in a large bowl. Whisk in oil.
2. Add in remaining ingredients and stir well. Chill and serve.

Caribbean Spicy Black Bean Salad

serves 4

Spicy Dressing
1/2 t. Salt
1/2 t. Red Pepper Flakes
1/4 t. Ground Allspice
1/4 t. Cumin
1/4 t. Oregano (dried)
1/4 C. Olive Oil
1 T. Apple Cider Vinegar
1 T. Sweetener

Salad
4 C. Black Beans (cooked), drained, rinsed
1 Bunch Watercress (large), chopped
1 C. Red & Yellow Pepper (mixed), diced
2 C. Corn Kernels (optional)
6 C. Baby Greens (loosely packed)
2 Scallions, sliced thinly

1. In a small bowl, whisk together dressing ingredients.
2. In large bowl, toss beans, watercress, peppers, celery, and corn kernels with 1/4 cup of dressing.
3. Arrange greens on 4 serving plates. Top each with bean mixture and then drizzle with remaining dressing. Sprinkle with scallion slices.

La Cabana Salad

1 Head-Curly Leaf Lettuce, (washed and drained)
1 Bunch Arugula, stemmed, washed
2 Tomatoes (ripe)
1 (8 oz.) Cake Tempeh, steamed
1 Sweet Red Pepper, cored & seeded
2 Beets, steamed & diced
2 Celery Stalks, sliced thinly

2 C. Mixed Cooked Beans, (navy, kidney or your choice)
Dressing:
2 T. Mustard (prepared)
2 T. Apple Cider Vinegar
2 T. Lemon Juice (fresh)
1/2 t. Sea Salt
3 T. Olive Oil
1/2 t. Red Pepper Flakes

1. To prepare salad, core lettuce and cut into 1/4" slices. In mixing bowl gently toss it with arugula.
2. Arrange in bottom of 6 shallow salad bowls, mounding it toward center. Cut each tomato into wedges. Cut tempeh and pepper into thin strips.
3. Arrange tomatoes, tempeh and pepper strips on top of lettuce in sunburst (radiating away from center, like spokes of a wagon wheel, alternating colors).
4. Rinse beets under cold water after steaming. Blot dry, dice. Mound beets, celery and beans in center of salad.
5. To make dressing, combine mustard, vinegar, lemon juice, salt and oil in a mixing bowl and whisk until salt is dissolved.
6. Whisk in red pepper flakes. Pour over salad and serve.

"Harmlessness is the highest religion."

JAIN (JAINISM) MAXIM

Cuban Black Bean Salad
serves 2

2 C. Black Beans (cooked), drained and rinsed	1/4 t. Cumin Powder
1/2 C. Red Bell Pepper, diced	3 T. Vinegar
1/2 C. Red Onion, diced	3 T. Olive Oil
1/4 C. Cilantro (fresh), chopped	1/4 t. Sea Salt
	1/8 t. Red Pepper

1. Place beans, red bell pepper, onion and cilantro in a salad bowl.
2. Stir together cumin powder, vinegar and oil in a cup. Pour over bean mixture and gently stir, coating evenly. Season with salt and pepper, to taste.

•Variation: Place all above ingredients in a food processor, along with 3 chopped garlic cloves and 1 T. lime juice. Process until creamy to make a dip.

Potato Salad
serves 6-8

	Blender Mixture
8 C. Cooked Potatoes, cubed	2/3 C. Oil
2/3 C. Celery, diced	1/3 C. Apple Cider Vinegar
1/4 C. Fresh Parsley, chopped	1 C. Tofu (soft), mashed
1/8 C. Scallion, diced	1 T. Bragg™ Liquid Aminos
1 C. Onion, diced	2-3 T. Mustard (prepared)
2/3 C. Carrot, grated	2 T. Rice Syrup
1 t. Dill Weed, dried	1/2 T. Garlic Powder
1 T. Nutritional Yeast	1/2 T. Onion Powder
1 t. Sea Salt	1 t. Spike™ Seasoning
1/4 t. Black Pepper	

1. Boil the cubed potatoes (approx. 4-5 lbs.) until soft, but still somewhat firm in texture. Drain and rinse. Chill to harden the potatoes.
2. In a bowl, mix the potatoes, celery, parsley, scallions, onion, grated carrot and dill weed. Sprinkle on the nutritional yeast, salt and pepper.
3. In a blender, blend the remaining ingredients, beginning with the oil. Pour this blended mixture over the potatoes in the bowl. Stir in to cover potatoes completely. Allow to marinate for several hours or overnight before serving.

> *"The problems of the world cannot possibly be solved by skeptics and cynics whose horizons are limited by obvious realities. We need men who can dream of things that never were."*
>
> JOHN F. KENNEDY (1917-1963)
> 35th President of the United States of America

Potato Salad a la 'Kate'

yields 1 large bowl

5 lbs. Red Potatoes
1/4 Red Onion, minced
3.4 oz. Capers (bottle)
1 C. Nayonaise™ or Veganaise™
1 T. Sweetener or Pickle Relish

1 Bunch Fresh Dill, chopped
1 Bunch of Scallions, minced
6 Celery Stalks, diced
Sea Salt, to taste
Black Pepper, to taste

1. Cut potatoes into chunks. Boil until soft. Drain and rinse.
2. Mix ingredients in with potatoes and stir. Chill and allow flavors to absorb.

Curried Potato Salad

yields 6 cups

2 lbs. Red Potatoes,
   scrubbed and cubed
1 T. Mustard Seed
1 t. Cumin Seeds
1 t. Curry Powder
1/8 t. Red Pepper Flakes
2 T. Lemon Juice (fresh)

1 t. Ginger (fresh), grated
1 t. Sea Salt
1 t. Olive Oil
1 Red Onion (small), chopped finely
2 Jalapeño Peppers, seeded & minced
1 C. Green Peas
1/4 C. Cilantro (fresh), chopped

1. Boil potatoes in salted water, just until tender (20-30 minutes), then drain.
   Cool slightly and dice small.
2. Toast mustard seeds, cumin seeds, curry, and pepper in a pan over low heat, until
   fragrant (about 1 minute). Transfer to large bowl, whisk in lemon juice, ginger, salt, then
   oil. Add onion, jalapeños and warm potatoes. Toss, then cool.
3. Add peas and cilantro.

Creamy Cole Slaw

yields 1 large bowl

1 Head Green Cabbage, shredded
2 C. Carrots, shredded
1/4 C. Onion, grated
3/4 C. Celery, diced
1/2 C. Oil
1/2 C. Apple Cider Vinegar

5 T. Fructose or Sucanat
1/2 T. Bragg™ Liquid Aminos
1/4 t. Dill Weed
1/2 T. Spike™ Seasoning
Lemon Juice, a squeeze
1 1/8 C. Tofu (soft), mashed

1. In a large bowl, mix together the cabbage, carrots, onion and celery.
2. In a blender, blend the remaining ingredients. Pour over the vegetables and allow to
   marinate for at least one hour before serving.

Greek Chick Pea Salad
serves 4-6

Vinaigrette
2 T. Water
2 T. Olive Oil
1/2 C. Tomato Juice
1 T. Tomato Sauce
1 Tomato, chopped
Hot Sauce, dash
2 T. Vinegar
2 T. Sweetener

1/4 t. Sea Salt
1/4 C. Tamari or Bragg™ Liquid Aminos
1/4 t. Garlic Powder
Salad:
3 C. Chick Peas (cooked), drained
2 Tomatoes, chopped 1/2" thick
2 C. Tofu (firm), crumbled
1/2 C. Black Olives (pitted), drained
2 Scallions, sliced
1/4 C. Parsley (fresh), chopped

1. Blend all vinaigrette ingredients in a blender about 15 seconds and set aside.
2. Combine all salad ingredients in a large bowl. Toss lightly.
3. Add vinaigrette to salad. Toss to distribute evenly and coat thoroughly.
   Cover and chill before serving.

Greek Lentil Salad
serves 4

2 C. Cooked Lentils (3/4-1 C. dry)
2 C. Cooked Quinoa (about 3/4 C. dry)
1/2 C. Olive Oil
1/4 C. Vinegar
4 Garlic Cloves, minced
1 T. Greek Oregano

1 Red Onion, minced
4 Ripe Tomatoes, chopped
1 C. Kalamata Olives (pitted), sliced
1/2 C. Tofu (firm), cubed
2 T. Nutritional Yeast
1/2 t. Salt & Pepper

1. Cook the lentils and quinoa separately and allow to chill. (see Cooking Guides for Grains & Beans, pages 18 and 19)
2. Combine olive oil, vinegar, garlic and oregano in small bowl and set aside.
3. Combine cooked lentils & cooked quinoa in bowl. Add onion, tomatoes, olives, tofu and nutritional yeast. Pour dressing over all and toss to mix well. Season to taste. Refrigerate salad at least 30 minutes before serving.

"A varied whole food vegan diet contains adequate levels of energy and protein to sustain good health in all age groups, as evidenced by studies of vegans across the world."

GILL LANGLEY, MA., Ph.D.
British author
Vegan Nutrition, U.K.

Jamaican Breadfruit Salad
serves 4-6

1 Breadfruit	1 1/2 C. Corn Kernels
2 C. Tofu (soft), mashed well	1 1/2 C. Green Peas
2 T. Tahini	2 Carrots, grated
2 T. Mustard	1 t. Hot Sauce
2 T. Nutritional Yeast	1 t. each: Salt, Red Pepper, Garlic Powder
1 Onion (small), grated	Paprika and Parsley to garnish

1. Peel the breadfruit and cut into 1" cubes. Bring to a boil in a pot of salted water, enough to cover breadfruit. Boil until soft, but not mushy, about 15 minutes. Drain and place in bowl. (Whole breadfruit can be baked in the oven, as well.) Let cool.
2. Mix together breadfruit, tofu, tahini, mustard, nutritional yeast, onion, corn, peas and carrots. Mix well, then season with hot sauce, salt, pepper and garlic powder. Garnish with paprika and parsley.

Garbanzo Salad
serves 4

2 C. Garbanzo Beans (soaked, cooked, and drained)	1-2 Garlic Cloves, minced
2 Carrots, grated	2 T. Tahini
1 Beet (medium), grated	2 T. Balsamic Vinegar
2 Green Onions, chopped	1 T. Water
1/4 C. Parsley (fresh), chopped fine	Sea Salt, to taste
	Black Pepper, to taste

1. See 'Cooking Guide for Beans' to prepare the garbanzo beans.
2. In a mixing bowl, combine beans, carrots, beets, onions and parsley together.
3. In a separate bowl, whisk together the remaining ingredients and pour over the bean mix. Toss well and serve over crisp garden greens.

> *"The obligations of law and equity reach only to mankind; but kindness and beneficence should be extended to the creatures of every species, and these will flow from the breast of a true man, as streams that issue from the living fountain.*
>
> PLUTARCH (46-120 AD.)
> Greek philosopher and moralist

3 Bean Salad
serves 6-8

2 C. Pinto Beans (small),
   soaked, cooked, and drained
2 C. Kidney Beans (cooked), drained
2 C. Green Beans (cooked and sliced)
1 Red Onion, sliced into crescent shape
2 Celery Stalks, diced
2 T. Balsamic Vinegar

1 1/2 T. Dijon Mustard
1 T. Tamari
2 T. Maple Syrup
1 t. Nutritional Yeast
2 T. Water
1 t. Basil (dry)

1. See 'Cooking Guide for Beans' for preparation of beans.
2. In a large bowl, combine beans, onion and celery together.
3. In a separate bowl, whisk all remaining ingredients together and pour over bean mix. Toss and chill. Allow at least 30 minutes for flavors to marry. Mix again and serve at room temperature.

Mushroom - Arugula Salad
serves 4

1/4 C. Veggie Stock or Water
2 T. Balsamic Vinegar
1 T. Sweetener
1/2 t. (each) Salt & Red Pepper
4 T. Olive Oil
4 Bunches Arugula (or 12 oz.),
   stems trimmed, washed & drained

4 Cloves Garlic, crushed
2 T. Nutritional Yeast
8 oz. Shiitake Mushrooms, stems
   discarded & caps cut into quarters
8 oz. Button Mushrooms, sliced
1 T. Parsley (fresh), chopped

1. In a small bowl, mix stock, vinegar, sweetener, salt, pepper and 2 tablespoons of oil.
2. Arrange arugula on large platter, then set aside.
3. In large skillet, (cast iron or non-stick) heat remaining olive oil on medium heat. Add garlic and cook just until golden brown. Add mushrooms and yeast and cook 8-10 minutes, until mushrooms are browned and liquid evaporates.
4. Add stock mixture to skillet. Cook 30 seconds, stirring. Immediately pour mushroom mixture over arugula. Top with parsley and a sprinkle of nutritional yeast.

"If there would come a voice from God saying, 'I'm against vegetarianism!' I would say, 'Well, I am for it!' This is how strongly I feel in this regard."

ISAAC BASHEVIS SINGER (1904-1991)
Yiddish Laureate of Literature
1978 Nobel Prize recipient

Cabbage, Carrot and Jicama Salad
serves 4-6

1/4 C. Cilantro or Mint Leaves
   (fresh), chopped
1/2 C. Lime Juice (fresh)
1/2 C. Maple Syrup
1/2 t. Sea Salt
1/4 t. Red Pepper (crushed)
5-6 Carrots, shredded

1 Head Green Cabbage (small),
   shredded
1 Jicama (medium), peeled & cut
   into 1/8" thick sticks
1/2 Red Pepper, cored & seeded,
   cut into 1/8" thick slices
2 T. Sunflower Seeds
1/2 C. Raisins (optional)

1. In large bowl, using a fork, mix chopped cilantro, lime juice, maple syrup, salt and crushed red pepper.
2. Add carrots, cabbage, jicama and red pepper. Toss.
3. Cover and refrigerate if not serving right away. Garnish with sunflower seeds & raisins.

Waldorf Salad
serves 4-6

3 C. Apples, peeled, chopped
1 T. Lemon Juice
1/2 C. Celery, chopped
1/2 C. Golden Raisins
1/2 C. Dark Raisins
1/2 C. Walnuts, chopped
1/2 C. Pitted Dates, chopped
Vanilla Tofu Yogurt
1/2 lb. Tofu (soft)

1/4-1/2 C. Apple Juice
1 t. Vanilla Extract
1 T. Sweetener
Vanilla Tofu Yogurt Dressing
1 1/2 C. Vanilla Tofu Yogurt
1 T. Grated Lemon Peel
1/4 t. Ground Nutmeg
1 T. Dry Sweetener

1. In a bowl, toss apples with lemon juice. Add celery, raisins, walnuts and dates.
2. Place Vanilla Tofu Yogurt ingredients in a blender or food processor. Homogenize. Chill.
3. Vanilla Tofu Yogurt Dressing: Place vanilla yogurt in bowl. Gently fold-in lemon peel, nutmeg and sweetener. Coat salad with dressing.

"Our task must be to free ourselves...
by widening our circle of compassion to embrace all living creatures,
and the whole of nature and its beauty."

ALBERT EINSTEIN (1879-1955)
German born, American physicist
1921 Nobel Prize Winner

Corn Relish
serves 4

4 Ears of Corn,
   kernels cut from cob, then cooked
2 Scallions (green part only), diced
2 Peppers, cored, seeded, and diced
2 Celery Stalks, trimmed, diced

Dressing
1/2 t. Cumin
1 T. Lime Juice
1 T. Sweetener
1 T. Broth (or water)
1 t. Garlic Powder
1 t. Salt and Pepper (each)

1. Combine corn kernels, green scallions, peppers and celery in mixing bowl. Toss gently.
2. Stir together cumin, lime juice, sweetener and broth.
3. Pour over salad and toss again. Season to taste with salt, pepper and garlic.

Light Garden Vegetable Soup
serves 4-5

1 Onion (medium), diced
2 C. Carrots, sliced
2 C. Cauliflower Flowerets
3 C. Zucchini, sliced in halves
3 Roma Tomatoes, cubed
Blender Ingredients
3 C. Water
3-4 T. Bragg's™ or Tamari
1 t. Dill Weed

1/2 T. Dr. Bronner's Bouillon™
2 T. Nutritional Yeast
2 1/2 C. Cooked Vegetables
   (mostly the carrots; no zucchini)
3 t. Miso (blonde)
1 t. Salt-Free Spike™ Seasoning
1 t. Onion Powder
1 t. Oregano (dried)

1. In a soup pot, sauté the onion in a little oil or water, then the carrots and cauliflower. When almost soft, add the zucchini and tomatoes. Cover and simmer until soft.
2. In a blender, blend the Blender Ingredients. (You will be blending some of the softened vegetables from the pot into this blender. Pick out the carrots and tomatoes, and do not blend the zucchini pieces). Blend well and pour back into the soup pot. Add more water for a thinner soup. Cook 15 minutes.

> *"We cannot know for sure whose domination came first, but we can see that today, the domination of women and the domination of animals, especially those exploited for food, are deeply intertwined."*
>
> CAROL J. ADAMS
> Author of: The Sexual Politics of Meat, Neither Man Nor Beast

Creamy Vegetable Soup

yields 9 cups

1 Onion, sliced	2 t. Spike™ Seasoning
2 Garlic Cloves	1 t. Garlic Powder
4 Carrots (medium) sliced	2 t. Onion Powder
3 Potatoes, cubed	2 T. Fresh Dill
Tamari, to taste	1 t. Herb Seasoning
2 Celery Stalks, sliced	1/4-1/2 C. Cashew Butter
8 C. Water or Stock	2-3 C. Assorted Vegetables (Peas, Broccoli, Zucchini, etc.)

1. Sauté onion and garlic in 1 T. of oil or water. Add the carrots and potatoes. Stir and add 2 cups of water and the tamari. Simmer. Add the celery when vegetables begin to soften.
2. When vegetables are soft, remove half the potatoes and carrots and blend in a blender with 2 cups of water, the remaining seasonings and cashew butter.
3. Return blended liquid to the pot and add the remaining vegetables and 4 cups of water. Let simmer for 15-20 minutes until flavors are blended and vegetables are soft. This soup is even better when it sits for a few hours, if you can wait that long!

Tomato Vegetable Soup

serves 6-8

1/4 C. Oil	1/2 C. Green Peas, fresh
2 Garlic Cloves, diced	10-12 C. Tomato Sauce/Stewed Tomato Juice
2 Onions, chopped	1/2 C. Bragg's™ or Tamari
1 Potato (large), cubed	1 t. Parsley
2 Carrots, sliced	1/2 t. Dill Weed
2 Celery Stalks, sliced	1/2 t. Garlic Powder
1/2 C. Broccoli, chopped	1/2 t. Sweet Basil
1/2 C. Cauliflower, chopped	1/2 t. Sea Salt

1. In a large soup pot, heat the oil over medium heat. Add garlic, onions, potato, carrots and celery. Sauté for 5 minutes. Season with half of the spices.
2. Add the remaining vegetables and cook for 3-4 minutes. Add the stock, reduce heat and simmer for one hour. Add the remaining seasoning, to taste.
3. When veggies are soft, spoon half of them, especially carrots and potatoes, from the soup into a blender. Add 2 cups stock from soup pot and purée for 1 minute.
4. Return mixture to the pot. Cook for 1 hour more over low heat and serve.

"We have committed the golden rule to memory;
let us now commit it to life."

EDWIN MARKHAM (1852-1940)
American poet

Vietnamese Noodle Soup

serves 4

6 C. Vegetable Stock or Water
1" Piece Fresh Ginger, chopped
2- 4 Scallions, chopped
4 T. Tamari
8 oz. Package Rice Sticks, broken up
1 lb. Tofu (firm), cubed

1 Onion (medium), sliced thinly
1 Bunch Basil (fresh), washed, chopped
3-4 C. Bean Sprouts
2 Jalapeño Chiles, sliced thinly
1 Lime, quartered

1. In a sauce pan, on medium heat, add the first four ingredients to make a broth. Simmer for 15 minutes.
2. Soak the rice sticks (noodles) in a separate pot, in warm water, for 30 minutes. When ready to serve, cook rice sticks in enough boiling water to cover noodles, for about 2-3 minutes and then drain.
3. Meanwhile heat broth and add tofu. Cook on medium heat for 2 minutes.
4. Divide drained noodles into 4 separate bowls. Also divide onion slices, basil, bean sprouts and chili slices into each bowl. Spoon the broth and tofu on top.
5. Serve the soup at once with a lime wedge.

Split Pea Soup

yields 3/4 of a big pot

3 C. (dry) Split Peas
1-2 Onions, diced
4-5 Carrots, sliced
1-2 Potatoes, cubed
1/4 t. Curry Powder

1 T. Dill Weed
1/4 t. Cumin
2 T. Bragg's™ or Tamari
1 T. Spike™ Seasoning
1 t. Sea Salt

1. Boil the split peas in their own separate pot with 6 or more cups of water.
2. In a big soup pot, sauté the onions in a little oil/water and then add the carrots and potatoes. Cook until soft and remove from heat.
3. When the split peas are cooked, scoop out 2 cups and mix in blender with 1 cup of water and the seasonings, except sea salt. Pour into soup pot.
4. Repeat the same process of blending another 2 cups of split peas and one cup of water.
5. Add remaining non-blended split peas into the soup pot. Season with sea salt at the end.

"My favorite quote says it all... 'Become a vegan/vegetarian: your body will respect you for your wisdom and the animals will love you for your compassion.'"

CASEY KASEM
American Top 40 radio personality

Summer's Pressure-Cooked Split Pea Soup

serves 6-8

3 T. Safflower Oil	1 1/2 C. Split Peas, rinsed
2 C. Onion, chopped finely	1 1/2 Carrots, sliced
1 T. Sea Salt	3 Celery Stalks, diced
2 T. Tabasco™	1 1/2 C. Tomatoes, cubed
7 Garlic Cloves, chopped finely	1/2 C. Cilantro, chopped finely
2 Potatoes (large), cubed	10 C. Water

1. Heat oil in pressure cooker on medium-high heat. Fry onions, salt, and tabasco for 3 minutes.
2. Add garlic and then the potatoes. Fry for 2 minutes. Add split peas, mix well, and add 4 cups of water. Cook for 3 minutes and then add carrots.
3. When water starts to boil, add celery. (Feel free to add as much celery as you like, as it enhances the soup.) Add 6 more cups of water. Put the top on the pressure cooker and cook on high heat until full pressure occurs. Then lower the heat to medium-low and cook for 5 minutes. Take off heat and place under cold water until pressure dissipates. Open and add the tomato and cilantro, and then return heat to high. Put the pot back on without the top and return to boil until tomatoes soften. Cook slightly and then serve.

Corn Chowder Soup

serves 6-8

3 T. Oil	3-4 Potatoes, diced
3 Onions (large), diced	2-3 Carrots, sliced
4 Garlic Cloves, minced	3 T. Bragg's™ or Tamari
5 C. Fresh Corn Kernels (cut from the cob)	1 t. Garlic Powder
3 T. Soy Powder	1/2 t. Basil
2 1/2 Quarts Water	1/2 t. Thyme
4 T. Tahini	1 t. Sea Salt

1. In a large pot, heat the oil. Add the onions and garlic and sauté for 3-4 minutes.
2. Mix in the corn. Sauté for 3-4 minutes more.
3. In a blender, combine 1/3 of the corn/onion sauté with 1 T. soy powder and 1/3 of the water and whiz. Set mixture aside. Repeat blending 2 more times with remaining 2/3 of corn/onion mixture, adding tahini to the final blender. A thick creamy texture is desired. Pour blended mixture back into soup pot.
4. Add remaining ingredients and cook (don't boil) on medium-heat until vegetables are soft.

"When we allow ourselves to feel our feelings, what should be intolerable becomes intolerable."

KENNY LOGGINS
American musician/singer

Cream of Cauliflower Soup
serves 6

2 C. Cooked Brown Rice	1/4 C. Bragg's™ or Tamari
5 C. Vegetable Stock	1/2 t. Garlic Powder
1 Head Cauliflower, chopped	1/4 t. Basil
2 t. Tahini	1/8 t. Cayenne
2 Celery Stalks, chopped	

1. Put 1/3 of cooked rice and 1/3 of stock in blender; purée at high speed for 1 minute, until creamy. Pour into large soup pot.
2. Do step 1 two more times.
3. Add 1/2 of the cauliflower to blender with water, tahini, and spices and blend at high speed for one minute. Add mixture into the soup pot.
4. Place over medium heat; add the remaining chopped cauliflower and celery.
5. Cook for approximately one hour, stirring often, until the cauliflower is tender.

Navy Bean Soup
serves 6-8

2 C. Navy or Pinto Beans	8 Garlic Cloves, diced
Approximately 10 C. Water	1 Carrot, sliced
1/3 C. Oil	1 Celery Stalk, sliced
1/4 C. Bragg's ™ or Tamari	1 t. Garlic Powder
2 Onions, diced	2 Bay Leaves

1. Soak the beans overnight in water to cover.
2. The next day, drain, rinse the beans and place in a large pot. Cover with water and place over medium heat (or use pre-cooked beans).
3. Add oil, Bragg's™ or Tamari, one of the diced onions, 4 garlic cloves, and spices. Cook for about one hour. Add the carrots, celery, remaining onion and garlic cloves.
4. Cook for approximately one hour more, until the carrots and beans are tender.
5. Remove bay leaves before serving.

> *To waste, to destroy our natural resources, to skin and exhaust the land instead of using it so as to increase its usefulness, will result in undermining in the days of our children the very prosperity which we ought by right to hand down to them amplified and developed."*
>
> THEODORE ROOSEVELT (1858-1919)
> 26th President of the United States
> Message to Congress, December 3, 1907

'Soup'erb Creamy Lima Bean
serves 6

1-2 T. Oil (optional)
1 Onion (large), diced
2 C. Carrots, sliced
2 C. Cauliflower Flowerets
6 C. Water
3 C. Lima Beans (cooked)

2 T. Bragg™ Liquid Aminos
2 T. Nutritional Yeast
1 t. Spike™ Seasoning
1 t. Dill Weed
1 t. Oregano (dried)
1 t. Garlic (granulated)
1/4 C. Miso

(Cook the Lima Beans before beginning the soup. See 'Cooking Guide for Beans' pg. 19).

1. In a soup pot, sauté the onion in a little oil (optional). Add the carrots and cauliflower and a little water, cover and steam.
2. In a blender, blend 2 cups of water with 1 cup of the cooked lima beans, 1 cup of the cooked carrots and cauliflower, Bragg Liquid Aminos and yeast. Pour back into the soup pot. Add 2 cups of water to the pot as well.
3. In the blender, again, blend 2 cups of water with 1 cup of the lima beans and pour into soup pot.
4. Add remaining flavorings (except miso) and the remaining 1 cup of whole lima beans to the pot and bring to a boil.
5. When soup reaches a boil, remove from heat. Take out 1-2 cups of the soup and mix with the miso in a bowl. Pour this mixture back into the soup pot. Serve.

Creamy Potato Soup
yields 1 large pot

3 Garlic Cloves
2 T. Oil
2 T. Water
2 Onions (large), diced
6 C. Potatoes, cubed
2 C. Carrots, sliced
6 1/3 C. Water

2 T. Cashew Butter
1 T. Spike™ Seasoning
2 T. Bragg™ Liquid Aminos
1/2 T. Sea Salt
1 t. Dill Weed
1/2 t. Black Pepper
Dill Weed (fresh), chopped

1. In a blender, blend the garlic cloves with oil and water. Pour into soup pot.
2. Sauté the onions in this garlic oil. When the onions are partially cooked, add the potatoes and then the carrots. Add 1/3 cup of water and cover, allowing the vegetables to soften. Stir frequently.
3. In a blender, blend 2 cups of water, cashew butter, Spike™, Bragg's™ and 1 cup of cooked potatoes from the pot. Blend well. Pour back into the soup pot.
4. In a blender again, blend 1 cup of the cooked potatoes and 2 cups of water. Pour back into the pot. Add 2 more cups of water, sea salt to taste, dill weed, pepper, and the fresh dill. Simmer for 15-30 minutes. Serve.

Vichyssoise Soup

serves 6

3 Leeks (medium)
2 T. Olive Oil
4 Potatoes (medium), peeled and diced
3 C. Water or Broth

2 C. Soy Milk
1/4 t. Sea Salt
1/4 t. Red Pepper

1. Cut and discard the roots and tough leaves from the leeks. Cut the leeks in half, length wise, and rinse under cold water to remove dirt. Cut the leeks crosswise in 1/4 inch slices. You should end up with about 2 cups.
2. In a medium sauce pan, over medium heat, add olive oil and leeks. Stir and cook for 5 minutes. Add potatoes and water and bring to a boil. Lower heat to low, cover and simmer for 30 minutes.
3. Transfer the leek mixture to a blender or food processor and blend until smooth. Return to pot and stir in soy milk, salt, and pepper.
4. If desired, chill the soup before serving or warm over low heat until soup is just heated through.

New Age Chowder

yields 10 cups

1 T. Safflower Oil
6-8 Pieces of Seitan, sliced thin
1/4 C. Water
3 Carrots, sliced thinly
3 Celery Stalks, diced (or Fennel Bulb)
1 Onion, diced
4 Potatoes (medium), peeled

3 C. Water
1 Bay Leaf
3 C. Soy Milk
1 lb. Tofu (firm)
1 C. Soy Milk (thick)
1/4 t. Garlic Powder
1/4 t. Sea Salt
1/8 t. Black Pepper

1. In a sauce pan, over medium heat, add oil and seitan. Cook about 5 minutes, until browned. Add 1/4 cup water, carrots, celery/fennel and onion.
   Cook until lightly brown, 6-8 minutes stirring occasionally.
2. Peel and cut potatoes into 1/2 inch cubes and add to pot with 3 cups water and bay leaf. Cook on medium heat for 10 minutes. Reduce heat to low, add soy milk and cover. Simmer for 10 minutes, until vegetables are tender.
3. Cut tofu into 1/2 inch cubes and add to soup. Cook covered for 3 minutes, then carefully stir in thick soy milk. Simmer on low for 3 more minutes. Discard bay leaf and season with garlic powder, sea salt and pepper to taste.

"Salmonella contamination is endemic in the poultry industry."

MICHAEL A. KLAPER, M.D.
American author and international lecturer

Coconut Ginger Soup 1

serves 5-6

1 Onion, chopped
3 Garlic Cloves, chopped
3-4 T. Ginger, chopped
1 t. Oil (or use water)
6 Carrots (large), sliced
1 Potato (large), cubed
2 Celery Stalks, diced

1 1/2 C. Coconut Milk
1 C. Nutritional Yeast
1 T. Spike™ Seasoning
2 T. Tamari
2 t. Cayenne (optional)
1/2 C. Peas (defrosted if frozen)

1. Sauté (using oil or water) onion, with the garlic and 2 T. of ginger. Add the carrots, potato and celery. Fill the pot with enough water to cover vegetables and let simmer.
2. In a blender, blend 2 cups of water with coconut milk, yeast and remaining ginger and spices. Add this to the pot when the veggies are beginning to get soft. Add the peas in at the end.
3. Let simmer for 10-15 minutes until flavors are blended. Serve warm.

Coconut Ginger Soup II

serves 5-6

1 Onion (large), sliced
1 T. Oil
3 Garlic Cloves (optional)
3-4 T. Fresh Ginger, diced
2 Potatoes (large), cubed
5 Carrots, sliced
2 Celery Stalks, diced

1 (14) oz. Can Coconut Milk
1 t. Sea Salt
1 t. Powdered Ginger
1 t. Onion Powder
2 t. Spike™ Seasoning
2-3 T. Bragg™ Liquid Aminos
1/2 C. Peas or Zucchini

1. In a soup pot, sauté the onion in oil or water, adding the garlic and half of the ginger, while onions soften. Add the potatoes, carrots and celery with enough water to cover the vegetables by an inch. Cover and simmer.
2. When the vegetables are softened, scoop out 1 1/2 cups of the vegetables and blend with 1 cup of water and the coconut milk. Add the rest of the ginger and seasonings. Blend well. Pour this blended mixture back into the pot.
3. Add the peas or sliced zucchini or any softer vegetable in bite-sized pieces. Cook until these vegetables are soft (approximately 10 minutes) adding more water if desired. Serve.

"Mankind's true moral test, its fundamental test (which lies deeply buried from view), consists of its attitude towards those who are at its mercy: animals."

MILAN KUNDERA
Czech author, poet, playwright
Author of, <u>The Unbearable Lightness of Being</u>

Coconut Curry Soup

Serves 5-6

5 Garlic Cloves	2 T. Cashew Butter
2 T. Oil	1 T. Curry
2 T. Bragg™ Liquid Aminos	1 t. Onion Powder
1-2 Onions (large), sliced	1 t. Garlic Powder
2 C. Carrots, sliced	2 T. (additional) Bragg's™ or Tamari
3 C. Potatoes, cubed	2 t. Spike™ Seasoning
1 (14) oz. Can Coconut Milk	1 C. Broccoli, Cauliflower, etc.

1. In a blender, blend the garlic with oil and 2 T. Bragg's. Pour into a large soup pot and sauté the onions in this garlic oil. When onions soften, add the carrots and potatoes with 1/2 cup of water. Cover and simmer.
2. When the vegetables are softened, scoop out 1 cup of the vegetables and blend with 2 cups of water and the coconut milk. Pour this back into the pot.
3. Pull out another cup of cooked veggies and blend with 2 more cups of water, cashew butter, curry and remaining seasonings. Pour this blended mixture back into the pot.
4. At this point, add some cauliflower and broccoli or any vegetables in bite-sized pieces. Cook until these vegetables are soft and serve.

Creamy Carrot Coconut Soup

Serves 6

1 T. Oil (optional)	1 (14) oz. Can Coconut Milk
1 Onion (large), sliced	1-2 t. Sea Salt
4 Garlic Cloves, diced	1 t. Onion Powder
8 C. Carrots, sliced	1 t. Garlic Powder
2 t. Bragg's™ or Tamari	6- 8 C. Water

1. In a soup pot, sauté onion in oil (or use 2-3 T. water). Add garlic in 2 minutes and stir.
2. When onions are softening, add carrots and stir in Braggs/Tamari, simmer on low for 3 minutes stirring often.
3. Add coconut milk, the rest of the seasonings and 4 C. water. Bring to almost a boil, cover and simmer on low until carrots are soft.
4. Let cool, then remove and blend 1/2 of the carrots and broth in a blender, using additional water if desired. Use caution when blending anything hot; it expands in blender and can push the top off. (Use less water for a thicker creamier soup.)

> *"The greatest man is he who chooses right with the most invincible resolution."*
>
> SENECA (8 BC.-AD. 65)
> Roman philosopher

Sea Vegetable Miso Soup
serves 4-6

4 Garlic Cloves, minced
2 Onions, diced
3 Carrots, sliced
2 Celery Stalks, diced
1 t. Onion & Garlic Powder
4 T. Bragg's™ or Tamari

1 t. Parsley Flakes
7 C. Water or Stock
Stick of Kombu / Sea Vegetable of Choice
6 T. Miso Paste
1 C. Noodles (cooked)

1. In a soup pot, sauté the garlic and onions in a small amount of oil or water. When onions are soft, add the remaining vegetables and seasonings (except miso).
2. Add the water or vegetable stock along with the sea vegetable of choice and simmer until all vegetables are soft.
3. Remove 1 cup of hot broth from pot and mix with the miso until blended. Pour this back into the soup pot. Stir. Add noodles. Serve.

'Soup'er Onion Soup
serves 4

3 Onions, sliced or diced
3 T. Bragg™ Liquid Aminos
3 T. Nutritional Yeast
1/4 C. Cashew Butter
1/2 C. Nutritional Yeast

2 T. Dr. Bronner's Bouillon™
1 T. Onion Powder
1/2 T. Garlic Powder
2 T. Miso (unpasteurized)
5 C. Water

1. In a medium size pot, sauté the onions in a little oil. Add Bragg's™ and yeast.
2. When onions are soft, pull out 1 cup and place them in the blender with 3 cups of water, cashew butter, 1/2 cup of nutritional yeast, bouillon, onion powder and garlic powder. Blend and pour back into the soup pot.
3. Bring to a boil and stir for 5-10 minutes. Remove from flame.
4. In the blender, blend the miso with 1 cup of water and return this to the soup pot. (Do not boil the miso.) Add 1 more cup of water to the pot, and serve.

"Forbear, O mortals, to spoil your bodies with such impious food!
There is corn for you, apples, whose weight bears down
The bending branches; There are grapes that swell
On the green vines, and pleasant herbs and greens
Made mellow and soft with cooking....
Earth is generous with her provision, and her sustenance
Is very kind."

OVID (43 B.C-17 A.D)
Roman Poet

Hearty Lentil Soup

serves 6

2 C. Dry Lentils	1/2 T. Garlic Powder
1 T. Oil	1/2 t. Dill Weed
2 Onions, chopped	3/4 C. Lentils, cooked
3 Garlic Cloves, diced	1/4 C. Tomato Paste
2 Celery Stalks, diced	1 T. Bragg's™ or Tamari
2 C. Carrots, sliced	1 T. Vegetable Bouillon
1 Eggplant, diced (optional)	1/4 C. Cooked Carrots
1 T. Nutritional Yeast	1/4 t. Cumin
1 T. Bragg's™ or Tamari	
Blender Ingredients	1 C. Zucchini, diced
2 C. Water	1 t. Sea Salt

1. Cook the lentils in a separate pot (see Cooking Guide for Beans pg. 19).
2. In a soup pot, sauté the onion and garlic in the oil and then add celery and carrots. Allow the carrots to soften and then add the eggplant. Add the yeast and Bragg's™, with a little water, and cover. Cook until carrots are soft.
3. In a blender, whiz half the blender ingredients. Pour into the soup pot. Repeat the blender process another time.
4. Add 2-4 cups of additional water. Add the zucchini.
5. Add 2-4 cups, or the desired amount of the remaining whole cooked lentils to the pot. Add the sea salt. Simmer until the zucchini is soft. Serve.

Light Lentil Soup

serves 5

1 T. Oil (optional)	Blender Ingredients
1 Onions, chopped	2 C. Water
3 Garlic Cloves, diced	1 t. Garlic Powder
2 Celery Stalks, sliced	1 t. Dill
3 C. Carrots, sliced	1 t. Salt-Free Spike™
2-3 Potatoes, cubed	1 t. Cumin
2 C. Dry Lentils (rinsed & soaked)	1 T. Tamari
1 T. Nutritional Yeast	1/4 C. Carrots (cooked)
Bragg™ Liquid Aminos, to taste	1 t. Onion Powder
Water as directed below	1 t. Sea Salt

1. In a soup pot, sauté (in oil) the onion and garlic until soft. Add celery, carrots and potatoes; and stir. Add the lentils along with the yeast and Bragg's, with enough water to cover the lentils by an inch. Cover and simmer. Add more water as necessary as the lentils cook.
2. When lentils are soft, remove 3/4 cup of lentils with some vegetables and whiz with the Blender Ingredients. Pour into soup pot. Add enough water for desired consistency. Simmer until the flavors blend.

Autumn Harvest Soup

Serves 5-6

1 T. Oil (optional)	1 t. Sea Salt
1 Onion (large), diced	2-3 T. Braggs™ or Tamari
1-2 Clove Garlic, diced	2 T. Nutritional Yeast
3 Carrots, 2 sliced, 1 grated	1 t. Salt-Free Herb Seasoning
1 Sweet Potato (large), sliced	1/4 t. Lemon Pepper
2 Potatoes (medium), cubed	6-7 C. Stock or Water
1 Butternut (or sweet squash), cubed	

1. Dice onion and garlic and sauté in oil or water. Add sliced carrots, potatoes, squash and sea salt to pot with enough stock to cover veggies. Let simmer on a low heat until vegetables are soft.
2. Remove 1/3 of the cooked vegetables with a strainer and blend with remaining stock until creamy. (Use less stock for a thicker soup). Add the remaining seasonings and blend again. Return mixture into soup pot and simmer for 10 more minutes.

•Delicious served immediately and even better the next day.

Minestrone Soup

yields 5-6 bowls

2 C. Cooked Beans (Pinto, Red, Kidney)	1/2 T. Onion Powder
1 Onion (large), diced	1/2 T. Garlic Powder
3 Celery Stalks, diced	7-8 oz. Pasta Ribbons
2 C. Carrots, sliced	1/4 C. Bragg™ Liquid Aminos
2 Zucchini, sliced & halved	1/2 t. Sea Salt
6 oz. Tomato Paste	1 T. Dill Weed
1/2 T. Parsley	1/2 T. Salt-Free Spike™
3 T. Nutritional Yeast	1/2 t. Black Pepper
1 1/2 T. Oregano (dried)	Basil Leaves (fresh), handful

1. Soak the beans for hours or overnight before cooking. Rinse, then cook them in a small pot and when soft, discard the water and rinse with fresh water. Set aside.
2. In a medium-sized pot, sauté the diced onion and celery. Add the carrots. When they partially soften add the zucchini.
3. In a blender, blend 2 cups of water with the tomato paste, parsley, yeast, oregano, onion and garlic powder. Return to the pot. Simmer for awhile.
4. Cook ribbon noodles, separately, until tender; then drain.
5. Pull out from the pot 1/2 cup of cooked carrots and place in the blender with 1 1/2 cups of water. Blend the carrots and water until creamy. Continue adding 1 1/2 cups of water, along with the Bragg's™, sea salt, dill weed, salt-free Spike™ and pepper until well mixed. Pour back into the pot.
6. Add a handful of fresh basil leaves. Remove before serving. Add 2 more cups of water to the pot. Stir and simmer.
7. Just before serving, add the pasta ribbons. (The shells will absorb the water.)

Great Gazpacho

serves 6
From: The Compassionate Cook by Ingrid Newkirk

3 C. Vegetable or Tomato Juice	2 T. Vinegar
1 Onion (medium), minced	1 t. Tarragon (dried)
2 Tomatoes (medium), diced	1 t. Basil (fresh), minced
1 Green Bell Pepper, minced	Cumin, pinch
1 Garlic Clove, crushed	Hot Sauce, dash
1 Cucumber (medium), diced	2 T. Olive Oil
2 T. Lemon Juice	Salt and Pepper, to taste

Combine all the ingredients and chill for two hours.

Mushroom-Barley Soup

serves 5-6

3/4 -1 C. Barley	2 T. Nutritional Yeast
2 Garlic Cloves (fresh), minced	5 T. Cashew Butter
2 Onions (small), diced	1 T. Onion Powder
4 C. Mushrooms, sliced	1/2 T. Garlic Powder
4 T. Bragg Liquid Aminos™	1 T. Sea Salt

1. Cook the barley in a big soup pot (1 cup dry barley to 3-4 cups of water).
   This soup is a 'hearty' soup. For a thinner soup, use only 3/4 of a cup of dry barley.
2. When the barley is completely cooked, remove it from the pot.
   In that same pot, sauté garlic, onions and then mushrooms.
3. In a blender, blend 1 1/2 - 2 cups water, Bragg's, yeast, cashew butter and seasonings.
   Pour this into the soup pot.
4. Cover the blades of the blender with some cooked barley. Add water to cover the barley and blend into a creamy consistency. Add 1-2 more cups of water to the blender and blend. Pour this into the soup pot.
5. Add the remaining cooked barley to the soup pot. Simmer for 25-30 minutes.
   (If soup sits for awhile, the barley will absorb some of the liquid and thicken the soup. To remedy this, add more liquid and seasonings.)

"The meat-laden, Western style diet, rather than leading us to an age of prosperity and health, has contributed to an epidemic of degenerative diseases. The nations who consume the most meats suffer the highest rates of death from heart attacks, strokes, cancer and diabetes."

MICHAEL A. KLAPER, M.D.
American author and international lecturer

Dips, Dressings, Sauces & Gravies

"He will be regarded as a benefactor of his race who shall teach man to confine himself to a more innocent and wholesome diet."

HENRY DAVID THOREAU (1817-1862)
American author, poet, and naturalist

Mediterranean Hummus
yields 5 cups

4 C. Chick Peas (cooked), drained
1 t. Onion Powder
1/2 C. Water
3-4 T. Tahini
1 t. Herb Seasoning
2 T. Bragg's™ or Sea Salt, to taste

1 t. Garlic Powder
1 t. Cumin
1/2 t. Sea Salt (optional)
Lemon Juice, to taste (optional)
Fresh Herbs and/or toasted Garlic
  (optional)

1. In a food processor (using the "S"- shaped blade), whiz half of each ingredient together. Stop intermittently to scrape the sides of the processor with a rubber spatula and continue to whiz until creamy smooth. Repeat with the other half of ingredients.
2. Chill and serve. The consistency should be somewhat soft as it hardens when refrigerated.

Bean Dip
5-6 servings

2 2/3 C. Pinto Beans (cooked)
3 T. Bragg's™ or Tamari
2/3 C. Tomato Paste
2 t. Garlic Powder

1 t. Onion Powder
1 t. Cumin
1 T. Apple Cider Vinegar
Jalapeños, diced, to taste (optional)

In a food processor (using the "S"- shaped blade), blend all ingredients. Chill.

(Upon being informed by doctors that he would die if he refused meat)

"My situation is a solemn one: life is offered to me on condition of eating beefsteaks. But death is better than cannibalism. My will contains directions for my funeral, which will be followed not by mourning coaches, but by oxen, sheep, flocks of poultry and a small traveling aquarium of live fish, all wearing white scarves in honor of the man who perished rather than eat his fellow creatures. It will be, with the exception of Noah's Ark, the most remarkable thing of its kind ever seen."

GEORGE BERNARD SHAW (1856-1950)
Anglo-Irish playwright
1925 Nobel Prize recipient

Versatile Tofu Onion Dip

yields 2 - 2 1/2 cups

1 Onion (large), diced, sauteed	1/2-3/4 lb. Tofu, rinsed well
2 T. Bragg™ Liquid Aminos	4-6 T. Water
3 T. Nutritional Yeast	1/2 t. Sea Salt
1/4 C. Safflower Oil	Garlic & Onion Powder, dash

1. In a fry pan, sauté 1 onion (preferably sweet) in a little oil or water.
2. Add a dash of Bragg's, yeast and water to the sauté. Cook until onions are translucent.
3. In a food processor, using the "S"- shaped blade, blend all ingredients until smooth.
4. Chill and serve as a dip.
   •Perfect for baked potatoes or combine with grains to make loaves and burgers.

Tofu Herb Dip

yields 3 cups

1 lb. Tofu	1 t. Garlic Powder
1/4 C. Oil	1 t. Onion Powder
4 T. Nutritional Yeast	1 T. Chives
1/2 C. Water	1 T. Parsley
2 t. Herb Seasoning	1 T. Dill Weed
2 T. Tamari/Bragg's™	1 T. Cilantro

Blend all ingredients together in a food processor using the "S"- shaped blade. (Add any favorite herbs.)

"Dill"icious Dip

yields 2-3 cups

1/8 - 1/4 C. Safflower Oil	Garlic & Onion Powder, dash
1/2 lb. Tofu, rinsed well	1 t. Spike™ Seasoning
1/4 - 1/3 C. Fresh Dill Weed	2 T. Bragg™ Liquid Aminos
4 T. Water	2-3 T. Nutritional Yeast

Blend ingredients together in a food processor, using the "S"- shaped blade. Chill. Serve.

"Ever occur to you why some of us can be this much concerned with animals' suffering? Because government is not. Why not? Animals don't vote."

PAUL HARVEY
American radio newscaster,
syndicated journalist

Creamy Tofu-Pesto Dip

yields 2-3 cups

1 C. Cashew Pieces (raw)	2 T. Nutritional Yeast
1/4 -1/3 C. Oil	2 T. Bragg's™ or Tamari
3/4 lb. Tofu	1/4 - 1/2 t. Sea Salt
1/3 C. Water	6 Garlic Cloves, diced, toasted
1 C. Basil (fresh), chopped	1 Clove Garlic (small)

1. Soak cashew pieces for 5-10 minutes and drain water.
2. In a food processor, using the "S"- shaped blade, blend oil with cashew pieces until creamy smooth.
3. Add tofu a little at a time. Add remaining ingredients. Blend. Chill and serve.

Cheezy Dip

yields 4-5 cups

1/4 -1/3 C. Oil	5 T. Nutritional Yeast
1 lb. Cake of Tofu, rinsed well	1/2 C. Water
1/4 C. Bragg's™ or Sea Salt, to taste	Garlic & Onion Powder, dash
	'VeganRella' ™ Cheese, grated (optional)

In a food processor, using the "S"- shaped blade, blend all ingredients until smooth and creamy.
- Add grated 'VeganRella' ™ non-dairy cheese and whiz for an even more flavorful dip.
- Also can be used as a topping for baked casseroles.

Nacho Cheeseless Dip

yields 2 cups

1 C. Tofu, mashed	1/4 C. Nutritional Yeast
2/3 C. Grated 'VeganRella' ™	2 T. Bragg's™ or Sea Salt, to taste
1/4 C. Oil	6 T. Water

In a food processor, blend all ingredients together, using the "S"- shaped blade.

- Use as a dip, spread on breads (as is or baked), a topping for baked potatoes or a sandwich spread. Add to cooked grain to make burgers and loaves.

"I believe that pity is a law like justice, and that kindness is a duty like uprightness."

VICTOR HUGO (1802-1885)
French poet, novelist and playwright

Pea Dip
yields 3 cups

2 1/2 - 3 C. Green Peas,
   (fresh or frozen, steamed lightly)
1/2 Onion (medium), chopped
3/4 lb. Tofu
1 T. Olive Oil

2 Garlic Cloves, chopped
Salt and Red Pepper, to taste
1/8 - 1/4 C. Water,
   (less water for a thicker dip)
1/8 t. Dill Weed

Place ingredients in a food processor. Using the "S"- shaped blade, pulse until creamy smooth. (Add favorite seasonings, to taste.) Chill and serve.

Creamy Carrot-Cashew Paté
5-6 servings

2 1/2 - 3 C. Cashew Pieces (raw)
4 Carrots (small), peeled, sliced
Garlic & Onion, to taste (optional)

1/3 C. Oil
3 T. Bragg's™ or Sea Salt, to taste
1/3 - 1/2 C. Water

1. Soak the cashew pieces in water for about twenty minutes, until soft, then drain the cashew pieces of excess water. If you over soak, they seem to lose some flavor.
2. In a food processor, blend the sliced carrots as finely as you can get them with the "S" - shaped blade. If you are using any fresh onion or garlic, add them at this time as well.
3. Add the oil and cashews a little at a time so as not to overwork the food processor and to enable the machine to blend them all to a smooth consistency. Add water and Bragg's. Stop the machine intermittently and scrape the sides with a rubber spatula to be sure that everything is getting blended. Creaminess is essential in a paté. Chill and serve.

Creamy Artichoke Dip
5-6 servings

1 T. Olive Oil
1 Onion (medium), chopped
4 Garlic Cloves, chopped

1/2 lb. Mushrooms
6-8 Artichoke Hearts, steamed
4 oz. Tofu (firm)

1. Stir fry the onions, garlic and mushrooms in oil. When soft, remove from fry pan.
2. Place steamed artichoke hearts and the stir fry into food processor and pulse until smooth. Add tofu and pulse again. Season to taste with favorite seasonings, i.e., garlic powder, sea salt, sweetener. Chill and serve.

"As long as there are slaughterhouses, there will be battlefields."

COUNT LEO TOLSTOY (1828-1910)
Russian novelist and philosopher

Zippy Parsley Dip

yields about 1 1/2 cups
Contributed by Wild Ginger Restaurant - Vegan Village, United Kingdom

2 - 2 1/2 oz. Parsley (fresh)
1 oz. Onion, diced
1 1/2 T. Vegan Mayonnaise

Salt and Pepper, to taste
Juice of 1 Lemon (to taste)
4 oz. Tofu, drained

1. Wash and drain parsley. Discard any dead leaves and stems.
2. Put all ingredients in a blender and blend well.

Sour Cream

yields about 1 cup

1 C. Tofu (firm)
2 1/2 T. Lemon Juice

1/4 t. Sea Salt
Water, to thin
1 T. Oil (optional)

In a food processor, using the 'S'- shaped blade, blend all ingredients to a smooth consistency. Chill and use as needed. Keeps for 2-3 days refrigerated.

Tofu Mayonnaise

yields 2 cups

1/3 - 1/2 C. Safflower Oil
3 T. Apple Cider Vinegar
1/2 lb. Tofu

1 t. Sea Salt
1 1/2 - 2 T. Fructose
Dash Lemon Juice (fresh)

In a blender or processor, blend liquid ingredients and tofu. This mixture might be thick, so add ingredients slowly, turning blender on and off. Keeps well in the refrigerator.

Oat Cheese

yields 1 1/2 cups

1/3 C. Rolled Oats
1/8 C. Tahini
2/3 C. Nutritional Yeast
1 T. Spike™ Seasoning
2-3 T. Lemon Juice

2 C. Water
1 T. Onion Powder
1 t. Garlic Powder
1 T. Dill (optional)
4 T. Arrowroot

1. Pulverize oats in a dry blender. Add remaining ingredients and blend.
2. Transfer to a sauce pan. Heat on medium-low flame until thickened, stirring constantly. (Do not bring to a boil.)
   • Use fresh for pizza and lasagna or transfer to a bread loaf pan, cool and refrigerate overnight. It will mold to a more solidified consistency.

Thousand Island Dressing

yields 3 cups

1/4 - 1/3 C. Oil	1 T. Mustard (prepared)
2/3 C. Water	1/3 C. Tomato Paste
1 T. Apple Cider Vinegar	1 T. Sweetener
1/2 lb. Tofu	1 T. Bragg™ Liquid Aminos
4 T. Sweet Relish:	Onion Powder, dash
(Cascadian Farm™- no honey)	Fresh onion, diced (optional)

1. In a blender, blend all ingredients except diced onion and half of the sweet relish.
2. Add in remaining relish and whiz for just 30 seconds. Good shelf life.

Tahini Dressing

yields 1 1/2 cups

1 C. Water	3 t. Tamari or Bragg's™
1/2 C. Tahini	Spices or Herbs of choice (optional)

1. In a blender, blend all ingredients. Use 1/4 cup less water for a thicker dressing to use in bakes and casseroles. Stays good for only two days in refrigerator.

•Variation: 1 t. curry powder may be added for a delicious curry-tahini dressing.

Quick Tahini Dressing in a Jar

Great for traveling!

1/2 C. Tahini	2 t. Bragg™ Liquid Aminos
2/3 C. Water	1 t. Nutritional Yeast (optional)

Place all ingredients in a jar and shake vigorously.

House Dressing

yields 3 cups

3/4 C. Water	1 t. Salt-Free Spike™
1/4 - 1/3 C. Oil	1/2 t. Onion Powder
1/2 C. Tahini	1/4 t. Garlic Powder
2/3 C. Tofu, mashed	2 T. Nutritional Yeast
2 1/2 T. Bragg™ Liquid Aminos	1 T. Spike™ Seasoning (original)
3 T. Mustard (prepared)	1/4 t. Vegit™ Seasoning

In a blender, blend all ingredients until creamy. Stays 2-3 days in refrigerator.

French Dressing
yields 5 cups

5 Carrots, sliced and steamed	Garlic & Onion Powder, to taste
1/4 - 1/3 C. Vinegar	2 1/2 T. Bragg™ Liquid Aminos
2/3 C. Olive Oil (or other oil)	2 T. Nutritional Yeast
1 2/3 C. Water or Carrot Stock	Dill Weed, dash
4 T. Sorghum or Rice Syrup	1 t. Oregano (dried)
7-8 T. Tomato Paste	1 t. Basil

1. Steam carrots in 2 cups of water. Save some of the carrot stock to use later.
2. In a blender, add liquid ingredients, tomato paste and steamed carrots. Blend. Add remaining ingredients; blend until creamy smooth. Chill before serving.
   • Will keep quite well in the refrigerator.

It's Italian! Dressing
yields 2-3 cups

1 C. Water	3 T. Nutritional Yeast
1 C. Olive Oil (or other)	2 1/2 T. Spike™ Seasoning
3 T. Apple Cider Vinegar	2 1/2 - 3 t. Rice Syrup
1 T. Oregano (dried)	1/2-1 t. Basil (dried)
1 t. Dill Weed	1 t. Onion Powder
1 t. Garlic Powder	Pepper, dash
1 Garlic Clove (fresh), diced	1 Onion Slice, diced

In a blender, blend all ingredients together. Keeps well in refrigerator.

Creamy Italian Dressing
yields 3 cups

1/2 C. Oil	2 T. Nutritional Yeast
1/3 C. Apple Cider Vinegar	Spike Seasoning™, Pepper, dash
1 C. Water	Onion Powder, to taste
2 T. Rice Syrup or Sucanat	Garlic Powder, to taste
1 T. Bragg™ Liquid Aminos	1 T. Oregano (dried)
1/2 lb. Tofu	1 t. Basil (dried)

In a blender, add liquids, then tofu and blend. Add spices and blend until creamy. Keeps well in the refrigerator.

"The greatness of a nation and its moral progress can be judged by the way its animals are treated."

MAHATMA GANDHI (1869-1948)
Hindu pacifist, spiritual leader

Sesame-Miso Dressing

yields 3 cups

1/2 C. Miso	3 Garlic Cloves, diced
1/4 C. Sesame Oil	3 T. Lemon Juice (fresh)
1/4 C. Oil	2 T. Sweetener
3/4 C. Water	1-2 T. Nutritional Yeast
1/2 t. Garlic Powder	1/2 t. Onion Powder

In a blender, blend all ingredients together. Keeps well in refrigerator.

Sweet and Sour Miso Dressing

yields 3-4 cups

4 T. Miso (preferably blonde)	3-4 T. Rice Syrup or Sucanat
1 1/4 C. Oil	5 t. Nutritional Yeast
1/2 C. Apple Cider Vinegar	1 C. Water

In a blender, blend all ingredients together. Keeps well in refrigerator.

Miso-Lemon Mustard Dressing

yields 2 cups

1/2 C. Lemon Juice (fresh)	1/4 C. Rice Syrup
2/3 -1 C. Oil	Pepper, dash
1/2 C. Water	1 T. Mustard
3-4 t. Nutritional Yeast	2 t. Miso

In a blender, blend until creamy smooth. Keeps well in refrigerator.

Lemon-Curry Dressing

yields 2 1/2 cups

1 C. Water	1/2 C. Oil
2 t. Lemon Juice (fresh)	1 T. Rice Syrup
1/4 C. Nutritional Yeast	1/2 t. Curry (mild)
1 T. Bragg™ Liquid Aminos	1/2 C. Tofu, mashed

In a blender, blend all ingredients until smooth. Keeps well in refrigerator.

Lemon-Ginger Dressing
yields 2 cups

1 C. Water	1 T. Tahini
1/2 C. Oil	1-2 T. Fresh Ginger, minced
2 T. Lemon Juice (fresh)	1 T. Bragg™ Liquid Aminos
1 T. Maple Syrup	2 T. Nutritional Yeast
1/4 lb. Tofu	1 t. Mustard (prepared)

In a blender, blend all ingredients together. Keeps well in the refrigerator.

Raw Avocado Dressing
yields about 2 cups

1/2 C. Olive Oil	1/4 C. Avocado
1/4 C. Basil (fresh)	2 T. Nutritional Yeast
1 Garlic Clove, minced	1 T. Bragg™ Liquid Aminos
1/2 t. Spike™ Seasoning	1 C. Water
1/4 t. Onion (granulated or powder)	2 T. Vinegar or Lemon Juice
	1/8 t. Cayenne Pepper (optional)

In a blender, blend all ingredients together. Keeps well in the refrigerator.

*Dilli*cious Salad Dressing
yields about 2 cups

1/4 - 1/3 C. Olive Oil	6 T. Lemon Juice
1/2 lb. Tofu	2-3 T. Rice Syrup
3-4 T. Bragg™ Liquid Aminos	1/3 C. Fresh Dill Weed
1 T. Nutritional Yeast	Garlic Powder, to taste
3/4 C. Water	Onion Powder, to taste

In a blender, blend all ingredients together. Chill and serve. Good shelf life.

Creamy Garlic Dressing
yields 2 cups

2/3 C. Water	7 Garlic Cloves, diced, toasted
1/3 C. Oil	2 T. Bragg™ Liquid Aminos
1/2 lb. Cake of Tofu	1/2 t. Garlic (Granulated/Powder)
1 t. Onion Powder	1 T. Nutritional Yeast

In a blender, blend all ingredients together. This dressing is for the real garlic lover!
Keeps well in the refrigerator.

> *"The best way to fight evil is by making energetic progress in the good."*
>
> The I CHING (Ancient Chinese Book of Changes)

Avocado Green Goddess Dressing
yields 2 cups

3/4 C. Water
1 Haas Avocado
3 T. Lemon Juice (fresh)

1 1/2 - 2 T. Bragg's™ or Tamari
Garlic & Onion Powder, dash
1/4 C. Herbs (fresh), chopped

In a blender, blend all ingredients together. Best eaten the night it is made.

No-Oil Tomato-Vinaigrette
yields 1 cup

2 T. Tomato Paste
2 T. Apple Cider Vinegar
3/4 C. Water
Lime Juice, dash

1 1/2 T. Rice Syrup
2 T. Nutritional Yeast
1 1/2 T. Bragg's™ or Tamari
1 T. Mustard (prepared)

In a blender, blend all ingredients to a creamy consistency.

Creamy Dijon Dressing
yields 1 quart

1/2 C. Oil
1 1/4 C. Water
2 T. Mustard (stone ground)
1 T. Blonde Miso

1/2 C. Nutritional Yeast
1 C. Tofu, mashed
1 T. Bragg's™ or Tamari
1/2 T. Lemon Juice (fresh)

In a blender, blend all the ingredients to a creamy consistency.

Lemon-Basil Dressing
yields 2 cups

1/4 C. Water
3/4 C. Oil
1/4-1/3 C. Lemon Juice (fresh)
1/3 C. Basil (fresh)

1 T. Bragg's™ or Tamari
4 T. Nutritional Yeast
2 T. Rice Syrup
Other Fresh Herbs (Optional)

In a blender, blend all ingredients together. Good shelf life.

"To dispose a soul to action, we must upset its equilibrium."

ERIC HOFFER (1902-1983) American philosopher

Cole Slaw Dressing

yields 2 1/2 cups

1/2 lb. Tofu
1/2 C. Brown Rice Vinegar
1/2 C. Safflower Oil
1/3 C. Lemon Juice, fresh
1-2 t. Spike™ Seasoning

2-3 T. Mustard
2 T. Sea Salt
1/3 C. Sweetener (Fructose)
Fresh Parsley, to taste

Blend all ingredients together. This dressing is used to make Cole Slaw.

Salsa

yields 2 1/2 cups

1 (14) oz. Can Diced Tomatoes
1/2 C. Onion, diced
1/2 C. Fresh Cilantro, chopped
8 oz. Tomato Sauce, unflavored
3 t. Nutritional Yeast
1 Lime, squeezed

Hot Chili Pepper, to taste
1 Garlic Clove, finely chopped
Jalapeno Pepper, to taste, diced
1/2 t. Sea Salt
1 t. Apple Cider Vinegar
1/4 t. Cumin

In a bowl, mix all ingredients together. Chill and serve.

Divine Cashew-Mushroom Gravy

yields 2-3 cups

3 Garlic Cloves, minced
2 Onions (small), diced
2 C. Mushrooms (fresh), sliced
2 C. Water
3 T. Nutritional Yeast

1 t. Garlic Powder
1 t. Onion Powder
3 1/2 T. Cashew Butter
2 T. Bragg's™ or Tamari
1/2 t. Sea Salt
1 T. Arrowroot Powder

1. In a small pot, sauté garlic and onions, then add mushrooms and simmer until vegetables are soft.
2. In a blender, blend remaining ingredients. Pour mixture into the pot and simmer until arrowroot thickens the gravy. Stir often.
   • This gravy is the perfect complement for mashed potatoes and loaves.

"Animal fats, especially those in milk, butter, cheese and meat, are highly saturated, and an excess intake of such foods may be partly responsible for the development of atheroma, which causes atherosclerosis."

FAMILY MEDICAL GUIDE, AMERICAN MEDICAL ASSOCIATION

Mushroom-Cheezy Gravy

yields 3 cups

1 Onion (medium), diced	1 T. Dr. Bronner's Bouillon™
1 C. Mushrooms, sliced	1 T. Bragg's™ or Tamari
2 C. Water	2 T. Arrowroot Powder
1 C. Nutritional Yeast	1-2 T. Molasses
1 t. Vegit™ Seasoning	1/2 t. Garlic Powder
1 T. Oil or Tahini	1/2 t. Sea Salt

1. In a small pot, sauté onion. When somewhat soft, add mushrooms.
2. In a blender, blend remaining ingredients.
3. Pour mixture into sauté and simmer on a low flame until gravy thickens.

Holiday Mushroom Gravy

yields 2 1/2 cups

2 C. Mushrooms, sliced	1 t. Garlic Powder
2 C. Water	1 t. Onion Powder
1/3 C. Tahini	2 t. Dr. Bronner's Bouillon™
2/3 C. Nutritional Yeast	4 t. Arrowroot Powder
2 t. Spike™ Seasoning	1/8 t. Black Pepper
1 t. Oregano (dried)	

1. Sauté mushrooms in a small pot until soft.
2. In a blender, blend all remaining ingredients together and pour into pot with mushrooms. Simmer on a low flame and stir gravy until it thickens.

Brook's Brown Gravy

yields about 5 cups

4 C. Water	1/4 C. Bragg's™ or Tamari
4 T. Whole Wheat Flour	1 t. Onion Powder
2 T. Nutritional Yeast	1/2 t. Thyme
	Salt and Pepper, a pinch

Mix all ingredients together and heat over a medium flame. Stir constantly until gravy thickens.

"Nothing will benefit human health and increase chances for survival of life on earth as much as the evolution to a vegetarian diet."

ALBERT EINSTEIN (1879-1955)
German born - American physicist
1921 Nobel Prize recipient

No Oil Miso-Mushroom Gravy
yields 2 1/2 cups

2/3 C. Onion, diced	1/2 T. Bragg's™ or Tamari
2 1/4 C. Mushrooms, sliced	1 1/2 T. Arrowroot Powder
2 C. Water	1/2 T. Wizards™ Worcestershire
3 T. Red Miso	(vegan Worcestershire Sauce)
1 1/2 T. Nutritional Yeast	1/2 t. Garlic Granules/Powder

1. In a small gravy pot, sauté the onion with a little water. Add the mushrooms and simmer, with lid on, until mushrooms are soft.
2. Meanwhile, in a blender, blend the remaining ingredients. Pour into the pot with the mushrooms and simmer on a low flame until gravy is thickened.

Rich Carrot-Coconut Sauce
yields 2-3 cups

1 C. Carrots, sliced	2 1/2 T. Bragg™ Liquid Aminos
1/2 -3/4 C. Water	1 T. Arrowroot Powder
1 1/2 C. Coconut Milk (can)	1/4 t. Garlic Granules
1/4 t. Curry Powder	4-5 T. Scallion, diced

1. Place the sliced carrots and the water in a small gravy pot, cover, and steam carrots until soft.
2. When carrots are soft, place them in a blender with remaining ingredients, except the scallions. Blend to a creamy consistency and pour into the pot. Simmer. Add the scallions while simmering. Stir continuously until gravy begins to bubble. Remove from flame.

Basil-Lemon Sauce
yields approximately 1 cup

1 C. Soy Milk or Nut Milk	1 T. Arrowroot Powder
2 T. Sunflower Oil (optional)	2 T. Lemon Juice
Sea Salt, to taste	2 T. Basil (fresh), chopped fine
White Pepper, to taste	

1. In a saucepan, combine all ingredients except lemon juice and basil and place over medium heat, stirring constantly.
2. When sauce thickens, add lemon and basil, stir well, and remove from heat.

"Go to your bosom, knock there and ask your heart what it doth know."

WILLIAM SHAKESPEARE (1564–1616)
English poet and playwright

Tartar Sauce

yields 2 cups

1 lb. Tofu	1 T. Mustard (prepared)
1/4 C. Oil	1/2 T. Sea Salt
1/4 C. Water	2 1/2 T. Lemon Juice
1 1/2 T. Sweetener (Fructose)	1 T. Nutritional Yeast
3-4 T. Sweet Relish	1/8 C. Onion, diced

1. In a food processor, blend all ingredients except the onion and 2-3 tablespoons of the relish. When mixture is smooth, fold in onion and remaining relish.
2. Chill and serve with lemon broil tempeh, breaded tofu fillet/cutlets, etc.

Chinese Sauce

4-6 servings

1/3 C. Oil	3 1/2 C. Stock
10 Garlic Cloves, chopped	4 T. Arrowroot Powder
1/2 t. Ginger (fresh), diced	1/3 C. Tamari
	1/2 C. Sweetener (Rice Syrup/Sorghum)

In a blender, blend all ingredients together and then transfer to a sauce pot and simmer on low heat until thickened.

Tasty Marinara Sauce

yields 10 cups

1-2 T. Olive Oil	1 t. Sea Salt
6 Garlic Cloves, diced	2 T. Garlic Powder
1 Onion, diced	2 T. Oregano (dried)
2 Bell Peppers, diced	2 T. Basil (dried)
8 -16 oz. Mushrooms (fresh) sliced	3 T. Sweetener
2 (12) oz. Tomato Paste Cans	2 t. Spike™ Seasoning
2 1/2 C. Water	1/2 t. Black Pepper
1 (16) oz. Tomato Sauce Can	1-2 T. Bragg's™ or Tamari
1 T. Onion Powder	2 T. Nutritional Yeast

1. In a large pot, sauté garlic in a little oil and a dash of water.
2. While it is simmering, add onion, peppers and then sliced mushrooms. (Be sure to tip the stems of mushrooms and wash them well).
3. When all vegetables are soft, add tomato paste, water, tomato sauce and remaining seasonings. Simmer and stir frequently for 30 minutes or longer.

Roasted Garlic and Basil Tomato Sauce

yields 1 medium sized pot

1 Whole Bulb of Garlic	1 C. Basil (fresh), chopped
1 Onion, small	1 T. Bragg™ Liquid Aminos
1/2 Green Pepper, diced	(or 1/2 t. Sea Salt)
1 T. Oil	2 Tomato Sauce Cans

1. Place entire bulb of garlic, with peel intact, in toaster oven for 10 minutes, until soft.
2. In a skillet, sauté onion and green pepper in oil (may substitute water). Sauté until onion is translucent.
3. Take garlic out of oven and peel. (It should be very easy to peel.) Dice it. Add diced garlic and chopped basil to sauté. Add Bragg's and stir for just a moment.
4. Add canned sauce (or 2 cans diced tomatoes). Let simmer for 20-30 minutes until flavors are blended, adding more salt or basil if desired.

Fresh Roma Tomato Garlic Sauce

yields 1 small pot

6 Cloves Garlic, peeled	1/2 C. Nutritional Yeast
1/4 C. Olive Oil	1/2 C. Water
1 Onion (medium), diced	2 t. Arrowroot
1 1/2 Bell Pepper, diced	1/2 t. Sea Salt
6-7 Roma Tomatoes, diced	1/4 t. Black Pepper

1. In a blender, blend garlic cloves and oil.
2. Pour into a large skillet. Add onion and sauté.
3. After one minute, add pepper and continue to sauté. Add diced tomatoes and cover. Allow to simmer for 5-10 minutes, until tomatoes are soft.
4. Remove 1 1/2 cups of the sauté (mostly tomatoes) and place back into blender. Add nutritional yeast, water and arrowroot as well. Blend.
5. Pour mixture back into skillet. Add salt and pepper. Simmer and stir until sauce thickens (about 5 minutes). Serve over pasta.

"A bear, who was kept in a zoological garden, displayed, so long as he had bread exclusively for nourishment, quite a mild disposition. Two days of feeding with flesh made him vicious, aggressive, and even dangerous to his attendant."

JUSTICE LIEBIG (1803-1873)
German chemist

Mr. Liebig became famous for research into protein. He concluded that plants are a primary source of protein, and that plant protein is equivalent to the protein found in animals.
Quoted in <u>The Ethics of Diet</u>, by Howard Williams, 1883.

Thai Coconut-Curry Sauce

yields 1 small pot

1 Onion (large), halved & sliced
2-3 Garlic Cloves, diced
1 (14) oz. Can Pure Coconut Milk
1 (14) oz. Can Water
1/2 t. Sea Salt

1/4 C. Cashew Butter
2 1/2 t. Curry (mild)
3 T. Bragg's™ or Tamari
4 t. Arrowroot

1. In a small pot, sauté onion slices and garlic.
2. In a blender, blend remaining ingredients.
3. When onions are soft, pour blended mixture into the pot and simmer for 10-15 minutes, stirring continuously, until it thickens. Serve over rice, Thai noodles or your favorite noodle with steamed vegetables.

Quick & Easy Vegetable Coconut-Curry Sauce

4-6 servings

1 Onion, sliced
3 Carrots (small), diced
1 Zucchini, sliced, halved
Blender Mixture
1 C. Vitasoy (non-dairy milk)
1 (14) oz. Can Coconut Milk

1 t. Curry
1 T. Bragg's™ or Tamari
1/2 t. Garlic, granulated
3 t. Arrowroot
1/4-1/2 t. Sea Salt

1. Sauté the onion in a saucepan with a small amount of oil. When onions are softened, add the carrots. Simmer until softened. Add the zucchini. Cover and simmer until soft.
2. In a blender, blend the remaining ingredients. Pour into saucepan and simmer, stirring frequently, until sauce thickens. Serve over noodles or rice.

Uncooked Tomato and Green Olive Sauce

serves 4

2 lbs. Tomatoes, chopped
12 Green Olives (large), pitted & chopped
1 Bunch Scallions, chopped
2 Garlic Cloves, chopped
1 T. Thyme (fresh), minced
2 T. Olive Oil

1 t. Salt
1 t. Pepper
1 t. Garlic Powder
1 t. Onion Powder
8 oz. Box of Pasta (cooked) or
4 C. Rice (cooked)

Place all the ingredients (except pasta/rice) in a blender or food processor. Pulse until creamy-chunky. Toss tomato-olive sauce over cooked pasta or rice

•Variation: Blend all ingredients except tomatoes. Then combine blended ingredients with tomatoes in a bowl. Toss in with pasta or rice.

Thai Peanut-Curry Sauce
yields 3 cups

4 Garlic Cloves, minced
2 Onions (small), sliced thinly
2/3 C. Peanut Butter
1 1/2 T. Curry Powder (mild)
1 1/4 T. Arrowroot Powder

2 C. Water
4-5 T. Molasses
1 T. Sucanat
3 T. Bragg's™ or Tamari
Cayenne (optional)

1. In a small pot, sauté garlic and onions with a little oil or water.
2. In a blender, blend remaining ingredients.
3. When onions are tender, pour blended mixture into pot with garlic and onions. Simmer until gravy thickens, stirring continuously.

Sweet Potato Spread
yields 4-5 cups

1 t. Oil
4 Sweet Potatoes (medium)
Seasonings, to taste

2 Onions (medium)
2 T. Blonde Miso

1. Pre-heat oven to 400°. Lightly oil a baking sheet and place sweet potatoes and onions on sheet. Bake until vegetables are soft, about 45 minutes. Remove from oven and allow to cool.
2. When cool enough to handle, peel both vegetables. Transfer vegetables to food processor. Add miso and purée, using the "S"- shaped blade, until smooth. Season, to taste, with garlic powder and favorite seasonings.

• Variation: Try using butternut squash and/or carrots instead of sweet potatoes. Another option would be to add 1/2 lb. of tofu to the processor.

Peanut Butter Tofu Spread
yields 1 1/2 cups

1/2 C. Peanut Butter
1/2 1b. Tofu
1/4 C. Sweetener

1/4 t. Vanilla
1/4 t. Cinnamon

Place all ingredients in food processor using the "S"- shaped blade. Pulse until creamy. If too thick, add 1/4 cup of water slowly to processor.

"The basis of my vegetarianism is not physical, but moral..."

MAHATMA GANDHI (1869-1948)
Hindu pacifist, spiritual leader

White Bean Topping-Italian Style

serves 4

4 C. Great Northern Beans or Navy Beans (cooked)	1/2 t. Basil
1/4 C. Water/Stock (or tomato sauce)	1/2 t. Oregano
1/4 C. Olive Oil	2 t. Onion Granules/Powder
1 T. Nutritional Yeast	1/2 t. Salt
3 Garlic Cloves, diced	1 T. Fresh Parsley, chopped
	2 Scallions, chopped

1. Combine beans, water or stock, oil, nutritional yeast, garlic, onion and seasoning in the food processor. Process to a smooth consistency, adding more liquid to reach desired consistency.
2. Transfer to bowl. Top with scallions and parsley. Serve at room temperature.

Mustard Marinade

yields 1 1/2 - 2 cups

1 C. Dijon Mustard	1 T. Sweetener (dry or liquid)
2 T. Olive Oil	2 Garlic Cloves, crushed
2 T. Vinegar	1 T. Ginger (fresh), minced
1 T. Tamari	1/4 t. Red Pepper
1 T. Bragg's™ or Tamari	1/4 C. Water

1. In a small bowl or blender, whisk or blend all ingredients. If mixture is too thick, add 1/4 cup of water to turn blades.
2. Serve over baked potatoes, etc. or as a dip.

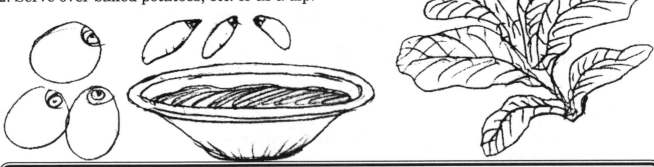

"We must not, in trying to think about how we can make a big difference, ignore the small daily differences we can make which, over time, add up to big differences that we often cannot foresee."

MARION WRIGHT EDELMAN
President of the Children's Defense Fund
1st African American lawyer admitted to Mississippi bar,
voted one of the '100 most influential women of the century' by Time Magazine.

Greek Style Garbanzo Dip for Artichokes
yield 2 1/2 cups

2 C. Garbanzo Beans (cooked)
1/4 C. Vegetable Stock
1/3 C. Lemon Juice
1 T. Garlic, minced
2 T. Olive Oil

2 T. Parsley, finely chopped
3 Scallions, sliced
1/4 t. Cumin Powder
1/4 t. Oregano (dried)

1. In a blender or food processor, place the beans, stock, lemon juice, garlic and olive oil. Process the ingredients until the mixture is smooth.
2. Transfer mixture to a bowl. Stir in the parsley, scallions, cumin and oregano.
3. Cover and refrigerate until ready to use. Spread the mixture on the individual artichoke leaves or use as a dip. (Enough Dip for 4 artichokes)

To Cook Artichokes: 4 Medium Artichokes

1. To cook and serve a whole artichoke, cut off the stem at its base so it will stand upright. Snap off the tough outer leaves and cut off the top quarter of the bud. You can also snip off the pointy tips of the exposed leaves and rub the cut portion of the artichoke with lemon to prevent discoloration. Place prepared artichokes in a bowl of water until ready to use.
2. Boil artichokes, by standing them in a deep pan, in 4-6 inches of boiling salted water. Add a little olive oil, lemon juice or herbs to the cooking water. Cover the pot and gently boil for 30-40 minutes until a petal near the center pulls out easily. Stand artichokes upside down to drain. Once cooked, artichokes are best served immediately. Serve with your favorite dipping sauce.

Pesto Sauce
serves 2-3

1 C. Raw Cashew Pieces (or Pine Nuts)
3-4 Garlic Cloves, diced, toasted
3 T. Water
2 T. Nutritional Yeast

1 T. Bragg's™ or Tamari
1/3 C. Cold Pressed Oil
1 C. Basil (fresh), chopped
Sea Salt, dash (optional)

1. Soak the cashew pieces in water for 5-10 minutes and then drain water off.
2. Pan-fry the garlic for 5 minutes until toasted.
3. In a food processor, blend all the ingredients together well, including the toasted garlic.

Zesty Barbecue Sauce
yields 3 cups

2 C. Water
1/4 C. Sorghum/Molasses
2/3 C. Tomato Paste
2 T. Vinegar
1/4 T. Garlic Powder
1/2 T. Onion Powder
1 T. Arrowroot

1 T. Hickory Smoke Flavor (Wright's)™
1 T. Molasses
1 T. Wizard's™ Vegetarian
    Worcestershire Sauce
1/2 T. Tamari
2 T. Dr. Bronner's Bouillon™

In a blender, blend all the ingredients. Pour into a small pot and simmer on low. Stir until it thickens. When it begins to bubble, remove from flame.

•If using molasses rather than sorghum, use 1 T. of Sucanat instead of the 1 T. Molasses.

Lemon-Tahini Dressing
yields 2 cups

1 C. Water
3/4 C. Tahini (thin)
4-5 T. Lemon Juice (fresh)

1 1/2 T. Bragg™ Liquid Aminos
1 Piece of Garlic (large)
Cayenne or fresh Herbs (optional)

In a blender, blend the above ingredients until creamy smooth.

Lemon/Miso/Mustard Dressing
yields 2 cups

1 C. Water
2/3 C. Oil
5 T. Lemon Juice (fresh)
3 T. Blonde Miso

2 T. Mustard (prepared)
3 T. Nutritional Yeast
1 T. Fruitsource®

In a blender, blend all the above ingredients. Keeps well in the refrigerator.

"A long habit of not thinking a thing wrong, gives it a superficial appearance of being right, and raises at first a formidable outcry in defense of custom. But the tumult soon subsides."

THOMAS PAINE (1737-1809)
English born American Revolutionary patriot and writer

Appetizers & Side Dishes

"It is my view that a vegetarian manner of living, by its
purely physical effect on the human temperament,
would most beneficially influence
the lot of mankind."

Tofu Rainbow Paté

yields 2 (1 1/2 quart) loaf pans

This recipe is a three layered dish. Each layer is mixed in the food processor and then poured into an oiled baking dish, each layer upon the previous layer.

First Layer
2 C. Carrots, sliced, steamed
3/4 lb. Tofu (medium-firm)
1 t. Bragg's™ or Tamari
1 t. Sea Salt
2 t. Arrowroot Powder

1/3 C. Oil
2 T. Nutritional Yeast
1 t. Garlic Powder
1 t. Onion Powder

1. In a food processor, using the "S"- shaped metal blade, blend steamed carrots. Add all the remaining ingredients and then blend until very smooth and creamy. Pour this mixture in each oiled bread pan, filling it 1/3 of the way up.

Second Layer
2 C. Beets, sliced, steamed
1/4 - 1/3 C. Oil
1 lb. Tofu (medium-firm)
1/2 t. Garlic Powder

1 T. Arrowroot Powder
3 T. Nutritional Yeast
1 t. Onion Powder
1 T. Bragg's™ or Tamari
2 t. Spike™ Seasoning

2. In a food processor, blend the beets first and then add remaining ingredients. Blend until very smooth and creamy, intermittently scraping the sides with a rubber spatula. Pour this mixture on top of the orange colored first layer in each loaf pan.

Third Layer
1 lb. Tofu (medium-firm)
3 T. Bragg's™ or Tamari
1 t. Onion Powder

1/4 -1/3 C. Oil
4 T. Nutritional Yeast
1 t. Turmeric Powder
1 t. Arrowroot Powder

3. Blend all ingredients together. Pour this blended mixture on top of the beet layer in each loaf pan. You should now have three distinctly colored layers in each loaf pan.
4. Bake, in a pre-heated oven, at 350° for 45-55 minutes. Allow to cool and then chill in refrigerator overnight or for many hours, so it can solidify.
5. Place a plate over the bread pan and flip each casserole; the paté should easily come out. Slice and serve.

> *"The animals share with us the privilege of having a soul."*
>
> PYTHAGORAS (circa 582-507 B.C.)
> Greek philosopher, mathematician, mystic
> "Father of Vegetarianism"

Mushroom Paté

yields 1 small cake pan

3 C. Mushrooms, sliced	1 3/4 lb. Tofu (medium-firm)
1 Small Onion, diced	1 1/2 T. Bragg™ Liquid Aminos
1 t. Sea Salt	2 T. Nutritional Yeast
Leftover Juice of Mushroom Sauté	1 t. Onion Powder
1 t. Spike™ Seasoning	2 t. Arrowroot Powder

1. Wipe mushrooms clean with a wet paper or cloth towel.
2. Sauté the mushrooms with a little oil and save the juice. Sauté the onion separately.
3. In a food processor, blend all the ingredients except the mushrooms.
   Fold in the mushrooms, without blending.
4. Place the mixture in an oiled cake pan. Bake at 350° until it cracks and turns light brown in color (35 minutes approximately). Allow to cool and then chill. Serve cold in slices.

Stuffed Mushrooms Incredible!

yields 10 large mushrooms

1. Wipe 10 large mushrooms clean with a wet cloth towel (stems removed). Marinate in:

2 T. Bragg's™ or Tamari	1/2 t. Garlic Powder

2. In a food processor, blend:

1/2 Onion (large), sautéed	1 T. Bragg's™ or Tamari
1 C. Tofu (soft), mashed	1 T. Oil
1 T. Spike™ or Vegit™ Seasoning	1 T. Nutritional Yeast

3. In a fry pan, grill (on high heat) the mushroom caps on the top side.
4. Remove them when sizzled on one side and place onto a small baking sheet.
5. In the same fry pan, using a little oil, fry:

2 Whole Wheat Bread Slices, cubed	
1/2 t. Spike™ Seasoning	1/2 t. Dill Weed
1 t. Oregano	1/2 t. Bragg's™ or Tamari

6. Add this toasted bread to the tofu mixture.
   In addition, season with 1/2 t. pepper and 1/2 teaspoon dill weed. Mix together well.
7. Spoon mixture into each mushroom cap and sprinkle with paprika.
   Pre-heat oven. Bake at 375° for 20-25 minutes.

"There's no reason to drink cow's milk at any time in your life. It was designed for calves, not humans, and we should all stop drinking it today."

DR. FRANK A. OSKI
former Director of Pediatrics,
Johns Hopkins University

Marinated Portabella Mushrooms

serves 4-6

Marinade
5 T. Toasted Sesame Oil
3 T. Vinegar
2 T. Tamari
2 T. Lemon Juice
2 Garlic Cloves, minced

To Grill
4-5 Portabella Mushrooms (remove stems
& wipe mushrooms clean with a paper or
cloth towel).
1 Bunch Watercress (large),
Vinegar, splash

1. For the marinade: mix the ingredients together in a bowl. To marinate, submerge 1 mushroom for just a few seconds. Remove, then shake to remove extra liquid.
2. To grill: Place mushrooms on a medium to hot grill. Cook 6 minutes and flip, using tongs, for another 5 minutes or until soft. While mushrooms are grilling, brush them with leftover marinade.
3. When fully cooked, place mushrooms on a cutting board. Slice into strips. Place watercress on each plate and splash with vinegar. Add salt and pepper. Add mushroom strips. Use grilled mushroom to make an excellent sandwich with hot sauce.

Grilled Portabella Mushrooms with Herb Baguette

serves 2

1 1/2 lbs. Portabella Mushrooms (whole)
2 t. Cumin, ground
2 t. Chili Powder
1 t. Cinnamon (ground)
1 T. Dry Sweetener

1-2 T. Olive Oil
1 French or Italian Baguette
3 Garlic Cloves, minced
1 t. Oregano (dried)
Salt and pepper, to taste

1. Wipe mushrooms clean with a damp paper towel or kitchen cloth. Cut stems off if too long. In a small bowl mix cumin, chili powder, cinnamon and sweetener together.
2. Brush mushroom and stems with 1 T. olive oil. Then place them in the bowl with the above seasonings, tossing well to coat mushrooms.
3. Cut baguette in half and then cut each piece in half length wise. Place on foil, crust side down. Brush with olive oil and sprinkle with garlic and oregano.
4. Place mushrooms on foil. Then place on grill away from direct heat and grill for 5 minutes. Place bread on the grill for 2-3 minutes to toast.
5. Serve mushrooms and baguette together after grilling.

"I will continue to be a vegetarian even if the whole world started to eat meat. This is my protest against the conduct of the world."

ISAAC BASHEVIS SINGER (1904-1991)
Yiddish Laureate of Literature,
1978 Nobel Prize recipient

Breaded Stuffed Mushrooms

yields 22 large mushrooms

22 Large Stuffing Mushrooms
<u>Mushroom Marinade Sauce</u>
2 T. Bragg's™ or Tamari
1 T. Apple Cider Vinegar
1/2 T. Garlic Powder
1 T. Oil
<u>Filling</u>
3 C. Tortillas, Chopped
2 C. Quinoa, cooked (or other grain)
   (see Cooking Guide for Grains)

1 1/2 C. Tofu (medium-firm) mashed
1 T. Salt-Free Spike™
1/2 T. Basil (dried)
1 1/2 T. Oregano (dried)
1 T. Onion (granulated/powder)
1/2 C. Nutritional Yeast
5 T. Bragg's™ or Tamari
4 T. Oil
2 T. Tahini

1. Wipe mushrooms clean with a damp towel and pat dry. Remove stems, making more space for the stuffing in the mushroom cap.
2. Place mushrooms in the marinade mixture and periodically stir.
3. In a large skillet, pan fry with a little oil, the chopped tortillas (corn and/or wheat, or bread). Add the grain, mashed tofu, spices and nutritional yeast.
   Stir and pan fry the stuffing mixture.
4. When finished, place in a bowl and add Bragg's™, 4 T. oil and tahini. Mix.
5. Oil the emptied fry pan. Place the marinated mushrooms in the fry pan with the stuffing side up. With a high flame, brown the mushroom caps for a couple of minutes and then remove from heat.
6. Fill each cap with stuffing. Pack it in tight and then put another spoonful on top.
   Bake at 350° until the mushrooms are soft and juicy.

Tempeh Chunks

yields 1 skillet

3 (8 oz.) Tempeh Cakes, steamed
4 T. Tamari
4 T. Nutritional Yeast

3 T. Oil
1/4 t. Garlic Powder

1. After steaming the tempeh, allow to cool. Then cut into bite-sized chunks.
2. Marinate in a mixture of the remaining ingredients. Stir periodically.
3. Oil a skillet and pan fry the chunks. Squirt with a little more Bragg's™ or Tamari and oil (optional) while frying. Easy and filling.

> *"There is no disease, bodily or mental, which adoption of a vegetable diet and pure water has not infallibly mitigated, wherever the experiment has been fairly tried."*
>
> PERCY BYSSHE SHELLEY (1792-1822)
> English poet

Curried Tofu Chunks
Serves 3

1 3/4 lb. Tofu (firm) 1/2" cubes	1 T. Tahini (thin) or Oil
1 T. Tamari	2-3 T. Nutritional Yeast
1/2 T. Dr. Bronner's Bouillon™	1/4 t. Onion Powder
1 t. Curry	Sea Salt, dash (optional)

1. Cube tofu and place in a bowl. Marinate in the tamari and bouillon for several minutes. Then add the remaining ingredients and stir.
2. Brown the chunks in a lightly oiled fry pan on both sides, approximately 10 minutes.

- Add the completed chunks to 2 cups of curried cooked grain of choice or serve them as an appetizer on a serving platter. (Each chunk has a toothpick through it.)
- Variation - add different seasonings other than curry, such as basil, oregano and dill weed. In addition, add a small amount of wheat germ or oat bran.

Breaded Eggplant Cutlets
serves 2-3

1-3 Round Eggplants (medium-large sized), peeled
Breading

1 C. Whole Wheat Pastry Flour	1 t. Herb Seasoning
1/2 C. Wheat Germ or Bran	1 t. Sea Salt
1/2 C. Corn Meal	1 t. Garlic Powder
1/2 C. Nutritional Yeast	1 t. Onion Powder

Tahini Dressing (thick): See recipe page 78

1. Steam eggplants until soft. Set aside to cool for a few minutes. Slice eggplant.
2. In a bowl, mix together all the breading ingredients.
3. Dip each piece of eggplant into the Tahini Dressing. Coat with the breading mixture. Pan fry, on both sides, in an oiled skillet. Drain on paper towel.

- Serve as is or in a sandwich.
- Variation - Cut tofu into chunks and prepare the same way. Serve a grain.

" 'Thou shalt not kill' does not apply to one's own kind only, but to all living beings; and this Commandment was inscribed in the human breast long before it was proclaimed from Sinai."

COUNT LEO TOLSTOY (1828-1910)
Russian novelist and moral philosopher

Tofu Cutlets-Quick and Easy

yields 7 cutlets

1 lb. Tofu, sliced into 7 slices

2 T. Tamari

Tahini Dressing: 2-3 T. Tahini, 2 T.
  Water and excess tamari marinade

3 T. Nutritional Yeast

2 T. Bran

Garlic Powder, to taste

Onion Powder, to taste

Favorite Seasonings (optional)

2 t. Salt-Free Spike™

1. Cut tofu into 7 slices and allow them to marinate in the tamari for 10 minutes. (Use the excess tamari to make the tahini dressing).
2. Make Tahini Dressing. Spread on the face-up side of each cutlet. Add half the nutritional yeast, bran and seasonings.
3. Place each cutlet, coated side down, in an oiled fry pan (medium heat).
4. While frying, coat the exposed cutlet sides with the remaining tahini dressing and seasonings. Cook until browned. Turn and cook for about 5 more minutes. Serve on a sandwich.
   •Variation: Dip tofu slices in a bowl of thick tahini dressing. Dip in breading. Pan fry.

Lasagna Roll-Ups

yields 8 rolls

8 Lasagna Noodles

Filling

2 C. Tofu, mashed (medium- firm)

1/4 C. Nutritional Yeast

1/4 C. Tomato Sauce

2-3 T. Tahini

1 T. Parsley

Sauce

1/2 t. Oregano

1/2 t. Basil

1/2 t. Onion Powder

1/2 t. Garlic Granules

Salt and Pepper, to taste

3 C. Tomato Sauce

1. Partially cook noodles. Drain.Rinse with cold water and drain again.
2. In a bowl mix together filling ingredients.
3. Lay out noodles and spread about 2 T. of filling on each. Roll up tightly and place seam side down on a 9" baking casserole. Pour sauce over roll-ups.
4. Cover and bake for 25 minutes at 350°. Sprinkle with nutritional yeast and serve.

Mock "Chicken" Tofu

yields 2 servings

1 lb. Tofu (firm)

2 T. Oil

1/4 t. Turmeric

2 t. Spike™ Seasoning

2 T. Bragg's™ or Tamari

1/3 C. Nutritional Yeast

1. Rinse and drain tofu. Cut into bite-sized chunks.
2. Heat oil in frying pan on medium heat. When hot, add the tofu and let cook until the one side is crispy.
3. Flip sides and brown tofu for another 5 minutes. Add the seasonings, cover, and simmer.

Grilled VeganRella™ & Tomato Sandwich

Grated 'VeganRella'™ Cheese
1-2 T. Oil
Bread Slices, quantity desired

1-2 Tomatoes, sliced
Nacho Cheeseless Dip (optional -
    see recipe pg. 75)

•This sandwich can be baked for a healthier choice or grilled in a fry pan for a more authentic taste.

1. Grate the VeganRella™ flavored cheese. The quantity will depend on how many sandwiches you are making.
2. If frying, spread grated VeganRella on two pieces of bread adding a slice of tomato to one piece. Grill on medium-high heat in an oiled fry pan for a couple of minutes. Then put one slice over the other, press down with spatula, cover with a lid and simmer for about a minute. Shut off flame and allow the VeganRella to melt.
3. If baking, simply spread grated VeganRella™ on bread or toast. Add a slice of tomato, then bake until 'cheese' is melted. Another option is to spread some Nacho Cheeseless Dip on slices of bread (instead of or with the VeganRella™), add a slice of tomato and bake until spread is golden in color.

California Grills
yields 2 sandwiches

6 Slices of Eggplant, 1/2" thick
3 T. Olive Oil
Salt and Pepper, to taste
1 Red Bell Pepper, halved lengthwise,
    cored and seeded

4 Slices Red Onion, 1/2" thick
2 Tomatoes, sliced 1/2" thick
4 Slices Whole Wheat Bread
1 T. Mustard

1. Pre-heat grill to medium high. Brush eggplant slices with olive oil on both sides, sprinkle with salt and pepper and grill 4-5 minutes on each side.
2. Grill the bell pepper halves, skin down, until charred. Place in a bag and seal (to steam) about ten minutes. Slip off charred skins and discard.
3. Lightly brush onion and tomato slices on both sides with oil and grill 5-7 minutes each side. Sprinkle with salt and pepper.
4. Brush both sides of bread with oil and grill or toast until golden brown.
5. For each sandwich, spread mustard on both pieces of bread, top one piece with 3 eggplant slices, 2 slices of onion, 1 sliced tomato and 1 red pepper half. Cover with the other slice of bread and cut in half to serve.

"Humans are not carnivorous by their anatomy, nor by their nature."

MICHAEL A. KLAPER, M.D.
American author and international lecturer

Tofu Spinach Philo Wraps
serves 4

1 Package Philo Dough Wraps
  (whole wheat or regular)

Spinach Filling
1/2 C. Vegetable Stock
1 Onion (medium), chopped
2 Garlic Cloves, diced
1 C. Mushrooms, sliced
2 C. Spinach, chopped

Tofu Filling
1 T. Oil
1 lb. Tofu (firm)
1/2 t. Garlic Granules
1/4 t. Sea Salt
1 T. Sesame Seeds
1/4 t. Paprika
1/4 t. Dry Mustard

1. In a skillet, over medium heat, put stock, onions and garlic. Cook until soft. Add mushrooms and spinach and let simmer for several minutes.
2. Drain the stir fry and remove from skillet and set aside.
3. In a bowl, mash tofu into a chunky batter and season with the seasonings. Add spinach filling and mix.
4. Spread one full sheet of Philo wrap flat out and lightly oil using a pastry brush or spray lightly with a vegetable oil spray.
5. Cut sheet into 2 pieces, place the tofu-spinach filling (about 3-4 T.) in center of each Philo dough piece. Fold dough, wrapping like a package or rolling up.
6. Repeat steps 4 & 5 until filling is used. Bake on an oiled baking sheet in a pre-heated oven at 350° for 20 minutes.

Broccoli-Almondine Casserole
Serves 3-4

3 Broccoli Heads (mostly flowers)
4- 6 Garlic Cloves, peeled
2-3 T. Olive Oil

3/4 C. Almonds, finely sliced
2 T. Bragg's ™ or Tamari
  (or salt substitute)

1. Wash broccoli and separate flowers into bite-sized pieces. Steam them until just tender. While broccoli is steaming, blend (in a blender) 2 cloves of fresh garlic with olive oil.
2. Finely chop the other 2 (or 4) cloves of garlic and sauté in a pan, using the garlic oil just made. Add sliced almonds to the cooking oil and toast them. Then add the Bragg's™ .
3. When broccoli is steamed, put in a baking dish and pour sauté mixture over it. Place in a warm oven, covered. Serve.

"Compassion alone stands apart from the continuous traffic between good and evil proceeding within us. Compassion is the anti-toxin of the soul."

ERIC HOFFER (1902-1983)
American philosopher

Middle-Eastern Broccoli with Sesame

yields 2 servings

1 lb. Broccoli
2 T. Sesame Seeds
1 T. Toasted Sesame Oil
2 t. Ginger (fresh), peeled & grated

1 T. Tamari
1/8 t. Red Pepper Flakes
1 T. Vinegar
2 Green Onions, chopped

1. Remove stems from broccoli and cut flowers into bite-sized pieces. Steam for 5-7 minutes until tender, yet firm, then drain.
2. Lightly toast sesame seeds in toaster-oven or frying pan.
3. Heat sesame oil in cast iron skillet or non-stick pan. Add ginger and cook for 30 seconds over low heat. Add tamari, red pepper and vinegar.
4. Stir broccoli into the sesame oil mixture and simmer for about 3 minutes to coat well.
5. Sprinkle green onions over broccoli with toasted sesame seeds.

"Cheezy" Onions

Serves 2-3

2 Onions, sliced or diced
2 T. Oil
3-4 T. Water

2 1/2 T. Bragg's™ or Tamari
5 T. Nutritional Yeast
Sea Salt & Pepper, to taste

In a fry pan, sauté the onions in oil, then add remaining ingredients. Continue to cook until onions are thoroughly soft and saucy. Serve as a topping or side dish.

Cabbage & Onion Sauté

yields 5 servings

1 T. Oil
4 Garlic Cloves, diced
2 Onions, diced
3 T. Tamari

3 T. Nutritional Yeast
1 Cabbage Head, shredded
3/4 t. Garlic Powder
1 t. Dill Weed

1. Sauté the diced garlic in a fry pan with a little oil. Add onions. Sauté until tender. Add a portion of the tamari and yeast to the cooking onions.
2. Add the cabbage to fry pan with remaining seasonings. Stir fry until soft.

> *"The high-minded man must take care more for truth than for what people think."*
>
> ARISTOTLE (384-322 B.C.)
> Greek philosopher, scientist, logician
> (student of Plato)

Tofu Caraway Cabbage

serves 4

2 T. Caraway Seeds
1 T. Sunflower Oil
3 Garlic Cloves, diced
1 Onion (large), diced
2 T. Water
2 T. Tamari

2 T. Apple Cider Vinegar
1 Head Cabbage (large), sliced
1/2 lb. Tofu (soft)
2 T. Lemon Juice
1/4 t. Sea Salt
Black Pepper, to taste (fresh)
1/4 C. Parsley (fresh)

1. In a skillet, heat the caraway seeds until they start to pop. Add oil and garlic and sauté. Add diced onion and cook until soft. Add water, tamari, and vinegar and stir well. Add the cabbage, cover, and simmer for 10-15 minutes or until cabbage is tender.
2. In a blender, combine tofu, lemon juice and salt. Blend until smooth. Pour over cabbage and heat 1 more minute. Season with fresh ground pepper and garnish with parsley.

Asparagus with Hollandaise Sauce

serves 3-4

1-2 Asparagus Bunches, trimmed
1 C. Tofu (soft) mashed
1/8 C. Oil
1/8 C. Lemon Juice
1 C. Water

1 T. Miso (blonde)
1 T. Bragg's™ or Sea Salt, to taste
1 T. Arrowroot Powder
1/2 t. Sea Salt
1/4 C. Nutritional Yeast

1. Cut or break the hard bottoms off the asparagus stalks. Steam the asparagus in a steamer basket until soft (approximately 5 minutes). Place in a casserole dish.
2. In a blender, blend the remaining ingredients and pour into a small pot. Simmer and stir frequently for about 10 minutes. Pour over asparagus.

Cream of Cauliflower

serves 4

2/3 C. Onion, diced
1 T. Oil (optional)
1 Stalk Celery, sliced
1 Whole Cauliflower, cut to bite-size
1 t. Sea Salt (or to taste)
1 1/2 C. Tofu (soft)

1 T. Lemon Juice
1 t. Onion Powder
1 t. Garlic Powder
4 T. Nutritional Yeast
1/4 t. Black or Lemon Pepper

1. In a fry pan, sauté onion in oil or a small amount of water, add celery, cauliflower and sea salt. Simmer on a low flame, adding water if needed.
2. In a blender, purée tofu thoroughly, with enough water to make into a cream, then add remaining ingredients. Pour over cauliflower, stir, and place in a casserole dish. Sprinkle with additional nutritional yeast, bake for 10 minutes on low and serve.

Baked Butternut Squash

yields 1 squash

1 Butternut Squash	1 T. Tamari
2 T. Oil	

1. Bake the squash in the oven until soft enough to cut in half (approximately one hour). Take it out and let it cool for a minute. Slice in half, lengthwise. Scoop out seeds.
2. Using a knife, cut lines in both directions down the inside of the squash halves, opening it up for a marinating mixture to seep in. (Don't cut through the shell.) Spread 1 to 1 1/2 T. oil on each half as well as 1/2 T. Bragg's on each half. Bake for another 10-15 minutes.

Yellow Summer Squash on the Half Shell

yields 14 halves

7 Yellow Crookneck Squash	1 t. Salt-Free Spike™
2 T. Nutritional Yeast	1 T. Tamari
1 t. Garlic Powder	4 T. Water
1/2 t. Oregano and Parsley (each)	1/2 T. Tahini (thin)

1. Wash the squash and slice in half, lengthwise.
2. Use a fork to pierce the squash, making grooves so that marinade mixture can seep into the squash. Line up each piece, grooves facing up, in a baking dish with sides.
3. Mix together the remaining ingredients and brush over the top of the squash. Pre-heat oven to 375°. Bake for 15-25 minutes until squash is very tender.

Spaghetti Squash on the Half Shell

yields 2 halves

1 Spaghetti Squash (large)	2 T. Tamari or Bragg's™
1 t. Onion Powder	1 t. Parsley Flakes
1/2 t. Garlic Powder	2 T. Nutritional Yeast
2 T. Water	

1. Place the squash in a pre-heated oven at 375° until it softens (approximately one hour). Remove from oven and cool enough to slice in half. Remove seeds. Place back in the oven to bake another 15 minutes. Make a mixture of the remaining ingredients.
2. Remove squash from oven and loosen the inside of the squash with a fork. Mix in the seasoning mixture and place back in the oven for another 10-15 minutes.

"Loyalty to a petrified opinion never yet broke a chain or freed a human soul."

MARK TWAIN (1835-1910)
American author and humorist

Spaghetti Squash Marinara

yields 2 halves

1 Spaghetti Squash (large)
1-2 T. Oil (Optional)
2 T. Tamari or Bragg's™

1 t. Garlic Powder
2 T. Nutritional Yeast
1/2 C. Tomato Sauce (see pg. 87)

1. Bake the squash in a pre-heated oven at 375° until soft enough to slice in half (approximately one hour). Remove from oven and cool before slicing. Remove seeds.
2. Using a fork, loosen up the squash. Mix remaining ingredients into both halves of the squash (using only half of the yeast and tomato sauce). Spread the rest of the sauce and yeast on top of squash. Bake until completely soft (another 20 minutes approximately).

Stuffed Tomatoes

serves 6

6 Tomatoes (large)
3 Green Onions, chopped
1 T. Balsamic Vinegar
1 T. Dijon Mustard
1/4 C. Parsley (fresh), chopped
2 t. Tahini

Fresh Ground Pepper, to taste
1/2 t. Basil
1/2 t. Oregano
Sea Salt, to taste
1 C. Basmati Rice (cooked)
Curly Lettuce, to garnish plate

1. Slice off the top 1/2 inch of the tomatoes and scoop out the flesh using a sharp knife and a spoon. Reserve the flesh in a bowl. Turn the tomato shells upside down on a towel to drain for 5 minutes.
2. Add the remaining ingredients to the reserve, except the rice and lettuce, stir and allow to marinate for 10 minutes.
3. With a slotted spoon, remove 1/3 of the mix and set aside for later as a garnish. Add the rice to the 2/3 mixture, stir, and allow to stand another 5 minutes.
4. Arrange the lettuce on 6 salad plates. Spoon the rice mixture back into the tomato shells, and place one on each plate. Top with remaining tomato mixture garnish and serve at room temperature.

> *"When I was 88 years old, I gave up meat entirely and switched to a plant-foods diet following a slight stroke. During the following months, I not only lost 50 pounds but gained strength in my legs and picked up stamina. Now, at age 93, I'm on the same plant-based diet, and I still don't eat any meat or dairy products. I either swim, walk, or paddle a canoe daily and I feel the best I've felt since my heart problems began."*
>
> DR. BENJAMIN SPOCK, M.D. (1903-1998)
> The famous "Dr. Spock"; pediatrician and author
> From: Nutrition Advocate, 1996

Stuffed Zucchini Boats

yields 12 boats

6 Zucchini, sliced in half lengthwise
1 Onion, diced
3 C. Mushrooms, sliced
2 T. Tamari or Bragg's™
2 C. Tofu, mashed
2 T. Oil

1 T. Nutritional Yeast
1/8 C. Water
1 t. Spike™ Seasoning
1/2 t. Salt-Free Spike™
1 t. Onion Powder
1 C. Grain of Choice (cooked)

1. Wash the zucchini and remove stem. Slice in half, lengthwise. Scoop out insides carefully but leave enough to make a firm container for the filling. Set zucchini insides aside.
2. Sauté the diced onion. When finished, remove and place in the food processor.
3. In the same fry pan, sauté the mushrooms with 1 T. Bragg's™. When finished, place in a mixing bowl.
4. Chop the zucchini insides into bite-sized pieces and then sauté with 1 T. Bragg's™. When cooked add it to the bowl with the mushrooms.
5. In the food processor (using the "S"- shaped blade), blend (along with the onion sauté) the remaining ingredients, beginning with the tofu, except for the grain. Add it to the bowl with mushrooms and zucchini. Add the grain and mix.
6. Oil a large baking pan and squirt with some Bragg's™. Place the zucchini halves in the pan and fill generously with the filling. Pre-heat oven and bake at 375°, on the lower shelf in the oven. Then switch to the upper rack. They are finished when filling is golden brown and the zucchini is soft, about 30-40 minutes.

Simply Delicious Baked Zucchini

yields 14 halves

7 Zucchini (smaller size)
1/3 C. Oil
4 T. Water

1 T. Nutritional Yeast
3 T. Tamari or Bragg's™
1/2 t. Garlic Powder

1. Slice each zucchini in half down the middle, lengthwise. (Slice in half again lengthwise if zucchini is large.)
2. Slide a fork from one end to the other, on the inside of the zucchini, using pressure, making grooves in each piece.
3. In a blender, blend the remaining ingredients.
4. Spoon this mixture into the grooves and bake in a pre-heated oven at 350° until soft and tender, about 20-30 minutes.

> *"An unrefined plant-based diet, together with appropriate exercise consistently followed, would eliminate most of the degenerative diseases that curse our Western world."*
>
> RAY FOSTER, M.D, FACS

Zucchini Pizzas
yields 6 half shells

3 Zucchini (medium), sliced in half
1 T. Oil
1 T. Tamari or Bragg's™
1 T. Water
1/2 t. Oregano (dried)

1/4 t. Dill Weed
1/4 t. Basil (dried)
1 C. Tomato Sauce
'Cheezy' Dip (see recipe pg. 75)

1. Slice the zucchini in half down the middle, lengthwise.
2. On insides of each piece, slide a fork from end to end, with pressure, to form grooves.
3. Make a marinade sauce of the oil, tamari, water, and herbs. Drop by spoon into the grooves evenly. Cover with tomato or marinara sauce. Then cover with "Cheezy" Dip and bake at 350° until zucchini are quite soft, 30-40 minutes.

Italian Eggplant Stir Fry
serves 4

3 Garlic Cloves, diced
1 Onion, sliced in half moons
1 Eggplant (large), cubed or diced
2 C. Mushrooms, sliced
1 Bell Pepper, sliced in strips
2 T. Tamari or Bragg's™

2 Tomatoes, cubed
1/4 C. Basil (fresh), chopped
1/3 C. Fresh Dill, chopped
1/4 t. Black Pepper
1 T. Nutritional Yeast
1 t. Sea Salt

1. In a skillet, sauté the garlic in a little oil and then the onion slices.
2. Add the eggplant and cover, allowing it to soften. In a couple of minutes, add the mushrooms and then the pepper. Season with tamari. Cover and simmer a couple more minutes. Add tomatoes and remaining seasonings. Simmer briefly until tomatoes are soft.

•Serve as is or over grain or pasta.

"In the American Journal of Clinical Nutrition, there was a recent series of letters and commentaries saying that people should probably get their omega-3 fats from vegetables and not from fish, because the omega-3 fish oils do seem to have a variety of negative effects, one of which is that they promote the production of free radicals. Free radicals can damage tissues and lead to cancer."

MILTON R. MILLS, M.D.
Physicians Committee for Responsible Medicine

Ratatouille

yields 1 large skillet

4 Garlic Cloves, diced	1 t. Garlic Powder
1 Onion, diced	1/2 t. Black Pepper
2 Bell Peppers, diced	2 t. Spike™ Seasoning
4 C. Mushrooms, sliced	3 T. Nutritional Yeast
7 C. Eggplant, cubed	4 t. Sweetener
2 Zucchini, diced	2 T. Oregano
2 T. Tamari	1/2 t. Dill Weed
1 (15) oz. Tomato Sauce Can	1/2 t. Sea Salt
3 T. Tomato Paste	2 T. Basil (dried)

1. In a large cast iron pan or skillet, sauté the garlic and the onions. When they are partially cooked, add the peppers and then the mushrooms. When they are softened a bit, add the eggplant. Season with the tamari, cover with a lid and allow to cook until soft. Add the zucchini pieces and cover again.
3. When the vegetables are almost cooked, add the tomato sauce and paste. Add all the remaining seasonings and spices and simmer, stirring frequently.
4. When sauce turns darker in color, shut off and allow to sit and absorb flavors.
   Serve as is or over grain or pasta.

Steamed Greens

<u>Greens of Choice</u>	
Collard Greens	Bragg's™ or Tamari
Kale (different varieties)	Oil (optional)
Mustard Greens	
Swiss Chard	
Bok Choy & Pok Choy	

1. Wash the greens well as they often have sand particles. Slice into small strips.
2. Steam using a steamer basket at the bottom of a pot. Fill with water, not to exceed the height of the steamer basket. (If water is filled too high, the greens will shrink as they cook and fall into the water).
3. Soft leaf greens, like chard, don't need anything added to them. When they soften they melt in your mouth. Collards, a thicker leaf, tend to need a dash of oil added to the pot to render them more tender.
   •The less the greens are steamed the more vitamins and nutrients are retained.

"All beings tremble before violence. All fear death. All love life. See yourself in others. Then whom can you hurt? What harm can you do?"

The BUDDHA (circa 563-483 B.C)

Indian avatar

Baby Bok Choy - Stir Fry

serves 4

8 oz. Shiitake Mushrooms (dried)	1 T. Sesame Oil
3 1/2 C. Water	1 T. Sweetener
2 T. Tamari	2 Heads Baby Bok Choy
2 T. Chili Sauce or 1/2 t. Red Pepper	1 T. Sunflower Oil
2 T. Arrowroot Powder	2 C. Sliced Mushrooms (fresh)

1. Soak shiitake mushrooms in water until completely soft, 15-20 minutes.
2. In a small bowl combine 1 cup of the soaking liquid with tamari, chili sauce, arrowroot powder, sesame oil and sweetener.
3. Slice the shiitake mushrooms. Cut off root end of bok choy and separate into stalks. Wash well. Cut crosswise into 1" slices.
4. Heat oil in a skillet or wok over high heat. Add fresh mushrooms and sauté until softened, about 1 minute. Add shiitake and bok choy and stir-fry 3 minutes. Add tamari mixture and cook until it thickens, about 2 minutes longer. Serve over rice or noodles.

Knishes

yields 2 dozen

1 Onion (medium), diced	3 T. Soy Powder + 6 T. Water,
1 C. Oil	(or egg replacer mixture for 3 eggs)
1/2 C. Potato Flour	1 t. Sea Salt
	4 C. Mashed Potatoes

1. Sauté onion in 4 tablespoons of oil and cool.
2. Knead remaining oil, potato flour, soy powder mixed with water and salt.
3. Roll out. Cut in 2" squares.
4. Place 1 teaspoon of browned onions on each square along with a spoonful of mashed potatoes. Fold and pinch edges together.
5. Place them on an oiled and floured baking sheet (or use baking papers). Bake for 25 minutes at 350° in a pre-heated oven.

> *"Lobsters are fascinating. They have a long childhood and an awkward adolescence. They use complicated signals to explore and establish social relationships with others. Their communications are direct and sophisticated. They flirt. Their pregnancies last 9 months. Some are right-handed, some left-handed. They've even been seen walking hand-in-hand. Some can live to be more than 150 years old, though few (1%) survive the world's most devastating predator- the species with whom lobsters share so many traits - the human being."*
>
> INGRID NEWKIRK
> National Director: People For The Ethical Treatment of Animals
> Quoted from: Save the Animals; 101 Easy Things You Can Do

Mediterranean Eggplant Sauté

serves 4-5

1-2 T. Oil	1-2 t. Cumin Powder
1/2 Onion (large), diced	1/8 t. Black Pepper
2 1/2 C. Mushrooms, sliced thick	1 T. Oregano
1 t. Garlic Granules	1 T. Nutritional Yeast
1-2 t. Onion Powder	1 C. Chick Peas (cooked)
1/2 t. Paprika	1 T. Tamari
2 1/2 T. Tamari	1 T. Vinegar
5 C. Eggplant, cubed	

1. Sauté the onion in the oil. When soft, add mushrooms; season with garlic, onion powder, paprika and tamari. Add the eggplant, cover, and let simmer for several minutes. Add the next four seasonings and cover again. Allow the eggplant to completely soften.
2. Place the chick peas in a cup with the tamari and vinegar and stir. Stir into the sauté and cook several minutes. Let sit with the lid covering it for at least 5 minutes. Serve.

Scalloped Potatoes

yields 1 large casserole

8 -10 Russet Potatoes, sliced thin	1 Onion, sliced
1/2 C. Oil	4-5 Garlic Cloves, sliced
1 C. Tofu, mashed	1 t. Onion Powder
1 C. Water	1/2 t. Garlic Powder
1 T. Bragg's™ or Tamari	Sea Salt and Pepper, to taste
3 T. Nutritional Yeast	Paprika
1 T. Cashew Butter	

1. Peel and slice potatoes. Place in water to prevent oxidation.
2. In a blender, blend oil, tofu, water, Bragg's, yeast and cashew butter.
3. In a large, oiled pan, mix blended sauce with sliced potatoes, onion and garlic. Pre-heat oven to 350° and bake. Stir periodically while baking.
4. When potatoes are almost thoroughly cooked (pull 1 out and test in 45 minutes), add sea salt and pepper, to taste. Sprinkle with paprika. Cook until potatoes are completely soft.

"People often say that humans have always eaten animals, as if this is a justification for continuing the practice. According to this logic, we should not try to prevent people from murdering other people, since this has also been done since the earliest of times."

ISAAC BASHEVIS SINGER (1904-1991)
Laureate of Literature,
1978 Nobel Prize recipient

Mashed Potatoes - Creamy Style

Serves 4-6

1 Onion, diced
7 C. Potatoes, cubed
2 T. + 3 T. Nutritional Yeast
4 t. Potato Stock

4 t. Oil or Cashew Milk
2 t. Bragg™ Liquid Aminos
1 t. Dill Weed
1 t. Sea Salt

1. Sauté the onion in 1 T. oil, 3 T. water and 2 T. nutritional yeast, until soft.
2. Boil a large pot of water and cook the bite-sized potato pieces until soft.
3. Drain the potatoes, saving a small amount of the potato water (stock). Mash the potatoes with the stock and all the remaining ingredients. Stir in the onion sauté.

•Serve with cashew-mushroom gravy or simple tahini dressing.

Traditional Potato Latkes -Vegan Style

serves 8

4 Idaho/Russet Potatoes (large)
   (about 2 1/2 lbs.)
1 Onion (medium)
1-2 t. Sea Salt

1/2 t. Black Pepper (fresh ground)
3 T. Tahini
2 T. Matzoh Meal (or wheat germ)
Safflower Oil

1. Coarsely grate the potatoes and onion with a hand grater or a food processor. Place in a colander. Set over a large bowl and squeeze out liquid.
2. Pour off the liquid from the bowl, leaving the potato starch that has settled to the bottom. Add the potatoes, onions, salt, pepper, tahini and wheat germ. Mix well.
3. Heat about 1/4 inch of oil in a large skillet over medium heat. Use a heaping tablespoon of batter to form each pancake. Flatten them with the back of a spoon as you add them to the skillet. Pan fry until golden brown, turning once. Add more oil and adjust the heat as needed. Drain on a paper towel before serving.

"The human body, the very one you're sitting in right now, has no nutritional requirement for animal flesh or cow's milk. It functions superbly without them, and this includes producing healthy offspring. Mothers who do not give milk or dairy products to their children are helping their children stay healthy, rather than depriving them."

MICHAEL A. KLAPER, M.D.
author and international lecturer
Pregnancy, Children, and The Vegan Diet

Potato Omelette

serves 4

3 Potatoes (large), grated	1/2 lb. Tofu, mashed
1 Onion (large), grated	1/4-1/2 t. Sea Salt
1/2 t. Sea Salt	1/2 t. Garlic Granules
1/8 t. Red Pepper (or black)	1/2 t. Onion Powder
2 T. Olive Oil	1/8 t. Paprika
1 Bell Pepper, chopped finely	1/8 t. Red Pepper

1. In a bowl, thoroughly mix the grated potato, onion, salt and pepper. Add this mixture to a skillet with 1 T. olive oil, over medium heat, and pan fry until potatoes and onions are golden brown. Add chopped bell pepper and cook for four more minutes.
2. In a bowl, mash tofu and season with salt, garlic granules, onion powder, paprika and red pepper. Add the cooked potatoes, onions and pepper to the tofu and mix well.
3. In the same skillet, over medium heat, add 1 T. olive oil. Place the tofu- potato batter in the pan. Lightly brown on one side and flip to brown the other.

Home Fries

serves 2-3

2 T. Oil	1 t. Onion Powder
4 C. Cooked Potatoes,	1/2 t. Sea Salt
(cubed in bite-sized pieces)	1/2 t. Paprika
1 1/2 T. Bragg's™ or Tamari	1/4 t. Black Pepper
2 T. Nutritional Yeast	

1. Heat 2 T. oil in a skillet on medium heat.
2. Place the bite-sized cubed potatoes (leftover potatoes work well) in the skillet and season with Bragg's™. Add the yeast and onion powder. If potatoes are sticking, add another tablespoon of oil. Just before the potatoes are browned, add the sea salt, paprika and pepper and pan-fry for another minute.

French Unfries

yields 2 small trays

7 Idaho/Russet Potatoes	1 t. Sea Salt
2 T. Oil	1 T. Nutritional Yeast
1 T. Bragg's™ or Tamari	1/2 t. Paprika

1. Peel and cut the potatoes into strips like French fries.
2. Place in a bowl and mix with the remaining ingredients.
3. Pre-heat oven to 375°. Lightly oil two small baking sheets (preferably lipped).
   Place the potatoes on the trays and bake for 20-40 minutes until golden brown, switching the trays halfway through. Use a spatula to flip the fries periodically.
4. Lightly salt, to taste.

Holiday Candied Yams

serves 4-6

5 Yams (medium-large) (or sweet potatoes), sliced	1 T. Nutritional Yeast
1 T. Bragg's™ or Sea Salt, to taste	1 T. Sucanat™
3-4 T. Maple Syrup	1 T. Vanilla
	1/8 C. Oil

1. Peel and slice the yams. Steam yams in a pot until softened, about 20-30 minutes.
2. In a blender, blend the remaining ingredients.
3. Place the yams (or sweet potatoes) in a casserole and pour blender mixture over them. Be sure to scrape the sides of the blender with a rubber spatula. Spread evenly on the yams and bake in a pre-heated oven at 350°. Stir occasionally and continue baking for about 1/2 hour. Allow to cool before serving.

Spanish Paella

serves 6

2 T. Olive Oil	Salt & Pepper, to taste
6 Cloves Garlic, minced	1/2 t. Paprika
1 Onion (medium), chopped	12 Asparagus Spears, cut into 2" pieces
2 C. Brown Rice (uncooked)	6 Broccoli Spears (large), thinly sliced
3 1/2-4 C. Broth	
1 t. Saffron, to taste	6 Seitan Strips, cubed
1 Green Bell Pepper, chopped	1 C. Green Peas
1 Red Bell Pepper, sliced	
2 Tomatoes, chopped	

1. In a large skillet, heat oil over medium-high heat. Add garlic and onion and sauté until onion is transparent, about 3 minutes.
2. Add rice, stir-fry until rice begins to brown, about 2 minutes. Add broth, saffron, bell peppers and tomatoes, mix well. Bring to simmer and add salt & pepper and paprika.
3. Cover and bake in a pre-heated oven at 350° until most of liquid is absorbed, about 25-35 minutes. Place asparagus, broccoli and seitan on top of mixture. Cover and bake until vegetables are tender and rice is done, about 7-10 minutes. Remove from oven and sprinkle on peas. Cover and let sit 2 minutes until peas are hot.

"If you change to a vegan diet, and do it very vigorously, you have enormous power. You can reverse heart disease. You can prevent it. You can, I believe, prevent most cases of cancer if you combine dietary changes with avoiding tobacco. You could prevent probably 70% or 80% of cancers, just by those steps alone. And, obviously, there's a whole host of other diseases that you would be able to live without."

NEAL BARNARD, M.D.
President: The Physicians Committee for Responsible Medicine

Thai'd Veggie Rolls
yields approximately 24 small rolls

1 Bunch Scallions	4 T. Orange Juice
1 T. Olive Oil	1/2 C. Cilantro, chopped
2 C. Carrots, shredded	1 T. Sesame Oil
2 C. Cabbage, shredded	1/2 t. Ginger Powder
2 Red Pepper, cut in thin strips	Salt and Pepper (to taste)
2 C. Snow Peas, sliced diagonally	12 Sheets of Nori, cut in half

1. Cut the green tops from the scallions and set aside. (You will need 24 strands for tying the rolls.) Mince enough of the white part of the scallion to make 1/4 cup and set aside.
2. Heat the olive oil over medium heat, in a large skillet or non-stick pan. Sauté minced scallions, carrots, cabbage, peppers and snow peas for three minutes. Add orange juice and continue cooking, uncovered, until juice is almost evaporated, about 3 minutes.
3. Place vegetables in a bowl and toss with cilantro, sesame oil and ginger powder. Salt and pepper to taste.
4. Lay out 1/2 sheet nori, and place 1 T. of vegetable filling in the center. Roll up carefully, and tie up each roll with a scallion top.
5. Serve with Thai Dipping Sauce. Recipe as follows:

Thai Dipping Sauce
yields 1 1/2 cups

3/4 C. Peanuts (dry roasted)	4 T. Tamari
2 Thin Slices Ginger (fresh), peeled	2 T. Rice Vinegar
2 Garlic Cloves, minced	1 C. Vegetable Stock (warm)
2 T. Sweetener	2-3 T. Lime Juice
1/2 t. Crushed Red Pepper Flakes	

1. Combine peanuts, ginger, garlic, sweetener, pepper flakes, tamari and vinegar in a blender or food processor. Process until smooth, adding stock slowly and blending on a low speed. As a final step add the lime juice. Serve at room temperature.

> *"Most nutrition professionals agree that moving away from an animal product-based diet to a plant-based diet is the single most important improvement Americans (and others who eat similarly) can do to improve their well-being. I personally have eaten vegan (totally vegetarian) for over 15 years and have raised my two children that way since birth."*
>
> GEORGE EISMAN, Registered Dietitian
> Co-Founder: Vegetarian Nutrition Practice Group; American Dietetic Association,
> Author of: <u>The Most Noble Diet</u>

Greek Souvlaki

serves 6

2 Garlic Cloves, crushed
1/2 t. Oregano
1/4 t. Red Pepper
3 T. Olive Oil
2 T. Lemon Juice
1 lb. Tofu (firm), cut into 1" cubes
1/2 t. Cumin
1/2 t. Salt

1 C. Flat-Leaf Parsley (leaves only)
1/2 C. Mint (fresh)
1/2 lb. Tofu (soft)
3 Red Bell Peppers
1 Onion (large),
  cut into 1/2" slices
1 Package of Flat Bread
4 C. Flat-Leaf Spinach, washed, drained

1. In a large bowl mix together garlic, oregano, pepper, 2 T. oil and 1 T. lemon juice. Add tofu cubes. Turn to coat tofu. Chill 1 hour.
2. In food processor, combine remaining lemon juice, cumin, 1/4 t. salt, parsley, mint and soft tofu. Process to creamy smooth. Pour into serving bowl. Chill. This makes herb sauce.
3. Over gas burner or under broiler, roast peppers, turning, until skins are blackened. Place in paper bag; close. Let cool. Peel peppers, discard skins, stems and seeds. Cut peppers into strips.
4. Remove tofu from marinade. In a large skillet, over medium heat, add remaining oil and onion slices and cook 2-3 minutes. Add in tofu cubes and cook another 3 minutes while turning. Sprinkle with remaining salt.
5. To Assemble: lay flat bread on counter. Top with spinach leaves, tofu cubes, onions and pepper strips; sprinkle with some of the herb sauce, and roll up into cones or cylinders. Serve with remaining sauce.

Peking Tempeh Tortilla Rolls

serves 6

2 C. Long Grain Brown Rice (cooked)
1 T. Sesame Oil
6 Scallions, cut into 1" pieces
2 T. Sesame Seeds (toasted)
2 C. Red Cabbage, shredded finely
1 C. Carrot, shredded
4 oz. Cake Tempeh, steamed & crumbled

3 T. Rice Vinegar
1/2 t. Salt
1 T. Ginger, grated
1/3 lb. Snow Peas (ends trimmed)
6 Flour Tortillas
6 T. Spicy Mustard

1. After cooking rice (see Cooking Guide for Grains), stir in sesame oil, scallions and sesame seeds. Set aside.
2. In a bowl, combine cabbage, shredded carrots, tempeh, vinegar, salt and ginger.
3. Bring small saucepan of water to a boil. Add snow peas; cook 30 seconds. Drain, rinse under cold water. Pat dry, cut lengthwise into thin strips. Add to cabbage mixture.
4. Lay tortillas flat on work surface. Spread each with 1/2 T. mustard. 1 inch from bottom edge, place a strip of cabbage mixture and top with strip of rice mixture.
5. Roll up until tortilla just covers ingredients, tuck in ends. Continue to roll into tight cylinder.

Vietnamese Spring Rolls

serves 8

<u>Sauce:</u>
- 3 T. Rice Vinegar
- 3 T. Soy Sauce
- 3 T. Lime Juice
- 3 T. Water
- 2 Scallions, minced
- 1 T. Sweetener
- 1 t. Ginger Root, grated
- 1/4 t. Red Pepper Flakes

<u>Rolls:</u>
- 3 oz. Rice-Vermicelli Noodles
- 8 Rice-Paper Wrappers
- 8 Lettuce Leaves (curly type)
- 2 Carrots, shredded
- 1 Red Bell Pepper, sliced
- 1 Ripe Avocado (firm, peeled, thinly sliced)
- 1 C. Cilantro Leaves, chopped
- 1 C. Peanuts, chopped

1. In small bowl, whisk all Sauce ingredients until sweetener is dissolved.
2. Fill medium saucepan 2/3 with water; bring to boil. Add noodles, cook until tender, about 2 minutes. Drain, rinse with cold water. Using scissors, cut noodles into 3" lengths.
3. Fill large bowl with hot water. Immerse wrappers, 2 at a time until soft, about 1 minute. Lay wrappers side-by-side between damp paper towels until ready to use.
4. On each wrapper, place 1 piece of lettuce along bottom, 1" from edge. Place some noodles, bell pepper strips, avocado slices and 2 T. each carrot, cilantro and peanuts.
5. Roll up until wrapper just covers filling, fold in ends. Roll into tight cylinders. Using serrated knife, cut in half crosswise. Cover with damp towel. Do not refrigerate. Uncover, serve with sauce.

Vegetable Curry

serves 8

<u>Curry Sauce</u>
- 1 1/2 C. Soy Milk (rich)
- 1 C. Corn Kernels
- 1 C. Coconut Milk (unsweetened)
- 1 T. Curry Powder
- 1 (1") Piece Fresh Ginger, (peeled, chopped)
- 2 Cloves Garlic (large)

<u>Vegetable Base</u>
- 1 Head Cauliflower (cut into florets)
- 5 Red Potatoes, cubed

- 1 lb. Carrots (peeled & quartered lengthwise, cut into 1" chunks)
- 1 Onion (large), sliced
- 1/2 lb. Mushrooms (small)
- 1/2 t. Cumin Seeds, (optional)

<u>Ingredients to set aside</u>
- 2 C. Chick-peas (cooked)
- 2 C. Green Peas
- Basmati Rice (cooked)
- Garnish, (chopped cilantro, roasted cashews)

1. In blender, purée: soy milk, corn kernels, coconut milk, curry powder, ginger root, and garlic until smooth. Pour into a large bowl.
2. Place vegetable base into a casserole dish. Pour curry sauce over vegetable base. Toss until vegetables are coated well. Bake in a pre-heated oven at 400° for 30-40 minutes, covered. Uncover, stir in chick-peas and green peas. Cover; bake 5 more minutes or until vegetables are tender. Serve over Basmati rice and top with garnish.

Quinoa Spicy Pilaf

Serves 6-8

1 C. Chick-peas (cooked)	1/4 t. Black Pepper
6 C. Quinoa (cooked)	1/4 t. Curry (mild)
1/4 t. Cayenne Pepper	1/2 t. Cumin
1/4 t. Paprika	2 T. Oil
1/2 t. Oregano (dried)	1 T. Bragg's™ or Tamari
1 T. Nutritional Yeast	1 t. Spike™ Seasoning
1/2 t. Onion Powder	1/2 t. Garlic Powder

1. Cook the chick-peas and drain (see Cooking Guide for Beans pg. 19). Cook the quinoa (see Cooking Guide for Grains pg. 18). Pre-heat oven to 350°.
2. Mix all the ingredients together in a casserole and bake for 20-25 minutes.
   •Serve as a side dish or as a bed for a vegetable medley and sauce.

Potato Rolls

yields 22 rolls

12 C. Potatoes (peeled and cubed)	1 t. Garlic Powder
1/8 C. Oil	1 t. Onion Powder
1 1/2 T. Bragg™ Liquid Aminos	1 t. Spike™ Seasoning
1 1/2 t. Sea Salt	1 T. Nutritional Yeast
1/4 t. Black Pepper	1/2 t. Dill Weed
1/4 C. Soy/Rice or Oat Milk	2 C. Peas (frozen)
	1 Package of Lumpia or Spring Roll Wrappers
	Cornstarch and Water Mixture

1. Boil the cubed potatoes until soft. Drain water. Place in a large mixing bowl and mash thoroughly. Add all the ingredients, except the Lumpia wrappers, peas, corn starch and water mixture. Mix well. Fold in the peas and mix again.
2. After opening the wrappers, place them in between two damp dish towels to keep them moist and easy to work with. (You can use Spring Roll Wrappers if you can't find Lumpia Wrappers). Place about 3 heaping teaspoons of potato batter onto the end of each wrapper. Roll up, folding sides in. (A mixture of cornstarch and water will make a glue for closing the wrappers or use a little oil.) Place each roll on an oiled baking sheet. When all rolls are on the baking sheet, baste each with oil (using a basting brush) on the tops and ends. Bake (or convect) in a pre-heated oven at 375° for 20-30 minutes until golden brown and crispy on the outside. Serve with Tofu Mayonnaise pg. 77.

> *"Running the ranch paid well; it was challenging; it was my family tradition. But my conscience told me that I needed to speak out about this industry - there's just too much that the cattle industry hides from the public."*
>
> HOWARD LYMAN
> former cattle rancher, international lecturer
> From: <u>Vegan: The New Ethics of Eating</u>, by Erik Marcus

Entrées

"As man advanced gradually in intellectual power and was enabled to trace the more remote consequences of his actions; as his sympathies became more tender and widely diffused, extending to men of all races, and finally, to the lower animals, so would the standard of his morality rise higher and higher."

CHARLES DARWIN (1809–1882)
English naturalist and biologist

Neat Loaf
yields 1 large skillet or casserole

2 Onions, diced, sautéed	1 T. Dr. Bronner's Bouillon™
1 Bell Pepper, diced, sautéed	1 1/2 C. Tomato Paste
4 C. Seitan, ground	5 t. Oregano (dried)
1 Tempeh Cake, ground	2 t. Salt-Free Spike™
2 C. Millet (cooked)	1 t. Cumin
1/4 C. Oil	1 t. Sea Salt
1/2 t. Black Pepper	2 T. Nutritional Yeast
1 C. Tofu, mashed	1-2 T. Oil

1. Sauté onions in a little oil. When soft, remove from fry pan and put aside half of the onions. Put the rest in a large mixing bowl. Sauté bell pepper and add to onions in bowl.
2. Using the "S"- shaped blade of the food processor, grind the seitan and then the tempeh. Fry together in a large skillet and season with salt flavorings (Bragg's, Tamari) and yeast.
3. When browned, place ground seitan & tempeh into the mixing bowl. Add cooked millet (see Cooking Guide for Grains).
4. In the food processor, blend oil, the onion sauté that was set aside, black pepper, tofu, bouillon and 1 cup of tomato paste. Stir this into the mixture in the large bowl. Add oregano, Spike™, cumin, sea salt and the other half cup of tomato paste. Mix well.
5. Place into an oiled casserole or large cast iron skillet. Sprinkle with extra nutritional yeast and 1-2 T. oil on top. Bake in a pre-heated oven at 350° for 50 minutes.

Easy Carrot-Grain Loaf
yields 1 loaf

2 C. Brown Rice (uncooked)	1 Onion (large), diced, sautéed
1 C. Grain of Choice (uncooked)	3 T. Nutritional Yeast
2 C. Carrots, grated	4 T. Bragg's™ or Tamari
1/2 lb. Tofu	7 T. Tahini Dressing (see recipe pg. 78)
4-6 T. Water	1/2 t. Sea Salt
Garlic and Onion Powder, to taste	2-3 T. Mustard (optional)

1. Cook grains and set aside to cool (see Cooking Guide for Grains).
2. In a food processor, blend all ingredients except grains and carrots to a smooth and creamy mixture. Add this mixture to the grains and carrots. Mix.
3. Place mixture into an oiled casserole and bake at 350° for 30 minutes or until golden brown.

> *"My refusing to eat meat occasioned an inconveniency, and I have been frequently chided for my singularity. But my light repast allows for greater progress, for greater clearness of head and quicker comprehension."*
>
> BENJAMIN FRANKLIN   (1706-1790)
> American statesman, inventor and author

Mexican Rice and Lentil Loaf

yields one 13" x 9" baking pan

1-2 T. Garlic Oil
1 Onion (large), diced
8 C. Brown Rice, cooked
1 C. Lentils (cooked), drained
<u>Processor Ingredients</u>
1/4 C. Oil
1 C. Tofu, mashed
1 C. VeganRella™ Cheese Alternative

2 T. Tamari
1 t. Garlic Powder
Onion sauté (the 1 diced onion)
<u>Final Ingredients</u>
1 t. Sea Salt
1 C. VeganRella™, grated
Paprika, sprinkle

1. Sauté the diced onion in garlic oil.
2. Place cooked rice and lentils in a large mixing bowl (see Cooking Guides).
3. In a food processor, blend the Processor Ingredients and add to rice and lentils. Mix well.
4. Add the sea salt and 'VeganRella'. Mix thoroughly and place in an oiled baking pan. Sprinkle with paprika. Bake in a pre-heated oven at 350° for 35-40 minutes.

Savory Carrot-Tofu Loaf

yields one 9" x 12" casserole

1 Onion, diced
3 C. Carrot, grated
2 lbs. Tofu, mashed
3 C. Millet, cooked
1 T. Salt-Free Spike™
1 T. Oregano (dried)
2 t. Garlic Powder
1 t. Spike™ Seasoning
1/2 t. Turmeric
3/4 C. VeganRella™, grated

<u>Blended Mixture</u>
1/3 C. Oil
1 1/2 C. Tofu, mashed
1/8 C. Bragg's™ or Tamari
1/8 C. Mustard
3 T. Nutritional Yeast
1 T. Onion Powder
Pepper, dash
1 t. Sea Salt

1. Sauté the onion.
2. In a large bowl, mix the grated carrot, tofu, millet and seasonings. Mix in the grated VeganRella™ cheese.
3. In a food processor, blend the remaining ingredients along with the sautéed onion.
4. Pour the wet mixture into the dry batter and mix thoroughly. Place in an oiled casserole dish and bake at 350° for 40-50 minutes, rotating casserole from top to bottom racks.

"The more noble a soul is, the more objects of compassion it has."

FRANCIS BACON (1561-1626)
English philosopher, statesman and essayist

Barley-Pecan Loaf

yields 1 large baking casserole

5 Garlic Cloves	1 T. Spike™ Seasoning
1/4 C. Oil	2 T. Nutritional Yeast
1 1/2 C. Tofu, mashed	8 C. Cooked Barley (2-3 C. dry)
1 C. Water	2 C. Carrots, grated
2 T. Tahini	1/2 C. Pecans, chopped
1/2 t. Curry	1 t. Paprika
1/2 t. Pepper	

1. In a blender, blend garlic cloves in 1/4 cup oil (just covering the blender blades). Blend in tofu, water, tahini and spices.
2. In a large bowl, combine blended mixture with the barley, pecans and carrots. Mix well.
3. Place into a large oiled casserole and sprinkle with paprika. Bake in a pre-heated oven at 350° for 45-60 minutes. Allow to cool before serving. Serve with a gravy.

Tofu Loaf

serves 4-6

2 Garlic Cloves, diced	2 T. Oil
1 Onion, diced	3 T. Tamari
1 Red Pepper, diced	1/2 t. Garlic Powder
1 Celery Stalk, diced	1 C. Nutritional Yeast
1 Carrot, diced or grated	1 C. Tahini or Peanut Butter
2 lbs. Tofu, mashed	1/2 t. Basil
4 Slices Whole Wheat Bread	1/2 t. Turmeric
	1/2 t. Oregano

1. In a medium-sized skillet, sauté garlic, onion, pepper, celery and carrot (in that order) in 1 tablespoon of oil. Season with 1 tablespoon of Tamari.
2. When vegetables are tender, add them to the mashed tofu in a bowl.
3. Cut bread into small crouton-sized pieces and quick-fry in: 1 T. Oil, adding 1 T. Tamari, 1/2 t. Garlic Powder and 5 T. Nutritional Yeast.
4. Add croutons, nut butter and remaining seasonings to tofu mixture. Stir well.
5. Place mixture in a well oiled casserole and bake in a pre-heated oven at 350° for 35 minutes. Allow to cool. Slide a butter knife along the sides and remove from casserole.

•Serve at holidays or any occasion with a gravy, or slice and use for sandwiches.

"Ethics are responsibility without limit towards all that lives."

ALBERT SCHWEITZER (1875-1965)
Alsatian philosopher and medical missonary
1952 Nobel Prize recipient

Millet-Tempeh Burgers

yields 16 burgers

1 Onion, diced
1 Tempeh Cake   2 T. Mustard
1 1/2 T. Bragg's™ or Tamari   1/4 t. Black Pepper
3 T. Nutritional Yeast   1 t. Garlic Powder
1/3 C. Oil   1 t. Onion Powder
1 C. Tofu, mashed   1 t. Spike™ Seasoning
1 T. Tahini   6 C. Cooked Millet (see Cooking Guide)

1. Sauté diced onion in 1 t. oil, 1 T. Bragg's™ and 1 T. yeast.
2. In a food processor, use the "S" - shaped blade to grind the tempeh into small chunks.
3. When onions are soft, remove from fry pan. Fry the ground tempeh with a small amount of Bragg's™, oil and 1 T. yeast.
4. In the food processor, blend: oil, tofu, tahini, mustard, 1 T. yeast and seasonings along with the sautéed onion.
5. In a large mixing bowl, combine together the cooked millet, tempeh and the blended creamy tofu mixture. Mix well.
6. Form into patties and bake in a pre-heated oven at 350° for 20-30 minutes, until crispy golden brown.

Peanut-Millet Burgers

yields 15 burgers

6 C. Millet (cooked)   1/3 C. Oil
1 C. Celery, diced   2 T. Bragg's™ or Tamari
2 C. Onion, diced   2/3 C. Vegetable Sauté
3/4 C. Tofu, mashed   1 T. Oregano
1/3 C. Peanut Butter   1 t. Cumin
3 t. Spike™ Seasoning   1/3 C. Water

1. In a bowl, set aside 6 cups of the cooked millet (see Cooking Guide for Grains).
2. In a fry pan, sauté celery and onion until soft.
3. In a food processor, use the "S"- shaped blade to blend all other ingredients, adding 2/3 cup of the celery and onion sauté and 1/3 cup water.
4. In a bowl, mix together the remaining vegetable sauté, millet and the blended mixture.
5. Shape into patties and bake in a pre-heated oven at 350° for 20-30 minutes, until crispy golden brown.

"We can easily forgive a child who is afraid of the dark. The real tragedy of life is when men are afraid of the light."

PLATO (ca. 428- 348 B.C.)
Greek philosopher

Indian Curry Loaf
yields (1) 9" X 7" Casserole

4 C. Cooked Lentils	1 t. Curry Powder
8 C. Cooked Short Grain Brown Rice	1 t. Cumin
<u>Blender Ingredients</u>	<u>Final Seasonings</u>
1 C. Tofu (mashed)	1/2 t. Sea Salt
1/4 C. Oil	1/2 t. Curry
1/2 C. Water	1/2 t. Cumin
1/8 C. Tamari	1/4 t. Turmeric

1. In a large mixing bowl, place the cooked lentils and rice (see Cooking Guides).
2. In a blender, blend all the Blender Ingredients. Pour into the mixing bowl and mix well with rice and lentils.
3. Add the Final Seasonings and mix again. Oil a shallow baking casserole and place the mixture into it. Firmly pack down and smooth the top. Bake in a pre-heated oven at 350° for 45 minutes. The top should have a light crust when done.

Veggie Kabobs with Marinated Tofu
yields 6 skewers

1 lb. Tofu (firm), drained, of excess water, frozen, cubed	1 Red Pepper, cut into 1" pieces
	1 Green Pepper, cubed
1 Red Onion (medium-sized), cut into 2" thick slices	12 Button Mushrooms, wiped clean with a damp towel, stems removed

Marinade

6 T. Mustard, (creamy)	8 T. Apple Juice & 8 T. Orange Juice
3 T. Rice Vinegar	1 t. Salt and Pepper
3 T. Olive Oil	2 Garlic Cloves, crushed

1. Unpack and drain water from packaged tofu. Place the whole block of tofu on a plate. Place another plate directly on top of tofu and place a weight atop plate, for example, a teapot filled with water. After 30 minutes, pour off collected water.
2. Repeat step one. After draining, cut into 4 small rectangles and wrap in plastic. Freeze 12-48 hours. (Freezing tofu makes it easier to handle and changes it's texture.) Unwrap and thaw by placing tofu in a bowl of hot water. Thaw all the way through (20-30 minutes).
3. Do not pull pieces apart until completely thawed. Gently squeeze and drain out the water.
4. Coat tofu completely with marinade ingredients. Marinate in a shallow dish for at least 2 hours. Remove from marinade, then marinate the vegetables.
5. Cut tofu into cubes, then thread onto metal skewers, alternating with veggies.
6. Grill over medium-hot fire for 10-12 minutes, turning occasionally. Brush with marinade frequently. Vegetables should be slightly charred on the outside, tender on the inside.

High Protein Quinoa Burgers
yields 24 medium burgers

10 C. Quinoa, cooked
3 C. Tofu (firm), mashed
<u>Food Processor Ingredients</u>
1/2 C. Oil
4 T. Bragg's™ or Tamari
1/2 T. Garlic Powder
1/2 T. Onion Powder
1 C. Tofu (firm), mashed

1/2 C. Tomato Paste
1/2 T. Spike™ Seasoning
1/2 C. Nutritional Yeast
2 T. Peanut Butter
3 T. Mustard
1 T. Tahini (thin)
Salt-Free Spike™, to taste
Favorite Seasonings, to taste
3/4 C. Water

1. In a large bowl, place the tofu and cooked quinoa (see Cooking Guide for Grains).
2. In a food processor, blend remaining ingredients with 3/4 cup water. Add blended mixture to quinoa / tofu mixture and mix well.
3. Form the mixture into medium-sized burgers. Place on to 2 oiled cookie sheets (12 on a sheet). Bake in a pre-heated oven at 350° until crispy on one side (25-30 minutes). Flip and continue to bake until the outside of the burgers are crispy (about 15 more minutes).

• This recipe yields enough to save some burgers for lunch box sandwiches.

Light and Easy Quinoa Burgers
yields 18 burgers

9 C. Quinoa, cooked
 (about 2 1/2 C. uncooked)
1 Onion, diced
1/2 C. Oil
2 C. Tofu, mashed
3 T. Bragg's™ or Tamari

2 T. Nutritional Yeast
3/4 t. Sea Salt
1/4 t. Black Pepper
1/2 T. Onion Powder
1/2 T. Garlic Powder
1/4 C. Water

1. Cook the Quinoa. When finished place in a large mixing bowl.
2. In a small fry pan, sauté diced onion until softened.
3. In a food processor, blend remaining ingredients with 1/4 cup of water, adding the onion sauté. Combine blended mixture with Quinoa in bowl. Mix well.
4. Form into small patties and place on an oiled baking sheet. Bake in a pre-heated oven at 350° until crispy on the top side (25-30 minutes). Flip and continue to bake until the outside of the burgers are crispy (about 15 more minutes).

"To avoid causing terror to living beings, let the disciple refrain from eating meat."

The BUDDHA (circa 563-483 B.C.)
Indian avatar

Chick-Pea-Tempeh Burgers
yields 11 burgers

2 Cakes Tempeh, ground	1/2 T. Spike™ Seasoning
1/4 C. Oil	1 t. Onion Powder
2 T. Bragg's™ or Tamari	1/2 t. Garlic Powder
2 1/2 C. Chick Peas (cooked)	1/2 C. Water
1 T. Tahini	Paprika for sprinkling

1. In a food processor, using the "S'- shaped blade, grind the tempeh into small pieces.
2. Sauté the ground tempeh in a fry pan with oil and Bragg's™.
3. In the food processor, combine all the ingredients (except for the tempeh and paprika) with 1/2 cup of water and blend well.
4. Mix tempeh with blended mixture. Form into burgers on an oiled baking sheet and sprinkle with paprika. Bake in a pre-heated oven at 350° for 30-40 minutes. Switch racks in the oven during baking time.

Super Vegan Burgers
yields 12 large burgers

1 C. Tofu, mashed	1 1/2 C. Oats
1 C. Tomato Paste	1/2 C. Sunflower Seeds, ground
1/4 C. Oil	2 T. Bragg's™ or Tamari
1 T. Hickory Smoke (optional)	2 1/2 C. Seitan, ground
1 1/2 T. Mustard	1/4 C. Nutritional Yeast
1 T. Garlic Powder	1 T. Spike™ Seasoning
1 T. Onion Powder	2 1/2 C. Cooked Millet
1 T. Salt-Free Spike™	

1. In a food processor, using the "S"- shaped blade, whiz together all of the ingredients in the first column. Set aside in a bowl.
2. In the same food processor, grind the oats and sunflower seeds to a fine meal. Add to the bowl.
3. Grind the seitan, using the "S"- shaped blade, and then add to the mixture.
4. Add the remaining ingredients and mix well. Form into large-sized burger patties and place on an oiled baking sheet. Bake at 350° until cooked, about 35-45 minutes.

> *"Other things being equal, I judge that a strict vegetarian will live ten years longer than a habitual meat eater, while suffering on the average, less than half so much from sickness."*
>
> HORACE GREELEY (1811-1872)
> American newspaper editor
> Founder of New York Herald Tribune

Sweet Potato and Black Bean Burger
yields 12-15 burgers

2 T. Oil
2 Onions (medium), diced
4 Garlic Cloves, minced
2 Carrots, grated finely
2 C. Black Beans (cooked)
10 Sun-Dried Tomatoes, (soaked in
  hot water until soft), coarsely chopped
2 C. Shiitake Mushrooms (dried), soaked
  in hot water until soft, coarsely chopped
2 Baked Sweet Potatoes,
  (scooped out of skin)

2 C. Quinoa (cooked)
1 1/2-2 C. Home-Made Bread Crumbs
  or Wheatgerm or Bran
2 T. Caraway Seeds
1 t. Sea Salt
1 t. Onion Powder
1 t. Red Pepper
1/2-1 C. Tomato Sauce
4 T. Mustard (creamy)
2 T. Balsamic Vinegar

1. Heat oil in a skillet over medium heat. Add onions and garlic and lower heat.
   Cook until lightly browned, several minutes. Add carrots, beans, tomatoes and
   mushrooms and cook an additional 4-5 minutes, stirring occasionally. Turn off heat.
   Mash slightly in pan, until beans are half crushed.
2. Place skillet mixture in large bowl with remaining ingredients, and mix thoroughly. If
   mixture is moist, add more bread crumbs.
3. Form into patties and cook over medium heat in oiled skillet, about 4 minutes on each
   side or until heated through and slightly crispy on the outside.
   (Patties can also be baked on a cookie sheet for 25 minutes at 350°.) Serve on a bun.

Polenta
serves 4

2 C. Polenta (coarse corn meal) (dry)
2 T. Spike™ Seasoning
1 t. Garlic Powder
1 t. Onion Powder

1 t. Basil (dried)
Cashew Pesto (see recipe pg. 75)
1/2 C. Mushrooms, sliced
  (or Zucchini or Onion)

1. Bring 7 cups of water to a boil. Add Polenta slowly, stirring with a whisk. Add all
   seasonings and continue to stir with whisk for about 7 minutes. When thickened and
   cooked, pour Polenta mixture into a dish and let cool. Refrigerate, allowing it to solidify.
2. When cooled, slice. Fry with a little oil or bake until the outside is crisp. Serve with fresh
   cashew pesto and top with sautéed mushrooms, sweet onions or zucchini.

---

*"Were it only to learn benevolence to humankind,
we should be merciful to other creatures."*

PLUTARCH (46-120. A.D.)
Greek philosopher, essayist and biographer

Creamy Polenta with Tempeh Onion Sauce

serves 4-6

Sauce

1 T. Olive Oil
1 1/2 Onions (medium), chopped
4 Garlic Cloves, minced
1 t. Oregano
1/4 t. Red Pepper Flakes

1 Cake Tempeh, steamed, drained, and coarsely chopped
2 Tomatoes (large), chopped
1/3 C. Vinegar (optional)
1 t. Sea Salt
1 T. Dry Sweetener

Polenta

4 C. Water
2 C. Corn Kernels
1 1/2-2 C. Stone Ground Yellow Cornmeal
1/3 C. Nutritional Yeast

Salt, to taste
Red or Black Pepper, to taste
1/4 C. Chopped Parsley (for garnish)
Olive Oil, (to drizzle on top)

To Prepare Tempeh-Onion Sauce:

1. Heat olive oil in a large skillet over medium-high heat. Add onions, garlic, oregano, red pepper flakes, and tempeh. Sauté, stirring frequently, until onions are tender, about 5 minutes. Then add tomatoes to skillet along with vinegar, salt and sweetener. Quickly bring to a boil. Reduce heat to low and simmer 15 minutes, stirring occasionally.

To Make Polenta:

2. Bring water to a low boil in a saucepan. Add in corn kernels. Slowly add in cornmeal, stirring constantly with a wooden spoon, until cornmeal no longer feels grainy (taste it to see), 5-6 minutes. Lower heat. Stir in nutritional yeast. Batter should be creamy and slightly runny. If too thick, add some hot water. Stir in salt and pepper to taste.
3. Spoon Polenta into shallow bowls. Top with tempeh-onion sauce. Sprinkle with chopped parsley. Drizzle some olive oil over top. Serve immediately.

"Consider the following statistics: one thousand acres of soybeans yield 1,124 pounds of usable protein; one thousand acres of wheat yield 1,043 pounds of usable protein. Now consider this: one thousand acres of soybeans or wheat, when fed to a steer, will yield only about 125 pounds of usable protein. These and other findings point to a disturbing conclusion: meat-eating is directly related to world hunger."

STEVEN ROSEN
American author: <u>Food for the Spirit</u>

(Figures reflect protein yield for an average day of the year.)

Lemon Broil Tempeh

serves 2-3

2 Tempeh Cakes
2 T. Lemon Juice
2 T. Bragg's™ or Tamari
1/2 lb. Tofu
4 T. Nutritional Yeast
2 T. Sweet Relish

2 T. Water
1/2 t. Garlic Powder
4 T. Lemon Juice
2 T. Bragg's™ or Tamari
Onion Powder, dash
1-2 T. Oil (optional)

1. Steam the 2 cakes of tempeh (in a steamer basket) about 5-10 minutes until they puff up. Cut each piece in half, down the center. Carefully cut each piece in half again, through the middle, to end up with 8 pieces.
2. Marinate the tempeh in 2 T. lemon juice and 2 T. Bragg's™.
3. In a blender or food processor, blend the remaining ingredients, beginning with the tofu. (Do not blend tempeh.)
4. Dip and thoroughly coat each piece of tempeh in this batter.
5. Place each piece on an oiled baking sheet and bake, in a pre-heated oven, at 350° until the coating turns golden brown. Serve with tartar sauce (see recipe pg. 86).

Tempeh Pizzas

serves 4-5

1/4 C. Vegetable Stock or Water
1 Onion (medium), chopped
1 Bell Pepper, chopped
8 oz. Tempeh (steamed 5 minutes)
3 T. Bragg's™ or Tamari
1 t. Oregano

1 t. Basil
1 t. Garlic Granules
1 t. Red Pepper Flakes
2 1/2 C. Tomato Sauce
6 Whole Wheat Pita Pocket Bread
   (or 8 Whole Wheat Tortillas)
Nutritional Yeast, to sprinkle

1. In a large skillet, sauté the onions and peppers in the vegetable stock or water. Crumble the steamed tempeh and add to the skillet. Stir in and cook for 5 minutes.
2. Add tamari, oregano, basil, garlic and red pepper flakes. Stir in tomato sauce. Simmer for another five minutes.
3. Put pita bread or tortillas on a baking tray and place under a hot broiler to toast lightly. When toasted, spread the tempeh mixture evenly over the bread, top with nutritional yeast and bake in a pre-heated oven at 375° for 10 minutes.

"Being all fashioned of the self-same dust,
Let us be merciful as well as just."

HENRY WADSWORTH LONGFELLOW (1807-1882)
American poet

Tempeh and Broccoli Rabe

serves 4

1 Tempeh Cake, cubed	1 C. Wheat Germ
1 lb. Broccoli Rabe or Broccoli	1/2 C. Fine Yellow Corn Meal
1 Onion (large), sliced	1-2 T. Olive Oil
2 Carrots, sliced thinly	2-3 T. Bragg's™ or Tamari
4 Garlic Cloves, chopped	2 T. Vinegar

1. In a large pot, steam tempeh, broccoli rabe, onions, carrots and garlic for 10 minutes, then drain.
2. Place steamed vegetables and tempeh in a casserole and season with wheat germ, corn meal, olive oil, Bragg's, and vinegar. Toss lightly to cover and bake for 15 minutes at 350°.

Tempeh Cacciatore

serves 4-6

2 T. Oil	2 T. Balsamic Vinegar
2 Tempeh Cakes, steamed and julienne	2 T. Garlic, minced
2 Yellow Crookneck Squash, sliced	1 T. Basil (fresh) or 1 t. dried
2 Carrots, julienne	1 T. Oregano (fresh) or 1 t. dried
1 Bell Pepper, sliced	2 T. Arrowroot Powder
1 C. Tomato Paste	Sea Salt and Red Pepper, to taste
2 C. Vegetable Stock	1/2 lb. bag Penne Pasta (cooked)

1. In a skillet, over medium heat, put 1 T. oil and tempeh. Sauté for 6-8 minutes, until tempeh starts to brown. Remove tempeh and set aside. Put 1 T. oil in skillet and add squash, carrots and pepper strips. Sauté until softened, about 8 minutes. Remove vegetables and set aside.
2. In the same skillet, add tomato paste, stock, vinegar, garlic and herbs. Stir well over medium heat about eight minutes. Sift in arrowroot powder and keep stirring until it homogenizes into a sauce and thickens. When sauce is thick, add cooked vegetables and tempeh, and stir until bubbly. Season with salt and pepper if desired.
3. Serve over cooked penne pasta.

"In all the round world of Utopia, there is no meat. There used to be, but now we cannot stand the thought of slaughterhouses. We never settled the hygienic aspect of meat-eating at all. This other aspect decided us. I can still remember as a boy the rejoicings over the closing of the last slaughterhouse."

H.G. WELLS (1866-1946)
English novelist and historian, <u>A Modern Utopia</u>

Tempeh Teriyaki
yields 1 large skillet

4 Tempeh Cakes, steamed & cubed
2-3 T. Sesame Oil
1 t. Tamari
1-2 Garlic Cloves, 1 T. Garlic, minced
4 T. Fresh Ginger, minced
Tamari, for marinating
1 Onion, sliced in half moons
10 Mushrooms, sliced
1/2 Green Bell Pepper, sliced

1 Red Bell Pepper, sliced in strips
3 1/2 C. Water
3 T. Dr. Bronner's™ Vegetable Bouillon
3 T. Molasses
1 T. Garlic Powder
1 T. Onion Powder
1 t. Ginger Powder
3 1/2 T. Arrowroot Powder
3 T. Miso (dark)
Nutritional Yeast, sprinkle

1. Steam 4 cakes of tempeh and let cool.
2. In a blender, blend together oil, tamari, garlic, 1 T. ginger and just enough water to cover the blades. It will blend into a thick, creamy marinade.
3. Cut tempeh into large bite-sized cubes and marinate in blended mixture along with extra tamari.
4. In a large sauce pot, sauté 3 T. fresh minced ginger and 1 T. minced garlic in sesame or other oil. Add onion, mushrooms and peppers and cook until softened, about 7 minutes.
5. In a blender, blend 3 1/2 cups of water, Dr. Bronner's™, molasses, garlic powder and onion powder, ginger powder, arrowroot and miso. Pour this mixture into pot with the vegetables. Stir constantly and allow to thicken.
6. In a large oiled cast iron skillet, fry tempeh chunks with a sprinkle of nutritional yeast. When they have browned a bit, add the thickened sauce to the cast iron skillet and bake for an hour at 350°, allowing the sauce to saturate tempeh chunks. (If using a regular skillet to fry tempeh, transfer to a casserole dish before baking) Serve over a grain.

"The man who becomes a thinking being, feels a compulsion to give to every will-to-live the same reverence for life that he gives to his own."

•••

"Reverence for life, for the smallest and most insignificant, must be the inviolable law to rule the world from now on. In so doing, we do not replace old slogans with new ones and imagine that some good may come out of high-sounding speeches and pronouncements. We must recognize that only a deep-seated change of heart, spreading from one man to another, can achieve such a thing in this world."

ALBERT SCHWEITZER (1875-1965)
Alsatian philosopher and medical missionary
1952 Noble Prize recipient

Teriyaki Vegetable Rice

serves 6-8

Teriyaki Sauce

2 T. Fresh Ginger, grated
  or 1 T. Ginger Powder
6 Garlic Cloves, minced
2 T. Sesame Oil

3 C. Pineapple-Papaya Juice
1/2 C. Tamari
2 t. Mustard (dry)
1/2 t. Cayenne Pepper

1. Combine all the above ingredients in a blender. Blend well and set aside.

2 Bunches Young Asparagus (fresh)
4 T. Arrowroot Powder
4 C. Teriyaki Sauce, (see above)
2 T. Sesame Oil
2 C. Broccoli Flowerets
2 C. Carrots, chopped

2 C. Cauliflower, chopped
1 Red Onion, peeled, cored
  & halved & cut into 1/4" strips
4-5 C. Basmati Rice (cooked)
4 T. Sesame Seeds, toasted in a
  dry skillet until lightly browned

2. Gently bend each asparagus stalk to break off the tough, woody ends. Cut the stems diagonally into 1 1/2-2" sections, leaving 2" of tips. Separate thicker lower stems from the thinner upper stems and tips.

3. Dissolve the arrowroot in 2 cups of the teriyaki sauce. Set aside. Heat half of the sesame oil in a large skillet over high heat. Add thicker asparagus stalks and stir-fry for 2 minutes. Add the broccoli, carrots and cauliflower. Stir-fry for 2 minutes. Then add 1 C. teriyaki sauce (without arrowroot). Cover and cook 2 minutes, or until vegetables are almost tender. Then remove from pan, cover and set aside.

4. Add remaining sesame oil to skillet and heat. Add remaining asparagus and red onion. Stir-fry 2-4 minutes. Add the last cup of teriyaki sauce (without arrowroot). Cover and cook for 2 minutes or until vegetables are tender.

5. Now add teriyaki sauce containing arrowroot to skillet and simmer 1-2 minutes, stirring.

6. Add vegetables that have been set aside, stirring continuously until sauce thickens.

7. Serve immediately over basmati rice with toasted sesame seeds.

> *"Meat, which contains cholesterol and saturated fat, was never intended for human beings, who are natural herbivores."*
>
> WILLIAM C. ROBERTS, M.D.
> Editor in Chief of American Journal of Cardiology
> Vol.66, October 1, 1990 pg. 896

Chinese Medley

yields 1 casserole

1 T. Oil Sesame	2 T. Sweetener
3 Garlic Cloves, minced	1 Zucchini, quartered, diced
1 Onion, sliced	2 C. Cauliflower, flowerets
1 Red Pepper, sliced	2-3 C. Broccoli, flowerets
12 Mushrooms, sliced in half	1 t. Garlic Powder
1/3 C. Almonds, blanched	2 C. Snow Peas
3 T. Bragg's™ or Tamari	2 C. Mung Bean Sprouts
2 Carrots, sliced diagonally	1-2 C. Bok or Pok Choy
4 C. Cabbage, shredded	1 T. Tamari
3 T. Apple Cider Vinegar	1/2 t. Ginger Powder

1. In a large skillet, with 1 T. oil, sauté garlic and onion. Add the pepper and mushrooms. Stir and cover to simmer. At one minute intervals, add all the remaining ingredients and seasonings. Stir and simmer each time. The snow peas, mung sprouts and greens should be added last and cooked for just a few minutes. Save the juices from the sauté for the Chinese sauce. Serve immediately over rice or add the following.

2. <u>Tempeh Chunks</u>

1-2 T. Oil	1 t. Ginger Powder
2 Cakes Tempeh, steamed, cubed	1/2 t. Garlic Powder
3 T. Tamari	1 t. Nutritional Yeast (optional)

In an oiled skillet over medium-high heat, pan fry the tempeh chunks with the ingredients listed, until crisped. Add to the vegetable medley.

3. <u>Chinese Sauce</u>

1 T. Oil	2 T. Apple Cider Vinegar
2 T. Garlic, minced, sauteed	5 T. Sweetener
3 T. Fresh Ginger, minced	1 t. Onion Powder
2 C. Water (juice from sauté)	1/2 t. Garlic Powder
2 T. Tamari	1/2 t. Ginger, ground
1/4 C. Sesame Oil	3 T. Arrowroot Powder
1-2 T. Sorghum	

In 1 T. oil, sauté the minced garlic and ginger. In a blender, whiz all ingredients and pour into a small pot. Simmer and stir until sauce thickens, never allowing a rapid boil.

4. Serve Chinese Medley over rice, add Tempeh Chunks and top with Chinese Sauce. Use sauce over your favorite chinese entrees, fried rice, eggless foo yung, spring rolls, etc.

"It is nearly fifty years since I was assured by a conclave of doctors that if I did not eat meat, I should die of starvation."

GEORGE BERNARD SHAW   (1856-1950)
Anglo-Irish Playwright; 1925 Nobel Prize recipient

Veg Foo Yumm!

yields 13 patties

Sauté Mixture
1 Onion, diced
2 C. Mushrooms, sliced
1 T. Tamari
1 C. Zucchini, diced
2 C. Snow Peas, tipped, cut
1-2 C. Mung Bean Sprouts
1 t. Ginger Powder
1 t. Garlic Powder
Bowl Mixture
2 lbs. Tofu (firm), mashed
1 C. Whole Wheat Pastry Flour
1/2 T. Onion Powder

2 T. Bragg's™ or Tamari
1 t. Sea Salt
1/4 C. Nutritional Yeast
1/4 t. Black Pepper
1 t. Baking Soda
1 T. Baking Powder
Blender Mixture
3/4 C. Water (liquid from sauté)
1 C. Tofu (soft), mashed
1/2 T. Onion Powder
1 T. Bragg's™ or Tamari
1 T. Ener-G® Egg Replacer
1/2 T. Spike™ Seasoning

1. In a fry pan, sauté (in water or oil) the onion. Add the mushrooms, tamari and zucchini and cook for 2 minutes. Add the snow peas, mung bean sprouts, seasonings and cover to simmer. After several minutes, remove from flame. Drain the liquid from the sauté and save.
2. In a bowl, mash the tofu and add the remaining Bowl Mixture ingredients.
3. In a blender, blend the blender ingredients. Add this blender mixture to the bowl mixture and mix. Finally, add the sauté to the bowl and mix thoroughly.
4. Oil 2 cookie sheets well. Drop batter onto the sheet by using a serving spoon. Flatten and form each of them into the shape of Foo Yung Patties (there will be about 13-14). Bake in a pre-heated oven at 375° for 50 minutes, switching racks in the oven to avoid burning the bottom batch. They will be golden-browned on the outside when ready.

"So many gods, so many creeds,
So many paths that wind and wind,
While just the art of being kind
Is all this sad world needs."

ELLA WHEELER WILCOX (1850-1919)
American poet and author
"The World's Need"

Delicious Curried Vegetables

1/8 C. Sesame or Safflower Oil
2 Onions (medium), chopped
2 T. Fresh Ginger, finely chopped
3 Garlic Cloves, finely chopped
1 t. Cumin
1/2 t. Turmeric
1/4 t. Cayenne
1 1/2 t. Curry Powder

1 t. Sea Salt (or salt substitute)
1 (16) oz. Can Tomato Sauce
  (or 2-3 Tomatoes, peeled)
1 Eggplant (medium), sliced, peeled
2 Potatoes, sliced and par-steamed
1 1/2 C. Fresh Spinach, washed & drained
  or other vegetables
1 1/2 C. Snow Peas

1. Sauté onions in oil, adding a little water if they stick to the pan. Add ginger and garlic, stirring frequently. When onions are translucent and the mixture is "melting" together, add spices and continue to stir.
2. Add tomato sauce or tomatoes. (Place tomatoes in very hot water for 5 seconds and the skins come off easily.) Mix together thoroughly.
3. Add vegetables, starting with the hardest (i.e. eggplant and potatoes). Let simmer until veggies are soft, but not overdone. Serve over rice or as is.

Curry Tempeh Cutlets

yields 12 cutlets

3 Cakes Tempeh, steamed and cooled
Marinade
1/3 C. Water
2 T. Bragg's™ or Tamari
1/4 T. Curry (mild)
2 T. Oil
Coating
1/3 C. Water

1 T. Cashew Butter
1 C. Tofu, mashed
1/2 t. Garlic Powder
2-3 T. Oil
3 T. Nutritional Yeast
1 T. Bragg's™ or Tamari
1 t. Curry (mild)

1. Cut each tempeh cake in half down the center and slice each piece in half through the middle, creating 12 pieces.
2. Put marinade ingredients in a bowl, and whisk with a fork. Add tempeh cutlets, allowing them to marinate, for approximately 1 hour.
3. In a blender, blend Coating ingredients. Pour mixture into a bowl and dip each cutlet into the coating. Get a good, thick coat on each piece and place on an oiled baking sheet. Bake at 350° until coating turns golden brown, about 30 minutes.

> *"Patients fed a vegan (meat and dairy free) diet during an intensive 12-day live-in program experienced an average reduction of 11% in total cholesterol levels. Most patients also lost weight and had improved blood pressure levels."*
>
> - JOURNAL OF THE AMERICAN COLLEGE OF NUTRITION, 1995

Curry Cous-Cous with Lima Beans
serves 5-6

2 C. Cooked Lima Beans
3 C. Water
1 T. Dr. Bronner's Vegetable Bouillon™
3 C. Whole Wheat Cous-Cous (dry)
2 t. Spike™ Seasoning
1/4 C. Scallion, diced

1/2 t. Curry Powder (to taste)
1/2 t. Cumin
1 t. Garlic Granulated/Powder
1/4 - 1/2 t. Sea Salt
1/4 t. Black Pepper (or cayenne)

1. Cook the lima beans (see Cooking Guide for Beans).
2. Boil water with the bouillon. When water boils, add the Cous-Cous. Cook for under a minute and then remove from flame. Cover and let steam cook for several more minutes. Fluff with a fork. Cover again.
3. Add the spices and beans. Mix with a fork. Serve with the following sauce.

1 C. Vitasoy™ (Creamy Original)
1 T. Rice Syrup
2 T. Nutritional Yeast
1/2 t. Curry Powder (to taste)

2 T. Miso (blonde)
1 T. Bragg™ Liquid Aminos
1 t. Arrowroot

4. Blend all ingredients together in a blender. Pour into a small sauce pot and simmer for approximately 8-10 minutes until sauce thickens.

Vegetable Cous-Cous
serves 6

3 C. Water or Vegetable Broth
2 C. Whole Wheat Cous-Cous
1 T. Oil
1 Cucumber (long), halved lengthwise, seeded, thinly sliced
1 Yellow Pepper, seeded, thinly sliced

1 T. Ground Cumin
1 t. Paprika
1/2 t. Salt
1/4 t. Red Pepper Flakes
4 C. Chick Peas (cooked)
1/2 C. Slivered Almonds

1. In a medium-sized saucepan, bring 2 cups of broth to a boil. Add cous-cous. Cover and remove from heat; set aside. In a skillet, over medium-high heat, add oil and vegetables. Sauté 2-5 minutes to soften. Add seasonings and mix.
2. Stir in chick peas and remaining broth. Cover and cook 2 minutes, until heated through. Stir in cous-cous. Transfer to a bowl and top with almonds.

"Animals have the same source as we have. Like us, they derive the life of thought, will and love from the Creator."

ST. FRANCIS ASSISI (1182-1226)
Christian Saint and mystic

Zucchini-Mushroom Baked Omelette

serves 4

1 Onion, diced
8-9 Mushrooms, sliced
2 Zucchinis (medium-size), diced
Bragg Liquid Aminos, dash
1/2 t. Dill Weed
Garlic and Onion Powder, dash
Nutritional Yeast, sprinkle for sauté

2 lbs. Tofu, mashed
2 T. Oil
1 t. Turmeric
2 T. Nutritional Yeast
2 T. Bragg's™ or Tamari
1/2-1 T. Spike™ Seasoning

1. Sauté onion, mushrooms, and zucchini with a little Bragg's™, dill weed, garlic and onion powder and nutritional yeast.
2. In a bowl, mix tofu, oil, turmeric, nutritional yeast, Bragg's™ and Spike™.
3. When vegetable sauté is finished, add to the tofu batter and mix well.
4. Flatten batter onto oiled baking sheet (batter should be about 1 inch high). Bake in a pre-heated oven at 350° for 30 minutes or until golden brown.

Zucchini Fritatta

serves 4

1 Onion, diced
3 Zucchini (medium-sized), diced
2 1/4 lbs. Tofu (soft), mashed
1/2 t. Curry (mild)
1 T. Garlic Powder
1 T. Spike™ Seasoning
1 T. Onion Powder
1/2 T. Ener-G® Egg Replacer

3 T. Bragg™ Liquid Aminos
2 T. Oil
2 T. Nutritional Yeast
1 t. Turmeric
1 t. Black Pepper
2 T. Spike™ Seasoning
3 T. Pastry Flour

1. Sauté onion and zucchini with a squirt of Bragg's™ and nutritional yeast.
2. In a bowl, mix tofu with all remaining ingredients. Add the sauté and mix.
3. Flatten mixture onto an oiled cookie sheet (the batter should be about 1 inch high). Bake in a pre-heated oven at 350° for approximately 1/2 hour, or until golden brown.

"The protein of animal muscle (steak, chicken, meat, fish fillets, etc.) is far more concentrated and acidic than the plant protein found in whole grains, legumes, and green vegetables. ...this concentrated, acidic protein load can leach calcium from the bones, contributing to osteoporosis."

MICHAEL A. KLAPER, M.D.
American author and international lecturer
<u>Vegan Nutrition: Pure and Simple</u>

Mushroom-Pepper Tofu Bake

yields 1 small cake pan

4-6 Mushrooms, sliced	1 3/4 lb. Tofu
2 t. Nutritional Yeast, for sauté	1 t. Sea Salt
Garlic Powder, to taste	1/2 t. Black Pepper
1 1/2 Onion, diced	2 T. Nutritional Yeast
	1 T. Oil & Bragg's™, for processor

1. Sauté mushrooms with a little water, nutritional yeast, and garlic powder.
2. Sauté the onion. When soft, set aside.
3. In a bowl, mash 3/4 lb. of the tofu. Add sea salt, pepper and yeast. Then add the mushrooms.
4. In a food processor, using the "S"- shaped blade, blend remaining 1 lb. of tofu with 1 T. oil, the onion sauté and a squirt of Bragg's™. Add the blended tofu mixture to the tofu-mushroom mix and stir them together.
5. Bake in a small, round oiled cake pan at 350° for 30 minutes or until the top turns golden brown.

A "Quiche to Build a Dream on"

yields 1 large skillet

1 Onion, diced	**Blender Ingredients**
1 T. Bragg™ Liquid Aminos	1/4 C. Oil
1/4 t. Garlic Powder	1 T. Bragg™ Liquid Aminos
10 oz. Mung Bean Sprouts	3/4 C. Tofu, mashed
2 lbs. Tofu, mashed	1/3 C. Water
1/2 t. Black Pepper	1 t. Onion Powder
1 t. Spike™ Seasoning	Add to batter at end
2 T. Nutritional Yeast	1/2 t. Sea Salt
3 T. Whole Wheat Pastry Flour	1/2 t. Baking Soda
	1 T. Nutritional Yeast

1. Sauté the diced onion in 1 T. Bragg's™ and garlic powder. When soft, add the mung bean sprouts and cover. Simmer for a minute.
2. In a bowl, mash the tofu and add the following 3 seasonings and flour.
3. In a blender, whiz the Blender Ingredients. Pour this into the mashed tofu. Add the sea salt, baking soda and yeast. Mix well.
4. Place in a large oiled skillet or casserole and bake at 375° for 30-40 minutes or until golden brown. Cool and allow to partially solidify before serving.

"The love for all living creatures is the most noble attribute of man."

CHARLES DARWIN (1809-1882)
English biologist and naturalist

Spinach-Mushroom Tofu Pie

yields one 13" x 9" x 2" baking pan

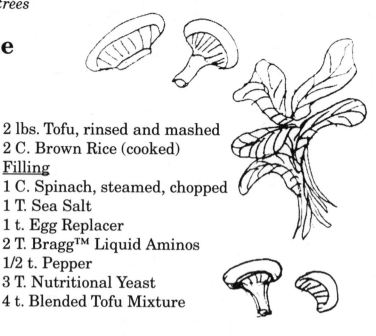

15 Mushrooms, tipped and diced

<u>Crust</u>
1 Onion, diced
1/2 C. Oil
1/2 lb. Tofu
Juice of Mushrooms Sauté
2 T. Nutritional Yeast
Bragg's™ or Sea Salt, to taste
3 C. Millet (cooked)
1 C. Brown Rice (cooked)
2 T. Whole Wheat Pastry Flour

2 lbs. Tofu, rinsed and mashed
2 C. Brown Rice (cooked)
<u>Filling</u>
1 C. Spinach, steamed, chopped
1 T. Sea Salt
1 t. Egg Replacer
2 T. Bragg™ Liquid Aminos
1/2 t. Pepper
3 T. Nutritional Yeast
4 t. Blended Tofu Mixture

1. Sauté mushrooms and onions (in a little oil or water) separately.
2. In a food processor, blend oil, tofu, onion sauté, juice from mushroom sauté, yeast, 1 T. Bragg's™ and favorite seasonings to taste. Hold out 4 teaspoons of this blended tofu mixture for pie filling.
3. In a mixing bowl, blend cooked millet, 1 cup cooked rice, pastry flour and your favorite seasonings with creamy tofu mixture. Mix well.
4. Pat this batter into a well oiled 13 x 9 baking pan, forming a crust around sides and bottom. Mold it in firmly.
5. In a bowl, mash 2 lbs. of tofu, add the rice and remaining ingredients listed in the filling. Add mushrooms. Mix well.
6. Pour this filling into the crust.
7. Bake at 350° until golden brown and firm, approximately 30-45 minutes. Serve with mushroom gravy for an elegant dish.

"Let a man begin to think about the mystery of his life and the links which connect him with life that fills the world, and he cannot but bring to bear upon his own life and all other life that comes within his reach, the principle of reverence for life."

ALBERT SCHWEITZER (1875-1965)
Alsatian philosopher and medical missionary
1952 Nobel Prize recipient

Gourmet Lasagna
yields 8 x 10" casserole

4 1/2 C. Tomato Sauce
10 oz. Package Lasagna Noodles
<u>"No-meat layer"</u>
1 C. Texturized Vegetable Protein
1-2 Cakes of Tempeh or
   2 Packs of Yves Just Like Ground!™
2-3 T. Oil
Bragg's or Tamari, to taste
1 1/2 T. Oregano
1/8 T. Basil
1 t. Garlic Powder
1/2 t. Sea Salt
1/2 t. Black Pepper
2 T. Nutritional Yeast

<u>Tofu "uncheese" Layer</u>
2 C. Tofu (soft), mashed
2 C. Tofu (firm), mashed
1 t. Sea Salt
2 t. Bragg's™ or Tamari
1/4 - 1/2 t. Black Pepper
1 t. Onion Powder
6 T. Nutritional Yeast
1 t. Oregano
4 t. Oil
<u>Cheesy Topping</u>
1 C. Tofu (soft), mashed
1 T. Bragg's™ or Tamari
4 T. Oil
5-6 T. Nutritional Yeast
1/2 t. Sea Salt

1. Partially cook the lasagna noodles in boiling water for 6-8 minutes. (Cook in a flat pan, if you have one.) Rinse noodles, separate, flatten out and set aside.
2. Place T.V.P in a bowl and pour 1 1/2 cups of boiling water over it. Cover and allow it to soak up the water. (You can substitute T.V.P. with Yves Just Like Ground!™)
3. In a food processor, grind tempeh with the "S"- shaped blade, into tiny chunks. Pan-fry the ground tempeh until slightly crisp with 2 T. oil and Bragg's. Add remaining spices and yeast. Mix in 1 cup tomato sauce and cook for 5-10 minutes. (If replacing tempeh or T.V.P. with Yves, Just Like Ground!™, simply cook it in the fry pan with oil and the seasonings).
4. When the water is absorbed in the T.V.P (you may need to drain it), add it to the tempeh in the fry pan. Season with Bragg's™. Sauté; remove from flame.
5. In a bowl, mash all Tofu Layer ingredients together. Chill.
6. In a food processor, homogenize the Cheesy Topping ingredients. Set aside.
7. Spread 3/4 cup tomato sauce over the bottom of an oiled 8" x 10" pan. Lay 4 noodles down and spread 1/2 cup tomato sauce over them. Flatten in the "no-meat" layer and pour another 3/4 cup of sauce over it.
8. Place another layer of 4 noodles, then spread another 1/2 cup of sauce over the noodles. Mash and flatten in the tofu layer and then another noodle layer. Spread 1 cup of tomato sauce over the noodles and sprinkle with oregano.
9. Spread and swirl the "Cheesy" Topping over top. Bake in a pre-heated oven for 40-50 minutes at 350°. Put the casserole on a shelf placed in the middle of oven for even baking.

"Compassion is the foundation of everything positive, everything good. If you carry the power of compassion to the marketplace and the dinner table, you can make your life really count."

RUE McCLANAHAN
American actress

Penne VeganRella™ Bake

serves 4-6

16 oz. Penne Pasta	2 t. Arrowroot
6 Garlic Cloves	1/2 t. Sea Salt
1/4 C. Olive Oil	1/4 t. Pepper
1 Onion, diced	1 C. Tofu, mashed
1 1/2 Bell Peppers, diced	1 VeganRella™ Package, grated
6-7 Roma Tomatoes (fresh), cubed	1/2 C. Water
1/2 C. Nutritional Yeast	4 t. Nutritional Yeast
1/2 C. Water	1/8 C. Bragg's™ or Tamari

1. In 4 quarts of boiling water, cook the Pasta al denté (about 4-5 minutes). Drain and rinse.
2. In a blender, blend garlic cloves and oil. Pour into a fry pan and add onion, peppers and tomatoes. Cook until soft (about 5-7 minutes). When done, ladle 1 1/2 cups of this sauce back into the blender, adding 1/2 cup of nutritional yeast, 1/2 cup water and the arrowroot. Blend and return to sauce. Add salt and pepper and simmer until thickened.
3. In a blender, blend mashed tofu, 1/2 of the grated VeganRella™, 1/2 cup water, 4 t. yeast, and 1/8 cup Bragg's™.
4. Pour the pasta into an oiled casserole and mix thoroughly with the blended 'cheesy' mixture. Mix in red sauce. Sprinkle with the remaining half of grated VeganRella™ cheese alternative. Bake in a pre-heated oven at 350° for 35 minutes.

Oil Free Whole Wheat Pizza Crust

yields 1 medium crust

2 1/2 t. Dry Active Yeast	2 t. dry sweetener
1 C. Water, warm	1 t. Molasses (or other sweetener)
1/2 t. Salt	3 C. Whole Wheat Flour

1. Dissolve yeast in 1/2 cup of warm water with salt and sweetener. Let sit for 10-15 minutes.
2. Separately, add molasses to 1/2 cup of warm water.
3. In a large bowl, combine the two liquids. Mix in flour and knead for about 10 minutes.
4. Let rise for about 15 minutes, punch down and roll out on a pizza pan, making a lip around the edges. Put on the sauce and toppings.
5. Bake in a pre-heated oven at 375° for about 25 minutes until bottom is crisp.

"If human civilization is going to invade the waters of the earth, then let it be, first of all, to carry a message of respect—respect for all life."

JACQUES COUSTEAU (1910-1997)
renowned sea explorer, film-maker

Vegan Pizza

yields 1 large Pizza

<u>Cheesy Topping</u>
1/3 C. Oil
1 lb. Tofu
4 T. Nutritional Yeast
4 T. Water
1/3 C. VeganRella™
2 T. Bragg's™ or Tamari
<u>Dough</u>
1 Active Dry Yeast Packet

2 C. Warm Water
2 T. Sweetener
2 t. Olive Oil
2 1/2 C. Whole Wheat Flour
2 t. Sea Salt
<u>Toppings</u>
Tomato Sauce
2 T. Fresh or Dried Basil and Oregano
Vegetables of Choice
Grated VeganRella™ Mozzarella

1. In a food processor, blend all the Cheesy Topping ingredients. Set aside.
2. Dissolve yeast in 1/2 cup of warm water with 1 T. of sweetener. Set in a draft-free place for approximately 15 minutes, until the yeast is activated and almost doubled in size.
3. While yeast rises, thoroughly mix together the flour and salt. Mix the remaining 1 1/2 C. water and oil, separately. Mix together the dry and the wet ingredients, adding the activated yeast last.
4. Turn out dough on a flat, floured surface and begin to knead. (If the dough is too wet and sticks to your fingers, add more flour.) Knead about 10 minutes until dough is smooth. Cover and let sit in a warm (not hot), draft-free place for 20-30 minutes.
5. Punch down and let rise again for 45 minutes until doubled in size. Roll into two small or one large circle, or rectangle depending on your pan. After rolling out the dough, let sit for another 25 minutes.
6. Spread the tomato sauce on the risen dough and then the cheesy topping. Sprinkle with herbs and grated VeganRella™ for an extra 'cheesy' treat. Top with veggies. Bake in a pre-heated oven at 375° for 20 minutes or until the bottom crust is golden brown.

Pizza Crust

yields 2 pizza crusts

1 Package Baking Yeast (fast rising)
1 C. Water, warm
1 t. Sweetener

2 t. Olive Oil
2 1/3 - 2 2/3 Whole Wheat Flour
Olive Oil, extra

1. Dissolve yeast and sweetener in warm water. Allow to bubble.
2. Add olive oil and flour. Knead into a ball. Let rise for 1/2 hour.
3. Divide dough into 2 equal parts. Roll each out into 8" circle or round pizza pan.
4. Brush with olive oil. Spread tomato sauce on top, add 2 cups of grated Vegan "cheese" and toppings. Bake in a pre-heated oven at 350°, until crust is lightly browned.

> *"All things must change to something new."*
>
> HENRY WADSWORTH LONGFELLOW (1807-1882)
> American poet

Calzone (pizza pie)

yields 6

Crust Use Pizza Crust recipe pg. 141 adding the following ingredients:

1/2 t. Salt-Free Spike™	1 T. Oregano (fresh)
1/2 t. Garlic Powder	1 T. Basil (fresh)
1 t. Onion Powder	

Sauce
2 1/2 C. Italian Tomato Sauce (see recipe pg. 86)

Tofu Filling

1/2 lb. Tofu, mashed	2 T. Nutritional Yeast
1 1/2 T. Bragg™ or Tamari	

Sauté together in 1-2 t. oil

1 Onion (medium) or 3 Scallions	2 Japanese Eggplants (small), sliced thin
3 Yellow Zucchini, sliced or diced	6 mushrooms, sliced

8 Slices Vegan Cheese or 1 C. Cheesy Topping (see pizza recipe pg. 141)

1. Follow the recipe for Pizza Crust, adding the additional crust ingredients to the dry mixture.
2. When dough is ready to roll out, cut in half, roll one piece flat onto a paper baking sheet. Cut into 3 large rectangles. Spread half of each rectangle with tomato sauce, keeping sauce away from the edges.
3. Mix the mashed tofu with Bragg's™ and yeast.
4. On the tomato sauce side of the rectangle put 1/6th of the tofu filling and sautéed vegetables, as well as a slice of vegan cheese or cheesy topping.
5. Fold the dry side of dough over each and seal edges, wrapping the underside up. Repeat process with the 2 other rectangles, and 3 more rectangles made from the second half of the dough. Fork air holes in the top.
6. Place paper baking sheets on a baking tray, and bake in a pre-heated oven at 375° for 20-30 minutes until crust is golden brown and firm.

---

*"Each time someone stands up for an ideal,
or acts to improve the lot of others, or strikes out against injustice,
they send forth a ripple of hope."*

ROBERT F. KENNEDY (1925-1968)
United States Attorney General and Senator
speech in South Africa, 1966

Italian Vegetable Polenta

yields a 9" by 9" casserole

4 C. Water
1 C. Polenta (coarse cornmeal)
1 t. Garlic Powder
1 T. Spike™ Seasoning
1 t. Oregano (dried)
1/2 t. Salt-Free Spike™
1/4 C. Fresh Basil, chopped
2 T. Nutritional Yeast

Filling
1 Onion, diced
1 Bell Pepper, diced
4 C. Eggplant and/or Zucchini, sliced

2 T. Bragg's™ or Tamari
4 C. Kale, sliced thin
  (or other green of choice)
1 t. Onion Powder
1 t. Parsley Flakes
1 t. Dill Weed
1/2 t. Sea Salt
1/2 C. Tomato Paste
1/2 C. Water
Pepper, dash

Topping
2 T. Nutritional Yeast
1 T. Oil

1. In a saucepan, bring water to a near boil. Add the Polenta. (Note: In order to prevent lumps, cornmeal is usually mixed with an equal amount of cold water and then stirred into the hot water -or- dry cornmeal is poured very slowly into hot water, stirring constantly.) Add the seasonings and the fresh basil. Stir constantly. Add the yeast and keep stirring until it thickens.

2. Pour into an oiled pan. Bake in a pre-heated oven at 350° for 25 minutes, and then remove. (After it has cooled, work it up on the sides as much as possible, forming a lip. It will slide down off the edges.)

3. In the empty saucepan, sauté the onion and pepper. Add the sliced eggplant (and/or zucchini) along with a drop of water if necessary. Season with Bragg's™. Cover and simmer. When vegetables are soft, add the thinly sliced greens and cover again for a minute. Add the seasonings, the tomato paste and water. Sauté and stir for 8 more minutes and then pour into the center of the Polenta crust.

4. Top with the yeast and oil and spread. Place the whole mixture back in the oven and bake for 30-40 minutes. Allow to cool and solidify a bit before serving.

"The first reason why I don't consume dairy products, and why I think other people should not, is the fat content. The fat is saturated fat, and you may as well be eating beef tallow. The fat in these dairy products encourages heart disease and numerous other problems. It's a risk factor for some forms of cancer as well."

NEAL BARNARD, M.D.
President of The Physicians Committee for Responsible Medicine,
Washington D.C.

Basil Tempeh Casserole
serves 6

3 Tempeh Cakes (5 grain)
3 T. Lemon Juice
2 T. Bragg's™ or Tamari
Blender Ingredients
1 C. Water
4 T. Lemon Juice
2 Garlic Cloves
1 C. Basil (fresh), chopped
1 C. Tofu, mashed
1/4 C. Nutritional Yeast
1 t. Sea Salt
1 t. Onion Powder
1 T. Bragg's™ or Tamari
1/2 t. Garlic Powder

Breading
1/2 C. Pastry Flour
1/4 C. Soy Powder
2/3 C. Nutritional Yeast
2 t. Salt-Free Spike™ Seasoning
1 t. Onion Powder
1/2 t. Sea Salt
Toppings
3 C. Mushrooms, sliced thin
1 T. Bragg's™ or Tamari
1/2 t. Garlic Powder
1 1/2 T. Nutritional Yeast
2 Tomatoes, cubed
1 t. Sea Salt
1 (6) oz. Can Black Olives, sliced

1. Steam the tempeh in a steamer basket.
2. Cut each cake into 6 strips and then cut each strip in half, making two long strips. Marinate in the lemon juice and Bragg's™.
3. In a blender, combine the Blender Ingredients.
4. Place the tempeh flat in a pan and pour the blender mixture over it. Refrigerate and allow to marinate for 1/2 hour. (Use any extra basil sauce to make salad dressing.)
5. In a separate bowl, combine the Breading ingredients and coat each marinated tempeh stick with the mixture. Pan fry. Let it crisp on one side, then flip and let the second side crisp. When finished place in a long casserole.
7. Sauté the mushrooms with Bragg's™, garlic powder, and 1/2 tablespoon of nutritional yeast. Set aside.
8. Sauté the tomatoes in a lightly oiled skillet with 1 T. of nutritional yeast and the sea salt. When cooked, combine with mushroom saute' and sliced black olives. Mix. Pour over the top of the tempeh and gently mix. Serve.

> *"There are many other sources of calcium besides the milk of cows. Green vegetables contain ample amounts of calcium as do grains, nuts, seeds, and many fruits and vegetables. My medical experiences affirm that many health problems respond extremely favorably after the removal of dairy products from the diet."*
>
> MICHAEL A. KLAPER M.D.
> American author and international lecturer
> Vegan Nutrition: Pure and Simple

Eggplant Parmesanless

yields (1) 8" x 10" casserole

2 Eggplant (large), peeled, thin sliced	1 T. Wheat Gluten Flour
1 Onion (large), sliced	1/3 C. Corn Meal
3-4 C. Tomato Sauce	2 T. Bran
2/3 C. Tahini	1/2 t. Dill Weed
1/2 C. Tofu, mashed	1 t. Garlic Powder
3 T. Bragg's™ or Tamari	1/4 t. Pepper
1/2 t. Sea Salt	1 t. Basil (dried)
4-5 C. 'Cheezy' Dip (see recipe pg. 75)	2 t. Spike™ Seasoning
2/3 C. Nutritional Yeast	1 T. Oregano
1 C. Pastry Flour	1 t. Onion Powder

1. Prepare the eggplant and onion.
2. In a blender or food processor, blend 1 cup water, tahini, tofu, Bragg's™ and salt. Pour into a large bowl.
3. In a food processor, make the 'Cheezy' Dip to use as a 'cheezy' topping.
4. In a separate bowl, make a breading mix with the remaining ingredients (nutritional yeast, flours, corn meal, bran and seasonings).
5. Dip eggplant slices into wet (tahini) batter and then into the breading mix. Don't move them around; just spoon the breading mix over the slices. (Avoid having your dry batter get clumpy or sticky from too much wet batter getting in it.)
6. Pan fry both sides of each cutlet in an oiled skillet until coating turns crispy brown. Stack them on a plate covered with a paper towel to absorb excess oil.
7. Spread 1/2 cup of tomato sauce across bottom of an oiled 8" x 10" casserole. Layer in the cutlets covering each layer with 1/2 cup tomato sauce and a good layer of tofu 'cheezy' topping. Layer in the onion slices. Repeat process, covering the last layer with 1 full cup of tomato sauce and the remaining cheezy topping. Bake in a pre-heated oven at 350° for 40 minutes. Cook an additional 15 minutes at 200°, then serve.

"In the next ten years, one of the things you're bound to hear is that animal protein is one of the most toxic nutrients of all that can be considered."

"Quite simply, the more you substitute plant foods for animal foods, the healthier you are likely to be. I now consider veganism to be the ideal diet. A vegan diet—particularly one that is low in fat—will substantially reduce disease risks. Plus, we've seen no disadvantages from veganism."

T. COLIN CAMPBELL, PH.D.
Nutritional biochemist, Cornell University, Ithaca, NY.
Director: Cornell-China-Oxford Project on Nutrition, Health and Environment 1983-1990

Stuffed Manicotti
yields 10 stuffed manicotti

8 oz. Package Manicotti Shells	1/2 t. Vegit
2-3 C. Tomato Sauce	1/2 t. Sea Salt
1 lb. Tofu (firm), mashed	<u>Cheesy Topping</u>
1 C. Tofu (soft), mashed	1/2 C. Water
1 lb. Spinach (fresh), sliced, steamed	3 T. Oil
1/3 C. Nayonaise™	1 C. Tofu (soft), mashed
3 T. Nutritional Yeast	1/4 - 1/3 C. Nutritional Yeast
1/4 t. Black Pepper	1 T. Bragg's™ or Tamari
2 T. Bragg's™ or Tamari	1/4 t. Sea Salt

1. Cook the shells al denté (about 5 minutes) in rapidly boiling water. Separate them and set aside.
2. Prepare (see recipe in sauce section) or have set aside the tomato sauce.
3. In a bowl, mash the tofu and mix with the remaining ingredients, except the Cheesy Topping ingredients.
4. Cover the bottom of a long casserole dish with tomato sauce. Stuff each manicotti shell with the tofu-spinach filling and place in the casserole. Cover with the remaining tomato sauce.
5. In a blender, blend all the Cheesy Topping ingredients. Pour this over the manicotti. Bake at 350° for 30-40 minutes. Cool slightly before serving.

Cashew Mushroom Alfredo Sauce over Noodles
serves 4

1 Onion, diced	1/4 C. Cashew Butter
3 Garlic Cloves, diced	2 T. Nutritional Yeast
1 T. Oil	1 t. Tarragon
1/2 Bell Pepper, diced	3 T. Bragg™ Liquid Aminos
5 C. Mushrooms, sliced thick	1 t. Onion Powder
3 T. Dill Weed (fresh)	2 t. Spike™ Seasoning
1/4 C. Water	1 t. Garlic Powder

1. Sauté onion and garlic in 1 T. oil or water. Add pepper and cook until soft. Add mushrooms and a minute later, add dill weed and stir.
2. In a blender, blend 1/4 cup of water with cashew butter and remaining seasonings. Pour over cooking vegetables. Simmer on low heat and stir for 5 minutes. Serve warm over noodles. (See cooking instructions on package of noodles. Use plenty of water.)

> *"A six-year study of 88,000 nurses by Boston's Brigham and Women's Hospital found that those who ate meat every day were more than twice as likely to get colon cancer as those who avoided meat."*
>
> NEW ENGLAND JOURNAL OF MEDICINE,
> 13 December 1990

Easy Linguine Mushroom Stroganoff

serves 4-6

1/2 Onion, diced	1/2 t. Garlic, granulated
4 C. Mushrooms, sliced	1/4 t. Black Pepper
2 T. Bragg's™ or Tamari	5 t. Arrowroot Powder
3 C. Vitasoy™ (Creamy Original)	1 t. Dr. Bronner's Bouillon™
2 1/2 T. Nutritional Yeast	1 t. Onion (granulated)
1/2 t. Sea Salt	16 oz. Linguine Noodles

1. In a large pot, sauté the onion and then add the mushroom slices, along with the Bragg's™. Cover and simmer until soft.
2. In a blender, blend the remaining ingredients, except the linguine. Pour this mixture into the pot with the onions and mushrooms. Simmer and stir frequently until sauce thickens.
3. In a separate large pot, boil 4 quarts of salted water with a dash of oil. Bring to a rapid boil and add the linguine. Cook until tender. Drain noodles well in a colander. Then place the linguine into the large pot of sauce and stir. Serve.

Mushroom-Eggplant Stroganoff

yields 1 large skillet

	Blender Ingredients
4 Garlic Cloves	2 C. Water
4 T. Oil	1/3 to 1/2 C. Cashew Butter
1/4 C. Water	4 T. Bragg's™ or Tamari
9 C. Eggplant, cubed small	3 T. Nutritional Yeast
2 C. Mushrooms, sliced	2 T. Arrowroot
1 T. Bragg's™ or Tamari	1/2 t. Sea Salt
1/2 T. Onion Powder	

1. In a blender, blend the garlic cloves with the oil and 1/4 cup water. Pour this into a large skillet and add the eggplant chunks. Stir and cover. Allow to simmer. Be sure to cook the eggplants until soft.
2. Add the mushrooms. Season with Bragg's™ and onion powder. Cover with lid and simmer until mushrooms are soft.
3. In a blender, blend the remaining ingredients. When vegetables are thoroughly cooked, add the liquid. Simmer and stir 5-10 minutes. Serve over linguine.

> *"I believe if the viewing of slaughter was required to eat meat, most folks would become vegetarians."*
>
> HOWARD LYMAN
> ex-cattle rancher, international lecturer
> Author of: Mad Cowboy

Saucy Italian Eggplant
Serves 3-4

3 Garlic Cloves, diced
1-2 T. Oil
1 Onion, sliced thin
1 Bell Pepper, sliced in strips
1 Eggplant (large), diced
2 T. Bragg's™ or Tamari
2 C. Mushrooms, sliced
2 Tomatoes, in large chunks

1/4 C. Fresh Dill and Basil (each), chopped
1/2 C. Nutritional Yeast
1/2 C. Water
1 t. Sea Salt
1 t. Oregano (dried)
1 t. Arrowroot Powder
Black Pepper, to taste (optional)

1. In a large skillet, sauté the garlic in the oil. Add the onion and pepper and sauté a minute or two, then add eggplant. Season with Bragg's™ and stir. Cover and simmer for a few minutes. Add the mushrooms and cover again for a minute or two. Finally, add the tomato chunks and fresh herbs.
2. When the tomatoes are soft, pull out 1/3 cup of the cooked tomatoes and place in a blender. Blend them with the yeast, water, spices and arrowroot.
3. Pour this back into the fry pan and simmer while stirring for a few minutes until it thickens. Serve over grain or noodles.

Rick Browning's Macaroni and 'Cheese'
Serves 3-4

4 C. Elbow Macaroni
1/2 C. Olive Oil
1/2 C. Whole Wheat Flour
4 C. Boiling Water
1 t. Sea Salt

1 1/2 t. Garlic Powder
Turmeric, dash
2 T. Tamari
1 C. Nutritional Yeast
Paprika, sprinkle

1. Cook the pasta in plenty of boiling water and drain.
2. In a pot, heat olive oil and whisk in flour. Whip in the boiling water, sea salt, garlic powder, turmeric and tamari. Then whip in the yeast. (Large flakes are best.)
3. Mix most of the topping with macaroni in a bowl. Place mixture in a casserole and top with the remaining creamy sauce. Sprinkle with paprika. Bake for 15 minutes at 350° in a pre-heated oven. Broil 2 minutes to brown the top after baking.

"Freedom! A fine word when rightly understood. What freedom would you have? What is the freedom of the most free? To act rightly."

JOHANN WOLFGANG VON GOETHE (1749-1832)
German philosopher

Greek Spaghetti

serves 3-4

16 oz. Spaghetti
4 Garlic Cloves
3 T. Oil
2 T. Bragg's™ or Tamari
1 Onion, sliced in half moons
4 Roma Tomatoes, cubed
1 Red Pepper, sliced in strips
1 Zucchini, diced
Blender Mixture

1 C. Vitasoy™ (or any non-dairy milk)
4 T. Lemon Juice (fresh)
1/4 C. Oil + 2 T. Cashew Butter
1 T. Rice Syrup
1/2 C. Water
4 T. Nutritional Yeast
3 T. Arrowroot
1/4 t. Black Pepper
1 (16) oz. Can Black Olives

1. Cook the pasta in rapidly boiling water and stir frequently. Drain and rinse.
2. In a blender, blend the garlic, oil and Bragg's™. Pour into a saucepan.
3. Sauté the onion. When softened a bit, add the tomatoes. Add the pepper strips and then the zucchini and cook until soft.
4. In a blender, blend the remaining ingredients, except the olives. Pour it into the sauce pan when the vegetables are soft. Stir and simmer until sauce thickens. Add the sliced olives to the thickened sauce. Serve over spaghetti.

Greek Rice and Tofeta

serves 4

2 C. Brown Basmati Rice (uncooked)
Tofeta Cheese
1 1/2 lb. Tofu Block (firm), crumbled
3 T. Tahini
1 t. Lemon-Pepper Seasoning
1 t. Herbamare™ (or sea salt)
3 T. Lemon Juice
1/2 T. Nutritional Yeast
Sauté
1 T. Oil
1/2 Red & 1/2 Yellow Pepper, diced

2 C. Mushrooms, sliced
4 Tomatoes (small), chopped
1 Bunch Spinach (large), chopped
1 T. Lemon Juice
1 T. Bragg's™ or Tamari
1 T. Wizard's™ Worcestershire
1/2 T. Garlic Granules
1 t. Black Pepper
1 T. Oregano
1 1/2 C. Black Olives, sliced
1/4 C. Pine Nuts

1. Cook the rice in water seasoned with a dash of oregano, lemon-pepper & garlic. Set aside.
2. Combine the Tofeta Cheese ingredients, stir well and chill to marinate.
3. Sauté the pepper and mushroom. Add tomatoes, then spinach and seasonings.
   Finally, add olives and pine nuts. Remove from flame. Cover.
4. Serve the sauté over the rice and top with the tofeta cheese.

*"Thanks be to God: since I gave up flesh and wine,
I have been delivered from all physical ills."*

JOHN WESLEY (1703-1791)
founder of Methodism

Greek Eggplant Moussaka
yields (1) 13" x 9" pan

2 C. Chick Peas, soaked/cooked/mashed
2 C. Cooked Millet
2 Eggplant (Medium)
<u>Flour Batter</u>
1/3 C. Gluten Flour
3/4 C. Pastry Flour
1/2 C. Nutritional Yeast
1 t. Garlic Powder
1/4 C. Bran
1/2 t. Onion Powder
1/2 t. Sea Salt
1 T. Oregano
1/2 T. Basil (dried)
1 t. Spike™ Seasoning
1/2 T. Salt-Free Spike™
<u>2 C. Tahini Dressing</u> (Substitute
 water for low-oil recipe.)

1 Onion (medium), diced
1 T. Tamari
12 oz. Tomato Paste Can
1 T. Oregano
1 T. Basil
1/2 - 2/3 C. Oil
1/2 C. Water
2 T. Bragg™ Liquid Aminos
1/2 T. Spike™ Seasoning

<u>Topping</u>
1 C. Tofu, mashed
1/2 C. Nutritional Yeast
1/4 C. VeganRella™, grated (optional)
1/4 C. Oil
1 T. Bragg™ Liquid Aminos
1/4 t. Sea Salt

1. Cook chick peas until soft. Cook millet (see Cooking Guide for Grains) and set aside.
2. Peel eggplant and slice into 1/4 inch slices.
3. Mix together Flour Batter ingredients, up through the Salt-Free Spike™.
4. In a separate bowl, place 2 cups of tahini dressing (or water). (See recipe for Tahini dressing pg. 78.) Dip eggplant slices in dressing and then lay them in the flour batter. Spoon flour mixture over each piece.
5. Fry each piece on both sides in an oiled pan and set aside on a plate.
6. Sauté the onion with 1 tablespoon of Tamari.
7. In a large bowl, combine tomato paste, cooked millet, onion sauté, oregano, basil, 3 cups chick peas (mashed or whizzed through the food processor), oil, water, Bragg's and Spike.
8. In a food processor, blend the topping ingredients and set aside.
9. Place half of the chick pea/tomato/millet mixture into a long, shallow, oiled baking pan and press it in firmly. Add a layer of breaded eggplant slices. Add the other half of the chick-pea mixture. Again, add another layer of the eggplant slices.
10. Finish by spreading on the topping. Bake in pre-heated oven at 325° for 40 minutes.

> *"One farmer says to me: 'You cannot live on vegetable food solely, for it furnishes nothing to makes bones with,' walking all the while he talks behind his oxen, who, with vegetable made bones, jerk him and his lumbering plow along in spite of every obstacle."*
>
> HENRY DAVID THOREAU (1817-1862)
> American author, poet, naturalist

Mexican Enchilada Pie

9 large servings

1 Can Black Olives, sliced (12-16 oz.)
1 1/2 Packages Corn Tortillas
<u>Red Sauce</u>
1/2 Onion (large), diced
2 Bell Peppers, diced
7 Mushrooms, sliced (optional)
1 1/2 C. Water
12 oz Can Tomato Paste
1 t. Garlic Powder
1/2 C. Fresh Cilantro, chopped
1 t. Cumin
2 T. Bragg™ Liquid Aminos
1/2 t. Chili Powder
1 Chili Pepper (optional), diced
<u>Tofu Layer</u>
2 lbs. Tofu (firm), mashed
1/4 C. Fresh Cilantro, chopped
2 T. Oil

3 T. Nutritional Yeast
1 t. Sea Salt
2 T. Bragg's™ or Tamari
<u>"Cheesy" Topping</u>
1 C. Tofu, mashed
2 T. Bragg's™ or Tamari
1/8 C. Water
4 T. Nutritional Yeast
1/2 t. Sea Salt
<u>"No-Meat" Layer</u>
3 C. Texturized Vegetable Protein
2/3 C. of the Red Sauce
1/2 t. Black Pepper
1 t. Onion Powder
1 t. Garlic Powder
2 t. Sea Salt
1 t. Cumin
3 T. Nutritional Yeast
•Garnish-Cilantro (fresh), chopped

1. In a saucepan, sauté onion and peppers, then mushrooms. Add water, tomato paste and seasonings. Stir and cook for 20-30 minutes. (This amount of sauce is just enough for the pie itself; additional sauce may be desired for serving.)
2. In a bowl, mix together all the ingredients of the Tofu Layer, and set aside.
3. In a food processor, blend together ingredients listed under "Cheesy" Topping.
4. Boil 4-5 cups of water. Pour the boiled water over the T.V.P. (texturized vegetable protein), cover and allow it to absorb all the water. Set aside.
5. Cover the bottom of a large, oiled casserole with one cup of the red sauce.
6. Layer the bottom with corn tortillas. Press in the tofu mixture, evenly.
7. Add another layer of corn tortillas and then another layer of red sauce.
8. When all the water is absorbed by the T.V.P (drain any excess water), add the remaining "No-Meat" Layer ingredients to it and mix. Place this layer on top of the casserole, and firmly pack it in.
9. Sprinkle with sliced olives and another light layer of red sauce. Again, cover with a layer of corn tortillas. Cover with a thick layer of red sauce and top with "Cheesy" Topping.
10. Garnish with sliced olives and chopped cilantro. Bake at 350° for 40-45 minutes.

> *"Common men talk bagfuls of religion but act not a grain of it, while the wise man speaks little, but his whole life is a religion acted out."*
>
> SRI RAMAKRISHNA (1836-1886)
> Indian (Bengali) Saint

Homemade Chili

yields (1) medium to large sized pot, approximately 14 cups

1 2/3 C. dry Beans (Pinto, Red or Kidney) soaked overnight and rinsed
5 Garlic Cloves, diced
1 Onion (large), diced
1 Bell Pepper, diced
12 oz. Can Tomato Paste
12 oz. of Tomato Sauce
1/4 C. Cilantro (fresh), chopped
1 C. Bean Stock (water beans were cooked in)
2 C. T.V.P (or ground tempeh/seitan)

1 T. Sweetener
1 T. Tamari
3 T. Nutritional Yeast
1 T. Cumin
1 T. Vegetable Bouillon
1/2 - 1 T. Chili Powder
1/4 t. Sea Salt
Garlic & Onion Powder, to taste
Jalapeno Peppers, diced, to taste

1. Cook beans one hour before beginning chili preparation.
2. In a separate pot, sauté garlic, onion and pepper. When cooked, add tomato paste, tomato sauce and all other ingredients except T.V.P. (texturized vegetable protein), beans and bean stock. Continue simmering.
3. Place T.V.P in a separate bowl. Cover with 2-3 cups boiling water and simmer, covered. The T.V.P will absorb the water. When it has absorbed all the water, add the T.V.P to the Chili pot that is simmering. Stir frequently. When beans are cooked thoroughly, add them to the pot and add 1 cup of the bean stock. Simmer for another 1/2 hour.
4. Serve in taco shells, over rice or with corn bread (see recipe that follows).

•Optional: grate some vegan cheese alternative over the top of chili tacos and bake in oven until it melts.

Crunchy Cornbread Recipe

1 1/2 C. Cornmeal
1/2 C. Pastry Flour
1/2 C. Rice Flour
1/2 C. Semolina
1 T. Sea Salt

4 t. Baking Powder, sifted
1/4 C. Oil
3-4 T. Sweetener
1 C. Rice Milk
Spices (Optional)

1. Mix dry ingredients together.
2. Whip wet ingredients and then stir into the dry ingredients.
3. Bake in a pre-heated oven at 350° for 30-40 minutes in an oiled skillet until toothpick comes out dry.

> *"I am only one, but still I am one. I cannot do everything, but still I can do something. I will not refuse to do the something I can do."*
>
> HELEN KELLER (1880-1968)
> American essayist

Burritos with Refried Beans
yields 6 Burritos

3 1/3 C. Pinto Beans (cooked)	2 t. Chili Powder
3 T. Tamari	1 t. Cumin
2/3 C. Tomato Paste	1 T. Apple Cider Vinegar
2 t. Garlic Powder	Diced Jalapeño Pepper, to taste
2 t. Onion Powder	6 Tortillas

1. In a food processor, using the "S"- shaped blade, blend 2 2/3 cups of the pinto beans (see Cooking Guide for Beans) with the remaining ingredients, except tortillas.
2. When blended, add 2/3 of a cup of whole pinto beans to the blended mixture.
3. Pan fry in an oiled skillet for several minutes.
4. Fill tortillas with the refried beans, diced tomato, diced onion, shredded lettuce, salsa, avocado and grated VeganRella™ (optional). Wrap filling in tortilla tucking in ends.

Southern Succotash
serves 4-6

1 1/2 C. Black Beans (dry), washed, soaked, and drained	1 Green Pepper, seeded & diced
2 Bay Leaves	2 Tomatoes, seeded and diced
3 Garlic Cloves, diced	2 C. Corn Kernels (fresh/frozen)
1 T. Oil	1/2 t. Sea Salt
1 Onion (medium), chopped	1/2 t. Cumin
1 Jalepeño Pepper, seeded and diced	1 T. Cilantro (fresh), chopped
1 Red Pepper, seeded & diced	2 t. Oregano (dry)

1. Boil the beans in water with the bay leaves until tender, about 1 hour. (See Cooking Guide for Beans.) Remove the bay leaves, drain, rinse and drain again.
2. In a large skillet, heat the oil to medium and sauté the garlic, onion and peppers for 3-4 minutes. Add the tomatoes, corn and spices. Stir frequently for another 2 minutes. Add the beans and cook 2 more minutes, stirring occasionally.
3. Serve with your favorite rice or grain.

"Today about 1.3 billion cattle are trampling and stripping much of the vegetative cover from the earth's remaining grasslands. More than 60 percent of the world's rangeland has been damaged by over-grazing during the past half century."

JEREMY RIFKIN
President: The Foundation on Economic Trends,
Author: <u>Beyond Beef: The Rise and Fall of the Cattle Culture,</u>
Dutton, New York

Black Bean Tostadas
serves 6-8

2-3 T. Oil
1 Onion, chopped
2 Garlic Cloves, minced
3 C. Cooked Black Beans
   (1 1/3 C. dry beans)
1/2 C. Cooking Liquid from Beans
1 t. Oregano (dried)

1 t. Cumin
Salt, to taste
8 Corn Tortillas
Green Chile Sauce
  (see recipe below)
1 C. Vegan Cheese Alternative, grated
2 C. Lettuce, shredded
2-3 C. Tomatoes, chopped

1. Heat 1 T. oil in a large skillet. Add onion and sauté over low heat until translucent. Add garlic and sauté. Add beans, liquid and spices. Sauté for 20-25 minutes, stirring occasionally. Be sure there is enough liquid to keep everything moist and bubbling. Remove lid at the end of cooking to evaporate moisture.
2. Heat 1-2 T. oil in a skillet. When oil is very hot, individually crisp tortillas on both sides. Drain on paper towels.
3. Place one tortilla on each dinner plate. Spread 1/2 cup black-bean mixture over each, followed by 2 T. of Green Chile Sauce. Sprinkle with 2 T. grated Vegan cheese alternative, shredded lettuce and chopped tomatoes.

• Optional: Spread vegan sour cream (see pg. 77) or yogurt (pg. 21) on tortilla.

Green Chile Sauce
1 T. Oil
1 Onion, finely chopped
1 Garlic Clove, minced
1 T. Flour

1 C. = (2) 4 oz. cans green chilies,
   drained and chopped
1/2 C. Water
1/2 t. Sea Salt

Heat oil in a small, saucepan. Add onion and sauté until translucent. Add garlic and sauté. Sprinkle in flour and cook, stirring until mixture begins to brown slightly. Stir in chilies, water and salt. Simmer over low heat for 15 minutes, covered.

"1.5 million deaths per year in the U.S. are from diseases associated with diets high in saturated fats and cholesterol. The major dietary sources of fat in the American diet are meat, poultry, fish, dairy products and fats and oils...Dietary cholesterol is found only in foods of animal origin...Reduce consumption of saturated fat and cholesterol... Increase consumption of whole grain foods and cereal products, vegetables and fruits."

THE SURGEON GENERAL'S REPORT
on nutrition and health, 1988

Southern Pot Pie
serves 6

Cornmeal Pastry

1 C. Whole Wheat Pastry Flour
1/2 C. Yellow Cornmeal, (fine grain)
1/2 t. Salt

2/3 C. Oil or 1 Stick Vegan Margarine,
 (cut in pieces)
1/4 C. Cold Water

Filling

2 T. Oil
3 Scallions, cut into 1/2" pieces
2 Carrots, diced
2 t. Chili Powder
4 T. Whole Wheat Pastry Flour
1 C. Soy or Rice Milk
1/2 C. Veggie Stock/Broth

1/2 lb. Tofu (firm), cubed
2 C. Black Beans (cooked)
2 C. Corn Kernels
1 Green Pepper, diced
1 Red Pepper, diced
1/4 t. Salt
1/4 t. Garlic Granules

Pastry
1. Combine flour, cornmeal, and salt in medium-sized bowl using a pastry blender. Cut in margarine or oil until mixture resembles coarse crumbs.
2. Sprinkle cold water, 1 T. at a time, over mixture. Toss lightly with fork until pastry is moist enough to hold together.
3. Shape pastry into a ball. Cover with plastic wrap. Pastry can be prepared and refrigerated for later use.

Filling
1. Heat oil in a large skillet over medium-high heat. Add scallions, carrots and chili powder. Cook, stirring occasionally, until carrots are slightly soft (about 5-8 minutes). Stir in flour, stirring constantly for 1 minute or until smooth and bubbly. Stir in soy milk and broth. Cook, stirring constantly until mixture thickens (1-2 minutes). Stir in tofu, black beans, corn kernels, peppers, salt and garlic granules.
2. Using a floured rolling pin, roll out the pastry on a lightly floured surface into a rectangle 1" larger than a baking casserole.
3. Spoon the filling into baking dish. Center pastry over filling. Fold overhang back over top of pastry. Press to form edge.
4. Using a sharp knife, cut vents in pastry. (Whole pie can be assembled several hours ahead and refrigerated).
5. Bake in a pre-heated oven at 350° for 35-40 minutes until pastry is golden brown and filling is bubbly.

"There is nothing more difficult to take in hand, more perilous to conduct, or more uncertain in its success, than to take the lead in the introduction of a new order of things."

NICCOLO MACHIAVELLI (1469-1527)
Florentine statesman

Maui Baked Beans
yields 1 large casserole

2 Garlic Cloves	1 T. Dr. Bronner's™ Bouillon
1/8 C. Oil	1 t. Garlic Powder
1/2 T. Tamari	6 C. Beans, cooked
4 C. Seitan, sliced and cubed	1/2 Onion, diced
4 T. Nutritional Yeast	1/3 C. Molasses
1/2 C. Tomato Paste	1/3 C. Tomato Paste
1/4 C. Molasses	1 T. Tamari
1/4 C. Oil	1/4 T. Onion Powder

1. In a blender, whiz garlic cloves with oil, tamari and 1 T. water. Pour garlic oil into a skillet and sauté cubed seitan for 5-10 minutes, adding 2 T. of nutritional yeast.
2. Blend 1 cup water, tomato paste, molasses, oil, 2 T. nutritional yeast, Dr. Bronner's™ and garlic powder. Add this blended mixture to a casserole dish with the beans, onion and seitan.
3. Bake covered at 350° for approximately 35 minutes, or until onions are soft. Remove from oven.
4. Blend molasses, tomato paste, tamari and onion powder. Mix into casserole leaving a lot of sauce on top. Bake for another 30-45 minutes, uncovered.

Red Potatoes and Aramé
serves 4

1 lb. Red Potatoes (small), washed	1/4 t. Garlic Granules
1 C. Aramé (seaweed)	2 T. Mustard
2 T. Parsley	1 T. Olive Oil
1/4 t. Sea Salt	2 T. Nutritional Yeast
1/4 t. Paprika	

1. Steam potatoes until tender, about 20 minutes. Drain and remove from pot. Cube and place in a casserole dish.
2. Cover aramé with water for 20 minutes and drain. Add parsley to soaked aramé, toss lightly and season with salt, paprika, garlic granules, mustard and olive oil. Add seasoned aramé to potatoes in casserole. Top with nutritional yeast. Serve warm or chilled.

"It ill becomes us to invoke in our daily prayers the blessings of God, the Compassionate, if we in turn will not practice elementary compassion toward our fellow creatures."

MAHATMA GANDHI (1869-1948)
Hindu pacifist, spiritual leader

Vegetable-Potato Kugel

6 Potatoes (large), peeled, grated
1 Onion (large), grated
1/2 C. Onion, diced
1/2 C. Carrots, diced
1/2 C. Cauliflower, diced
1/2 C. Broccoli, diced
1 1/2 t. Sea Salt
1/2 t. Onion Powder
1 1/2 t. Garlic Powder

1-2 T. Oil
4 T. Nutritional Yeast
1 t. Baking Soda
1/4 C. Parsley, diced
1/4 C. Fresh Dill Weed, diced
1/2 C. Peas (frozen)
1/2 C. Matzoh Meal (optional)
Paprika, sprinkle

1. Sauté diced vegetables with 1-2 T. oil and 1/2 t. each of sea salt, garlic and onion powder, as well as 2 T. nutritional yeast.
2. Grate the potatoes and onions, strain of excess water and mix with vegetable saute'. Add baking soda, 1 t. sea salt, 1 t. garlic powder, 2 T. yeast, parsley, dill weed, peas and matzoh meal.
3. Place in a well-oiled, shallow pan and pat down. Oil the top for browning and sprinkle with paprika. Bake at 375° for about 30 minutes.

Herb Roasted Potatoes and Sweet Potatoes

serves 6, Quick & Easy

4 Sweet Potatoes (medium)
4 Baking Potatoes (medium)
4 Garlic Cloves, minced
2 T. Olive Oil
2 T. Water
1 T. Orange Rind, grated

1 T. Thyme (dried)
1 T. Oregano (dried)
1 t. Rosemary (dried)
1 t. Tamari
1/4 t. Red Pepper

1. Peel and cut each potato and sweet potato lengthwise into 8 pieces and combine in one large bowl.
2. Combine garlic, olive oil, water, and seasonings in a small bowl. Add this herb mixture to the potatoes and toss to coat.
3. Place the entire mixture into a baking casserole dish and cover with tin foil. Bake in a pre-heated oven at 400° for 45-50 minutes or until the potatoes are tender.

> "A study of 45,619 male health workers by Harvard School of Public Health found that men with the highest intake of potassium, contained in fruits and vegetables, reduced their risk of kidney stones by 50 percent, while those who ate the most animal protein increased their risk by 33 percent."
>
> NEW ENGLAND JOURNAL OF MEDICINE,
> March 25, 1993

Potato-Zucchini Pancakes/Fritters

yields approximately 12 pancakes

2-3 Zucchini, (medium-sized), trimmed
1/3 C. Soy Powder plus 2/3 C. Water
1 lb. Russet Potatoes, scrubbed
4 Scallions (large), chopped

4 T. Unbleached Flour
1/4 t. Salt
1/4 t. Garlic Granules
4 T. Oil

1. In food processor, fitted with a shredding blade, grate the zucchini.
2. In a large bowl, whisk soy powder and water and then add grated zucchini.
3. Peel potatoes and grate immediately in food processor. Blot dry on paper towels. Add potatoes to zucchini in bowl along with scallions, flour, salt and garlic granules. Stir well.
4. In a large skillet, over medium-high heat, put 2 T. oil. Using 1 T. per pancake, drop batter into skillet making 5-6 pancakes. Press mounds of batter flat with back of spoon or spatula. Cook 4-5 minutes until crispy. Turn carefully. Cook 4-5 minutes longer until golden.
5. Remove pancakes and place on paper towel to remove excess oil.
6. Repeat procedure using remaining batter and additional oil as needed. Serve with apple sauce or tofu yogurt.

Potato Tofu Stir Fry

serves 4-6

10 Red Potatoes (small)
1 lb. Tofu (firm), cubed
1/2 t. Sea Salt
1/2 t. Garlic Powder
1/2 t. Paprika
1/8 t. Red Pepper

4 T. Olive Oil
3 T. Nutritional Yeast
1/8 C. Vegetable Stock
4 Garlic Cloves, chopped
2 Onions (medium), diced

1. In a sauce pan, cover potatoes with water and bring to a boil. Cook until potatoes are tender, yet firm. Do not over cook. Drain and slice thinly.
2. Marinate tofu by placing it in a bowl with spices, 3 T. olive oil, yeast and stock. Stir and let sit for 25 minutes.
3. In a large skillet, over medium heat, add the remaining olive oil, garlic and onions, and sauté for three minutes. Add the tofu marinade and sauté for 4-5 minutes until tofu starts to brown. Add the potato slices and cook for 3 minutes more. Re-season to taste if desired. (Variation: Bake for 20 minutes).

"It is man's sympathy with all creatures that first makes him truly a man."

ALBERT SCHWEITZER, M.D. (1875-1965)
Alsatian philosopher and medical missionary;
1952 Nobel Peace Prize recipient

Potato Wellington

yields 2 rectangular, 12" loaves

Dough
1/2 C. Oil
1/4 C. Orange Juice
1 t. Spike™ Seasoning
1/4 t. Garlic Powder
1/4 t. Onion Powder
1/2 t. Dill Weed
2 C. Whole Wheat Pastry Flour, sifted

Potato Filling
7 C. Potatoes (cooked), mashed
   (about 4 lbs. potatoes, uncooked)

1 Onion, diced
2 T. Bragg™ Liquid Aminos
4 t. Oil
2 T. Nutritional Yeast
2 t. Dill Weed
2 t. Garlic Powder
2 t. Sea Salt
2 t. Onion Powder
4 T. Potato Stock

1. Whisk oil and orange juice together. Mix dough spices and flour together. Mix the dry into the wet forming a ball of dough. (Dough should be moist but not sticking to bowl.) Chill for 15 minutes.
2. In a fry pan, sauté onion with 1 T. Bragg's™, 1 T. oil, 2 T. nutritional yeast, and 3 T. water, creating a cheesy onion sauté. Cook until onions are soft.
3. Cut potatoes into small chunks and boil. Drain when cooked. Mash. Add onion sauté to potatoes and mix with all remaining seasonings, potato stock, remaining 3 T. oil and 1 T. of Bragg's™. Set aside to cool for wrapping in the dough.
4. Separate dough in half. With a rolling pin, roll out each piece of dough into a long rectangles between two sheets of wax paper.
5. Place potato filling along the center of the dough rectangles leaving enough dough on both sides to fold over the potatoes. Pinch or fold in the ends and seal. Fork vents into the top.
6. When potato filling is folded into the dough, transfer loaves onto baking sheet, flipping so the seam is on the bottom. Bake in a pre-heated oven at 350° until the crust turns golden brown.

• Serve with gravy. A wonderful holiday dish or dinner party favorite.

"So much more efficient is a vegetarian diet that less than one half the current agricultural acreage would be needed. The rest could revert to the wild, producing enormous savings in water and energy. We would not have to cut down forests and destroy habitats to create land on which to grow feed for livestock. We wouldn't have to force our acreage and squeeze every last possible yield from it. We could dispense with synthetic fertilizers and toxic pesticides, and still have vast surpluses of food. Our world would be a far greener one, with far less pollution, cleaner air, cleaner water and a more stable climate."

JOHN ROBBINS
author: Diet for A New America,
quoted from: The Animals' Voice Magazine, Volume 2 #1,
article entitled, "The Ground Beneath My Feet"

Stuffed Baked Potatoes

yields about 15-17 potatoes

10 lb. Potatoes	1-2 Onions (large), diced
4 Garlic Cloves	4-5 T. Nutritional Yeast
6 T. Oil	4 C. Tofu, mashed
3+ T. Bragg's™ or Tamari	1 t. Sea Salt
4 C. Mushrooms, sliced	Paprika, for sprinkling

1. Bake potatoes in oven. When soft, make a slit in the top of each potato, and another crossing it. (Don't slit all the way to edges.) Push both ends towards the middle, opening the potato & loosening it from its skin. (Use a towel to protect your fingers from burning.) Allow them to cool.
2. In a blender or processor, blend garlic in 3 T. oil and 1 T. Bragg's™. Pour into a large fry pan.
3. Add mushrooms and sauté. When finished, drain mushroom juice and put it in the food processor. Set the mushrooms aside in a large mixing bowl.
4. In the same fry pan, sauté the diced onions with a splash of Bragg's, water and yeast.
5. Using a food processor, purée half the onion sauté with 2 cups of mashed tofu, 2-3 T. oil, 2 T. Bragg's, 2 T. yeast. Add to the mushrooms in the large mixing bowl. Repeat this step. Mix in the sea salt.
6. Scoop the potatoes out very carefully (don't hurt the shape of the skins, for stuffing purposes). Mash potatoes together with the tofu-mushroom mixture.
7. Stuff each potato skin with this mixture. Sprinkle with paprika and bake again at 325° for 25-30 minutes. This is an easy gourmet treat everyone will enjoy!

Potato Kugel- Mike Dunetz Style

yields 1 shallow 10" x 6" casserole

5 lbs. Potatoes (about 7 large Russet)	1/4 C. Oil (plus oil for baking)
1 Onion (large), or to taste	1 t. Garlic Powder
2 t. Baking Powder	2 t. Sea Salt or 1 T. Bragg's™
1/2 C. Matzoh Meal	1 t. Herb Seasoned Salt
1/2 t. Black Pepper	2 t. Onion Powder
2 t. EnerG Egg Replacer & 4 T. Water, mixed	
(or see Vegan Baking Guide for egg substitutes)	

1. Grate potatoes and onion into a mixing bowl. Add remaining ingredients. Mix.
2. Oil a shallow casserole dish and pour mixture into it. Spread a light layer of oil on the top. Bake in a pre-heated oven at 375° for an hour or more, until browned on top.

"...the wolf shall dwell with the lamb...the lion shall eat straw like the ox...and no one shall hurt nor destroy in all of God's holy mountain."

THE BIBLE
ISAIAH 11: 6-9

Holiday Stuffed Butternut Squash
Serves 4

2 Butternut Squash
2 C. Brown Rice (cooked)
1 C. Walnuts, chopped
1/2 C. Pecans, chopped
1 C. Onions, chopped
1/2 C. Celery, chopped
1/2 C. Pepper, chopped
3 Slices of Toast

1/2 t. Basil
1/2 t. Oregano
1/2 t. Cumin
2 T. Tamari
3 T. Tahini
1/2 t. Garlic Powder
1/2 t. Onion Powder
1/2 t. Spike™ Seasoning

1. Slice butternuts in half, scoop out seeds.
2. Bake in a pre-heated oven at 350° for 20-30 minutes, until tender.
3. Remove from oven and let cool. Scoop out insides and mix with rice (save shells).
4. Sauté vegetables and add them to mixture. Add seasonings, nuts and tahini.
5. Slice the toast into small squares like croutons and add to mix.
6. Stuff mixture into hollowed butternut squash shells.
7. Bake for another 20 minutes and serve with gravy.

Holiday Sweet Potato Pie
yields 2 pies

Crust
1/4 C. Oil
1 C. Tofu, mashed
2 T. Bragg™ Liquid Aminos
3 C. cooked Brown Rice (short-grain)
1 C. Carrots, grated
Filling
3 Sweet Potatoes (large), sliced, steamed

1/2 T. Arrowroot Powder
Sea Salt, dash
1 T. Sucanat™
4 T. Maple Syrup
2 T. Nutritional Yeast
4 T. Oil

1. Steam sweet potatoes in a pot using a steamer basket. When soft, allow to cool.
2. In a food processor, blend oil, tofu and Bragg's™ adding 1-2 T. water.
3. In a large mixing bowl, place blended mixture and the rice. Add the grated carrots. Mix thoroughly.
4. Press rice mixture into 2 oiled pie plates, evenly along the sides and bottom, forming a pie crust.
5. In a food processor, blend all filling ingredients. Pour this mixture into the two pie shells.
6. Bake in a pre-heated oven at 350° for 30-35 minutes until crust looks golden brown. Cool.

> *"A believer, a mind whose faith is consciousness, is never disturbed because other persons do not yet see the fact which he sees."*
>
> RALPH WALDO EMERSON (1803-1882)
> American philosopher, poet and essayist

Savory Shep'heart's Pie

serves 8

2 lbs. Potatoes, peeled and
   cut into 1" cubes
3/4 C. Soy Milk (or any non-dairy milk)
1 T. Olive Oil
1/4 C. Nutritional Yeast
1/4 t. each Salt, Garlic Powder, & Oregano
1 1/2 lbs. Seitan, (ground-up in food
   processor with "S"- shaped blade)
1/2 t. Sea Salt
1 Onion (medium), chopped finely

1 Yellow or Red Bell Pepper (large),
   cored, seeded & cut into strips
4 Garlic Cloves, crushed
3 Tomatoes, cubed
1 C. Broth (water from cooked veggies)
2 T. Tamari
1/2 t. Rosemary Leaves, chopped
   or 1/4 t. dried, crumbled
1/2 t. Hot Red Pepper Flakes
4 T. Whole Wheat Flour

1. In a large sauce pan, add enough water to potatoes to cover them by 1" and bring to a boil. Reduce heat to medium. Simmer, covered, 15-20 minutes until tender.
2. Drain potatoes well. Return potatoes to saucepan. Add soy milk, olive oil, nutritional yeast, salt, garlic granules, and oregano. Mash potatoes just until smooth. Set aside.
3. In a large oiled skillet, over medium-high heat, combine ground seitan and 1/2 t. salt. Cook, stirring frequently, until lightly browned (about 5 minutes). Then place in a lightly oiled square baking dish.
4. Wipe skillet clean. Lightly oil and place over medium-high heat. Add onion, pepper and garlic. Cook 3-4 minutes, stirring frequently, until vegetables are tender, yet still firm. Add tomatoes, 1/2 C. broth, tamari, rosemary and red pepper flakes. Bring to low boil. Reduce heat to low and simmer, while covered, 5 minutes.
5. Meanwhile, in small bowl, stir remaining 1/2 cup broth into flour until blended and smooth. Stir this into mixture in skillet. Simmer 2 minutes longer, stirring constantly until slightly thickened.
6. Remove from heat. Gently stir vegetable mixture onto baking dish with seitan. With a spatula, swirl mashed potatoes into a layer over vegetables.
7. Bake in a pre-heated oven at 350° for 20 minutes until tips of potato swirls are golden.

"Tenderness and mercy and gentility, and all the spiritual qualities that set man off so greatly from beasts of prey, are lacking in the lion, tiger, wolf and other carnivores. The claim that man has evolved to such a high mental plane and spiritual plane that he must have meat is exactly the opposite of the facts. He must crush and harden his higher nature in order to hunt and fish and prey."

DR. HERBERT M. SHELTON (1895-1985)
Father of Modern Natural Hygiene

Thanksgiving Shep'heart's Pie

serves 5-6

1 Loaf of Bread, cut into small cubes
2 Onions, diced   2 T. Oregano
3 Garlic Cloves   1/2 T. Onion Powder
3 Celery Stalks   4 T. Nutritional Yeast
3 T. Bragg's™ or Tamari   1/4 C. Water or Stock
1/2 T. Garlic Powder   Mashed Potatoes (see recipe pg. 111)
1/4 C. Oil   (Use 5 large Potatoes)
3 T. Tahini   Paprika, sprinkle

1. Cut bread into small cubes, the size of croutons.
2. Sauté the onions, garlic and celery in 1 T. of the oil and Bragg's™ until soft.
3. Mix the remaining seasonings and liquids and pour over bread cubes. Stir fry. (optional)
4. Stir the vegetable sauté into the bread mixture (stuffing). Press into the bottom of an oiled long baking dish.
5. Make mashed potatoes.
6. Place mashed potatoes on top of stuffing. Sprinkle with paprika and bake in a pre-heated oven at 350° for 25 minutes.

Veggies Taj Mahal

serves 6
From: The Compassionate Cook
by Ingrid Newkirk & People for the Ethical Treatment of Animals

1 T. Vegetable Oil   1/2 t. Cayenne Pepper
1 T. Vegan Margarine   1 1/2 C. Onions, chopped
2 Garlic Cloves, minced   1 C. Tomatoes, chopped
3/4 t. Ground Cinnamon   2/3 C. Carrots, sliced
1/2 t. Ground Cardamom   1 C. Peas (frozen), thawed
1 1/2 t. Ground Cumin   2 C. Potatoes (white and/or sweet),
1 T. Coriander (fresh), minced   peeled and diced
1/2 t. Fennel Seeds   Salt, to taste
3/4 t. Turmeric   3/4 C. Water
2 t. Ground Ginger   1/4 C. Slivered Almonds

1. Heat the oil and the margarine in a large frying pan over medium heat. Add the garlic and the spices all at once and reduce the heat to low. Cook for approximately 1 minute, making sure not to burn the spices.
2. Add the onions and sauté for a few more minutes, until soft. Add the tomatoes and stir in the carrots, peas, potatoes, salt and water. Bring to a boil over high heat, cover and reduce the heat to a simmer. Cook until the potatoes are soft, about 15 to 20 minutes.
3. Serve the veggies over a bed of rice and garnish with slivered almonds.

Hungarian Sweet & Sour Stuffed Cabbage
yields 1 large casserole

1 Cabbage Head (large)
2 C. Seitan, ground
2 C. Rice (cooked)
1 C. Quinoa or Millet (cooked)
1 C. Texturized Vegetable Protein
1 Garlic Clove, diced finely
1 Onion, diced finely
1 T. Oil
1 (12 oz. can) Tomato Paste
<u>Tofu Mixture</u>
1/2 lb. Tofu

2 t. Spike™ Seasoning
1/4 C. Water
4 T. Nutritional Yeast
2 T. Tamari
1 t. Sea Salt
1/4 t. Parsley
1/2 t. Oregano
1/2 t. Garlic Powder

1 (12 oz. can) Tomato Paste, &Water (to thin)
Lemon Juice, to taste
Sweetener, to taste

1. Boil water in a large pot. Insert 1 head of cabbage (core removed, which reduces the cooking time).
2. While cabbage is cooking, grind the seitan in a food processor, using the "S"- shaped blade. Cook the rice and quinoa (see Cooking Guide for Whole Grains). Pour boiling water over the T.V.P. and let it absorb the water.
3. Stir-fry garlic and onion in 1 T. oil.
4. Place all the above ingredients and the tomato paste in a large mixing bowl.
5. In a food processor, blend the Tofu Mixture ingredients. Add this mixture to the grains.
6. Carefully remove cabbage leaves and let cool for 5 minutes. Put 1-2 tablespoons of batter in each leaf and roll up, making sure the batter is completely covered with leaf.
7. Make a mixture of tomato paste, lemon juice and sweetener. Cover the bottom of a baking dish with this mixture. Place rolls on top of mixture. Before adding second layer, spread more mixture on top of rolls. End with the tomato paste sauce on top of rolls. (Add a little water while baking, if necessary.) Bake, in a pre-heated oven, at 350° for 1 hour. Cool a little before serving.

• Stuffed cabbage stores well in the freezer.

"Devoted as I was from boyhood to the cause of the protection of animal life, it is a special joy to me that the universal ethic of 'Reverence for Life' shows the sympathy with animals which is so often represented as a sentimentality, to be a duty which no thinking man can escape."

ALBERT SCHWEITZER, M.D. (1875-1965)
Alsatian philosopher, medical missionary;
1952 Nobel Peace Prize recipient

Festive Stuffed Chard Leaves
yields 18-19 chard rolls

2 Onions (small), diced	3-4 T. Oil
1-2 Bell Pepper, diced	2-3 T. Spike™ Seasoning
2 Celery Stalks, diced	1 1/4 T. Curry Powder (mild)
2 C. Mushrooms, sliced	4 C. Brown Rice (short grain)
6 T. Bragg's™ or Tamari	1 C. Pecans or Walnuts, chopped
5 T. Nutritional Yeast	1 T. Vegetable Bouillon
5 Carrots, grated	2 T. Oregano
1-2 T. Garlic Powder	1/2 T. Basil
1-2 T. Onion Powder	1/2-1 T. Dill Weed
1 1/2 lb. Tofu (soft), cubed small	18 Swiss Chard Leaves (large)

1. In a fry pan, with a dash of oil, sauté onions, peppers, celery and mushrooms with 2 T. Bragg's and 1 T. yeast. Add carrots along with garlic and onion powder. Remove from fry pan and put in a large mixing bowl.
2. Cut tofu into small pieces and place in fry pan with a dash of oil. Sauté them with 2 T. Bragg's™, 1 t. Spike™, dash of garlic and onion powder and 1/4 T. curry powder.
3. Add tofu, rice and chopped nuts to the bowl and mix together well.
4. Add oregano, basil, 2 T. Spike, 4 T. nutritional yeast, dill weed, 3 T. oil, bouillon and 1/2 T. curry powder. Mix well.
5. Lightly oil 2 long casserole pans. Remove the thick bottom stem of each chard leaf. Drop 3-4 spoonfuls of mixture on to each leaf, starting at the top, thinner part of the leaf. Roll (from top down) pressing sides in, if possible, and place the rolled leaf into the pan. Pack each wrap closely together.
6. Cover lightly with your favorite gravy (or a mixture of oil, Bragg's™ and water) and bake in a pre-heated oven at 350° until leaves are tender, approximately 35-40 minutes.

"It takes less water to produce a year's food for a pure vegetarian than to produce a month's food for a meat-eater."

Diet for a New America, Stillpoint Publishing

"Livestock today consume 80% of the corn, 95% of the oats and almost all of the soybeans grown in the United States. They consume enough grain and soybeans to feed over five times the entire human population of the country. If people ate the grains directly, instead of cycling them through livestock, the benefits to the ecosystem would be staggering........."

Quoted from: The Animals' Voice Magazine, Volume 2 #1,
"The Ground Beneath My Feet"

JOHN ROBBINS
author: Diet for A New America, May All Be Fed
and Reclaiming Our Health, HJ Kramer Publisher

Eggplant Tomato-Tahini Bake
yields 1 large baking casserole

2-3 Eggplants (medium-sized)	2 T. Tamari
3 Ripe Red Tomatoes (large)	2 t. Salt-Free Spike™
1 Onion, sliced	Garlic Oil for Sauté
1 1/4 C. Water	3 C. Mushrooms, halved
3/4 C. Tahini	1 T. Tamari
2 Garlic Cloves (fresh)	1/4 C. Scallion, diced
1/4 C. Nutritional Yeast	Paprika

1. Slice eggplant in thin slices. Slice the tomato and onion.
2. In an oiled casserole dish, place a layer of eggplant covered with a layer of sliced tomato and onion.
3. In a blender, blend water, tahini, garlic, yeast, tamari and Spike™.
4. Pour a thin layer of the blended mixture over the layered vegetables. Then add another layer of vegetables along with some more dressing.
5. Fill almost to the top with layers of tomato, onion, eggplant and sauce, leaving some sauce out for later. Begin baking at 375° in a pre-heated oven.
6. Make some garlic oil in a blender by blending garlic with oil. In a small fry pan, sauté the mushrooms that are cut in half, in the garlic oil. Season with tamari.
7. When eggplant is partially cooked, remove from oven. Mix the mushroom sauté with the sauce saved from step 5. Pour this mixture over the top of the casserole, and spread out evenly. Sprinkle with diced scallions and paprika. Bake until eggplant is melt-in-your-mouth soft, approximately 1 hour.

• Variation, try a zucchini tahini bake. Replace eggplant and tomatoes (if desired) with zucchini and extra onions. This bake will take a little less cooking time and is also rich and delicious.

"I know a lot of people are on a continuum, evolving their diet from red meat to chicken, to fish, and to dairy products - finally evolving to a vegan diet, completely free of animal products. If you are on this continuum - if you are moving towards a pure vegetarian diet, I urge you not to linger in 'chicken-and-fish land' too long. Besides having large amounts of concentrated protein, which can leach calcium from the bones, today's fish is by far the most polluted of all the flesh foods. Fish flesh regularly contains toxic chemical pollutants known to cause cancer, kidney failure, nerve damage and birth defects. For this reason, I really feel that fish does not offer much at all in the way of a health food, and if it's the last vestige of animal products remaining in your diet, have no compunction about letting it swim off your plate altogether."

MICHAEL A. KLAPER MD.
American author and international lecturer
<u>Vegan Nutrition: Pure and Simple</u>

Seitan (Wheat-Meat)

Wheat gluten *is the natural protein portion of wheat that is extracted after wheat is milled into flour. In its processed form, wheat gluten is a fine tan flour consisting of about 75-80% protein.*

Seitan *is made from wheat gluten flour and can be used for many purposes. It is one of the best meat substitutes for flavor absorption as well as texture. It is high in protein and low in fat. Once prepared, it can be sliced into strips and served with different sauces or ground for tacos, lasagna, chili, etc.*

Seitan (Basic Recipe)
yields 5 pieces

18-20 C. Water	3 t. Herb Seasoning
1/2 t. Sea Salt	1 t. Onion Powder
4 1/2 C. Gluten Flour	1 t. Oregano
1/2 C. Nutritional Yeast	3 1/2 C. Water
1 t. Garlic Powder	1/4 C. Molasses
1 t. Basil	1/4 C. Tamari
1 t. Sea Salt	

1. Add sea salt to the water and bring to a boil.
2. In a medium-sized bowl, combine the dry ingredients (flour, yeast & spices). Stir well.
3. In a separate bowl or measuring cup, mix together the remaining liquids.
4. Add this to the dry mixture and mix thoroughly until dough is consistent (solid and firm, yet not dry).
5. Pour onto tray and knead dough until air is kneaded out. Form a rectangle loaf on the tray and cut into even pieces approximately 3" x 3".
6. Place the cut dough into boiling water. Boil for 45-50 minutes.
7. Remove one piece and cut to see if it is done. (It will be firm all the way through).
8. Take out and cool on a tray. If not for immediate use, leave in larger pieces and freeze. Keeps well in freezer for months. When removing seitan from freezer, defrost first then prepare as directed in recipe.

> *"The individual is capable of both great compassion and great indifference. He has it within his means to nourish the former and outgrow the latter... Nothing is more powerful than an individual acting out of his conscience, thus helping to bring the collective conscience to life."*
>
> NORMAN COUSINS
> American journalist, author, lecturer

Sweet and Saucy Seitan Stew

serves 4-6

3-4 Garlic Cloves, diced	2 T. Herb Seasoning
2 Onions (small), chopped	3 T. Tamari
1 Pepper, chopped	1 t. Cumin
6 Carrots, sliced	1-2 T. Oregano
3 Potatoes, cubed	6 T. + 1 C. Tomato Purée
2 Sweet Potatoes, cubed	5 Seitan Chunks (large),
1 Beet (small), cubed	(cubed into bite-size pieces)
1 t. Onion Powder	3-4 T. Garlic Oil
1 t. Garlic Powder	Tamari & Nutritional Yeast, for sauté
1 t. Dill Weed	Pepper & Basil, to taste

1. In a large pot, sauté garlic cloves, onions and then pepper in a little oil/water. After a few minutes, add carrots and soften them a bit; then add potatoes and beet. Allow to simmer with onion powder, garlic powder, dill weed, herb seasoning, 2 T. tamari, 1/2 t. cumin, oregano and 6 T. tomato purée. (Add a little water if necessary.)
2. While the vegetables are cooking, fry seitan in garlic oil, tamari and nutritional yeast.
3. When the carrots are soft, remove 2 cups of them and place in a blender. Blend with 1 cup of tomato purée and a dash of tamari. You may need to add a little water to get the blades moving.
4. Pour this blended mixture back into the stew pot and stir. Add the seitan and mix. Simmer and add pepper and basil. Allow to sit and absorb flavors after simmering. Serve alone or over grains.

•Optional: Add some steamed cauliflower, broccoli, eggplant or zucchini. If no more vegetables are being added and a saucier stew is desired, blend more carrots and tomato purée together or add water.

"An animal has feelings; an animal has sensitivity; an animal has a place in life, and the vegan respects this life that is manifest in the animal... The vegan thus has an enlightened and advanced sense of responsibility."

H. JAY DINSHAH
President: American Vegan Society, author and lecturer
quoted from Out of the Jungle

Seitan Stir Fry

yields 1 large skillet

4 C. Seitan, sliced
3 Garlic Cloves
1/4 C. Oil
2 T. Tamari
1 Onion (large), in half slices

1 Pepper, sliced in strips
1 Tomato, cubed
4 T. Nutritional Yeast
1/4 t. Pepper
1 t. Sea Salt

1. In a blender, blend garlic cloves, oil and 1 tamari. Pour half of this blended mixture into a large skillet. Add onion slices and pepper and when they soften, add tomato. When all the vegetables are almost cooked, remove from skillet and put aside.
2. Pour remaining garlic-oil mixture into the skillet and add sliced seitan. Season seitan with 1 T. tamari and the yeast and allow to crisp on both sides.
3. Add sautéed vegetables back to the skillet. Season with pepper and salt. Cook for 5-10 more minutes, allowing seitan to absorb the flavors.

Roast Beef NOT!

serves 4-5

4-5 C. Seitan, sliced in strips
2 T. Oil
2 T. Tamari
3 T. Nutritional Yeast
Sauce Ingredients
2 1/2 C. Water
1/4 C. Nutritional Yeast
1/2 C. Tomato Paste

1 1/2 T. Tamari
1/8 C. Miso (blonde)
2 T. Molasses
1/4 t. Turmeric
1/4 t. Black Pepper
1/2 T. Parsley Flakes
1 T. Onion Powder
1/2 T. Garlic Powder

1. Grill or pan fry the seitan slices in the oil and season with tamari and yeast. Brown on both sides.
2. In a blender, whiz the Sauce Ingredients. Pour into a saucepan and simmer for 25 minutes. Stir frequently, *never* bringing sauce to a rapid boil.
3. Pour sauce over the seitan and pan fry once again or bake in the oven. (Baking in the oven or letting it sit in the refrigerator with the sauce will allow the seitan to absorb the sauce and its flavors.)
•Optional: grill some sliced onions and mix in.

> *"The Christian argument for vegetarianism is simple: since animals belong to God, have value to God and live for God, then their needless destruction is sinful."*
>
> REV. DR. ANDREW LINZEY
> Anglican (Episcopalian) Priest and University Chaplain
> professor, author of 13 books

Seitan Peppersteak
yields 1 large skillet

Seitan Slices (enough to fill a large skillet)
Garlic Oil (optional), Oil blended with Garlic Cloves, dash of Tamari
<u>Sauce</u> (yields 4 C. of Peppersteak Sauce)

4-5 Garlic Cloves, diced	1 1/2 T. Arrowroot
2 Onions, sliced like half moons	1 t. Herb Seasoning
2 Peppers, thinly sliced (1 red)	1 C. Tomato Paste, or thick tomato sauce
8 Mushrooms, sliced	1/2 T. Garlic Powder
3 C. Water	1 t. Onion Powder
3 T. Vegetable Bouillon	2 T. Nutritional Yeast
1 1/2 T. Basil (dried)	3 T. Sorghum or Molasses
1/2 T. Veggie Pepper (or Black Pepper)	1 1/2 T. Tamari

1. Slice the seitan into slices and then in half.
2. In a blender, blend 2-3 garlic cloves with 2-3 T. oil and some tamari. Pour the garlic oil into a cast iron skillet and sauté the seitan pieces in it. Add nutritional yeast, tamari and seasonings, to taste. (For decreased oil intake, don't sauté the seitan in garlic oil. Simply add sauce to the seitan and bake.)
3. In a saucepan, using a dash of oil (or water) sauté the garlic cloves, then the onions, peppers and mushrooms (in that order). Cover and allow to soften.
4. In a blender, whiz the remaining ingredients. Pour in with the vegetables. Simmer over a low flame and stir, 20-30 minutes, until the arrowroot thickens the sauce.
5. Add most of sauce to seitan in skillet, stir. Bake for 30-40 minutes at 275°. Add remaining sauce, warm and serve.

Seitan Sloppy Joes
yields 1 large skillet

4 C. Seitan, ground	4 C. Marinara Sauce
1-2 T. Oil	(see recipe pg. 86)
1 t. Garlic Powder	3 T. Molasses
Pepper, a dash	1/2 T. Tamari

1. In a food processor, grind the seitan.
2. In a large skillet, sauté the ground seitan in oil; season with garlic powder and pepper. Add the marinara sauce, molasses, and tamari to the seitan in the pan. Stir and simmer. Serve over whole wheat buns or bread.

> *"Moderation in temper is always a virtue.*
> *But, moderation in principle is always a vice."*
>
> THOMAS PAINE (1737-1809)
> English born American Revolutionary patriot, author

Baked Ziti with Seitan

yields (1) 4 quart casserole

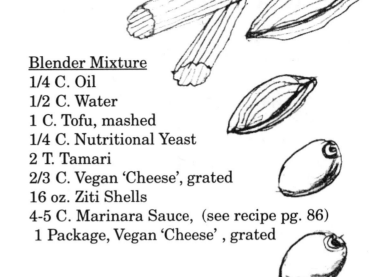

4 C. Seitan, sliced
4 Garlic Cloves
1/8 C. Olive Oil
1/3 C. Water
1 T. VeganRella™ Cream Cheese
1/4 C. Nutritional Yeast
1/2 t. Sea Salt
1 1/2 T. Nutritional Yeast

Blender Mixture
1/4 C. Oil
1/2 C. Water
1 C. Tofu, mashed
1/4 C. Nutritional Yeast
2 T. Tamari
2/3 C. Vegan 'Cheese', grated
16 oz. Ziti Shells
4-5 C. Marinara Sauce, (see recipe pg. 86)
 1 Package, Vegan 'Cheese' , grated

1. Slice seitan in thin slices and set aside.
2. In a blender, blend the garlic cloves with the oil, water, VeganRella™ cream cheese and yeast. Pour this blended mixture into a large skillet.
3. Place the seitan slices in the skillet or fry pan, simmer, stirring thoroughly. When most of the liquid is absorbed, sprinkle with sea salt and 1 1/2 T. nutritional yeast. Continue cooking to brown seitan on both sides. Remove from heat.
4. In the blender, whiz Blender Mixture ingredients, up to the ziti shells in column 2.
5. Boil water and cook the ziti, but don't overcook. Drain and rinse.
6. Oil a baking dish. Place seitan and ziti in the casserole with most of the tofu blender mixture (save enough to layer the top of the casserole). Stir 2 cups of marinara sauce into the pasta and seitan. (Optional: sprinkle grated vegan 'cheese' throughout the pasta and seitan.)
7. Flatten down the pasta and then layer 2 more cups of marinara sauce on top. Spread the remaining tofu blender mixture on top of the sauce and sprinkle with more vegan 'cheese'.
8. Bake in a pre-heated oven at 350° for 45 minutes, rotating casserole from bottom to top rack in the oven for even baking. A gourmet delight!

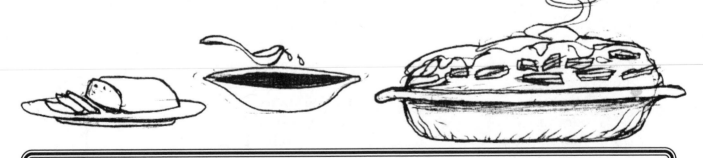

"This (video footage from the movie Babe) is the way Americans want to think of pigs. Real life "Babes" see no sun in their limited lives, with no hay to lie on, no mud to roll in."

MORLEY SAFER
'Pork Power',
60 Minutes, ABC television show, aired 9 /19 / 97

Baked Seitan and VeganRella™ Tacos
yields 18 small tacos

2 T. Oil
1 Onion, diced
3 Garlic Cloves, diced
2 Bell Pepper, diced
2 C. Mushrooms, sliced
1/2 C. Fresh Cilantro, chopped
Hot Chili Pepper, to taste, diced
1 (12) oz. Can Tomato Paste
1 1/2 C. Water
4 T. Nutritional Yeast

1 T. Sweetener
1 t. Herb Seasoning
1 1/2 t. Cumin
4-5 C. Seitan, ground
2 T. Oil
2 T. Tamari
1 T. Garlic, granulated
12-18 Taco Shells
VeganRella™ Cheese Alternative, grated

1. In a large pot, sauté the onion and garlic in 2 T. oil. Add the peppers; then the mushrooms. Cover and simmer until vegetables are soft. Add cilantro, chopped small. Add the chili pepper, tomato paste and water. Stir. Add 2 T. yeast, sweetener, herb seasoning and cumin. Stir and simmer.
2. In a food processor, using the "S"-shaped blade, whiz seitan pieces to get an imitation ground-meat consistency.
3. Oil a fry pan with 2 T. oil and pan fry the seitan. Season with tamari and 2 T. nutritional yeast. When browned, add this to the cooked red sauce. Season with granulated garlic and stir together.
4. Crisp the taco shells for several minutes in the oven; then remove. Line all the shells up in a casserole pan. Fill them with the taco mixture. Sprinkle grated VeganRella™ on the top of each shell and bake until it melts.
   •Optional: add shredded lettuce, diced tomato and onion, after removing shells from the oven.

Seitan Barbecue
serves 4-5

4-5 C. Seitan, sliced
2-3 T. Oil
2-3 T. Tamari
2-3 T. Nutritional Yeast (optional)
<u>Sauce Ingredients</u>
2 C. Water
1/4 C. Sorghum
2/3 C. Tomato Paste
2 T. Apple Cider Vinegar

1/4 T. Garlic Powder
1/2 T. Onion Powder
1 T. Hickory Smoke Flavor
  (Wright's Concentrated)
1 T. Molasses
1/2 T. Tamari
1 T. Arrowroot Powder
2 T. Vegetable Bouillon

1. Pan fry the sliced seitan in the oil and season with tamari. Add yeast, and brown on both sides. Shut off flame.
2. In a blender, blend the remaining Sauce Ingredients and pour into a saucepan. Simmer and stir for about 25 minutes, never bringing sauce to a boil.
3. For a quick and easy BBQ, simply add some of the sauce to the seitan and pan fry. A second option is to add the sauce to the seitan slices and bake in the oven, allowing the seitan to absorb the flavors.

Seitan Kabob

From: The Gentle Persuasion Cookbook by Brook Katz
serves 6-8

Pepper Glaze Sauce
1/4 C. Water
1/3 C. Vinegar
1/3 C. Tamari
1/2 C. Sweetener
1 T. Arrowroot
1/4 t. Black Pepper

6-8 Skewers
1 lb. Seitan, cubed
12-16 Shallots (or onion chunks)
2 Bell Peppers (large pieces)
1 C. Pineapple, cubed

1. Combine Sauce ingredients in a sauce pan. Stir over low heat until thickened.
2. Alternately add to each skewer, the seitan, shallots, pepper and pineapple.
3. Brush kabobs with pepper glaze and grill or broil.
4. Turn once, brush again, then serve.

Seitan-Macaroni and 'Cheezy' Casserole

yields an 8" x 12" casserole

1 lb. Macaroni Noodles
1 C. Water
3/4 C. Tofu, mashed
Lemon Juice, one squeeze
1/4 C. Oil
1 T. Tamari
1/2 t. Sea Salt
1/4 C. Nutritional Yeast
Garlic & Onion Powder, to taste
1 T. Tahini

1 T. Oil
3 C. Seitan, bite size chunks
Garlic & Onion Powder
1 T. Nutritional Yeast
Final Topping Ingredients:
1/2 C. Water
1/3 C. Tofu, Mashed
1 T. Cashew Butter or Tahini
2 T. Oil
1/2 t. Sea Salt
6 T. Nutritional Yeast

1. In boiling water, cook pasta.
2. In a blender, blend the water, tofu and remaining ingredients in first column.
3. When noodles are cooked, drain, and set aside in an oiled casserole dish.
4. In an oiled skillet, pan fry the seitan chunks with garlic/onion powder & yeast.
5. Add the seitan chunks to the pasta in the casserole and pour the blended mixture over.
   Mix. Bake in a pre-heated oven at 350° for 20 minutes, stirring periodically.
6. In a blender, blend the Final Topping ingredients. Pour over the casserole and bake for
   20-30 more minutes.

> *"It's about time, and it's about changes, and it's about time."*
>
> JOHN DENVER (1942-1997)
> American singer and song writer

Seitan with Spicy Peanut Sauce

From: The Gentle Persuasion Cookbook by Brook Katz
serves 6-8

2 T. Nutritional Yeast
8 oz. Peanut Butter (natural)
3 1/2 C. Water
2 T. Tamari

Cayenne Pepper, to taste (1/8 t.)
2 t. Arrowroot
2 lbs. Seitan, cubed
2 lbs. (dry weight) Flat Wide Noodles
(cooked, rinsed, and drained)

1. In a saucepan, combine all ingredients, except arrowroot, seitan, noodles and 1/2 cup of water.
2. Combine the arrowroot with the reserved 1/2 cup of water and then add to main mixture. Cook over medium heat, stirring frequently until sauce thickens, and then add seitan.
3. Stir well and serve over noodles.

Seitan Knishes

From: The Gentle Persuasion Cookbook by Brook Katz
yields 16-20 knishes

Crust
1 t. Baking Yeast
1/2 C. Warm Water
1/3 C. Oil
1/2 t. Sea Salt
2 C. Whole Wheat Pastry Flour
Filling
1 T. Oil
2 Onions (large), diced

4 Garlic Cloves, minced
2 Carrots, chopped
1/8 C. Tamari
1 T. Sage
1 T. Thyme
2 lbs. Seitan, ground
1/2 C. Water

1. In a bowl, put yeast, water, oil and salt, and mix well. Set aside for 1 minute. Add flour and mix. Knead for several minutes and set aside (covered with cloth) in a warm spot. Allow to rise.
2. In an oiled skillet, sauté onions, garlic and carrots for 5 minutes. Add tamari and spices and sauté for another minute. Add seitan and water. Cover and simmer for 10 minutes. Remove from heat.
3. Roll out crust between waxed paper until about 1/4" thick. Cut in 2 1/2" squares, and place a spoonful of filling on each one. Bring four corners up to top and pinch together.
4. Place on an oiled cookie sheet and bake in a pre-heated oven at 350° for 12-15 minutes.

> *"The Utopians feel that slaughtering our fellow creatures gradually destroys the sense of compassion, which is the finest sentiment of which our human nature is capable."*
>
> SIR THOMAS MOORE (1779-1852)
> Irish author and poet

Hungarian Goulash

serves 6

2 T. Oil	1 Cabbage (small), shredded
2 Onions (large), sliced	3 C. Tomatoes, diced
2 Garlic Cloves, chopped	3 C. Vegetable Broth
1/4 C. Paprika	1/2 t. Sea Salt
3-4 Potatoes, cubed and boiled	1/4 t. Red Pepper
2 lbs. Seitan, cut into bite sized cubes	1 C. Soy Milk (thick)

1. In a sauce pot, heat oil over medium heat. Add onions and cook for 7 minutes. Stir in garlic and cook for 4 minutes longer, stirring often. Add paprika and cook for 30 seconds.
2. Add cubed potatoes to the pot, when softened.
3. Add seitan, cabbage, tomatoes (with their juice), broth, salt and pepper. Heat on high until boiling; then let simmer on low heat for about 30 minutes. Lastly, stir in the soy milk, and heat thoroughly. Do not boil.
4. Serve over your favorite noodles.

Sweet and Sour Seitan

yields 1 large skillet

8 C. Seitan, cut in thin strips	2 T. Vegetable Bouillon
2 T. Tamari	1/4 C. Tomato Paste
2 T. Oil	2 T. Sweetener
4 Garlic Cloves	1 T. Oil
1 t. Fresh Ginger, minced	1 t. Garlic Powder
1/4 C. Apple Cider Vinegar	1 t. Onion Powder
1/3 C. Sorghum	1 t. Ginger Powder
1 1/2 C. Water	1 T. Arrowroot

1. In a blender, blend tamari, oil, garlic cloves and fresh ginger until smooth.
   Pour into a large skillet and add the seitan. Pan fry the seitan stirring frequently.
2. In a blender, blend remaining ingredients and pour into a small sauce pan.
   Stir and simmer until thickens. Mix into the seitan in the skillet.
3. Bake in a pre-heated oven at 350° for 30 minutes. Allow to cool and marinate.

"If you have men who will exclude any of God's creatures from the shelter of compassion and pity, you will have men who will deal likewise with their fellow men."

ST. FRANCIS of ASSISI (1182-1226)
Christian Saint and mystic

Creole Seitan Gumbo

serves 6

1 C. Vegetable Broth	3 C. Vegetable Broth
1 lb. Seitan, cut into bite sized cubes	1 C. Okra, chopped
2-3 T. Oil	1-2 T. Vegan Hot Chili Sauce
1/4 C. Whole Wheat Pastry Flour	1/4 t. Thyme (dried)
2 Celery Stalks, diced	1/4 t. Oregano (dried)
Green Pepper (medium), diced	3 Nori Sheets (roasted)
1 Onion (medium), diced	3 C. Brown Rice, cooked

1. In a sauce pot, over medium heat, add 1 cup of broth and seitan and cook about 10 minutes, turning often. Remove seitan from pot and set aside.
2. Add oil to the pot and heat over medium heat. Then stir in flour using a whisk until blended. Cook on low, stirring frequently until flour is dark brown, but not burned. (Add a little water/ broth if necessary.) Add celery, green pepper and onion. Cook for about 10 minutes, stirring occasionally until tender.
3. Return seitan to the pot and gradually stir in 3 cups of broth, okra, hot chili sauce and herbs, heating to a boil. Reduce heat to low, cover and simmer for about 15 minutes. Crumble up sheets of roasted nori, add to pot and simmer for another 2 minutes. Serve in bowls with a scoop of hot rice in the center.

African Stew

serves 4

2 T. Oil	5 C. Vegetable Broth or Water
1 Onion (medium), chopped	1/2 t. Sea Salt
4 Garlic Cloves, chopped	1 C. Bulgur
1/2 t. Paprika	1/2 C. Cilantro (fresh), chopped
1/8 t. Crushed Red Pepper	1/4 C. Mint (fresh), chopped
1 C. Tomatoes, diced	2 C. Garbanzo Beans (cooked)

1. Heat oil in a sauce pot, over medium heat. Add onion and sauté until tender, about 5 minutes. Stir in garlic, paprika and crushed red pepper, and cook 2 more minutes stirring constantly. Add tomatoes & vegetable broth/water and bring to a simmer. Stir in salt and bulgur. Cover and reduce heat to a simmer, stirring occasionally, until bulgur is tender (about 25 minutes). Remove from heat, uncover and cool.
2. Place stew in food processor. Add cilantro and mint. Process until almost smooth. Return stew to pot, stir in garbanzo beans, and re-heat.

> *"Let he that would move the world, first move himself."*
>
> SOCRATES (469-399 B.C.)
> Greek philosopher and teacher

South of the Border Stew with Tempeh and Tofu
serves 6

1 lb. Tofu (firm), cubed	5 Potatoes (medium)
1 Tempeh Cake, cubed	8-10 C. Vegetable Broth
3 Celery Stalks, cut into thirds	2 t. Sea Salt
3 Carrots (medium), cut into thirds	1/4 C. Lime Juice (fresh)
2 Onions (medium), cut into quarters	1/4 C. Cilantro (fresh), chopped
2 C. Corn Kernels	<u>Garnishes</u> 2 Avocados, cut into
1/4 t. Red Pepper Flakes	1/2 inch cubes, & Tortilla Chips.

1. In a sauce pan, combine tofu, tempeh, celery, carrots, onions, corn, red pepper, three whole potatoes (peeled), and 8-10 cups of broth. Cook on high heat until boiling, reduce heat, cover and simmer for 30 minutes.
2. Scoop out the cooked whole potatoes along with 1 cup of the soup broth and mash the potatoes with the broth, then return them to the pot. Dice the remaining 2 potatoes, and add to broth. Heat on medium-high heat to boiling, then reduce heat and simmer for 10 minutes or until potato pieces are tender. Test with a fork.
3. Just before serving, stir the salt, lime juice & cilantro into the stew. Serve with garnishes.

Moroccan Vegetable Stew
serves 5

1 T. Oil	1/2 C. Pitted Prunes, chopped
2 Carrots (medium), cut into 1/4" slices	1/4 t. Cinnamon
1 Butternut Squash (medium), peeled and cut into 1 inch cubes	1/2 t. Sea Salt
	1/4 t. Crushed Red Pepper
1 Onion (medium), chopped	1 1/2 C. Water
3 1/2 C. Garbanzo Beans (cooked)	2 C. Cous-Cous
3 C. Tomatoes, diced	2 T. Cilantro or Parsley (fresh), chopped
2 C. Water	

1. In a large skillet, over medium high heat, add oil, carrots, squash and onion. Cook until golden brown, about 10 minutes.
2. Stir in garbanzos, tomatoes, water, prunes, cinnamon, salt and red pepper. Heat to a boil. Reduce heat to low, cover and simmer for 30 minutes or until the vegetables are tender.
3. In a separate pot, boil 2 cups of water, add Cous-Cous, stir well, cover and remove from heat. Let sit for 3-5 minutes. Remove cover and fluff grain with a fork.
4. Stir cilantro or parsley into stew and spoon over Cous-Cous to serve.

> " *'Do unto others as you would that they should do unto you' applies to animals, plants and things, as well as to people...*"
>
> ALDOUS HUXLEY (1894-1963)
> English novelist, author of: <u>Brave New World</u>

Succulent Succotash

serves 6

2 T. Oil
2 T. Garlic, minced
2 C. Onion, chopped
1 Red Bell Pepper, diced
2 Jalapeño Peppers, seeded & diced
2 C. Tomato Sauce

1 1/2 lbs. Butternut Squash, peeled/cubed
2 C. Corn Kernels
Salt and Pepper, to taste
1/2 t. Garlic Powder
2 C. Baby Lima Beans (cooked)
1/3 C. Cilantro (fresh), minced

1. In a large skillet, over medium heat, sauté garlic in 2 T. oil. Stir frequently until garlic turns golden brown. Add onion, bell pepper and jalapeño and continue cooking, stirring frequently, for another minute.
2. Add tomato sauce, squash, corn, salt, pepper and garlic powder and continue to cook over medium heat, covered, for 20-30 minutes or until squash is tender. Stir in lima beans and cook, covered, for another 2-5 minutes. Stir in cilantro just before serving.

Roasted Vegetables with Topping

serves 4-6

8 Red Potatoes (small)
12 Zucchini Squash (small)
12 Carrots (small)
1 Bunch Golden or Red Beets (small)
3-4 Red Onions (small)
1/2 lb. Button Mushrooms
2 Red Bell Peppers

1/4 C. Olive Oil
1/4 C. Bragg's™ or Tamari
1/4 C. Balsamic Vinegar
1/4 C. Sweetener
3 Garlic Cloves, minced
1 T. Fresh Ginger, minced
3 T. Fresh Herbs, chopped

1. Pre-heat the oven to 400°. Scrub potatoes, squash, carrots and beets. Peel the onions and leave whole. Wipe mushrooms clean with a damp towel. Core and seed the bell peppers and cut into strips. Place all the vegetables together in large mixing bowl.
2. In a small bowl, whisk together the remaining ingredients, to make a topping.
3. Pour this topping over the vegetables. Stir to coat evenly. Place the vegetables in a roasting pan.
4. Roast the vegetables until they become tender, (about 1 hour) turning them over and brushing on more topping, from roasting pan, every 15 minutes.
5. Serve immediately.

> *"But for the sake of some little mouthful of meat, we deprive a soul of the sun and light, and of that proportion of life and time it had been born into the world to enjoy."*
>
> SENECA (C.5 - C.E.65)
> Roman philosopher, tutor to Nero

'Rawsome' Recipes

"Now does not nature produce enough simple vegetarian food for thee to satisfy thyself? And if thou art not content with such, canst thou not by mixture of them make infinite compounds?"

LEONARDO DA VINCI (1425-1519)
Italian artist, sculptor, scientist, inventor

Live Foods

In the pages ahead you will find a bountiful array of uncooked dishes, such as colorful and nutritious salads, sauces, loaves, essene breads, smoothies, desserts and other fresh delights. This section also includes directions for growing sprouts and making sprouted breads and crackers.

In a totally raw food diet, lunches and dinners can center around tossed salads and fruit and/or vegetable trays with sauces and dips. A fruit salad can be prepared in minutes and served as a light breakfast or lunch. The water and fiber content of fruit is high, yet the sugars are burned easily, thus making fruit less fattening. Fully ripened fruit is sweeter, more digestible and has greater nutritional value than immature fruit. For example, a green banana has 2% fruit sugar while a ripe one has 20%.

Live foods are packed with minerals and vitamins and are a good foundation for a healthy vegan diet. These live foods add valuable nutrients to enhance your personal optimum health and contain the necessary enzymes to break themselves down, thus providing more energy with less digestive effort.

Each person must find his or her point of balance between cooked and raw foods. This balance may change with the seasons, with your needs for nutrition and your evolving tastes. We hope this section will encourage people to increase their intake of live, fresh fruits and vegetables, seeds, nuts, sprouted grains and legumes, by offering recipes that make this transition easy and incredibly delicious.

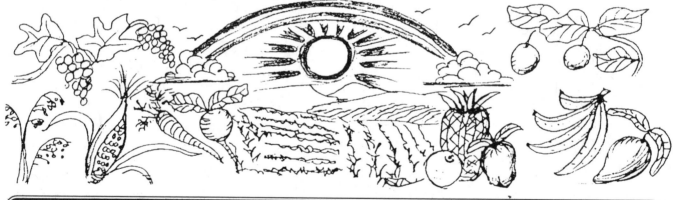

"Raw plant food is beautiful. Creating and eating this food is an art. Every ingredient is a new color. Each meal is a cloud or a stream or a flower — a piece of the magnificent painting that you are becoming. Every bite is a detailed brush stroke on your work of art in progress. What we see as the world is only a reflection of the work of art we are inside. We find that once we become pure and polished within, everything outside of us also becomes that and more. To me, the raw vegan ideal represents not only a way to live in peace, love and harmony with Nature and the animals, but also it represents the highest aspirations of beauty in the human spirit."

DAVID WOLFE
international lecturer
author of <u>The Sunfood Diet Success System</u>

'Veganic' Gardening and Composting

Veganic gardening uses no animal by-products. By growing our food veganically, there is greater hope of eliminating transmittable diseases, bacteria, etc. Some organic gardeners use by-products of the slaughterhouse industry or other animal ingredients, such as bone meal, blood, sludge, urea, fish parts, etc. Furthermore, some organic fertilizers, including manures, are derived from unethical raising and use of animals. We appreciate that organic growers do not use dangerous pesticides and chemicals. However, we encourage them to become veganic for an even richer soil. Veganic gardening is a healthier, more compassion- ate alternative.

Reaping what you sow runs deep into the soil. We have been able to successfully create a rich, nutritious soil from the simple use of our compost (fruit/vegetable peels, etc.), leaves, the use of grass clippings from mowing the lawn and from any of the trimmings of trees and bushes that are in the green, soft state. (The woody material takes a longer time to break down.) Untreated sawdust, as well as seaweed, are ingredient that can be used. This is a recipe for a basic veganic soil to be seasoned with whatever nutrition is needed, depending on your location and choice of crops. If rock dust or dolomite can be obtained, it would be a wonderful addition.

1) Save all fruit and vegetable peels and leftovers in a covered compost bucket in your kitchen. When full, take to an outdoor compost pile or an already made compost container.

2) Compost piles should be somewhere near the garden, away from the house, in a shady cool spot. Begin a pile with the compost and cover with whatever assortment of covering material you have available (grass clippings, hay, leaves, etc.). The object is to create layers of food material and then covering material to allow aeration.

3) When the pile reaches a few feet high, place an extra amount of cover material on it. Cover with a plastic sheet to protect it from rainfall and to contain its heat. Then let nature's master recycling plan take its course for about two to three months.

4) After that time period, the pile needs to be uncovered and turned. Turning requires the flipping of the entire pile so that the bottom of it becomes the top. Again cover it and your soil should be ready within a couple of months. You can make or buy a compost container that has moveable layers to make this job easier.

5) The manure of a **pet** horse, bunny rabbit or cow (naturally vegan animals) is the only exception to a veganic system that can be utilized in the compost, though you are possibly adding an animal-derived bacteria to your soil. Manure, in and of itself, is a good natural fertilizer for any trees or bushes.

> *"To live without killing is a thought which could electrify the world, if men were only capable of staying awake long enough to let the idea soak in."*
>
> HENRY MILLER (1891-1980)
> American author
> The Henry Miller Reader (1959)

Growing Wheatgrass

Supplies needed:
1. Large wide mouth jars; 2. Screens or other porous cloth; (cheese cloth, screening, nylon stockings); 3. Strong rubber bands to hold screen on; 4. Wheat berries; 5. Healthy soil in trays.

Wheatgrass Juice is a rich, green chlorophyll drink extremely high in enzymes and nutrition. Wheatgrass is easy to grow and insures a supply of fresh, alive vitamins and minerals. It can be juiced or simply chewed to extract the juice and remove pulp.
Sprouted wheat berries can be made into delicious essene breads. See recipes pg. 213.

Use about 1 1/2 C. dry Wheat berries to grow one garden flat of wheatgrass.

1. Begin by inspecting the seeds. Make sure they are clean by rinsing them in a jar. Next, fill the jar with water two inches above berries. Let soak 10-12 hours.
2. Pour out water and rinse again. Cover the mouth with screening and hold in place with a strong rubber band. Place jar on a rack, at an angle, to drain. Cover with a towel or shade cloth. Continue rinsing and draining 2-3 times a day for 2-3 days until the tail on the sprout is at least 1/8 inch long.
3. The sprouted wheat berries can be planted to grow wheatgrass or used in this sprouted state to make essene breads.
4. To prepare soil, a good mixture is 75% top soil and 25% peat moss. Or 50% top soil, 25% compost and 25% peat moss. Or you can use a prepared potting soil. Mix soil in a bucket or box. Fill trays at least 1 1/2 inch thick with soil. We have also had great success with growing wheatgrass in raised garden beds. Use 15 lbs. dry wheat berries for a 4' x 10' raised bed, flipping soil over after harvesting.
5. Sprinkle berries on top of soil, keeping them close but not piled on each other.
6. Water and cover with a shade cloth. Keep them shaded for the first 3 days and then partially shaded for the remaining days. Water at least once a day. In hot climate, water more often.
7. Harvest in 5-7 days from planting. Wheatgrass harvesting requires a sharp knife, scissors or grass clipper. Cut at least 1/2 inch above the base. Cut fresh, only what you need, and let the rest continue growing. It is overgrown at 8-9 days. The second growth does not have the same potency, so it is suggested to harvest only once, and then compost roots & soil.
8. Problems may occur which can usually be solved by a slight change in the growing process. Mold may grow if the seeds are too damp, planted too closely or have poor ventilation. Use shade cloth to increase aeration, and water less. Sparse crop can happen if the seeds were soaked too long or not watered properly. Pale grass may be caused by insufficient sunlight. Protect it from birds. (Wheat berries can be attractive to some animals and birds.) Wheatgrass likes filtered sunlight better than direct hot sunlight.
9. It takes approximately 7 days from soaking to harvest. 1 pound wheatgrass should yield at least 10 oz. of wheatgrass juice.

Recommended Wheatgrass Juicers: (See page 296 for more detailed information.)
Green Power Juicer - Wheateena Wheatgrass Juicer - Miracle Wheatgrass Juicer

Sprouting

A tiny seed appears lifeless. Then quite magically, with the help of fresh water, air and sunshine, a sprout comes forth, bursting with life. It's packed with enzymes, vitamins and nutrients that contain the elements the body needs for optimum growth and health. Sprouts are rich in chlorophyll and are a great source of protein.

Growing sprouts is great fun and well worth the effort. It is a quick, easy and inexpensive way to always get fresh vital nutrients into your diet, even if you are living in an area that does not have fresh foods in season. The process is rewarding as well as meditative, and will pay for itself many times over. The cost of the seeds is nominal and they grow into a bounty of nutrition.

Sprouts are full of vitamins and minerals in their purest form, which are easily digested with the help of the many enzymes they contain. They are actually germinated seeds, legumes and grains that, in the sprouting process, become powerful enzyme-makers, converting carbohydrates into simple sugars, complex proteins into amino acids and fats into fatty acids. These conversions make the assimilation and absorption of their valuable nutrients easier. For example, the nutrient content of grains, seeds and legumes can increase 10%-20% when they are sprouted. Many sprouted grains and legumes also contain the essential amino acids. Sprouts are a wonderful way to insure that you are getting the nutrition your body needs.

"*Sprouts and immature greens are the most nutritious and live, raw, organic foods that are available on this planet.*"

VICTORAS P. KULVINSKAS, M.S.
Author: <u>Survival into the 21st Century</u>
21st Century Publications, Fairfield, Iowa

*S*prouts: hydroponic jar, bag or basket method

SUPPLIES:
1. Wide mouth glass jars (in different sizes).
2. Screens or cheese cloth can be used to cover the opening of the jar.
   Cut the screen to fit over the jar's mouth (usually about a 6" square).
3. Use a strong rubber band to secure the screen.
4. Seeds can be purchased at most health food stores. Measure out the quantities listed below:

UNHULLED SEEDS:
Alfalfa -- 1 1/2 T.
Clover -- 1 1/2 T.
Radish -- 1 1/2 T.
Fenugreek-- 1 1/2 T.

LEGUMES:
Lentil -- 3/4 C.
Adzuki Beans -- 3/4 C.
Mung Beans -- 3/4 C.
Green Peas -- 1 C.
Garbanzo Beans -- 1 C.

GRAINS:
Wheat, soft --1 C.
Millet -- 1 1/2 C.
Rye -- 1 C.
Barley -- 1 C.
Quinoa -- 1 C.

SOAKING:
1. First inspect and remove the broken seeds.
2. Place them in a jar, rinse and drain.
3. Fill jar with spring or filtered water, about 2-3 inches above seeds or legumes. Soak overnight, approximately 8 hours.
4. After 8 hours, drain water. (This water can be used for house plants.)

RINSING & DRAINING: Rinse soaked seeds. Place jars in a rack or bowl (mouth down) at a 45 degree angle so the air can circulate. Make sure seeds do not totally cover mouth of jar. Cover with a towel to keep dark for the first days. This will ensure germination. Rinse and drain 2-3 times a day. Legumes and grains do not need the sunlight and will be ready in 1-2 days when the sprout tail is 1/8 inch long. For unhulled seeds, such as alfalfa, clover and radish, continue rinsing and draining for 2-3 more days and place in indirect sunlight until the leaves are deep green.

HARVEST: To harvest grains and legumes, just rinse and serve. For unhulled seeds and some legumes (such as mung beans), place in a container and submerge the sprouts until the hulls rise to the surface. Skim them off and place sprouts back in the jar to drain. Refrigerate all sprouts after they are fully sprouted to maintain freshness. They will last 5 - 7 days in refrigeration. Once wheat berries are sprouted, they can be used to make uncooked Essene breads and other healthy treats.

> *"God said, 'Behold! I have given you every herb bearing seed which is upon the face of all the earth, and every tree, in which is the fruit of a tree yielding seed. To you it shall be for meat.'"*
> *THE BIBLE, GENESIS 1:29*

Sprouts: planted

SUPPLIES:
1. fresh seeds or berries
2. healthy soil
3. garden flats or cafeteria trays with holes
4. box or basket with holes to drain, or gutters around the side.
5. strainer or screening material for rinsing seeds before planting

    1 3/4 C. Sunflower seeds (whole) for one flat of sprouts
    1 2/3 C. Buckwheat seeds for one flat of sprouts

SOAKING: Inspect seeds. Rinse once in jar and then fill with spring water 2-3" above seeds. Soak for 12 hours.

RINSING & DRAINING: 2-3 times a day for 1-2 days until the sprout shoot is growing.

SOIL PREPARATION: A good mixture is 75% top soil & 25% peat moss or 50% top soil, 25% peat moss and 25% compost. A prepared potting soil can also be used. A small amount of fresh sand, rock dust or kelp/seaweed adds to potency of the sprouts. Mix soil in a bucket or box, and fill trays at least 1 inch thick with soil.

PLANTING & GROWING: Sow seeds onto soil and spread out. Seeds should touch, but not be bunched on top of each other. Water them daily and cover with shade cloth or towel. After 3 days uncover and put in indirect sunlight. More sun = larger leaves.

HARVESTING: Harvest 5-8 days from planting when sprout is just over 2" tall with deep green leaves. Harvest with a serrated knife or scissors, trying not to pull plants up by the roots. Take hulls off with fingers. Brushing the tops of the sprouts before harvesting helps to remove the hulls.

POSSIBLE PROBLEMS: Problems may occur which can usually be solved by a slight change in the growing process. Mold may grow if the seeds are too damp, planted too closely or have poor ventilation. Use a shade cloth to cover instead of towels or newspaper and water less. Sparse crop can happen if the seeds were soaked too long or not watered properly. Pale sprouts may be caused by insufficient sunlight.

"When men have learned that when they harm a living thing, they harm themselves, they surely will not kill, nor cause a thing that God has made to suffer pain."

LEVI
The Aquarian Gospel of Jesus the Christ
transcribed from the Akashic records

Breakfast

Applesauce
yields 1 bowl

10 Apples, small
2 T. Date Sugar

1 t. Cinnamon
1/8 t. Nutmeg (optional)

1. Peel and core apples.
2. Blend all ingredients in a food processor with the "S"- shaped blade.

Fresh Fruit Salad
Serves 1-2

1 Avocado
1 Mango
1 Banana

1 Papaya or Peach
1 Orange
1/8 C. Raisins

1. Peel and slice each piece of fruit into a bowl, mix and serve.
   •Optional: Squeeze fresh orange juice over fruit bowl and sprinkle on sunflower seeds.

Sunflower Milk
yields 1 quart

1 Quart Ice Water
2/3 C. Sunflower Seeds

Dash of Vanilla (optional)
2-3 Dates (pitted), soaked in 1/2 C. Water

1. Place sunflower seeds in a blender (just covering the blades of the blender).
2. Cover the seeds with only one cup of water and blend to a purée, adding water if needed.
3. Add the dates and vanilla. Be sure to get the little pieces of seeds off the sides of the blender to avoid a gritty milk. When the purée becomes difficult to whiz, add more water until the paste is a very smooth consistency, then fill almost to the top with ice cold water and blend briefly. (Don't fill blender to the top or it will overflow when blending.)

• This milk is quick, easy and delicious over breakfast cereals. Use raw cashews in place of sunflower seeds for a rich, cream-like, whiter milk.

"The fate of animals is of greater importance to me than the fear of appearing ridiculous; it is indissolubly connected with the fate of men."

EMILE ZOLA (1840-1902)
French novelist and critic

Almond "Milk"
yields 1 blender

1/3-1/2 C. Almonds	3-4 Dates (pitted), soaked in 1/2 C. Water
4 C. Ice Cold Water	Almond Extract, dash

1. Cover the blades of the blender completely with almonds.
   Then pour 3/4 cup of water or (enough water to cover the almonds plus a little extra) into the blender and purée until smooth and creamy.
2. Pour a little water down the sides of the blender, getting all the little pieces of grit to fall into the purée. When completely smooth, with no grit, add ice cold water to fill the blender nearly to the top. Add a drop or two of almond extract. Blend until homogenous.

   • For a smoother consistency, strain before serving.

Granola Mix
yields approximately 8 cups

4 C. Rolled Oats	1 C. Raisins
1/2 C. Almonds, chopped	1/3 C. Figs, chopped
1/2 C. Pecans, chopped	1/3 C. Dates, chopped
1/2 C. Walnuts, chopped	1/2 C. Sunflower Seeds
1/2 C. Oat or Wheat Bran	1/2 -1 C. Date Sugar
1 C. Shredded Coconut	1 t. Cinnamon

1. Mix all ingredients together in a bowl and then store in a sealed container in the pantry.

   •Serve with sunflower or almond milk.

"Diabetes is not necessarily a one-way street. Early studies suggest that persons with diabetes can improve and, in some cases, even cure themselves of the disease by switching to an unrefined, vegan diet."

ANDREW NICHOLSON, M.D.
Physicians Committee for Responsible Medicine
Good Medicine Magazine, Winter 1997

Tasty Dried Granola

yields 1 quart

1 Papaya (large & ripe)	3 C. Whole Oats
1 Banana	1/2 C. Raisins (soaked 10 min.)
3 t. Cinnamon	1/4 C. Walnuts (soaked 10 min.)
1 1/2 t. Vanilla	1/4 C. Pecans (soaked 10 min.)
1/2 C. Date Sugar	1/4 C. Dried Banana

1. In a food processor, using the "S"- shaped blade, whiz the papaya, banana, cinnamon, vanilla and date sugar. Add oats and whiz again. Mixture should be thick and sticky. Place in bowl.
2. Place nuts, raisins and dried banana in the food processor and whiz lightly.
3. Fold chopped nuts and dried fruit into the mix.
4. Drop onto dehydrator sheet rack so it looks like granola. Dehydrate at 105° for 6 hours or until desired crunchiness.

Health Cereal

yields 1 bowl

1 C. Buckwheat groats	1/4 C. Soaked Raisins
1 Banana, sliced	

In a bowl, place the buckwheat groats and sliced banana. Add the soaked raisins and use the sweet water from the soaked raisins to pour over the buckwheat.

Almond-Raisin Whip

yields 1 cup

2/3 C. Almonds, soaked	2 Dates (pitted), soaked
1/2 C. Raisins, soaked in 1/2 C. Water	

1. Soak the almonds overnight.
2. In a blender, blend the ingredients together. Use as a spread on Essene bread.

"The vegetarian movement ought to fill with gladness the souls of those who have at heart, the realization of God's kingdom on earth."

COUNT LEO TOLSTOY (1828-1910)
Russian novelist and moral philosopher

Salads Galore

Tossed Dressed Salad

serves 5

1 Head Romaine Lettuce
1 Small Onion, thinly sliced
1 C. Bell Pepper, diced
1/2 Pint Cherry Tomatoes, halved
1 Long Seedless Cucumber, sliced
2-3 T. Nutritional Yeast

1/2 - 1 T. Herb Seasoning
1/2 t. Garlic (granulated)
1/8 t. Black Pepper
2 T. Apple Cider Vinegar
2 T. Lemon Juice (fresh)
1-2 T. Bragg™ Liquid Aminos
1/2 T. Olive Oil

1. Wash the lettuce and allow to drip dry.
2. Dice the vegetables and add to the lettuce. Sprinkle with dry seasonings.
3. Just before serving, add the vinegar, lemon juice, Bragg's™ and olive oil. Toss several minutes. Serve immediately.

Garden Salad

serves 4-5

1 Head Leaf Lettuce
1/2 C. Purple Cabbage, shredded
3 Swiss Chard Leaves, shredded
Broccoli & Cauliflower Flowerets
5 Spinach Leaves (large), chopped

4 Carrots, grated
2 Beets, grated
1 Cucumber, sliced
1-2 Tomatoes, diced small
1 Bell Pepper, sliced

1. Wash the greens and allow to drip dry in a strainer.
2. Cut the vegetables into bite-sized pieces or grate.
3. Toss the grated carrots, shredded purple cabbage, sliced pepper, broccoli and cauliflower flowerets in the salad. (Peel the broccoli stalks and slice for salad.)
4. Don't mix in the grated beet as it turns the salad red; decorate the top with it. Place the cucumbers and tomatoes around the edges of the salad; don't mix in. (Tomatoes and cucumbers mixed in will limit the shelf life of the salad.)

• Taking time to prepare a beautiful salad will help you enjoy eating more live foods.

> *"No great improvements in the lot of mankind are possible until a great change takes place in the fundamental constitution of their modes of thought."*
>
> JOHN STUART MILL (1806-1873)
> English author and philosopher

Sprout Salad

serves 4

4 C. Sprouts (any combination)
1/2 Head of Lettuce or Spinach
2 Slices Purple Onion, diced small
4 Carrots, grated

3 Mushrooms, sliced
1 Cucumber, peeled, diced
1 Bell Pepper, sliced
1 Tomato, diced

Toss all ingredients except the cucumbers and tomatoes. Toss with dressing. Add cucumber and tomato to the top.

Champion Carrot Salad

serves 4

2 C. Carrots, grated
1 C. Tahini Dressing (thick) pg. 204
Garlic & Onion Powder, dash

1 Stalk Celery, diced finely
1/4 Onion, diced small
Sea Salt, to taste
1 T. Dill Weed or to taste

1. Grate carrots through a Champion® Juicer. (Rather than assembling with the juicing screen, assemble leaving that space open.) Another option is to use a food processor or grater and grate as fine as possible.
2. Mix all ingredients together. Chill. Garnish with extra dill weed.

Oriental Cabbage Salad

serves 5

1 Small Head Cabbage, grated
1/4 C. Purple Cabbage, grated
2-3 Carrots, grated
1 Scallion, diced
3 Stalks Celery, diced
2 Garlic Cloves (fresh), diced

2 T. Fresh Ginger, diced
2 T. Miso (blonde)
2 t. Bragg's™ or Sea Salt, to taste
2 t. Vinegar (raw)
1 T. Date Sugar
4 T. Water (or more if needed)

1. Grate cabbage and carrots; dice the celery and scallion; mix together in a bowl.
2. In a blender, whiz the garlic and ginger with the miso, Bragg's™ , vinegar, sweetener and water. Be sure to thoroughly blend the ginger and garlic.
3. Pour the mixture over the vegetables and mix well. Marinate and chill for an hour before serving.

> *"Love all God's creatures, the animals, the plants.*
> *Love everything to perceive the divine mystery in all."*
>
> FYODOR DOSTOEVSKY (1821-1881)
> Russian novelist

Curry Cauliflower Salad
serves 3

2 1/2 C. Cauliflower, chopped
1/2 C. Leeks or Scallion, diced
1 1/2 C. Carrots, grated
3 t. Bragg's™ or a dash of sea salt

1/4 C. Raw Tahini
1 t. Curry (mild)
1/4 C. Water

1. Place the vegetables into a small bowl.
2. In a separate cup, mix together the tahini and remaining ingredients.
3. Pour over the vegetables, mix and allow to marinate before serving.

Rainbow Raw Salad
yields 5-6 servings

1/2 C. Zucchini, grated
3/4 C. Red Pepper, diced
1 C. Carrot, grated
1/2 C. Purple Cabbage, grated
1 Stalk Celery, diced small
2 1/2 C. Broccoli Flowerets
1/3 C. Scallions, diced

1/2 Tomato, diced
1/4 C. Lemon Juice (fresh)
2 T. Oil
2 T. Bragg's™ or Sea Salt, to taste
1/2 T. Herb Seasoning
2 T. Nutritional Yeast
1/2 t. Black Pepper

Mix all ingredients together in a bowl. Allow to marinate a short time and serve.

Grate Beet Salad
yields 6 cups

5 C. Beets, grated
3/4 C. Onion (sweet), diced
Dressing
1 C. Water
1 T. Onion, diced

1/2 C. Tahini (raw)
2 T. Apple Cider Vinegar (raw)
2 T. Nutritional Yeast
1 Garlic Clove

1. Grate the peeled beets (approximately 4-6 beets) and place in a mixing bowl. Add the diced onion.
2. In a blender, mix the Dressing ingredients. Pour over the shredded beets. Marinate several hours and serve.

"And thou shalt eat the herb of the field."

THE BIBLE, GENESIS 3:18

Vibrant Italian Salad

yields 4-6 servings

3 C. Tomatoes (fresh), cubed
2-3 C. English Cucumbers, peeled, sliced
1/2 Onion (medium), diced small
1 1/2 C. Broccoli Flowerets

Blender Ingredients
1/4 C. Water
1/4 C. Olive Oil (cold pressed)
1 t. Onion Granules
1 Garlic Clove
1 t. Garlic Powder

1 T. Date Sugar
1 T. Bragg's™ or Sea Salt, to taste
3 T. Nutritional Yeast

Final Additions
1 1/2 Avocado (large), cubed
1 t. Spike™ Seasoning
1/4 C. Vinegar (raw)
1/2 T. Basil
1 T. Oregano
1/4 t. Black Pepper
1/2 - 1 t. Sea Salt

1. Place the tomatoes, cucumber, onion and broccoli flowerets in a large mixing bowl.
2. In a blender, whiz the Blender Ingredients. Pour over vegetables to marinate for an hour.
3. After marinating, add the avocado and Final Additions. Stir and serve.

Mexicavo Salad

serves 4-6

4 Ears of Corn, kernels off cob
4 Tomatoes, diced
1/4 C. Green Pepper, diced
1 Bunch Pok Choy or Bok Choy
1/2 C. Sweet Onion, diced

Blender Ingredients
1/4 C. Apple Cider Vinegar
1/4 C. Oil (optional)

1 t. Nutritional Yeast
2 T. Bragg's™ or Sea Salt, to taste
1 Garlic Clove (small)
Pepper, dash
1 t. Herb Seasoning

Final Ingredients
5-6 Haas Avocado, cubed
1/2 C. Cilantro (fresh), chopped

1. Place the first 5 ingredients in a bowl.
2. In a blender, whiz the Blender Ingredients.
   Pour onto vegetables in bowl and allow to marinate for 1/2 - 1 hour.
3. Finally, just before serving, add the avocado and fresh cilantro. Stir well and serve.

"We have a great deal more kindness than is ever spoken. Despite all the selfishness that chills like east winds, the world, the whole human family, is bathed with an element of love, like a fine ether."

RALPH WALDO EMERSON (1803-1882)
American philosopher, poet and essayist

Spinach and Sprout Salad
serves 5

2 C. Spinach (fresh)
1 C. Clover and/or Alfalfa Sprouts
3 Carrots, grated
1 Shallot, sliced

2 T. Lemon Juice, fresh
3 T. Nutritional Yeast
1 T. Fresh Dill, or 1 t. dried
1 T. Bragg's™ or Sea Salt, to taste

1. Cut larger spinach leaves to bite size. Mix with sprouts, carrots and shallot.
2. Add remaining ingredients and mix well. Serve fresh or slightly chilled.

Pink Passion Salad
serves 5-6

1 Head Green Cabbage (small)
1/2 Head Red Cabbage (small)
1 Beet, grated
1 Red Pepper, diced
1 Tomato, diced
2 T. Fresh Basil, chopped

2 Red Onion Slices, diced
1 Lemon/Lime, juiced
3 T. Bragg's™ or Sea Salt, to taste
4 T. Nutritional Yeast
2 T. Fresh Dill, chopped
2 T. Olive Oil
Fresh Herbs of Choice (optional)

1. In a bowl, mix vegetables and dress with the remaining ingredients.
2. Chill for several hours before serving, allowing it to marinate.

Sprouted Lentil Salad
4-5 servings

4 C. Sprouted Lentils
2 Carrots, grated
1/4 C. Onion, diced
1/4 C. Parsley, chopped
2 T. Olive or Other Oil

1/4 C. Water
1/4 C. Lemon Juice, fresh
1 T. Bragg's™ or Sea Salt, to taste
1 T. Rice Syrup (optional)
3 T. Nutritional Yeast

1. In a bowl, mix together the sprouted lentils, grated carrots, diced onion and fresh parsley.
2. In a blender, blend the remaining ingredients. Pour over the vegetables and mix. Chill and serve. Nutritious and delicious!

"Recognize the eternal essence that exists in every living thing and shines forth with inscrutable significance from all eyes that see the sun!"

ARTHUR SCHOPENHAUER (1788-1860)
German author and philosopher

Aramé (Sea Vegetable) Salad

serves 4-6

1.75 oz. Package of Aramé
4 C. Water
1 Tomato, diced
1 Onion (small), diced
1 Cucumber, diced
1 Garlic Clove, diced

2 T. Olive Oil
2 T. Bragg's™ or Sea Salt, to taste
1 T. Apple Cider Vinegar (raw)
1/2 t. Spike™ Seasoning
1/2 Red Bell Pepper, diced

1. Rinse aramé and soak in 4 cups of water for 1/2 hour.
2. Drain. Add remaining ingredients. Toss and serve.

Parsley Salad

serves 2-4

1 Bunch Parsley, chopped
1 Can of Olives (small), pitted, sliced
2 Garlic Cloves, diced
1 Tomato, diced (optional)

2 T. Lemon Juice
1-2 T. Olive Oil
Bragg's™ or Sea Salt, to taste

Mix ingredients in a bowl. Serve.

Delightful Sprout Salad

serves 4-5

1 1/2 C. Cabbage, finely grated
1/2 C. Lentil Sprouts
  (or other sprouted legume)
1/2 C. Clover or Alfalfa Sprouts
2 Carrots, grated
1 Bell Pepper, diced
1/8 C. Sunflower Seeds

Dressing
1 T. Lemon Juice
2 T. Basil
2 T. Dill (fresh), chopped
1 T. Bragg's™ or Sea Salt, to taste
2 T. Nutritional Yeast
3 T. Raw Tahini

1. Combine grated and diced veggies, sprouts and seeds.
2. Mix dressing ingredients separately; then pour over the top of the vegetables. Mix thoroughly and let marinate for at least 1/2 hour.

"...We can judge the heart of a man by his treatment of animals."

IMMANUEL KANT (1724-1804)
German philosopher

Sprouted Quinoa Salad
serves 4

1 C. Sprouted Quinoa
1 Tomato (small), diced
1/2 Red Pepper, diced

1/2 T. Vinegar
1 T. Bragg's™ or Sea Salt, to taste
1 T. Nutritional Yeast
2 t. Mustard (optional)

1. Soak Quinoa for 6 hours and sprout for one day, to maintain freshness.
2. Mix all ingredients together in a bowl. Allow to marinate 10 minutes before serving.

Pok Choy Miso Salad
yields 8 cups

6 C. Pok Choy or Bok Choy
2 Stalks Celery, diced
2 C. Grated Carrot
Dressing Ingredients
1 Garlic Clove, pressed

2 T. Miso
1 T. Oil (optional)
1 T. Parsley, chopped
1 T. Water (2 T. if no oil)

1. Chop the pok choy and mix with celery and carrot.
2. Mix Dressing Ingredients in a cup to liquefy the miso. Pour over salad. Mix well.

Golden Caesar Salad
yield 1 medium-sized salad bowl

12 C. Baby Mixed Greens (loosely packed),
   (Tot Soy, Bok Choy, Spinach, Mustard)
1 Yellow Bell Pepper, sliced thinly
6 Mushrooms, sliced thinly
Sprinkle
1/2 C. Macadamia Nuts (raw)
1/2-1 T. Nutritional Yeast

1/4 t. Sea Salt
Dressing Ingredients
3 dates (pitted) soaked in 1/2 C. Water
1 T. Mustard (stone ground)
2 T. Olive Oil (cold-pressed)
1/2 t. Nutritional Yeast
1/4 t. Sea Salt

1. Fill salad bowl with (washed and dried) baby mixed salad greens, pepper and mushrooms.
2. Sprinkle: In a small blender cup or blender, place macadamia nuts, yeast and salt.
   Pulsate enough to chop nuts into small pieces but not a paste. Set aside.
3. In a blender, whiz the Dressing Ingredients. Toss the salad with the dressing just before
   serving. Sprinkle with macadamia topping.

"I wish no living thing to suffer pain."

PERCY BYSSHE SHELLEY (1792-1822)
English Poet

Sprouted Mung Bean Salad

serves 5

5 C. Sprouted Mung Beans
2 C. Carrot, grated
2 C. Pok Choy, Spinach
  or Chard, chopped
1 T. Apple Cider Vinegar (raw)
1 t. Oregano (dried)

2 T. Lemon Juice + 2 T. Oil
1/4 t. Garlic Powder
1 t. Herb Seasoning
3 t. Nutritional Yeast
1/2 t. Dill Weed
2 1/2 T. Bragg's™ or Sea Salt, to taste

Mix all ingredients together in a bowl. Allow to marinate before serving.

Creamy Cole Slaw

serves 4

1 C. Cashew Pieces
5 T. Lemon Juice (fresh)
2 T. Oil (cold pressed)
2 t. Onion Powder
1 t. Garlic Powder
2 T. Nutritional Yeast

1/2 t. Sea Salt, to taste
3 T. Apple Cider Vinegar (raw)
2 t. Sweetener
1 T. Raw Tahini
1 Head of Cabbage, shredded
2 Carrots, grated

1. Place the cashew pieces in a blender, filling to the 1 cup line. Add water to the 1 1/2 cup line and let soak for 10 minutes. Add the remaining ingredients to the blender, except for the cabbage and carrots. Blend.
2. Place the shredded cabbage and carrots in a bowl and add the blender mixture. Mix. Chill and allow to marinate. You may want to add more flavor before serving.

Spicy Raw Slaw

serves 4-5

1 Cabbage Head (small), shredded
2 C. Beet, grated
1/4 C. Onion, diced
2 T. Raw Tahini
1 T. Apple Cider Vinegar (raw)

2 T. Bragg's™ or Sea Salt, to taste
1/2 t. Curry (mild)
1/4 t. Cumin
1 T. Water

Mix all ingredients together in a bowl. Marinate for an hour before serving.

"...If man was what he ought to be, he would be adored by the animals..."

HENRI-FREDERIC AMIEL (1821-1881)
Swiss philosopher

Cucumber and Cherry Tomato Salad

serves 3-4

1/2 Pint Cherry Tomatoes, halved
2 Long Seedless Cucumbers, diced
1 Onion (small and sweet), diced
1/2 C. Bell Pepper, diced
1 T. Olive Oil
1 1/2 T. Apple Cider Vinegar
1 T. Nutritional Yeast

1/4 t. Garlic, granulated
1/8 t. Black Pepper
1/4 t. Dill Weed
1/2 t. Oregano, dried
1 T. Bragg's™ or Sea Salt, to taste
1/2 t. Salt-Free Seasoning

In a bowl, mix all ingredients together. Stir. Marinate before serving.

Cucumber Vinaigrette

3-4 Servings

4 C. Cucumbers, sliced
4 t. Olive Oil (cold-pressed)
1 t. Herb Seasoning
1 1/2 T. Apple Cider Vinegar (raw)
1 T. Date Sugar

1/2 Onion, sliced thin
1 T. Nutritional Yeast
1 1/2 T. Bragg's™ or Sea Salt, to taste
1 t. Oregano (dried)
1 T. Lemon Juice (fresh)
1/4 t. Pepper

Mix all ingredients together in a bowl. Chill and marinate for an hour. Serve.

Guacamolé Dip

serves 2-3

5 Avocados (Haas or Small)
1/2 Red Onion (small), diced
2 1/2 t. Lemon Juice (or lime)
1 Tomato, diced
1 Garlic Clove, minced

1/2 t. Herb Seasoning
1/2 t. Garlic Powder
Cayenne Pepper, dash
1 t. Bragg's™ or Sea Salt, to taste

Mash the avocados and mix in the remaining ingredients. Serve as a dip or spread.

> *"I am conscious that meat eating is not in accordance with the finer feelings, and I abstain from it whenever I can."*
>
> ALBERT SCHWEITZER, M.D. (1875-1965)
> Alsatian philosopher and medical missionary
> 1952 Nobel Peace Prize recipient

Tossed Confetti Cabbage

serves 4-6

1/2 Head Green Cabbage, grated	1 T. Nutritional Yeast
2 Beets (medium), grated	3 T. Brown Rice Vinegar (raw)
3-4 Carrots, grated	1/4 C. Sunflower Seeds
1 1/2 T. Olive Oil (cold-pressed)	1 T. Bragg's™ or Sea Salt, to taste

1. In a food processor, grate the cabbage, beets and carrots and place in a bowl.
2. Sprinkle olive oil over cabbage and toss. Add remaining ingredients, toss and serve.

Stuffed Avocados

serves 4

2 Large Avocados (hard shelled)	2 T. Bragg's™ or Sea Salt, to taste
2 Scallions, diced	1/2 t. Herb Seasoning
1-2 Cucumbers, diced	1/2 t. Garlic Powder
2 Tomatoes, diced	1 t. Sesame Seeds
2-3 Carrots, grated	2 T. Nutritional Yeast
1/2 C. Lentil Sprouts	Lemon Juice, dash

1. Slice the avocados in half and remove the pit. Gently scoop out the avocado.
2. Mix avocado with remaining ingredients in a bowl. Squeeze in a dash of lemon juice and place back into the shells. Decorate the top with colorful raw veggies and serve.

Avocado-Tomato Jubilee

serves 2-4

5 Avocados (small), cubed	2 Red Onion Slices, diced
1-2 Tomato, cubed	1 1/2 T. Bragg's™ or Sea Salt, to taste
2 T. Fresh Dill Weed, chopped	Cayenne Pepper, dash (optional)
1 T. Lemon Juice, fresh	

Mix all ingredients together in a bowl and serve.

"What is philosophy but a continual battle, an ever-renewed effort to transcend the sphere of blind custom and so become transcendental."

THOMAS CARLYLE (1795-1881)
Scottish-born English historian, biographer and essayist

Avocado Marinade

serves 4

5-6 Haas Avocados	1 Onion (small), diced
2 T. Bragg's™ or Sea Salt, to taste	1 T. Apple Cider Vinegar (raw)
1 T. Raw Tahini	1/2 t. Garlic Powder
2 T. Nutritional Yeast	Fresh Lemon Juice, 1 squeeze

1. Cut the avocados in half and remove the pit. Slice into sections and scoop out with a spoon. (You want to have big sized chunks.)
2. In a bowl, mix all other ingredients with the avocado chunks. Chill and serve.

Avocado - Carrot Salad

serves 5

3 Avocados (medium-large sized)	1/2 C. Red (Bermuda) Onion, diced
3 T. Lemon Juice (fresh)	1/2 t. Sea Salt
1 T. Bragg's™ or Sea Salt (to taste)	1 C. Carrots, grated
1/2 C. Scallions, chopped	

1. Slice the avocados into bite-sized pieces and place in a medium-sized bowl.
2. Add the remaining ingredients and mix well. Chill and serve.

Shiitake- Snow Pea Salad

2-4 servings

1 Avocado (large), skinned, pitted, cubed	1/2 C. Mushrooms (Shiitake) stemmed & sliced
1/2 lb. Snow Peas (in pods), washed and stemmed	1 Lemon, juiced
1/2 C. Mung Bean Sprouts	2 T. Sesame Oil
3 Scallions, chopped	2-3 t. Bragg's™ or Sea Salt, to taste
1 Bunch Watercress, washed & chopped	Black Pepper (fresh), to taste
	Sesame Seeds, for garnish

1. In a mixing bowl, combine avocado and vegetables together and lightly toss.
2. In a separate bowl, whisk the lemon, oil, Bragg's™ and pepper together. Pour over the vegetables and toss again.
3. Place in serving bowl and garnish with sesame seeds.

"Nothing cruel is useful or expedient."

CICERO, MARCUS TULLIUS (106-43 B.C.)
Roman orator and statesman

Jicama Heaven (Jicama is a Mexican root vegetable)
serves 4

3 C. Jicama, half grated, half diced
1/2 C. Red pepper, diced
1/4 C. Tomato, diced

1 t. Herb Seasoning
2 T. Lemon Juice
1 t. Bragg's™ or Sea Salt, to taste
1 t. Fresh Dill, chopped

1. Dice and grate jicama and stir in with the vegetables.
2. Season with remaining ingredients and mix well. Serve chilled.

Sprouted Bean Salad
serves 4-5

3 C. Sprouted Beans (a mixture
   of Lentil, Adzuki and Peas)
1 C. Carrot, grated
2 Tomatoes, diced

2 T. Nutritional Yeast
2 - 3 t. Bragg's™ or Sea Salt, to taste
2 t. Vinegar (raw)

1. Sprout beans as directed on the sprouting page in the beginning of this chapter.
2. Rinse and drain sprouts and mix with remaining ingredients. Let sit for at least 10 minutes to enhance the flavors. Serve.

Simple Cabbage Salad

1 Head Cabbage (small), shredded
2 T. Lemon Juice

2 T. Bragg's™ or Sea Salt, to taste
3-4 T. Raw Tahini

Mix all ingredients together. Let chill for a few hours or serve immediately.
• Optional- Add 1/4 onion or scallion, diced.

"Parents usually educate their children merely in such a manner that however bad the world may be, they may adapt themselves to its present conditions. But they ought to give them an education so much better than this, that a better condition of things may thereby be brought about by the future."

IMMANUEL KANT (1724-1804)
German philosopher

ABC Salad (Almond/Beet/Carrot)
serves 4

1 3/4 C. Almonds (soaked)
1 C. Beet, grated
2 Carrots, grated

1 1/2 t. Bragg's™ or Sea Salt, to taste
1-2 T. Raw Tahini
1 1/2 t. Nutritional Yeast

1. Soak 1 3/4 cup of almonds for at least 2 hours, drain and slice.
2. Mix almonds with grated vegetables and seasonings. Refrigerate for 15 minutes before serving.

Lemon-Walnut Salad
serves 6

2 C. Walnuts
4 C. Carrots, grated
1 1/2 C. Red Cabbage, shredded
1/8 C. Sweet Onion, diced

4 T. Lemon Juice
2 T. Nutritional Yeast
2 T. Bragg's™ or Sea Salt, to taste

1. Soak walnuts for 1 hour; rinse, drain and slice.
2. Grate and dice vegetables and mix in with the walnuts. Add the remaining seasonings and stir well.

Cucumber & Snow Pea Salad
serves 4

2 C. Cucumber Slices
1 C. Snow Peas
1/4 C. Red Pepper, sliced
1/2 C. Broccoli Flowerets

1 T. Vinegar (raw)
1 T. Bragg's™ or Sea Salt, to taste
2 T. Fresh Dill

1. Peel and slice cucumber; mix with vegetables. Add the seasonings and herbs.
2. Chill before serving.

> *"Compassion is a natural human quality, not the province of a particular religion. But unless we cultivate it in relation to ourselves and others, we will never achieve peace."*
>
> TENZIN GYATSO, 14th DALAI LAMA
> Tibetan Buddhist priest

Chinese Cabbage - Pecan Salad
serves 4-5

1 Head Chinese Cabbage, finely chopped	2 T. Bragg's™ or Sea Salt, to taste
1 C. Carrot, grated	2 T. Vinegar (raw)
1 C. Pecans, chopped	2 T. Nutritional Yeast
1 Sweet Yellow Pepper	1/2 t. Herb Seasoning

Mix all ingredients in a bowl. Allow to marinate and serve.

Dressed Spinach Salad
serves 2-4

4 C. Spinach, washed, chopped	2-3 Tomatoes (small), chopped
1/2 Yellow Pepper, seeded, diced	1 T. Oregano
2 C. Mushrooms, sliced	1 1/2 T. Olive Oil
1 Long English Cucumber, sliced	2 T. Bragg's™ or Sea Salt, to taste
2 C. Carrots, grated	2 T. Vinegar (raw)
1/4 C. Raw Cashews	1 T. Nutritional Yeast
2 T. Onion, diced	1/2 t. Black Pepper

1. Wash the spinach and let it dry. Tear into bite-sized pieces.
2. In a bowl mix spinach with remaining vegetables and cashews.
3. Add the remaining ingredients. Toss. Chill and Serve.

Creamy Curry Sprouted Lentil Salad
serves 4-6

4 C. Sprouted Lentils	1/2 C. Water
2/3 C. Onion, diced finely	1 C. Cashews (soaked a little)
1 C. Carrot, shredded	2 T. Bragg's™ or Sea Salt, to taste
Sauce Ingredients	1/2 T. Curry (mild)
1/8 C. Oil (cold pressed)	1 T. Lemon Juice

1. Place the first 3 ingredients in a bowl.
2. In a blender, blend the Sauce Ingredients into a thick creamy sauce. Pour over the vegetables. Mix well. Chill and allow to marinate for several hours before serving.

"The eating of meat extinguishes the seed of great compassion."

The BUDDHA (circa 563-483 B.C.)
Indian avatar

Raw Veggie "Tuna"
serves 4-6

3 lbs. Carrots, peeled, grated
2 Celery Stalks, diced
1 Bell Pepper, chopped
1 Red Onion (small), diced
1 1/4 C. Almond "Mayo" (see recipe below)

1 Tomato (large), diced
2 T. Bragg's™ or Sea Salt, to taste
1 t. Sea Salt
2 t. Kelp

Mix all ingredients together and serve.

Almond "Mayo"
yields 2 1/4 cups

1 C. Almonds
3/4 C. Water
1 T. Onion Powder
1 t. Sea Salt

2-3 T. Date Sugar
1 Lemon, juiced
1/4 C. Oil (cold-pressed)

1. In a food processor using the "S"- shaped blade (or with a strong blender) thoroughly blend almonds with water. Add the remaining ingredients, except the oil. Process.
2. Slowly add oil, while processing, and mixture will thicken. Chill.

Brazil Nut "Mayo"
yields 3 cups

2 C. Brazil Nuts
1/8 C. Olive Oil
1 t. Sea Salt, to taste

1/2 C. Lemon Juice
1/2 C. Water

1. In a food processor, using the "S"- shaped blade, process the brazil nuts.
2. Slowly add oil while still processing. Add remaining ingredients. Whiz. Chill.

Among the noblest in the land—
Though man may count himself the least—
That man I honor and revere,
Who without favor, without fear,
In the great city dares to stand,
The friend of every friendless beast."

HENRY WADSWORTH LONGFELLOW (1807-1882)
American poet

Dressings, Dips, Soups and more!

Green Goddess Dressing
yields 2 cups

3/4 C. Water
1 Haas Avocado
3 T. Lemon Juice (fresh)

1 - 2 T. Bragg's™ or Sea Salt, to taste
Garlic & Onion Powder, dash
1/4 C. Herbs (fresh)

In a blender, blend all ingredients together. This is a healthy raw dressing, best eaten the day it is made.

Avocado Dressing
yields 2 cups

1/2 C. Olive Oil (cold pressed)
1/4 C. Basil (fresh)
1 Garlic Clove, minced
1/2 T. Fresh Herbs
1/4 t. Onion Powder
1/8 t. Cayenne Pepper (optional)

1/4 C. Avocado
2 T. Nutritional Yeast
1 T. Bragg's™ or Sea Salt, to taste
1 C. Water
2 T. Lemon

In a blender, blend all ingredients together. Keeps well in the refrigerator.

Tahini Dressing
yields 1 1/2 cups

1 C. Water
1/2 C. Raw Tahini

3 t. Bragg's™ or Sea Salt, to taste
Curry or other Spices, to taste (optional)

In a blender, blend all ingredients.
Use 1/4 cup less water for a thicker dressing to use in bakes and casseroles.
•Stays fresh for a couple of days in the refrigerator.

"Every man who has ever been earnest to preserve his higher or poetic faculties in the best condition, has been particularly inclined to abstain from animal food."

HENRY DAVID THOREAU (1817-1862)
American author, poet, naturalist

Cucumber-Walnut Dressing
yields 2 cups

1 C. Water
1/2 C. Walnuts
1 Cucumber
2 t. Bragg's™ or Sea Salt, to taste
3-4 t. Nutritional Yeast

1 Tomato (small)
  (or 1/2 of a large tomato)
1/2 t. Garlic Powder
2 Parsley Bunches
1/2 t. Onion Powder

In a blender, blend all ingredients together.

Tomato Vinaigrette
yields 1 1/4 cups

3/4 C. Tomato, diced
1/2 C. Cucumber, diced
2 T. Red or Green Onion, diced
2 T. Lemon Juice
1 T. Bragg's™ or Sea Salt, to taste
1 T. Olive Oil (optional)

1 T. Nutritional Yeast
Garlic-Pepper, dash
1/4 t. Onion Granules
2 T. Water
1/2 - 1 T. Oregano
1/2 T. Basil

In a blender, blend all ingredients together until creamy. Chill and serve.

Sunny Dressing
yields 2 1/4 cups

3/4 C. Sunflower Seeds,
  soaked a few minutes in water
1 1/2 C. Water
2 T. Raw Tahini
2 T. Parsley (fresh), chopped
1 T. Red Onion, diced

1/2 C. Scallion, diced
1/4 t. Garlic-Pepper
Cayenne Pepper, dash
3/4 T. Nutritional Yeast
1 1/2 T. Bragg's™ or Sea Salt, to taste
2 T. Fresh Herbs of Choice

In a blender, blend the seeds with 1/2 cup of water until creamy and smooth. Add the remaining water and ingredients. Blend, chill and serve.

"New opinions are always suspected and usually opposed, without any other reason, but because they are not already common."

JOHN LOCKE (1632-1704)
English philosopher

Sweet Dill Dressing
yields 2 cups

6 Dates (pitted), soaked in 1 1/2 C. water

1 C. Dill (fresh), packed into cup	1 T. Nutritional Yeast
1/4 C. Lemon Juice (fresh)	1 T. Mustard
1/4 C. Olive Oil (cold pressed)	2 T. Miso (unpasteurized)

1. In a blender, blend date soak water, dates and dill to a smooth consistency.
2. Add remaining ingredients and mix thoroughly.

Chinese Dressing
Yields 2 Cups

1/4 C. Olive Oil	2 t. Miso
2 Cloves Garlic, diced	1/4 C. Raw Tahini
1/2 t. Ginger, peeled, diced	1/4 t. Sea Salt
7 Dates, pitted, soaked in 2 C. Water	1 t. Mustard (optional)

1. In a blender, mix olive oil, garlic and ginger with 1 cup of date soak water, thoroughly blending the garlic and ginger pieces.
2. Add dates with remaining water and ingredients and blend until smooth.

Fresh Salsa
yields 1 small bowl

1 C. Fresh Tomatoes, diced	3 T. Onion, diced
1 Tomato (medium-sized)	1/4 C. Cilantro (fresh), chopped
1/2 T. Bragg's™ or Sea Salt, to taste	1/4 t. Herb Seasoning
1/2 T. Apple Cider Vinegar (raw)	Hot Pepper, to taste, minced
1 T. Nutritional Yeast	Cayenne, to taste (optional)

1. In a small bowl, place the diced tomatoes.
2. In a blender, blend the one tomato with Bragg's™, vinegar and yeast. Pour this onto the diced tomatoes.
3. Add the onion, cilantro, herb seasoning and pepper. Mix and chill.

"Vegetarianism is the cure for 99% of the world's problems. Think about it..."

CASEY KASEM
American top 40 radio announcer

Pesto Sauce
serves 2-3

1 C. Pine Nuts (or Raw Cashews)	1 T. Bragg's™ or Sea Salt, to taste
3-4 Garlic Cloves, diced	1/3 C. Olive Oil (cold pressed)
3 T. Water	1- 2 C. Basil (fresh), chopped

1. Soak the pine nuts in water for 5-10 minutes and then drain water off.
2. In a food processor, blend all the ingredients together until smooth.

Spicy Mexican Tomato Sauce
serves 4

1 lb. Tomatoes, chopped	1 Green Pepper, chopped
1 Red Onion, diced	1 T. Lemon Juice
3 Garlic Cloves (large), diced	Sea Salt, to taste
1 Jalapeño Pepper, seeded & diced	Fresh Pepper, to taste
3 T. Cilantro (fresh), minced	1 t. Chili Powder
1 Red Bell Pepper, chopped	1 t. Cumin

1. Blend tomatoes, onion, garlic and jalapeño pepper in a blender. Place in a bowl and add cilantro, peppers, lemon juice and seasonings.
2. Allow to stand 30 minutes at room temperature. Stir and re-season if needed.

Nacho Sauce
yields 2 cups

1 C. Cashews, soaked	2 t. Mexican Blend Spice
1/4 C. Water	1/2 t. Garlic Powder
1/2 C. Salsa, fresh	1 t. Onion Powder
3 T. Nutritional Yeast	1/2 t. Kelp
1 t. Bragg's™ or Sea Salt, to taste	1 t. Lemon Juice

1. Soak cashews for 5 minutes and drain. Thoroughly blend with water in a food processor, using the "S"- shaped blade. When creamy, add the remaining ingredients and blend.
3. Serve with sunflower corn chips or as a dip.

(looking into an aquarium)
"Now I can look at you in peace; I don't eat you any more."

FRANZ KAFKA (1883-1924)
Austrian-Czech author

Italian Tomato Sauce (rich and creamy)
yields 2 1/2 cups

1 Tomato (whole)	1 T. Oregano
2 t. Bragg's™ or Sea Salt, to taste	1/2 C. Basil (fresh)
2 T. Nutritional Yeast	1/4 C. Olive Oil (cold pressed)
3 oz. Sun-Dried Tomatoes, soaked	3 Dates (pitted)

1. Place dried tomatoes in a bowl and cover with water. Soak for at least 1 hour (until soft). Cover dates with water and soak for 20 minutes.
2. Place all ingredients in a blender, including soak water and blend thoroughly, adding more water only if needed. Sauce should be thick and creamy.
3. This sauce is great for Italian dishes. It is used in the Pizza and Stuffed Pepper recipes.

Chinese Sauce
yields 1 1/2 cups

1/4 C. Olive Oil (cold pressed)	1 t. Miso
2 Cloves Garlic, diced	7 Dates (pitted) soaked in 1 C. water
1/2 t. Ginger, diced	1/4 t. Sea Salt
1 t. Mustard (optional)	

1. Blend olive oil, garlic and ginger with 1/2 cup date soak water, blending thoroughly. the garlic and ginger pieces. Add the rest of the ingredients and blend.

• Serve over soaked and sprouted wild rice with diced vegetables.

Miso Tahini Dipping Sauce
yields about 1 1/2 cups

2/3 C. Water	2 T. Nutritional Yeast
1 1/2 (rounded) T. Miso	1/2 t. Mustard
1/2 C. Raw Tahini	1/2 t. Lemon Juice (fresh)

In a blender, thoroughly blend all ingredients. Place in a small bowl and circle with fresh vegetables. Use as a dip for a platter or as a spread for sprouted breads and crackers.

Curry Almond Sauce (use with Mock Salmon Loaf - page 217)

1/2 C. Almonds, soaked	1/4 t. Herb Seasoning
1 C. Carrot Juice	1/2 t. Tomatillo Juice
2 t. Curry Powder	

1. Soak and drain the almonds. Blend all ingredients in a blender, until creamy. Add more almonds for a thicker sauce.

Pesto Paté

yields 3 cups

1 C. Brazil Nuts
1 1/2 C. Walnuts
1/2 C. Almonds
1/2 C. Parsley (fresh), firmly packed
3 1/2-4 C. Basil Leaves (fresh),
    firmly packed

3/4 C. Water
1 Garlic Clove
1 t. Onion Powder
1/2 t. Garlic Powder
2 T. Olive Oil (cold pressed)
3/4 t. Sea Salt
1/3 C. Nutritional Yeast

1. Soak all nuts 15 minutes; then drain and rinse. In a food processor, using the "S"-shaped blade, whiz the basil and parsley. Remove from processor.
2. Process the drained nuts and remaining ingredients until smooth.
3. Add the basil and parsley and whiz until creamy. Chill before serving.

Cashew-Carrot Paté

yields 3 servings

2 Carrots, peeled and chopped
1 Celery Stalk, chopped
2-3 Garlic Cloves, diced
Sweet Onion, 1 slice

1 C. Cashews (soaked for 1/2 hr.)
1 T. Bragg's™
1/4 C. Olive Oil (cold pressed)
Sea Salt, to taste

1. In a food processor, blend the vegetables as fine as you can get them with the "S"-shaped blade.
2. Drain the water from the cashews. Add to processor and whiz along with remaining ingredients. (Or use soaked almonds or sunflower seeds instead of cashews.)
Stop periodically and scrape sides with a rubber spatula. Continue to blend until creamy.
3. Chill and serve.

"I have lived primarily on sprouted seeds, beans, grains and nuts for more than two decades. Not only have I healed my body of colitis and arthritis following such a regimen, but I have also achieved a greater level of vitality and health than I had even as a child-and I am no child at seventy seven. And my hair has returned to its natural brown color, too!"

ANN WIGMORE, D.D. (1909-1994)
teacher, author, living foods proponent
quoted from: <u>The Sprouting Book</u>,
Avery Publishing Group

Pink Paté

yields 1 soup-sized bowl

1 Garlic Clove, diced
1/2 C. Sweet Onion, diced
2 T. Oil (cold pressed)
1-2 T. Bragg's™ or Sea Salt, to taste

1 3/4 C. Cashews (soaked 10 min.)
1 C. Beet, grated
Corn Kernels from 1 Cob

1. In a food processor, whiz the garlic, onion and liquids first; then add the softened cashew pieces. Add the beet and corn kernels. Whiz until smooth and creamy, occasionally scraping sides with a rubber spatula.
2. Chill to solidify before serving.

Sunny-Almond Paté

serves 2-4

2 Carrots (small), sliced
1/4 of a Beet, sliced
2 Onion Slices
1/2 C. Almonds, soaked
1/2 C. Sunflower Seeds, soaked

2 T. Bragg's™ or Sea Salt, to taste
4 T. Water
2 T. Oil (cold pressed)
1 t. Herb Seasoning

1. In a food processor, blend the carrots, beet and onion finely using the "S"- shaped blade. Add the soaked nuts and remaining ingredients. Blend until smooth and creamy. Use a rubber spatula to scrape the sides periodically.
2. Chill before serving, allowing it to solidify. Great as a healthy spread for sandwiches or Nori rolls.

Raw Hummus

serves 4

1 1/2 C. Garbanzo Beans, sprouted
3 T. Parsley (fresh), finely chopped
1 1/2 T. Raw Tahini
2 Garlic Cloves

2 T. Lemon Juice
2 t. Herb Seasoning
1 t. Cumin

In a food processor homogenize sprouted garbanzo beans. Blend in remaining ingredients and bring to a smooth consistency. Chill and serve.

"Pity melts the mind to love."

JOHN DRYDEN (1631-1700)
English poet and playwright

Creamy Corn Soup

yields 3 cups

2 1/2 C. Sweet Corn Kernels
1/4 C. Raw Tahini
1 C. Date Soak Water

1 T. Nutritional Yeast (optional)
1- 2 T. Green Onion, chopped
1/4 t. Sea Salt

Remove corn from cob. Blend all ingredients in a blender and serve. (If corn is very sweet, filtered water can replace date water.)

Corn Sesame Chowder

yields 3 cups   *recipe from: Optimum Health Institute*

2 C. Corn (removed from cob)
1 1/2 C. Sesame Milk
1 Green Onion
1/3 Avocado

1 t. Liquid Vegetable Seasoning
  (or Sea Salt, to taste)
1/4 t. Coriander
1/8 - 1/4 t. Nutmeg (fresh), grated

1. Blend sesame seeds (1/3 C.) with a small amount of water and purée. Add additional water to make 1 1/2 cups of milk.
2. Put 1 1/3 cups of corn and remaining ingredients in a blender. Blend until very smooth (about 3 minutes).
3. Put remaining kernels of corn into individual bowls, add soup, stir and serve.

Spinach Cilantro Soup

yields 3 1/2 cups   *recipe from: Optimum Health Institute*

3 C. Spinach Leaves
1 C. Cilantro (fresh)
1 1/2 C. Tomato Juice (fresh)
1 C. Carrot Juice (fresh)
1 Avocado (large)

2 Cloves Garlic
4 Green Scallions
1/2 t. Kelp
1/2 t. Basil
1/2 t. Onion Powder

1. Wash and remove stems from spinach and cilantro.
2. Place juice and all ingredients in a Vita-Mix or strong blender. Blend thoroughly and serve fresh or chilled.

"The conscience is God's presence in man."

EMANUEL SWEDENBORG (1688-1772)
Swedish theologian, scientist and philosopher

Rawsome Entrées

Oat Groat Energizer

serves 4-5

2 C. Oat Groats (soaked 10-12 hrs.)	2 T. Bragg's™ or Sea Salt, to taste
2 Celery Stalks, diced small	4 T. Fresh Lemon Juice
1 C. Sprouts, chopped	2 T. Oil (cold pressed)
(buckwheat or sunflower)	2 T. Nutritional Yeast
2 T. Onion, diced	Cayenne Pepper, dash
2 T. Parsley (fresh), chopped	

Drain the oat groats. Mix all ingredients together in a bowl. Allow to marinate before serving.

Sunflower Vegetable Burgers

yields 8-10 burgers

1/2 C. Almonds	5 Carrots, grated finely
4 C. Sunflower Seeds	1 Beet, grated finely
2 Celery Stalks, diced	3 T. Bragg's™ or Sea Salt, to taste
1/2 Bell Pepper, diced	1 T. Raw Tahini
2 Scallions/small Sweet Onion, diced	3 T. Nutritional Yeast

1. Soak the almonds 4-5 hours and the sunflower seeds for at least 1/2 hour. Drain the nuts and seeds.
2. Dice celery, pepper and onions and place in a bowl.
3. Put the drained seeds through the Champion® juicer to homogenize (not juice) or put them into a food processor and make into a paste. Save 1/2 cup of whole sunflower seeds for texture.
4. Mix the paste with the diced vegetables. Add the finely grated carrot and beet.
   (These can also be put through the champion juicer for a smoother consistency.)
   Add the seasonings, tahini and nutritional yeast, and mix well.
5. Form into patties and dehydrate for 3 hours (in the oven at 105°) until dry on the outside, and firm. They can also be left un-dehydrated.

"To admit that we have the right to inflict unnecessary suffering is to destroy the very basis of human society."

JOHN GALSWORTHY (1867-1933)
English novelist and dramatist
Recipient of 1932 Nobel Prize for literature

Mexican Mostadas

Serves 5-6

Tostada

2 C. Flax Seeds	Cumin, pinch
1 1/4 C. Fresh Water	1 t. Garlic Powder
4 T. Bragg's™ or Sea Salt, to taste	1 t. Onion Powder
2 T. Nutritional Yeast	1 C. Grated Carrots
1 T. Mexican Spice	1 C. Pumpkin Seeds (raw)

1. Mix together water, Bragg's™, nutritional yeast, Mexican spice, cumin, onion powder and garlic powder. Add flax seeds and let sit for 30 minutes, until gelled.
2. Add carrots and pumpkin seeds; mix.
3. Spread onto Teflex® sheets into four flat circles per sheet.
4. Dehydrate at 103° for 2 hours (in dehydrator or oven). Flip to other side and dehydrate 2 more hours or until crispy.

Guacamole for Mostadas

6 Haas Avocados
1 Cob Sweet Corn
1 6-oz. Can Olives
1 t. Bragg's™ or Sea Salt, to taste

1. Mash avocados. Cut corn off the cob. Slice olives.
2. Mix all ingredients together until creamy.

Salsa: Double the Fresh Salsa recipe (page 206) and add one clove garlic, finely diced.

Other ingredients: Sunflower or Alfalfa Sprouts

Putting together Mexican Mostadas

1. Spread guacamole on tostada.
2. Spread salsa on guacamolé.
3. Top with fresh sprouts and a spicy nasturtium flower.
4. Serve immediately for maximum tostada crispness.

> "Truth is the secret of eloquence and of virtue, the basis of moral authority. It is the highest summit of art and life."
>
> FREDERICK AMIEL (1821-1881)
> Swiss philosopher and poet

Beets-a Pizza

yields 6-7 small pizzas

Crust
2 C. Flax seeds, after soaking 10 min.
1 C. Beet, grated
2 C. Sunflower Seeds, soaked 15 min.
3 Ears of Corn (medium)
1/4 C. Onion
2 T. Basil (fresh)
1 T. Oregano (fresh)
1 t. Onion & Garlic Powder (each)
1 Clove Garlic (large)
1 t. Sea Salt

Red Sauce
1 Whole Tomato
2 t. Bragg™ Liquid Aminos
2 T. Nutritional Yeast
3 oz. Sun-Dried Tomatoes
1 T. Oregano
1/2 C. Basil (fresh)
1/4 C. Olive Oil (cold pressed)
3 Dates (pitted), soaked 10 min.

White Sauce
2 1/2 C. Brazil Nuts (soaked)
1 1/2 T. Lemon Juice
1-2 t. Sea Salt
1 t. Bragg™ Liquid Aminos
1 - 1 1/4 C. Water
1/4 C. Nutritional Yeast

Toppings
1 C. Beets, grated
1 C. Carrots, grated
2 Tomatoes, diced
1 C. Olives, sliced
1/2 C. Basil (fresh), chopped
1/2 C. Onion, diced

Final Topping
1 C. Walnuts or Almonds
1 T. Nutritional Yeast
2 t. Oregano (dried)
1 T. Basil (dried)
1 t. Sea Salt

1. Crust: soak flax seeds, adding dry seasonings to the water. In a food processor, using the "S"- shaped blade, chop the beet into fine pieces. Add soaked sunflower seeds to the processor and whiz to a paste, adding a little water if necessary. Remove from processor. Place remaining Crust ingredients, including soaked flax seeds, into processor and blend. Combine with first mixture. Thoroughly mix in a bowl. Form into 3-4" flat circles on dehydrator sheets and dehydrate for 5-7 hours until crust is firm. (Remember to flip crusts over half way through)
2. Red Sauce: soak dates and dried tomatoes until soft, with just enough water to cover. Blend all ingredients in a blender, with date and tomato soak water.
3. White Sauce: drain Brazil nuts & whiz ingredients in a food processor until smooth.
4. When ready to serve, place dehydrated crust on a plate. Spread on red sauce and then white sauce. Top with grated beets, carrot, diced tomato, olives, onion and fresh herbs.
5. Blend Final Topping ingredients in a food processor and sprinkle on top.

Raw Parmazano (alternative topping for pizza)

yields 3/4 cup

1/2 C. Almonds, ground
1/4 C. Nutritional Yeast

1/2 t. Spike™ Seasoning

1. Grind almonds in a food processor using the "S"- shaped blade.
2. Put in a jar and add nutritional yeast and Spike™.
3. Sprinkle on your salad, pasta, raw pizza, etc.

Pesto Pizza
yields 6 small pizza pies

Raw Pizza Crust
4 C. Sprouted Wheat Berries
1 t. Onion Powder
1 t. Basil (dried)
1 t. Oregano (dried)
1/2 t. Garlic Powder
Pesto Sauce
1 C. Pine Nuts
1-2 Garlic Cloves, diced
1-2 C. Basil (fresh), chopped

1/8 C. Water
2 T. Bragg's™ or Sea Salt, to taste
1 T. Nutritional Yeast
Toppings
1/8 C. Carrots, grated
3/4 C. Carrot & Beet, grated
1-2 Tomatoes, diced
1/3 C. Onion, diced
1/3 C. Peppers, diced
1/3 C. Mushrooms, sliced

1. Put sprouted wheat berries through a Champion® juicer. Use the juicing screen. This will remove some of the excess gluten. Discard the liquid.
2. Thoroughly mix the remaining dough ingredients in with the wheat berries.
3. Press dough into small, personal-sized circles on flat dehydrating sheets (4 per sheet). Dehydrate at 100° for 3 hours; turn over and continue for another three hours until dough is firm but not dried out. (If you don't have a dehydrator, place the pizza crusts in an oven at 100° for several hours, or use a solar dryer.)
4. Blend all pesto sauce ingredients in a food processor until creamy. Spread on finished rounds of pizza crust.
5. Top with the toppings and serve.

Stuffed Sweet Peppers
yields 10

10 Sweet Yellow Peppers (young)
2 Tomatoes, diced
1 Cucumber, diced
2 T. Basil, chopped (fresh)

1/4 t. Sea Salt
2 T. Nutritional Yeast
Italian Tomato Sauce (pg. 208)

1. Cut stem end off peppers, and remove with core and seeds. Trim off and save any good pepper from this. Place peppers in a dish with sides where they fit tight and hold each other up.
2. Dice the extra pepper pieces and mix in a bowl with tomato, cucumber, basil, sea salt and nutritional yeast.
3. Make Italian Tomato sauce and mix 1/2 cup of the sauce in with the tomato cucumber mixture. Pour this into each pepper, filling to just below the top.
4. Top the peppers with extra tomato sauce and sprinkle with the Raw Parmazano (pg. 214).
5. Serve with extra tomato sauce on top or on the side.

Tasty Wild Rice Burritos
Serves 5

2 C. Wild Rice = 4 C. Sprouted	1 6-oz. Can Olives
3 T. Bragg's™ or Sea Salt, to taste	2-3 Avocados, cubed
1/4 t. Cumin	1-2 Tomatoes, diced
2 T. Nutritional Yeast	1/8-1/4 C. Cilantro, chopped
1 Clove Garlic, diced finely	Chard Leaves or Lettuce Leaves

1. Soak wild rice for 2 nights, draining and rinsing after the first day, and again before use.
2. Mix Bragg's™, cumin, nutritional yeast, and garlic into sprouted rice, stir together.
3. Dice olives, avocados, tomatoes and cilantro, fold into rice mixture.
3. Wrap like a burrito in full lettuce or chard leaves.

Stuffed Tomatoes
Serves 4

4 large Tomatoes, ripe but not soft	1 t. Sea Salt
2/3 C. Carrot, grated	1 T. Cilantro, chopped
1 C. Avocado, cubed	1 t. Lemon Juice
1/2 C. Avocado, mashed	1 T. Dill, chopped (optional)

Sauce

Drained Juice from Tomatoes	1 t. Bragg's™ or Sea Salt, to taste
2 T. Cashews (soaked & drained)	1 t. Lemon Juice
3 T. Avocado	

1. Remove stem and slice 1/8" off the top of the tomato. Scoop out the inside and put it in a strainer, over a bowl. Save the liquid, on the side, for the sauce.
2. Mix strained tomato insides with other stuffing ingredients (all but the sauce ingredients). Then fill the tomato shells with this mixture. Place on a serving plate.
3. In a blender, blend Sauce ingredients, adding water only if needed. Sauce should be thick. Pour over tomatoes. Garnish and serve.

"The highest realms of thought are impossible to reach without first attaining an understanding of compassion."

SOCRATES (469-399 BC.)
Greek philosopher

Seed Balls

serves 12   *recipe from: Optimum Health Institute*

1 Green Pepper	1/2 C. Sesame Seeds
1 Bunch Green Onions	1 C. Sunflower Seeds
1 Bunch Celery	1 T. Dehydrated Basil
1 Yellow Onion	1 T. Caraway or Dill
1 Bunch Parsley	1-2 t. Dulse (a seaweed)
3 Zucchini (small)	1-2 t. Garlic Powder

1. Finely mince green pepper, green onions, celery, yellow onion and parsley. Place in a bowl. Shred zucchini and add to the bowl. Mix.
2. Grind seeds to a fine powder and add to mixture. Grind basil and either caraway or dill. Add and mix well. Add dulse and garlic and mix thoroughly.
3. Form into balls. Dehydrate at 102° until firm, but not hard; about 6 hours.

Mock Salmon Loaf with Almond Curry Sauce

Serves 4   *recipe from: Optimum Health Institute*

2 C. Almonds (soak & drain)	2 t. Kelp
2 Carrots (medium)	1 t. Curry Powder
1 C. Celery, diced	1/4 C. Carrot Juice
1/2 C. Green Onions, diced	1/4 C. Tomatillo Juice

1. With a Champion juicer, using the blank insert, homogenize the almonds and carrots alternating one and the other.
2. In a bowl mix celery, onion, seasonings and juice. Add the homogenized carrots and almonds; then mix thoroughly.
3. Shape mixture into a loaf. (Also delicious made into veggie burgers and dehydrated.)
4. Top loaf or burgers with Curry Almond sauce (pg 208) .

The Optimum Health Institute of San Diego
6970 Central Ave., Lemon Grove, CA. 91945
Telephone # (619) 464-3346
E-Mail Address: optimum@optimumhealth.org

"Love animals: God has given them the rudiments of thought and joy untroubled. Do not trouble their joy, don't harass them, don't deprive them of their happiness, don't work against God's intent."

FYODOR DOSTOEVSKY (1821-1881)
Russian novelist

Italian Zucchini Boats

yields 4 boats

2 Zucchini
1/2 T. Lemon Juice
1 t. Bragg's™ or Sea Salt, to taste
1/8 C. Oil (cold pressed)
2 C. Carrot & Beet (each), grated
1/2 t. Oregano
1/2 t. Basil

1/2 t. Garlic Powder
2 t. Nutritional Yeast
1/4 C. Scallion, diced
1/2 t. Dill Weed
1/2 t. Herb Seasoning
1 T. Apple Cider Vinegar (raw)

1. Wash the zucchini. Remove the stem. Slice in half lengthwise. Scoop out insides carefully (avoid breaking the outer shell).
2. Place the zucchini shells in a shallow plate or dish with lemon juice, Bragg's™ and oil to marinate (1/8 C. water can replace oil).
3. Grate the insides of the zucchini, carrots and beets. Mix all together and season with the remaining ingredients.
4. Fill the shells with the grated vegetable mixture. Chill and serve.

Raw Nori Rolls

yields 6 rolls

6 Nori Sheets
2 C. Paté or Spread
1 C. Carrots, shredded
1 C. Beets, shredded
1 Avocado, sliced

4 C. Sunflower Sprouts or Baby Greens
1 C. Marinated Mushrooms (combo of: Oil, Bragg's, Spices and Vinegar or Lemon)
Dipping Sauce
1 t. Bragg™ Liquid Aminos & 2 T. Water
1 t. Nutritional yeast & dash Cayenne

1. Lay out the Nori sheets. Place a scoop of paté on each sheet (see recipes pg 209 & 210), keep the paté at the bottom of the sheet and spread to the edges.
2. Sprinkle with beet and carrot shreds. Add sliced avocado. Layer Sunflower sprouts. Top with marinated mushrooms. Roll up tightly.
3. Slice the roll into 6-8 rounds. Serve with a bowl of dipping sauce.

"Veganism isn't just a strict vegetarian diet; it is a complete philosophical viewpoint. It is practical in outlook, simple to understand and aspires to the highest environmental and spiritual values. I am sure it holds the key to a future lifestyle for a humane planetary guardianship..."

HOWARD LYMAN
ex-cattle rancher turned vegan
international lecturer; author: Mad Cowboy

Dehydrated Breads and Crackers

Sprouted Breads

Sprouted breads have been around for centuries. These "breads" now born again in the new age, are becoming a staple in the raw food diet. The whole wheat berries will have more gluten and make a sweeter more doughy bread. Juicing the wheat berries first takes the gluten out and makes a lighter, crisper bread. Directions for sprouting wheat berries are given on page 182.

Sweet Wheat Bread
yields 8 loaves

4 C. Sprouted Wheat Berries	1/4+ C. Raisins
2 Small Bananas, sliced	1 T. Maple Syrup (optional)

1. Juice wheat berries in a Champion® Juicer, removing gluten.
2. Mix in raisins, bananas, and sweetener.
3. Flatten or make small thin loaves on a tray to dehydrate. Dehydrate for 5 hours. Flip over for another 3-4 hours until bread is firm and not sticking to tray.

Herb Essene Bread
yields 8-10 loaves

4 C. Sprouted Wheat Berries	3 T. Parsley (fresh)
1/2 C. Carrots, finely grated	2 T. Basil (fresh)
Sea Salt (or other seasoning), to taste	(or substitute favorite herb)

1. Homogenize wheat berries through the Champion Juicer. (Use the juicing screen, to remove some gluten and excess liquid.)
2. Mix in grated carrots, seasonings and herbs to dough.
3. Flatten or form into thin loaves and put on trays to dehydrate. Dehydrate four hours; flip over and continue dehydrating until firm. (You may use a solar dryer which will take a little longer, approximately 12 hours.) If a dehydrator is not available, dehydrate in the oven below 101°.

> *"In fact, every kind of creature that does not eat meat was there, living peaceably and happily with the others in this land where vegetable food abounded..."*
>
> HUGH LOFTING (1889-1947)
> British author
> from: Dr. Dolittle's Post Office

Sunflower - Wheat Essene Bread
yields 8-10 rounds

4 C. Wheat Berries, sprouted	1 T. Basil (fresh)
2 1/2 C. Sunflower Seeds, soaked	1 T. Oregano (fresh)
1 C. Beet, grated	1 t. Onion Powder
1/2 C. Carrots, grated	1 t. Garlic Powder
1 t. Sea Salt	

1. To make crust, homogenize sprouted wheat berries and drained sunflower seeds through a Champion®, or blend in a food processor. Thoroughly mix in the remaining ingredients.
2. Press into rounds (4 to a sheet); dehydrate for 5-7 hours, or until crust is firm.

Raw Chapati
yields 1 large chapati

4 C. Sprouted Wheat Berries	2-3 t. Fresh Herbs
3 T. Sesame Seeds	1 t. Olive (or other oil)

1. Juice wheat berries through Champion® Juicer; mix in Spike™ or other seasoning.
2. Lightly oil the baking sheet or dehydrating tray and sprinkle with sesame seeds. Roll or flatten out dough and place on sheet, on top of the sesame seeds.
3. Dehydrate at 101° for 3 hours; flip over for another 2-3 hours or until crust is firm.

Carrot Sunflower Crackers

3 C. Sunflower Seeds	2 Garlic Cloves
1/2 C. Walnuts	3 T. Basil (fresh), chopped
7 Carrots (large)	1/4 Onion
2 Beets	1- 2 T. Fresh Herbs

1. Homogenize all ingredients, except seasoning, through a Champion® Juicer.
2. Mix well, adding the seasoning.
3. Roll or flatten onto dehydrating tray and dehydrate for 4 hours at 104°. Cut to cracker size, spread out on tray and continue to dehydrate until crisp. (Longer drying will increase the crispness)

"I do not see any reason why animals should be slaughtered to serve as human diet when there are so many substitutes.
After all, man can live without meat."

TENZIN GYATSO, 14th DALAI LAMA of Tibet
Tibetan Buddhist priest

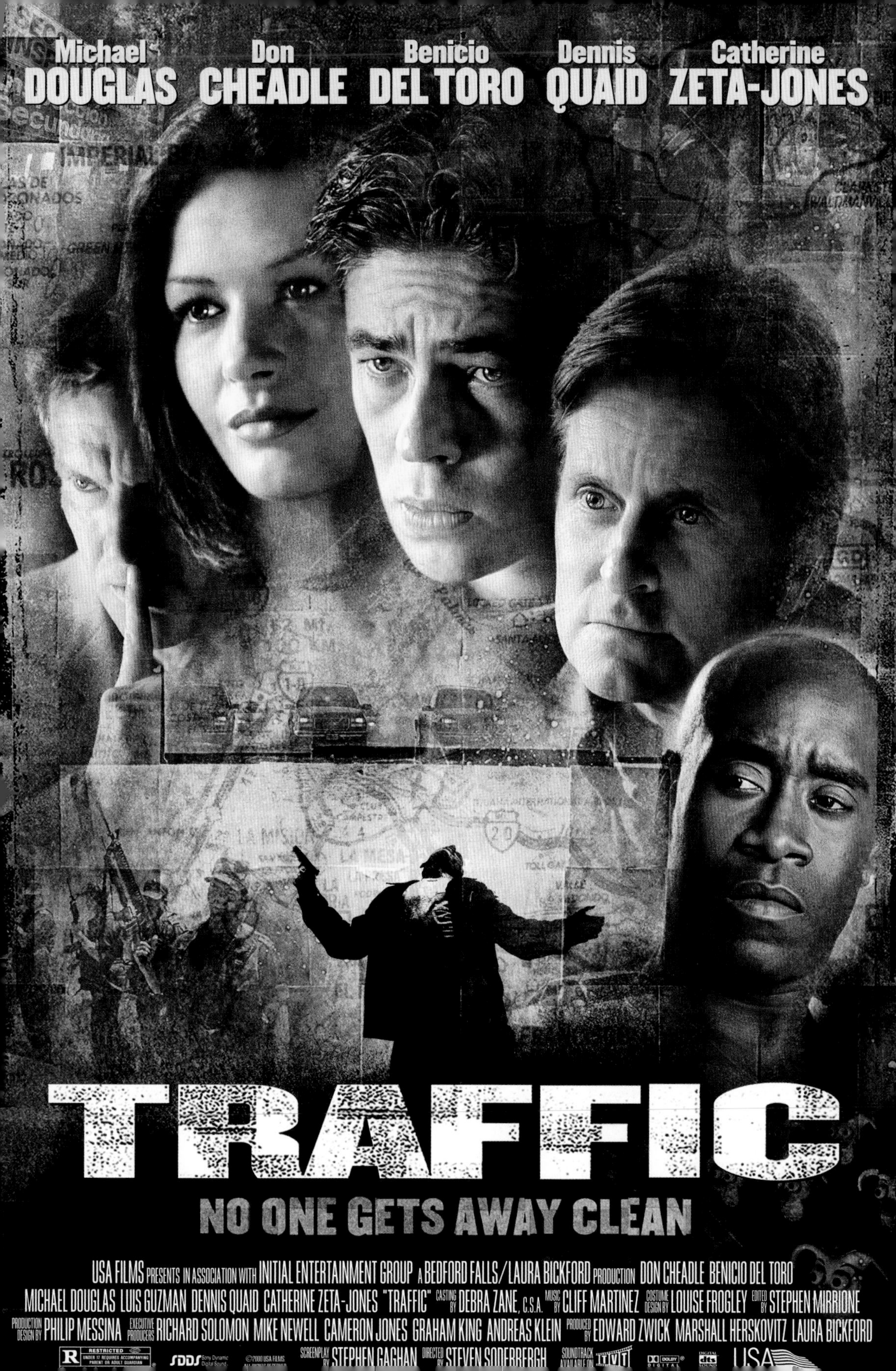
Michael DOUGLAS
Don CHEADLE
Benicio DEL TORO
Dennis QUAID
Catherine ZETA-JONES
TRAFFIC
NO ONE GETS AWAY CLEAN
USA FILMS PRESENTS IN ASSOCIATION WITH INITIAL ENTERTAINMENT GROUP A BEDFORD FALLS/LAURA BICKFORD PRODUCTION DON CHEADLE BENICIO DEL TORO
MICHAEL DOUGLAS LUIS GUZMAN DENNIS QUAID CATHERINE ZETA-JONES "TRAFFIC" CASTING BY DEBRA ZANE, C.S.A. MUSIC BY CLIFF MARTINEZ COSTUME DESIGN BY LOUISE FROGLEY EDITED BY STEPHEN MIRRIONE
PRODUCTION DESIGN BY PHILIP MESSINA EXECUTIVE PRODUCERS RICHARD SOLOMON MIKE NEWELL CAMERON JONES GRAHAM KING ANDREAS KLEIN PRODUCED BY EDWARD ZWICK MARSHALL HERSKOVITZ LAURA BICKFORD
R RESTRICTED UNDER 17 REQUIRES ACCOMPANYING PARENT OR ADULT GUARDIAN
SDDS Sony Dynamic Digital Sound
©2000 USA FILMS
SCREENPLAY BY STEPHEN GAGHAN DIRECTED BY STEVEN SODERBERGH
SOUNDTRACK AVAILABLE ON
DOLBY DIGITAL
DIGITAL dts SOUND
USA

This winter, Amazon.com hosts the official movie website for "Traffic."

TRAFFIC, a new film from director Steven Soderbergh (OUT OF SIGHT, ERIN BROCKOVICH), deals with the high-stakes, high-risk world of the drug trade, as seen through a series of interrelated stories. The U.S. President's new Drug Czar (Michael Douglas) must deal with his increasingly drug-addicted teenage daughter; an undercover DEA agent (Don Cheadle) becomes involved in the dangerous world of dealers and informants; a Mexican policeman (Benicio Del Toro) finds himself caught in a web of corruption; and a pampered wife (Catherine Zeta-Jones) living in upscale suburban America takes over her husband's drug empire with the help of her scheming lawyer (Dennis Quaid).

TRAFFIC opens nationwide January 12th, 2001.

Visit www.amazon.com/traffic for:

◆ **Exclusive Amazon.com streaming video interviews**
   with:
   Michael Douglas
   Catherine Zeta-Jones
   Benicio Del Toro
   Don Cheadle
   Director Steven Soderbergh

◆ **The movie trailer and photo gallery**

◆ **Cast and crew biographies and filmographies**

◆ **Local movie showtimes** (starting January 12th, 2001)

◆ **Production notes and discussion board**

"Bold in scope, 'Traffic' showcases Steven Soderbergh at the top of his game, directing a peerless ensemble cast in a gritty, multi-faceted tale that will captivate you from beginning to end...by far one of the best movies of the year."
Mark Englehart, Amazon.com Film Editor

"★★★★★ This is Steven Soderbergh's best film...The superb ensemble cast is uniformly outstanding...This is a must-see and one of the most ambitious films to come out of the studio system in years."
Amazon.com Customer Comment

W W W . A M A Z O N . C O M / T R A F F I C

USA
FILMS

R RESTRICTED
UNDER 17 REQUIRES ACCOMPANYING
PARENT OR ADULT GUARDIAN
Pervasive Drug Content, Strong Language,
Violence And Some Sexuality.

amazon.com

Sunflower- Corn Chips

2 1/2 C. Sunflower Seeds (sprouted)	1 1/2 C. Corn Kernels (fresh)
2 Carrots	1/2 t. Sea Salt
1/2 C. Flax Seeds (soaked) =1/4 C. Flax Seeds with 1/4 C. Water	

1. Soak 1 2/3 cups of dry, hulled sunflower seeds (when sprouted = 2 1/2 C.)
2. Peel and cut carrots and blend in a food processor with the "S"- shaped blade until finely chopped. Add remaining ingredients and blend thoroughly.
3. Press into chip circles on Teflex® sheets and dehydrate for 5-6 hours until crispy, flipping half way through. Serve with your favorite dip or Nacho Sauce (pg. 207).

Carrot-Sesame Crackers

Carrots, (30 small or 20 medium-sized)	3/4 C. Almonds (soaked)
1 Beet, sliced	1/4 C. Walnuts
2 Garlic Cloves	1/4 C. Basil (fresh)
3 C. Sunflower Seeds (soaked)	2-3 t. Spike™ Seasoning
1/4 C. Parsley (fresh)	1/2 C. Sesame Seeds

1. Peel the carrots and homogenize through the Champion® Juicer with the rest of the ingredients, except the sesame seeds and Spike™. (Do not juice.)
2. Thoroughly mix together in a bowl, adding the Spike™ Seasoning and sesame seeds.
3. When mixed, roll or press onto dehydrating sheets. Dehydrate for 3-4 hours at 104° on one side; turn and dehydrate for 3 more hours on the second side, until crisp.

Sunflower Spread (for crackers)

2 C. Sunflower Seeds (soaked 1 hr.)	2 T. Fresh Dill
5 Carrots, peeled and sliced	1 T. Bragg's™ or Sea Salt, to taste
3 T. Water	3 T. Nutritional Yeast
2 T. Fresh Herbs	1/4 C. Onion, diced

In a food processor, blend carrots and sunflower seeds using the "S"- shaped blade. Add water to help blade spin; then add the remaining seasonings. Serve chilled.

" On a diet of raw plant foods, the diseased cells heal, the emaciated ones recuperate, the inactive regain their vitality... Raw nutrients spread throughout the body, relax the organs, and grant health, strength, vigor, long life and success."

ARLIN, DINI, & WOLFE
American authors
Nature's First Law; The Raw Food Diet

Rawsome Treats and Beverages

Frozen Banana

1. Freeze only very ripe bananas (brown speckles on the peel).
2. When bananas are ripe, remove peel. Tip ends if necessary and cut away any bruised spots. Place in a plastic bag and freeze overnight or longer.
3. Use frozen bananas for smoothies, sorbét, yogurt and "Nice Cream" (a soft ice cream alternative). Slice banana and dip in carob sauce or tahini-maple syrup sauce for a quick and delicious treat. Homogenize frozen bananas through a Champion® Juicer, alone or with nut butter, for a soft ice cream.

Banana 'Nice' Cream

6 Bananas, frozen
2 T. Raw Tahini (variation: Almond or other Nut Butter)

1. Homogenize frozen banana through a Champion® Juicer. Add tahini or nut butter for a richer ice cream. (Blend in food processor if you don't have a Champion.) Eat immediately or freeze for a firmer 'Nice Cream'.
   •Variation: Make a serving of Carob-Tahini Fudge (pg. 225) and swirl through the 'Nice Cream'.

Banini or Vanilla (Malted) Shake
yields 1 blender

Ice Cold Water
4 Bananas, peeled & frozen, sliced
1 t. Vanilla

1/4 C. Raw Tahini
1 T. Maple Syrup
1 Banana (fresh), peeled

1. In a blender, start with 1 cup of ice cold water. Add the remaining ingredients and blend. If too thick, add more water. Sweeten to taste.

   • Suggested variations: strawberry banini, carob banini, carob-mint banini

Carob Smoothie

1 C. Ice Cold Water
1 3/4 C. Frozen Banana Slices
2 1/4 T. Nut Butter or Tahini

1 T. Date Sugar or Maple Syrup
1 T. Carob Powder
1/8 t. Mint Oil (optional)

In a blender, blend all the ingredients. Use ice cold water for best results.

222

Orange-Banana Smoothie

> 1 C. Orange Juice (fresh)
> 1 1/2 C. Banana, frozen and sliced (peels removed before freezing)

Blend together in a blender. Refreshing and delicious!

Fresh Mango Smoothie

yields 2 glasses

> 1 Mango (medium size Hayden)   1 1/2 C. Banana, frozen and sliced
> 1 C. Orange Juice (fresh squeezed)

1. Remove the fresh mango from pit and place in a blender (include juice). Add the orange juice.
2. Add the frozen banana slices, a little at a time, and blend. Serve immediately.

Tropical Fruit Smoothie

yields 4 cups

> 1 Papaya (fresh or frozen)   2 Bananas (peeled & frozen), sliced
> 1 C. Mango (fresh)   1 1/2 C. Orange or Pineapple Juice (fresh)
> 1/2 C. Pineapple, cubed

Cut the fruit into small pieces and place in a blender; add half of the juice and blend. Add the remaining juice and blend thoroughly.

Summer Harvest Blend

yields 4 cups

> 2 Bananas (peeled & frozen), sliced   2 Peaches or Nectarines
> 1 C. Strawberries   1 1/2 C. Apple Juice
> 1/2 C. Blueberries or Raspberries

Slice the bananas and peaches. Place half of the fruit in a blender with half of the juice and blend. Add the remaining fruit and juice and blend thoroughly.

"The gods created certain kinds of beings to replenish our bodies...they are the trees and the plants and the seeds."

PLATO   (circa 428-347 B.C.)
Greek philosopher

Papaya Pleasure Smoothie
yields 3/4 of a blender

2-3 Strawberry Papayas (fresh/small)	1/2 t. Vanilla
1 C. Ice Cold Water	1-2 T. Maple Syrup
2 Bananas (peeled & frozen), sliced	1 Banana (fresh)

In a blender, blend all ingredients.

Fresh Fruit Sorbét
serves 2-3

3 Bananas (peeled & frozen), sliced	1/2 C. Pineapple (frozen), sliced
1 C. Mango (frozen), sliced	1/2 C. Orange Juice (fresh)
1 C. Papaya (fresh or frozen)	

Mix all ingredients together in a food processor (or Vita Mix®) a little at a time, blending into a cream. Delicious served immediately. • Variation: Freeze to make sherbet.

Wheatgrass/Orange Juice Cocktail
Serves 2

2 C. Orange Juice (fresh)
2 oz. Wheatgrass Juice (fresh)
Squeeze of Lime

Mix the above ingredients and drink immediately for full vitality.

Aloe-Orange Julius

1 1/2 C. Orange Juice
4 T. Fresh Aloe (scooped out from skin)
1 oz. Wheatgrass Juice (optional)

Blend aloe with orange juice until smooth. Add wheatgrass juice and blend again. Serve.

> *"It ill becomes us to invoke in our daily prayers the blessings of God, the Compassionate, if we in turn will not practice elementary compassion towards our fellow creatures."*
>
> MAHATMA GANDHI (1869-1948)
> Hindu pacifist, spiritual leader

Coconut-Cashew Balls

yields 12 balls

3/4 C. Cashew Pieces
6 Medjool Dates, pitted
3 T. Maple Syrup

3 T. Raw Tahini
6 T. Coconut (fresh), shredded or grated

1. Place all the ingredients in a food processor and blend, using the "S"- shaped blade.
2. Roll into balls and refrigerate or freeze before serving.

Carob Tahini Fudge

yields about 2 cups

1 C. Carob Powder
1/2 C. Raw Tahini
2 Dates, pitted, soaked in 1/8 C. water

1/4 C. Maple Syrup
1/8 C. Water

Blend all ingredients thoroughly in a food processor. Freeze and serve.

Carob Chunkies

yields 8 chunkies

1/3 C. Raw Tahini or Nut Butter
1/4 C. Carob Powder
1/4 C. Maple Syrup

1/4 C. Sunflower Seeds
1/3 C. Raisins
1/4 C. Shredded Coconut

Mix ingredients in a bowl. Drop by spoonful onto a plastic plate and freeze.

Maple-Coconut Treats

yields 9-10 balls or cookies

1 1/4 C. Coconut (fresh), grated
1 C. Raisins
3 T. Maple Syrup

4 Dates (Medjool), chopped
1/3 C. Raw Tahini

1. Mix all ingredients together in a bowl.
2. Form into cookies and refrigerate, or freeze for a more solid treat.

"Let us ask what is best, not what is customary..."

SENECA (c. 5 B.C.-A.D. 65)
Spanish-born Roman philosopher, statesman, scholar

Raw Apple Pie

yields 1 pie

Crust
1/4 C. Water (or date soak water)
3/4 C. Walnuts, soaked
1/2 C. Almonds, soaked
3/4 C. Pecans, soaked
8 Dates, pitted, soaked
1 C. Raisins
1 1/2 C. Oats
1 t. Apple Pie Spice

Filling
2-3 Bananas (ripe), sliced
1 T. Maple Syrup
6 C. Apples, peeled, cored, grated
6 Dates, pitted, chopped
1/4 C. Lemon Juice, (optional)
    with additional sweetener
1/2 C. Raisins (optional)
Garnish: Pecans, Strawberries, Raisins

1. Soak all nuts, dates and raisins for 20-30 minutes.
2. In a food processor, using the "S"- shaped blade, blend the oats and pie spice (cinnamon, nutmeg and allspice combination) until it becomes a flour. Remove from processor. Optional: blend in 1/4 cup of dry almonds.
3. Add the date soak water, dates, raisins and nuts to the processor and blend. Add the oat flour mixture to it. Batter should be fairly dry; if too wet add some more oats.
4. Press into a pie shell.
5. Slice 2 bananas into 1/4" rounds. Lay each slice flat next to each other to cover the pie shell bottom.
6. In the food processor, blend the maple syrup, 1 cup of the grated apples and 1 banana, until creamy.
7. Add mixture to the remaining 5 cups of grated apples. Optional: add 1/2 cup raisins and/or 1/4 cup lemon juice (if adding lemon juice, add more maple syrup). Add dates. Mix.
8. Place the filling into pie shell on top of banana slices. Garnish with pecan halves and raisins or strawberry slices. Chill for several hours and serve.

Blueberry Cream Pie

yields 1 pie

Crust
1/4 C. Dates, pitted, soaked
1/2 C. Walnuts
1/4 C. Almonds

Filling
2-3 Bananas (medium)
1 lb. Blueberries (fresh or frozen)
1/2 C. Dates (pitted)

1. In a food processor, using the "S"- shaped blade, blend the 3 crust ingredients well.
2. Pat mixture into bottom and sides of a pie plate, forming a crust.
3. Slice the bananas into 1/4" rounds, leaving 1/4-1/2 of 1 banana for the creamy filling. Spread a layer of banana pieces on the bottom of the pie shell, covering it completely.
4. In a food processor, blend 1 1/2 cups of the blueberries with the remaining piece of banana and 1/2 cup of dates. Mix in the remaining blueberries (whole). Pour this over the sliced bananas in the pie shell. Chill and serve.

Raw Fruit Pie

yields 1 pie

<u>Crust</u>
2/3 C. Whole Oats
2/3 C. Walnuts
1/3 C. Cashew Pieces
3/4 C. Dates, pitted
1/3 C. Almonds, soaked 15 minutes
2 T. Maple Syrup

<u>Filling</u>
1 Apple, peeled, diced small
1/2 C. Raisins
1 Mango (large, or 2 small)
2 Bananas (ripe), sliced
2-3 Kiwi Fruit
2 T. Agar-Agar

1. In a food processor using the "S"- shaped blade, grind the oats into a flour. Then blend all ingredients in the first column,
2. Sprinkle a little carob on the bottom of the pie plate, then press batter into it, forming a crust. (The carob helps to keep it from sticking.)
3. Place the apple, 1 sliced banana, 1 diced kiwi fruit and raisins in the pie shell.
4. In a processor, blend the large mango and one ripe banana. Add 2 tablespoons of agar-agar. Pour this mixture over the fruit and mix together.
5. Decorate the top with sliced kiwi fruit and/or strawberries and raisins. Chill for several hours before serving.

Tropical Mango-Banana Pie

yields 1 pie

<u>Crust</u>
3/4 C. Almonds, soaked 15 minutes
3/4 C. Pecans
3-4 Dates, pitted
1/2 C. Raisins, soaked 1 minute

<u>Filling</u>
2 C. Mango (2 Mangoes)
1 1/2 Bananas
2 Bananas, sliced
Fruit (of choice), sliced
1/2 C. Raisins

1. In a food processor using the "S"- shaped blade, blend the crust ingredients. Remove and press evenly into pie plate and chill.
2. In food processor, blend mango and banana.
3. Slice 2 bananas into 1/4" rounds and layer on the bottom of the pie crust. Cover with sliced fruit of choice and sprinkle in the raisins. Spread in some of the mango-banana sauce and mix it with the fruit. Pour remaining sauce on top.
4. Decorate and chill for several hours. (Place in the freezer 1/2 hour before serving.)

> "...Again, there may be some people in the future who...being under the influence of the taste for meat, will string together in various ways sophistic arguments to defend meat eating... But...meat eating in any form in any manner and in any place is unconditionally and once for all prohibited."
>
> The BUDDHA (circa 563-483 B.C.)
> Indian Avatar, <u>Lankavatara Scripture</u>

Outrageous Raw Pie Crust

yields 2 pie crusts

1 3/4 C. Rolled Oats
1 3/4 C. Pecans/Walnuts/Almonds (mix)
4 Dates, pitted, soaked 10 minutes
1 1/2 t. Vanilla

3/4 t. Cinnamon
1/4 C. Macadamia Oil (cold pressed)
1/2 C. Dried Bananas
3/4 C. Maple Syrup

1. In a food processor using the "S"- shaped blade, grind the oats. Remove oats and set aside. Add the nuts and chop, finely. Then, add all the remaining ingredients into the food processor and blend. Mix with the oats.
2. Shape into a pie plate and fill with your favorite fruit medley.

Marble Nice Dream Pie

yields 1 pie

Crust
1/3 C. Shredded Coconut (dried)
1/2 C. Walnuts
1/2 C. Almonds
1/3 C. Raw Carob

1/2 t. Vanilla
6 Dates, soaked 10 minutes
1/2 C. Sunflower Seeds, soaked 15 minutes
1/3 C. Raisins

1. Blend crust ingredients in food processor using the "S"- shaped blade.
2. Sprinkle a little dry carob into the bottom of the pie plate. Press crust into pie plate.

Carob Sauce
4 T. Raw Tahini
8 Dates, soaked 10 minutes
1/2 t. Vanilla

1 Banana, peeled & frozen
3/4 C. Raw Carob
Date soak water, small amount

Blend in blender until thick and creamy. Place in freezer until ready to use.

Nice Dream Filling
12 Bananas, peeled & frozen
15 Dates, soaked 10 minutes

5 T. Raw Tahini
2-3 T. Coconut, shredded

1. Homogenize through Champion® Juicer, alternating ingredients.
2. Mix half of the 'Nice Dream' filling with the carob sauce, to make carob 'Nice Dream'
3. Put the carob and vanilla 'Nice Dream' into the pie crust and swirl. Top with shredded coconut. Freeze overnight. Remove from freezer 5 minutes before serving.

> *"Slowly but surely, humanity realizes the dreams of the wise."*
>
> ANATOLE FRANCE (1844-1924)
> French novelist, poet and critic
> 1921 Nobel Prize recipient

Angel's Fig Bars
yields 32 delicious raw goodies!

<u>Crust</u>
3 C. Rolled Oats
1 1/2 C. Walnuts
1 1/2 C. Almonds
25 Dates (soaked in water 10 minutes)
1/2 t. Cinnamon
1 1/2 t. Vanilla

<u>Filling</u>
80 Black Mission Figs (small),
  de-stemmed, soaked 10-15 minutes
1 C. Dates, soaked in water
1 t. Vanilla

1. In a food processor, using the "S"- shaped blade, process the oats into a flour.
   Remove from the processor.
2. Process the nuts to a fine consistency. Add oat flour and blend. Remove from processor.
3. Return half the mixture to the processor and add half of the soaked dates, 1/4 t. cinnamon
   and 1/2 t. vanilla. Process together and then remove. Do the same with the other half.
   Remove from processor.
4. In the food processor, blend the soaked figs with 1 cup of the date soak water, along with
   1 t. of vanilla.
5. Take half the crust and roll it on to a flat cookie sheet. (Wax paper on top will prevent the
   crust from sticking to the rolling pin.) Cut into 2" by 2" squares and set aside.
6. Take the rest of the crust, roll it on to a flat cookie sheet and evenly spread all of the fig
   mixture on top.
7. Place the pre-cut squares of crust on top of the fig filling. Cut each square through to the
   bottom crust .
8. Lift each fig bar off the tray with a spatula on to a serving dish or into a sealed container
   to stay fresh. It will keep well in the refrigerator for about a week.

> "A raw and living food diet is loaded with enzymes, crammed with
> vitamins and minerals, abundant in oxygen, complete with
> available proteins, and is especially high in fiber. "

BRIAN R. CLEMENT
<u>Hippocrates Health Program;</u>
A Proven Guide to Healthful Living
Hippocrates Publications

Carob Coconut Cookies

yields 12 cookies

1 C. Carob Powder	1/4 C. Maple Syrup
1/2 C. Coconut (fresh), grated	1/4 C. Water
1 Banana	1/2 t. Vanilla
3 Dates, pitted, soaked 10 minutes	1 C. Shredded Coconut

1. In a food processor, thoroughly blend all ingredients, except the shredded coconut.
2. Spread the shredded coconut on a tray. Scoop out 2 tablespoons of the blended mixture and place on the dry shredded coconut. Flatten and turn over so the coconut coats the entire outside.
3. Place flat on a sheet for dehydration and repeat with the rest of the carob mixture. Dehydrate or freeze for 2 hours to help the cookie maintain form.

Oat Cookies

yields 18 medium cookies

3 Bananas (ripe)	1 C. Oat Flour
2 T. Maple Syrup	4 C. Whole Rolled Oats
2 t. Vanilla	3/4 C. Raisins
1/2 C. Date Sugar	1/2 C. Walnuts, chopped
3 t. Cinnamon	1/2 C. Almonds, chopped

1. Mix bananas, maple syrup, vanilla and date sugar. Separately mix the remaining 3 dry ingredients. Add the dry to the wet and mix. Soak raisins, walnuts and almonds for 15 minutes. Chop nuts and fold with raisins into the cookie batter.
2. Pat into cookies and dehydrate at 104° for 1 hour, flip, and dehydrate for 1 more hour.
   • Variation: Use the same batter (sprinkled on dehydrator sheet). Dehydrate until firm.

Date-Nut Cookies

yields 15 cookies

1 C. Figs, de-stemmed, soaked 10 min.	1/2 C. Raisins, soaked 2 minutes
1/2 C. Dates, pitted	1/4 C. Shredded Coconut
1 C. Pecans, soaked 2 minutes	1 T. Raw Tahini
1/2 C. Walnuts, soaked 2 minutes	

1. In a food processor, blend the figs first. Add the remaining ingredients and blend again.
2. Form into small cookies and place in the refrigerator to solidify.

> *"...The principle of nonviolence necessitates complete abstention from exploitation in any form."*
>
> MAHATMA GANDHI (1869-1948)
> Hindu pacifist, spiritual leader

Just Desserts

"The average age (longevity) of a meat-eater is 63. I am on the verge of 85 and still at work as hard as ever. I have lived quite long enough and am trying to die, but I simply cannot do it. A single beef-steak would finish me, but I cannot bring myself to swallow it. I am oppressed with a dread of living forever. That is the only disadvantage of vegetarianism."

GEORGE BERNARD SHAW (1856-1950)
Anglo-Irish author and playwright

Apple Pie
yields 1 pie

Crust
1 3/4 C. Whole Wheat Pastry Flour   1/2 C. Oil
1/4 C. Soy Powder or Pastry Flour   1 t. Vanilla
1/4 C. Orange Juice

1. Combine flour and soy powder in a bowl.
2. Thoroughly mix wet ingredients together in a separate bowl.
3. Mix dry ingredients into the wet. Dough should be wet enough to hold together and dry enough not to stick to your fingers. It is best to use this dough immediately for easier rolling. (Or chill sealed until ready to use.)
4. Split dough in half, leaving 1 slightly larger. Roll each half between 2 pieces of wax paper, (dampen a flat surface and place wax paper on it, flattening to remove bubbles) or use flour to keep it from sticking. Roll from the center outward, until even, 1/8-1/4" thick.
5. Place the larger rolled dough in pie plate (sides & bottom); gently press into the corners.

Filling
5-6 medium apples   1 1/2 t. Cinnamon
  (preferably Rome Beauty)   1/4 C. Sucanat™ or other dry sweetener
1 t. Vanilla   Nutmeg & Allspice, a dash (optional)

1. Peel and core apples. Cut into bite-sized pieces. Mix with other ingredients.
2. Place apples into pie crust. Cover with second piece of rolled dough, seal edges with fingers or a fork, and make a few air holes on the top with fork. Bake in a pre-heated oven at 350° for 25-30 minutes, until crust is golden brown.

Apple Crisp
yields 1 medium-sized baking casserole (9" x 12")

8 C. Apples, peeled and sliced   1 C. Sweetener (or Maple syrup)
1/2 C. Cashew Milk or Rice Milk   1/4 t. Nutmeg
2 C. Rolled Oats   1/4 t. Allspice
1 3/4 C. Pastry Flour   1 t. Cinnamon
   1/2 C. Oil or Vegan Margarine (melted)

1. Cover the bottom of a baking dish with the sliced apples.
2. Pour the cashew milk (2/3 C. cashews blended with 1 quart water will make a blender of cashew milk OR 1 rounded t. cashew butter blended with 1/2 C. water) or rice milk over apples.
3. Mix together all dry ingredients, including sweetener.
4. Add oil or melted vegan margarine to dry mixture and mix well. Crumble over the top of the apples, covering them thoroughly.
5. Bake in a pre-heated oven at 350° for about 40 minutes, until browned on top and apples are soft (test with a fork).

Apple Turnovers
yields 10-12

Filling	Dough
5 C. Apples, peeled, (cut into small pieces)	1 3/4 C. Whole Wheat Pastry Flour
1 1/2 t. Cinnamon	1/4 C. Soy Powder
1/4 t. Nutmeg	1/4 t. Cinnamon
1/4 t. Allspice	1/4 C. Orange Juice, cold
1/4 C. Dry Sweetener	1/2 C. Oil
	1 t. Vanilla

1. Filling: Mix together apples, spices and sweetener. Set aside.
2. Dough: Mix dry ingredients together in a bowl.
3. In a separate bowl, mix wet ingredients, using a whisk to homogenize orange juice and oil.
4. Slowly pour dry mixture into wet batter. Mix thoroughly, using your hands at the end to knead in flour. Dough should not be too dry so that it falls apart, but dry enough not to stick to your fingers. It is best to use this dough immediately for easiest rolling or chill (well sealed) until use.
4. On wax paper, roll dough into a long rectangle and cut into squares (about 6).
5. Place the apple filling in the squares one at a time and fold the dough corner to corner, making a triangle, and seal the edges. (It can be folded any way as long as it seals the apples in).
6. Place the turnovers on a tray lightly oiled, or on baking paper. Bake in a pre-heated oven for 30 minutes at 350° until browned on top and bottom.

Chocolate Mousse I
serves 3-4

1 lb. Tofu (soft, not silken)	4 T. Cocoa Powder
3 T. Oil (not a strong-flavored oil)	2 T. Carob Powder
1/2 T. Tahini	1/3 C. Maple Syrup
6 T. Sweetener	1 t. Vanilla

Chocolate or Carob Chips (dairy-free), melted (optional)

In a food processor, blend all ingredients until smooth and creamy, scraping sides with a rubber spatula periodically. Chill in parfait glasses before serving.

"The question is not, Can they reason? nor, Can they talk? but, Can they suffer?"

JEREMY BENTHAM (1748-1832)
English philosopher
An Introduction to: The Principles of Morals and Legislation, 1789

Rich Chocolate Mousse II

serves 3

1 C. Sunspire™ (dairy-free) Chocolate Chips, melted	4 T. Maple Syrup
2 T. Carob Powder	2 T. Oil
2 T. Cocoa Powder	5 T. Sweetener (dry)
1/3 C. Water	1/2 C. Tofu (soft), mashed

1. Soften chocolate chips in a bowl by placing them in a warm oven.
2. In a food processor, first blend carob and cocoa powder with water and the melted chips. Then, homogenize all ingredients together thoroughly. Scrape the sides of the food processor with a rubber spatula and then whiz again.
3. Pour into 3 parfait glasses and refrigerate for a few hours. Serve chilled.

Chocolate Cream Pie

yields 1 pie

<u>Crust</u>

1/2 C. Oil	2 1/2 C. Whole Wheat Pastry Flour
1/3 C. Orange Juice	1 t. Baking Soda
1/2 C. Sweetener (dry)	

1. In a bowl, whisk together oil, orange juice and sweetener.
2. Sift flour and baking soda. Add dry ingredients to the wet and mix.
3. Chill batter for a few minutes to make rolling easier.
4. With a rolling pin, roll out batter between 2 pieces of wax paper, from the center out. Pat evenly into an oiled pie plate.
5. Bake in a pre-heated oven at 350° for 10 minutes.

<u>Filling</u>

1/3 C. Oil	1/3 C. Maple Syrup
1 lb. Tofu	4 T. Cocoa Powder
4 T. Carob Powder	4 T. Sweetener (dry)
	1 T. Arrowroot

1. In a food processor, blend all ingredients together, using the "S"- shaped blade.
2. Pour into partially baked pie shell. Bake for 30-35 minutes or until cream filling cracks.
3. Chill and allow to solidify before serving.

> *"Destiny, or karma, depends upon what the soul has done about what it has become aware of."*
>
> EDGAR CAYCE (1877-1945)
> American psychic diagnostician, clairvoyant
> holistic health proponent, author

Banana Dream Pie

yields 1 pie

Crust
2 C. Whole Wheat Pastry Flour
1/4 C. Date Sugar
1/4 t. Sea Salt
1/2 t. Cinnamon
1/3 C. Oil
1 T. Water or Nut Milk
1/8 C. Sorghum/Liquid Fruitsource
1/8 C. Molasses

Filling
3-4 Bananas (ripe)
1 t. Vanilla
1 T. Lemon Juice
1/2 C. Oil
1 C. Date Sugar
1/4 C. Sorghum/Fruitsource
1/4 t. Sea Salt
2 1/2 C. Tofu
2 T. Arrowroot

1. To make the crust: Mix the dry ingredients together. Mix the oil, water, sorghum and molasses. Add to the dry and work with your fingers.
2. Oil a 9" pie plate. Pat dough on bottom of pie plate and half way up the sides; pressing it in evenly.
3. Partially bake for 10 minutes and then remove from oven.
4. In a food processor, using the "S"- shaped blade, blend the filling ingredients until creamy.
5. Pour batter into the partially baked pie shell. Bake in a pre-heated oven at 350° for 20-25 minutes. Remove from oven. Cool and refrigerate for 3-4 hours. Serve.

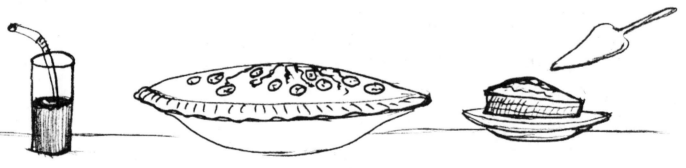

"In my humble opinion, non-cooperation with evil is as much a duty as is cooperation with good."

•••

"I do not regard flesh-food as necessary for us at any stage and under any clime in which it is possible for human beings ordinarily to live. I hold flesh-food to be unsuited to our species."

MAHATMA GANDHI (1869-1948)
Hindu pacifist, spiritual leader

"Cheesecake" Custard Pie

yields 1 9" pie

Crust

1/4 C. Orange Juice	2 C. Whole Wheat Pastry Flour
1/3 C. Oil	1 1/2 t. Baking Soda
1/2 C. Sweetener (dry)	

1. In a bowl, whisk orange juice, oil and sweetener.
2. Sift pastry flour and baking soda.
3. Pour dry ingredients into wet and stir to make a dough.
4. Chill for 5-10 minutes. Roll between two pieces of wax paper from the center out. Place into an oiled pie plate, evenly pressing it around sides and bottom.
5. Bake in a pre-heated oven for 5 minutes at 350° and then remove from oven.

Filling

2 1/2 C. Tofu, mashed, drained of water (over 1 lb. of tofu)	7 T. Sweetener (dry)
1/3 C. Oil	1/2 t. Vanilla
6 T. Nutritional Yeast	1/2 t. Sea Salt
6 T. Lemon Juice (fresh)	2 T. Arrowroot
2 T. Maple Syrup	1 t. Ener-G™ Egg Replacer

1. Blend all ingredients in a food processor.
2. Pour into the pie shell and bake for 35 minutes or until crust is golden brown.
3. Cool and refrigerate, allowing to solidify before serving.

Vanilla-Maple Pudding

serves 2-3

1/2 - 3/4 lb. Tofu	2 T. Tahini
4 T. Maple Syrup	3-4 T. Fructose
1 T. Oil	1 1/2 t. Vanilla

1. In a food processor, whiz ingredients, periodically scraping sides with a rubber spatula.
2. Blend until creamy smooth. Chill and allow to solidify before serving.

• Variation: Serve in a parfait glass with layers of chocolate mousse (see recipe pg. 234).

"All great truths begin as blasphemies."

GEORGE BERNARD SHAW (1856-1950)
Irish playwright and social reformer,
1925 Nobel Prize recipient

Sweet Brown Rice Pudding
serves 8

3 1/2 C. Water
1 C. Short Grain Brown Rice (uncooked)
1/2 t. Sea Salt
1/2 C. Raisins
1/2 C. Sucanat™

1/4 C. Maple Syrup
1 1/2 C. Non-Dairy Milk (soy, rice, nut)
1 t. Vanilla Extract
1/2 t. Cinnamon

1. In a medium-sized pot, bring water to a boil. Stir in rice and salt. Reduce heat to low. Cover, simmer 45-50 minutes or until rice is very soft. Uncover and boil gently 5 minutes or until most of the water evaporates. Stir in raisins, sweeteners and milk. Mix well.
2. Cook 12-15 minutes, on medium-low heat, until rice absorbs most of the milk and mixture is thick (pudding will thicken as it cools).
3. Pour into shallow (heat safe) bowl. Allow to cool. Add vanilla and cinnamon and stir. Chill, stirring occasionally. Serve.

Jewish Noodle Pudding
yields 1 medium-sized baking dish

1 lb. Flat Wide Noodles (not egg)
1 lb. Tofu (firm), mashed well
1/2 C. Sweetener (mixture of liquid & dry)
1/4 C. Soy Milk or Cashew Milk
1/3 C. Oil
1/4 C. Tahini

1 T. Vanilla
1 t. Cinnamon
Nutmeg, a pinch
2/3 C. Raisins, (soaked in water
　　　15 minutes and drained)

1. In a large saucepan, cook noodles in plenty of boiling water for 10-12 minutes.
2. Place tofu in a medium-sized bowl and mash. Then add sweetener, soy milk, oil, tahini, vanilla, cinnamon and nutmeg. Fold in and mix very well. Mix in soaked raisins.
3. Place cooked noodles in a casserole dish and add tofu mixture, tossing lightly. Bake in a pre-heated oven at 325° for 25 minutes. Sprinkle cinnamon atop.

•Variation: Add 1/2 cup of chopped apricots or apples.

> *"First it was necessary to civilize man in relation to man. Now it is necessary to civilize man in relation to nature and the animals."*
>
> VICTOR HUGO (1802-1885)
> French poet, novelist and playwright

Carob Pudding

yields 5 cups

1 1/4 C. Tofu
1 1/4 C. Cashew Butter
Water, to blend
2 t. Vanilla

1/2 C. Carob
3/4-1 C. Dry Sweetener
5 T. Arrowroot

1. In a blender, blend tofu and cashew butter with water, until creamy. Add remaining ingredients and blend thoroughly.
2. Pour into a saucepot and heat on low, stirring continuously until it bubbles through the center. When it bubbles, it will be thickened. Pour immediately into small cups, refrigerate and serve chilled.

Rich Nut Pudding

Serves 2-3

3 C. Macadamia and Cashew nuts
2 t. Vanilla
8 T. Arrowroot

1 1/2 C. Dates (pitted), soaked
overnight in 4 1/2 C. water
(or in boiling water if not soaked)

1. In a food processor or blender, whiz all ingredients (in 2 batches).
2. Pour into saucepan over medium-heat.
3. Stir constantly with a whisk until it bubbles. Remove from heat and pour into cups. Cool and refrigerate. Serve.

Coconut Date Pudding

serves 4

1 C. Dates (pitted)
4 1/2 C. Boiling Water
1 (14) oz. Can Coconut Milk

8 T. Arrowroot
Cinnamon, to sprinkle

1. Soak dates in the boiling water for 5 minutes. In a blender, whiz the coconut milk with the soaked dates and their soak water. Add the arrowroot and blend.
2. Pour into a saucepan over medium-heat. Stir constantly with whisk until thick. Once it bubbles, turn heat off.
3. Pour into cups. Cool and refrigerate. Sprinkle with cinnamon on top of each cup.

"It is almost a definition of a gentleman to say he is one who never inflicts pain."

CARDINAL NEWMAN (1801-1890)
English Cardinal

Fluffy Carob Cake
yields 2 cake pans

2 C. Tofu Milk (thick)
2/3 C. Oil
2 t. Vanilla
1/2 C. Maple Syrup
1 1/2 C. Sweetener (dry)

3 C. Whole Wheat Pastry Flour
3/4 C. Carob
  (or Cocoa Powder), sifted
1 1/2 t. Baking Soda
1/2 t. Sea Salt

1. In a blender, make 2 cups of thick tofu milk using 7-8 oz. of soft tofu and adding water. Start with a small amount and add more until you reach the 2 cup mark on the blender.
2. Add oil, maple syrup, vanilla and sweetener to the blender and blend.
3. In a bowl, sift all dry ingredients and mix.
4. Pour the blender mixture into the bowl and mix well. Batter will be loose.
5. Pour batter into 2 small oiled cake pans, filling half way, leaving room for cakes to rise.
6. Bake in a pre-heated oven at 350° for approximately 40 minutes, or until a toothpick comes out dry. Allow to cool before slicing. Perfect cake every time!

• Use this recipe for making cup cakes, as well. Pour batter into an oiled muffin tin.

'Peacetime' Cake
yields 1 cake

'The wartime cake' came to be when eggs and milk were rationed during World Wars. Here's the updated vegan version:

Wet
1 C. Sweetener (dry)
1 1/4 C. + 2 t. Water
1/3 C. Oil
2 C. Raisins

Dry
2 C. Whole Wheat Flour
1 t. Baking Soda
1 t. Baking Powder
1/2 t. Salt
1/2 t. Nutmeg
2 t. Cinnamon
1/2 t. Cloves (ground)

1. Oil and flour a 9" cake pan or loaf pan.
2. In a saucepan, mix all the Wet ingredients. Boil for 3 minutes. Cool.
3. Sift flour, baking soda and powder. Combine with salt & spices in a mixing bowl. Stir.
4. Add Wet to the Dry and mix.
5. Pour batter in cake pan and bake in a pre-heated oven at 325° for 50 minutes.

> *"The obvious is that which is never seen until someone expresses it simply."*
>
> KHALIL GIBRAN (1883-1931)
> Lebanese poet, author and artist

Ambrosia Cake

yields (2) 9" cakes

2 1/2 C. Sweetener (dry)	3 C. Pastry Flour
1/2 C. Oil	2 t. Baking Soda
2 1/2 C. Tofu Milk (tofu and water)	1 T. Baking Powder
2 t. Vanilla	1/2 t. Sea Salt
1 t. Almond Extract	1 C. Shredded Coconut
1 t. Lime (or Lemon) Extract	

1. Mix together sweetener, oil, vanilla, extracts and tofu milk (8 oz. tofu and 1 1/2 C. water).
2. In a separate bowl, sift remaining dry ingredients. Add shredded coconut. Mix.
3. Mix the dry into the wet. Divide batter into two lightly oiled cake dishes.
4. Bake in a pre-heated oven at 350° for 45 minutes or until a toothpick comes out dry.

•Serve with a white frosting (page 244) and a fruity topping (optional) over the frosting.

Carrot Cake

yields (2) 9" cakes

1 C. Tofu Milk (thick)	1/2 t. Allspice
3/4 C. Safflower Oil	2 t. Cinnamon
1 3/4 C. Sweetener (dry)	1/8 t. Cloves (ground)
4 C. Whole Wheat Pastry Flour	1 C. Raisins
1 1/2 t. Baking Soda	1 3/4 C. Carrots, grated

1. In a blender, put 1 cup of thick tofu milk (4 oz. tofu and 1/2 C. water). Add oil and Sucanat™ (or other dry sweetener), and blend.
2. Into a large bowl, sift the dry ingredients, mixing in the raisins and carrots.
3. Pour wet mix into the dry ingredients and stir well.
4. Pour into 2 small cake pans or a large baking dish.
   Bake in a pre-heated oven at 350° for 40-50 minutes or until a toothpick comes out dry.
5. Spread the following Frosting over the cake once cooled:

2 C. Tofu, mashed	1 1/2 C. Sucanat™ (or other sweetener)
1/2 C. Cashew Butter	3/4 t. Cinnamon
1/2 C. Peanut Butter	•Optional: 1-2 T. Maple Syrup for flavor

In a food processor, blend all ingredients. Chill before spreading on cake.

"It should not be believed that all beings exist for the sake of the existence of man..."

MAIMONIDES (Rabbi Moses ben Maimon) (1135-1204)
Spanish-born, Jewish rabbi, physician, philosopher, scholar

Chocolate Zucchini Cake

yields (2) 9" cakes

Dry
4 T. Cocoa Powder
2 1/2 C. Pastry Flour
1/4 t. Sea Salt
1/2 t. Baking Powder
1-1 1/2 t. Baking Soda, sifted

3/4 C. Oil
2 C. Sucanat™
2 T. Soy Powder & 4 T. Water
3/4 C. Tofu Milk (soft tofu & water blended)
1 t. Vanilla
2 C. Grated Zucchini

1. In a bowl, combine dry ingredients, sifted.
2. Whisk oil, sweetener, soy mixture, tofu milk and vanilla in a separate bowl.
3. Mix the dry and wet together well.
4. Add grated zucchini to batter.
5. Pour into 2 oiled 9" cake pans.
6. Bake in pre-heated oven at 350° for 30 to 40 minutes or until a toothpick comes out dry.
   • (Optional - top with 1/2 cup dairy-free carob chips.)

Vanilla Cake

yields (2) 9" cakes

2 1/2 C. Tofu Milk
3 t. Vanilla
1 t. Almond Extract or Oil
3/4 C. Oil
2 C. Sweetener (dry)

3 3/4 C. Pastry Flour
2 t. Baking Soda
2 t. Baking Powder
1/2 t. Sea Salt

1. In a blender, make tofu milk by blending 8 oz. tofu with 1-1 1/2 cups of water.
2. In a bowl, whisk together all ingredients in the first column.
3. Sift together dry ingredients.
4. Add the dry to the wet batter. Mix well.
5. Pour batter into 2 lightly oiled cake pans, filling each half way.
6. Bake at 350° in a pre-heated oven for 40- 45 minutes, or until a toothpick comes out dry.

• Mix tahini & maple syrup, to taste, for a quick and delicious frosting.

> *"The fact is that there is enough food in the world for everyone. But tragically, much of the world's food and land resources are tied up in producing beef and other livestock-food for the well-off, while millions of children and adults suffer from malnutrition and starvation."*
>
> DR. WALDEN BELLO
> Executive Director, Food First/
> Institute for Food and Development Policy

Marble Cake

yields (2) 9" cakes

2 1/2 C. Tofu Milk (thick)	3 3/4 C. Pastry Flour
3 t. Vanilla	2 t. Baking Soda
1 t. Almond Extract or Oil	2 t. Baking Powder
3/4 C. Oil	1/2 t. Sea Salt
2 C. Sweetener (dry)	

1. In a blender, begin with 8 oz. soft tofu and blend with 1 1/2 cups of water. Add water and/or tofu until you reach the 2 1/2 cup line on the blender.
2. In a bowl, whisk together all ingredients in the first column.
3. Sift together dry ingredients (second column). Add the dry to the wet batter. Mix well.
4. Split batter in half. Pour 1 half into 2 oiled cake pans, leaving it to one side.
5. Add the following ingredients to the half of batter still in the bowl. (If too thin, add more flour, if too thick, add more milk):

> 1/3 C. Carob
> 1/4 C. Sweetener
> 1/4 C. Tofu Milk

6. Add the carob batter to the other side of each cake pan and then fold in.
7. Bake at 350° in a pre-heated oven for 40-45 minutes or until a toothpick comes out dry.

Holiday Fruitcake

yields (2) 9" round cakes or 9" x 13" rectangle

2/3 C. Oil	
2 C. Sweetener (dry)	8 oz. Tofu
2 t. Vanilla	1 1/2 C. Water
1/2 t. Almond Extract	1/2 C. Raisins
1 1/2 T. Orange Juice	1/2 C. Walnuts, chopped
3 3/4 C. Whole Wheat Pastry Flour	1/2 C. Dates or Figs, chopped
1/2 T. Baking Soda	1/2 C. Apple, diced (or Banana)

1. In a bowl, whisk together the oil, sweetener, vanilla, almond extract, and juice.
2. In a separate bowl, sift together the flour and baking soda.
3. In a blender, blend the tofu and water.
4. Add the dry ingredients and the tofu mixture alternately to the wet ingredients. Stir well. Fold in the raisins, chopped fruit and nuts.
5. Pour batter into oiled and floured pans. Bake in a pre-heated oven at 350°. For small round cake pans, bake 25-30 minutes. For a rectangle, bake 35-40 minutes or until a toothpick comes out dry.
   • Ice with vanilla or orange frosting.

Crumb Cake
yields (2) 9" cake pans

4 C. Whole Wheat Pastry Flour
2 C. Sweetener (dry)
1 t. Cinnamon
1 t. Ginger Powder
3/4 t. Nutmeg
2/3 C. Oil
1 C. Raisins

1 C. Walnuts, chopped
1 3/4 C. Tofu Milk,
   (mixed with 4 t. Vinegar)
1 1/2 t. Baking Soda, sifted
2 t. Baking Powder, sifted
2 T. Ener-G™ Egg Replacer,
   (mixed with 4 T. Water)

1. Sift flour and combine with sweetener and spices in a bowl.
2. Mix in oil and set aside 2 cups of this crumbly mixture.
3. Stir raisins and walnuts into the remaining crumbly mixture.
4. To make tofu milk: blend 8 oz. soft tofu with 1-1 1/2 cups of water in a blender.
5. Add tofu milk, baking soda, baking powder and egg replacer mixture to batter. Mix.
6. Oil two small cake pans and pour thick batter in to them. Sprinkle the 2 cups of crumbly mixture on top.
7. Bake in a pre-heated oven at 375° for 40 minutes or until a toothpick comes out dry.

"Cheesecake"
yields 8 slices

Crust
2 C. Whole Wheat Pastry Flour
1 t. Baking Powder
1/4 t. Sea Salt
1/4 C. Sweetener (dry)
1/8 C. Maple Syrup
1/3 C. Oil (Safflower)
2 T. Water/Orange Juice

Filling
1 lb. Tofu (silken or soft)
4 T. Lemon Juice
1/4 t. Sea Salt
1 t. Arrowroot
1/2 - 3/4 C. Raw Sugar/Fructose
1/2 t. Vanilla
2 T. Nutritional Yeast

1. Sift the flour, baking powder and salt in a bowl. Mix the remaining crust ingredients in a separate bowl. Add the dry to the wet and mix.
2. Press dough into a 9" pie pan. Bake in a pre-heated oven 5-7 minutes at 350°; remove.
3. In a food processor, blend the filling ingredients until smooth. Pour into the pie crust.
4. Return to the oven for 15-18 minutes, or until the tofu turns pale yellow. Remove. Let cool and chill before serving.

"How narrow we selfish, conceited creatures are in our sympathies! How blind to the rights of all the rest of creation!"

JOHN MUIR (1838-1914)
American conservationist, naturalist, Sierra Club founder

Strawberry Tall Cake
yields 2 short or one tall cake

Cake
2 1/2 C. Tofu Milk	3 3/4 C. Pastry Flour
3/4 C. Oil	2 t. Baking Soda
1/2 t. Almond Extract	2 t. Baking Powder
3 t. Vanilla	1/2 t. Sea Salt
1 T. Orange Juice	1 t. Orange Rind, grated
2 C. Dry Sweetener	1 t. Lemon juice (optional)

1. In a blender, whiz 8 oz. soft tofu with 1 to 1 1/2 cups of water. Add tofu/water until you reach the 2 1/2 cup line on the blender. Tofu milk is thicker than store bought soy milk.
2. Whisk together all ingredients in the first column.
3. Sift together flour, baking soda and powder. Combine with remaining ingredients.
4. Add the dry to the wet batter and mix.
5. Pour batter into 2 oiled cake pans, filling each half way.
6. Bake at 350° in a pre-heated oven for 40- 45 minutes or until a toothpick comes out dry.

Frosting
Frosting	Strawberry Glaze
2 C. Tofu (soft)	1 Pint Strawberries, sliced
1/2 C. Sweetener	2 T. Arrowroot
1/2 C. Cashew Butter	2 T. Strawberry Jam
1 t. Vanilla	1 C. Fresh Strawberries, sliced

1. In a food processor, using the "S" - shaped blade, blend the frosting ingredients until creamy.
2. In a saucepan, heat the sliced strawberries with arrowroot and jam until the arrowroot thickens (20-30 minutes), stirring often.
3. To make one tall cake, use both cakes. For two short cakes, cut each cake in half horizontally (when cooled) using a sharp, serrated knife.
4. Spread cashew frosting on bottom layer. Pour enough of the strawberry glaze to cover the frosting. Put the second layer of cake on top of this and fully frost the top and the sides with the cashew frosting. Lay out fresh sliced strawberries on frosting and then pour the glaze on top letting it drip down the sides.
5. Serve immediately or refrigerate until serving.

White Cake Frosting
frosts 2 + cakes

1 1/3 C. Tofu (soft), pressed into cup	4 T. Sweetener (dry), Fructose
3 t. Cashew Butter	(fructose makes a whiter frosting)
2 T. Maple Syrup	

In a food processor, blend all ingredients together. Chill to solidify before using.

Chocolate/Carob Frosting

frosts 2 cakes

1 1/3 C. Tofu, mashed (pressed into cup)   4 t. Cashew Butter
4 T. Maple Syrup   5 T. Sweetener (dry)
2 T. Carob Powder   1 T. Cocoa Powder

In a food processor, blend all ingredients together. Chill before using.

Macadamia Nut Frosting

frosts 2 cakes

1 C. Tofu (soft), mashed   3/4 C. Sucanat™ + 1/3 C. Maple Syrup
1 C. Macadamia Nut Butter   1 t. Vanilla

In a food processor, blend all ingredients until smooth and creamy. Chill before using.

Melted Chocolate Chip Frosting

frosts 1-2 cakes

4 T. Water   1/4 C. Carob Powder
1-2 C. Chocolate Chips (non-dairy) 1/2 C. Sweetener (dry)

1. Melt all ingredients together in a small pot but do not boil. Stir.
2. Pour over cake. Allow to cool and solidify. Refrigerate until serving.

Peanut Butter Frosting

frosts 2-3 cakes

2 C. Tofu (soft), mashed   2 t. Vanilla
1/2 C. Peanut Butter   1/4 C. Maple Syrup
1 1/2 C. Sweetener (dry)   1/4 C. Tahini

In a food processor, blend ingredients thoroughly. Chill before using.

"Peace above all earthly dignities:
a still and quiet conscience."

WILLIAM SHAKESPEARE (1564-1616)
English poet and playwright

Cashew Icing

1 C. Cashew Butter
8 oz. Tofu (soft)

1 C. Sweetener (Fructose)
2 t. Vanilla

Blend all ingredients in a food processor, using the "S"- shaped blade.

Carob Sundae Sauce

1/2 C. Water
4 T. Carob Powder
2 T. Sucanat™ or Maple Syrup

3 T. Peanut Butter (heaping)
1 T. Rice Syrup

In a blender, blend all ingredients until smooth and creamy. Pour over homemade Banana-Peanut Butter 'Nice' Cream (which is a variation of Banana 'Nice' Cream on page 222), Imagine® Food's Rice Dream or Organic Soy Delicious™.

Chocolate Sauce

2 Squares Unsweetened Chocolate
1/3 C. Water
1/2 C. Sweetener (dry)

3 T. Vegan Margarine
1/2 t. Vanilla

1. Melt chocolate squares in water over low heat. Stir constantly.
2. Add sweetener. Bring to a boil for 2 minutes or until slightly thickened.
3. Add margarine and vanilla. Simmer and stir. Cool.

Frozen Carob Fudge

1/2 C. Water
6 T. Carob Powder
4 T. Sweetener (dry)

4-5 T. Peanut Butter
2 T. Rice Syrup or Sorghum

1. In a food processor, blend all ingredients.
2. Pour into a small, shallow, plastic container. Cover and freeze. Eat in the frozen state.

"Within 24 hours of birth, more than 90% of calves are taken away from their mothers forever."

ERIK MARCUS
<u>Vegan; The New Ethics of Eating,</u> McBooks Press

Almond Cookies
yields 34 cookies

2 1/2 C. Almonds, ground
2 C. Whole Wheat Pastry Flour
1 t. Baking Soda, sifted
1/2 t. Baking Powder, sifted
1 1/2 - 2 C. Sweetener (dry)

1/2 - 3/4 C. Water or Sunny Milk (pg. 22)
1 t. Almond Oil or Extract
3/4 C. Oil
1 t. Vanilla

1. Sift dry ingredients (except sweetener) together in a bowl.
2. Blend sweetener and remaining wet ingredients in a blender or with a whisk.
3. Add dry ingredients to the wet. Mix. Form into cookies. Place on lightly oiled baking sheets. Bake in a pre-heated oven at 350° for about 10 minutes or until golden brown.

Simple Almond Cookies
yields 25- 30 cookies

1/2 - 3/4 C. Oil
1 1/2 C. Sweetener (dry)
4 C. Whole Wheat Pastry Flour

3 1/2 T. Arrowroot Powder, sifted
2 C. Almonds, ground
1 1/2 C. Walnuts, ground

1. Mix oil and sweetener. Sift flour and arrowroot separately. Combine and add nuts.
2. Roll into cookies and bake at 350° for approximately 12-15 minutes, until golden brown.

Nutty Chocolate Chip Cookies
yields 48 cookies

2 1/2 C. Whole Wheat Pastry Flour
1 t. Baking Soda, sifted
2 C. Rolled Oats (quick cooking)
1/2 t. Sea Salt
1 T. Ener-G® Egg Replacer
1 3/4 C. Sweetener (dry)

1 C. Vegetable Oil
2/3 C. Tofu Milk (thick) (1/3-1/2 C. tofu, mashed, blended with 1/4 C. Water
2 t. Vanilla
10-12 oz. Vegan Chocolate Chips
1 C. Walnuts, chopped

1. Sift flour, baking soda and egg replacer into a bowl, and combine with oats and salt.
2. Blend sweetener, oil, tofu milk and vanilla in a blender.
3. Add wet mixture to the dry and stir. Add chocolate chips and walnuts. Mix.
4. Drop by spoonful onto an oiled cookie sheet (or baking paper). Bake in a pre-heated oven at 375° for 12-13 minutes.

"All that is needed for the triumph of evil, is that good men do nothing."

EDMUND BURKE (1729-1797)
Irish born English statesman, orator and writer

Crispy Almond Cookies

yields 20-25 cookies

1/2 C. Oil
1/2 C. Maple Syrup
1 T. Vanilla

1/4 C. Soy Powder
1 1/2 C. Pastry Flour
1 C. Almond Meal

1. Mix all ingredients together.
2. Form batter into cookies and bake in a pre-heated oven at 350° for 10-15 minutes, until bottoms are brown. Allow to cool and harden before eating.

Carob-Peanut Butter Cookies

yields 15 cookies

1 C. & 3 T. Pastry Flour
1/4 C. Carob (or Cocoa Powder)
1/4 t. Baking Soda, sifted
1/4 C. Oil

2 T. Sweetener
1 t. Vanilla
3/4 C. Peanut Butter

1. In a bowl, sift flour, carob and baking soda. Mix.
2. Mix the remaining ingredients separately. Mix dry into the wet to form a stiff, thick batter.
3. Roll spoonfuls of batter into balls and flatten onto an oiled cookie sheet (or baking paper).
4. Bake at 350° in a pre-heated oven until cracks appear on top and the bottoms begin to harden, approximately 8-10 minutes.

Carob Cookies

yields 20 cookies

2 1/4 C. Whole Wheat Pastry Flour
7 T. Carob Powder
1 t. Baking Soda
1/2 C. Maple Syrup

1/2 C. Sweetener (dry)
1/2 C. Oil
2 t. Vanilla
1/4 C. Tofu, mashed

1. Pre-heat oven. In a bowl, sift flour, carob and baking soda.
2. In a blender, blend sweeteners, oil, vanilla and tofu .
3. Add wet mixture to the dry and mix well.
4. Drop a teaspoon of batter for each cookie onto an oiled cookie sheet or baking paper.
5. Bake at 375° for 8-10 minutes or until cracks appear on top and the bottom begins to harden.

> *"You cannot make yourself feel something you don't feel. But you can make yourself do right, in spite of your feelings."*
>
> PEARL S. BUCK (1892-1973)
> American author

Carob-Coconut-Cashew Cookies

yields 24 cookies

2 1/2 C. Pastry Flour, sifted
6 T. Carob, sifted
1/2 t. Baking Soda, sifted
1/2 C. Shredded Coconut
1/2 t. Ener-G® Egg Replacer

Blender Ingredients
1/4 C. Oil
1/2 C. Cashew Butter
1/2 C. Water
1/2 T. Vanilla
1 C. Sweetener (dry)

1. Into a bowl, sift flour, carob and baking soda. Add shredded coconut and egg replacer.
2. In a blender, blend remaining ingredients. Pour wet ingredients into the dry. Mix together.
3. Oil a cookie sheet. Form batter into 24 small cookies (roll the batter into balls and then press down on sheet). Bake in a pre-heated oven at 350° for 10-15 minutes. Rotate trays while baking. Cookies are done when small cracks appear on the top and the bottom has hardened a bit. Allow to cool; then serve.

Coconut Cookies

yields 24 cookies

1/2 C. Maple Syrup
1/2 C. Sweetener (dry)
3/4 C. Oil
2 t. Vanilla
2 T. Soy Powder & 4 T. Water (mixed)

1 1/2 t. Almond Extract
3 C. Pastry Flour
1 1/4 t. Baking Soda, sifted
1 1/2 t. Baking Powder
3/4 C. Shredded Coconut

1. Combine sweeteners, oil, vanilla and soy powder mix and extract; whisk well.
2. Sift dry ingredients in a separate bowl, except coconut. Add coconut and stir.
3. Add dry ingredients to the wet and mix. Roll into cookies.
4. Bake at 350° in a pre-heated oven for 12-15 minutes or until bottom and top are golden brown. Allow to cool and harden before eating.

"Women who eliminate dairy products from their diet often experience great improvement in their menstrual cycle. One study found that women with PMS consumed five times more dairy products than women without PMS."

JOHN ROBBINS
American Author
Reclaiming Our Health
HJ Kramer Publisher

Pistachio Coconut or Cashew-Coconut Cookies

yields 30-35 cookies

2 C. Pistachios or Cashews, ground
1 C. Oats, ground
1 C. Shredded Coconut
1/2 C. Whole Wheat Flour
1/4 t. Sea Salt
1/2 t. Baking Powder

1 t. Baking Soda
1 C. Sweetener (of choice)
1/2 C. Oil
2 T. Soy Powder,
  mixed with 1/4 C. Water

1. In a medium bowl, stir cashews or pistachios with oats and coconut. Sift in flour, salt, baking powder and baking soda.
2. In a larger bowl, combine sweetener, oil and soy powder mixture.
3. Add dry ingredients into the wet. Mix well. Roll and flatten onto an oiled cookie sheet (or use baking papers).
4. Bake in a pre-heated oven at 350° for 12-15 minutes.

Light and Fluffy Spice Cookies

yields 30 cookies

4 C. Whole Wheat Pastry Flour
1 t. Egg Replacer
1 1/2 t. Baking Soda
3 t. Cinnamon
1/2 t. Nutmeg
1 t. Allspice

1/2 C. Maple Syrup
3 t. Vanilla
1/2 C. Oil
1/4 C. Tofu, mashed
1/2 C. Sweetener (dry)
1 C. Raisins (soaked and drained)

1. In a bowl, sift flour, egg replacer, baking soda and spices.
2. In a blender, whiz remaining ingredients, except the raisins soaked in water.
3. Pour wet mixture into dry; add raisins. Mix well. If batter is sticky, add a bit more flour.
4. Roll into balls and flatten onto an oiled cookie sheet (or use baking papers).
5. Bake at 350° in a pre-heated oven for approximately 10 minutes or until cookies crack a little on top and the bottoms becomes somewhat hardened.

"I will not kill or hurt any living creature needlessly, nor destroy any beautiful thing, but will strive to save and comfort all gentle life, and guard and protect all natural beauty upon the earth."

JOHN RUSKIN (1819-1900)
English author

Holiday Spice Cookies

yields 3 dozen

2/3 C. Oil	1 t. Baking Soda
1 1/4 C. Sweetener (dry)	4 t. Cinnamon
4 T. Tahini & 8 T. Water	1/4 t. Allspice
1 T. Vanilla	1/8 t. Nutmeg
4 C. Whole Wheat Pastry Flour	1 C. Raisins (soaked and drained)

1. In a large bowl, combine oil, sweetener, tahini and water mixture and vanilla. Mix well.
2. In a separate bowl, sift the flour, baking soda and spices. Stir in raisins.
3. Mix the dry mixture into the liquid mixture and stir to a smooth consistency.
4. The batter should be fairly dry. Roll batter into small balls and form into cookies. Place on an oiled cookie sheet. Bake in a pre-heated oven at 350° for 8 to 10 minutes, until bottoms are slightly browned.

Carob Chip Cookies

yields about 35 cookies

4 C. Whole Wheat Pastry Flour	1 Tofu Block, 2" by 2"
1 t. Baking Soda	1/2 C. Maple Syrup
2/3 C. Oil	1/2 t. Vanilla
1/4 C. Water (or less)	1 C. Carob Chips (Non-Dairy)
1/3 C. Sweetener (dry)	

1. In a bowl, sift together pastry flour and baking soda.
2. In a blender, blend remaining ingredients, except for carob chips. (Tofu is an egg replacer).
3. Pour wet mixture into the dry and mix thoroughly. If batter is sticky, add a bit more flour. Add the carob chips and mix. Shape into cookies.
4. Bake in a pre-heated oven at 350° until the cookies crack a bit on top (approximately 10 minutes). Rotate trays half way through, so they get evenly baked on the top and bottom.

> "....Why is compassion not part of our established curriculum, an inherent part of our education? Compassion, awe, wonder, curiosity, exaltation, humility—these are the very foundation of any real civilization..."
>
> YEHUDI MENUHIN (1916-1999)
> world-renowned violinist
> from: Just for Animals

Chips A' High Cookies
yields 35 cookies

4 C. Whole Wheat Pastry Flour
2 t. Baking Soda
1/2 t. Sea Salt
2 t. Egg Replacer mixed with 4 T. Water

1 C. Oil
2 t. Vanilla
3/4 C. Sweetener (dry)
1 1/4 C. Sunspire (non-dairy) Chocolate Chips

1. In a bowl, sift together flour, baking soda and salt.
2. In a separate bowl, mix together egg replacer mixture, oil, vanilla and sweetener.
3. Add dry ingredients to the wet batter. Stir in chocolate chips.
4. Drop a tablespoon of batter at a time onto a lightly oiled cookie sheet.
5. Bake in a pre-heated oven at 350° for 10-15 minutes or until cracks appear on top. Bottom should be lightly browned.

Oatmeal Chewies
yields 18-24 large cookies

2/3 C. Oil
3/4 C. Sweetener (dry)
3/4 C. Maple Syrup
1/2 C. Water
2 t. Vanilla
2 C. Whole Wheat Pastry Flour

1 t. Baking Soda
1/3 t. Sea Salt
3/4 t. Cinnamon
4 t. Soy Powder
6 C. Oats
1 1/2 C. Raisins

1. With a whisk, blend together oil, sweeteners, water and vanilla until fluffy.
2. Sift together flour, baking soda, sea salt, cinnamon and soy powder. Add dry to the wet and stir.
3. Add oats and raisins; mix thoroughly. Shape into cookies (large or smaller) and place on an oiled cookie sheet or baking paper.
4. Bake in a pre-heated oven at 350° for 12-17 minutes or until golden brown on the bottom.

•Optional: add 1-2 teaspoons of Maple or Almond Flavoring.

"People are the only animals that drink the milk of the mother of another species. All other animals stop drinking milk altogether after weaning. It is unnatural for a dog to nurse from a giraffe; a child drinking the milk of a mother cow is just as strange. It is not surprising that problems ensue from this inherently unnatural act."

MICHAEL A. KLAPER, M.D.,
American author and international lecturer
from: <u>Pregnancy, Children, and The Vegan Diet</u>

Outrageous Cookies
yields 2 dozen cookies

3 C. Whole Wheat Pastry Flour
1 T. Baking Powder
1/2 t. Sea Salt
1/2 t. Baking Soda
2 T. Egg Replacer,
   mixed with 3 T. Water

3/4 C. Oil
1 C. Sweetener (dry)
2 T. Maple Syrup
2 t. Vanilla
1/2 C. Raisins
1/2 C. Walnuts

1. Sift flour, baking powder, salt and baking soda into a bowl.
2. Mix wet ingredients together, including the sweeteners. Add the dry to the wet. Add raisins and walnuts. Mix.
3. Roll the cookies into balls and flatten onto an oiled cookie sheet (or baking paper). Bake in a pre-heated oven at 350° for 14-15 minutes. Allow to cool before serving.

• Use a vegan soy margarine in place of oil for a butter-type cookie.

Thumbprint Cookies
yields 1 dozen

1 1/4 C. Whole Wheat Pastry Flour
1/2 t. Baking Soda
1 C. Walnuts, finely chopped
1 T. Egg-Replacer,
   mixed with 2 T. Water

1/3 C. Oil
1/3 C. Sweetener
1/2 t. Vanilla
1/2 t. Almond Extract
5 oz. Fruit-Sweetened Jam

1. Sift together flour and baking soda in a mixing bowl. Add chopped walnuts.
2. Mix the water and egg-replacer with the oil, vanilla and almond extract.
3. Add the liquid to the dry. Mix well and chill in the freezer for 5-10 minutes.
4. Roll dough into small balls and flatten somewhat on an oiled cookie sheet or baking paper. Press thumb gently into center. Fill with jam.
5. Bake in a pre-heated oven at 350° for 10-13 minutes.

"...There slowly grew up in me an unshakable conviction that we have no right to inflict suffering and death on another living creature, unless there is some unavoidable necessity for it."

ALBERT SCHWEITZER, M.D. (1875-1965)
Alsatian philosopher and medical missionary;
1952 Nobel Prize recipient

Fruitie Tootie Thumbprint Cookies
yields 25 cookies

4 C. Whole Wheat Pastry Flour
1 t. Baking Soda
1/8 C. Water
1/4 C. Maple Syrup
1 C. Oil

2 T. Lemon/Lime Peels, grated
1/4 C. Tofu, mashed
3/4 C. Sweetener (dry)
1 t. Vanilla
10 oz. Fruit-Sweetened Jam

1. In a bowl, sift flour and baking soda.
2. In a blender, blend remaining ingredients well, except for the jam.
3. Pour wet mixture into the dry batter and mix. If batter is too sticky, add a little more flour.
4. Roll into little balls and flatten somewhat on an oiled cookie sheet, or use baking paper. Put a thumb print in the middle of each cookie and fill with 1/2 teaspoon jam.
5. Bake in a pre-heated oven at 350° for 10-15 minutes or until golden brown.

•A festive holiday cookie for any occasion.

Christmas Gingerbread Cookies
yields 30 cookies

1/4 C. Oil
1/2 C. Sweetener (dry)
3/4 C. Molasses
1/3 C. Water
3 1/2 C. Pastry Flour

1 t. Baking Soda
1/2 t. Allspice
1 t. Cinnamon
3/4 t. Ginger Powder
1/2 t. Cloves (ground)
1/4 t. Sea Salt (optional)

1. Whisk the wet ingredients, including sweetener, together in a bowl.
2. Sift the dry ingredients together in a separate bowl.
3. Pour wet ingredients into the dry and mix thoroughly.
4. Cover the batter and place in refrigerator for several hours.
5. Roll batter out between two pieces of wax paper and use cookie cutters to form shapes.
6. Bake in a pre-heated oven at 350° for 10-15 minutes or until golden brown.

"The world has been harsh and strange.
Something is wrong; there needeth a change."

ROBERT BROWNING (1812-1889)
English poet

Oatmeal Cookies
yields 28 cookies

6 C. Oats
2 C. Whole Wheat Pastry Flour
1 1/2 t. Baking Soda
1/2 t. Sea Salt
2 t. Cinnamon
2 C. Sweetener (dry)

2/3 C. Oil
2/3 C. Water
1/4 C. Tofu (soft)
2 t. Vanilla
1 C. Raisins

1. Place oats in a large bowl. Sift in flour, baking soda, salt and cinnamon.
2. Blend the sweetener, oil, water, tofu and vanilla in a blender. Pour the wet into the dry and mix well.
3. Fold in the raisins. Mix again.
4. Oil a baking sheet (or two). Form the dough into cookies and place on a tray. Bake in a pre-heated oven at 350° for 15 minutes.

Wheat-Free Chocolate Chip Cookies
yields 1 dozen+ cookies

Wet
1 C. Sweetener (dry)
1/4 C. Oil
1/2 C. Tofu
1/4 C. Rice or Soy Milk
1 T. Vanilla

Dry
1 C. Oat or Spelt Flour
1 C. Rice or Barley Flour
1/2 t. Baking Soda
1/2 t. Baking Powder
Add
1 C. Carob/Chocolate Chips (Dairy-free)

1. In a large mixing bowl, whisk together all the ingredients in the first column.
2. Sift dry ingredients into a separate bowl. Mix the dry into the wet ingredients.
3. Add chips to the dough and gently stir.
4. Roll out into 1/2" balls and flatten on to an oiled and floured cookie sheet.
5. Bake in a pre-heated oven at 350° for 10-15 minutes or until golden brown.

- Variation: Use 1/2 cup raisins and 1/2 cup chopped nuts instead of chips.
- Variation: Use: 1 T. ground flaxseed mixed with 3 T. water instead of oil for an oil-free cookie.

"It is madness to think that one can solve a problem with the same thinking that created it."

ALBERT EINSTEIN (1879-1955)
German-born American physicist
1921 Nobel Prize recipient

Ginger Snaps
yields 3 1/2 dozen cookies

4 C. Whole Wheat Pastry Flour	1 1/4 C. Molasses
1 t. Baking Powder	2 1/2 T. Ginger Juice (fresh)
2 T. Ener-G® Egg Replacer	1 C. Oil
1 1/2 t. Cinnamon	2 t. Vanilla
1/4 t. Allspice	1 3/4 C. Sweetener (dry)

1. Sift together dry ingredients (except sweetener) in a bowl. Whisk together the wet ingredients with the sweetener in a separate bowl. (Put ginger through a juicer.)
2. Add dry ingredients to the wet and mix until thick.
3. Drop by the spoonful onto an oiled cookie sheet, forming small cookies.
4. Bake in a pre-heated oven at 375° for 10-18 minutes.

Vanilla Cakies
yields 2 dozen

1/2 C. Oil	1 1/2 T. Vanilla
1/2 C. Maple Syrup	2 1/8 C. Whole Wheat Pastry Flour
2 T. Egg Replacer mixed with 2 T. Water	1/2 t. Baking Soda

1. In a blender, whiz wet ingredients: oil, maple syrup, egg replacer mixture & vanilla.
2. In a bowl, sift together the flour and baking soda. Pour the wet into the dry and mix.
4. Drop batter by the spoonful onto an oiled cookie sheet. Bake in a pre-heated oven at 375° for approximately 10 minutes or until bottom is crispy brown.

Brownies
yields 8-9 pieces

1/3 C. Tofu Milk (tofu & water)	1/3 C. Sweetener (dry)
1/2 C. Oil	2/3 C. Whole Wheat Pastry Flour
1/2 t. Vanilla	1/2 C. Carob Powder
1/3 C. Maple Syrup	1 t. Baking Soda

1. In a blender, blend tofu milk (see Baking Guide), oil, vanilla, and sweeteners.
2. In a separate bowl, sift flour, carob powder and baking soda.
3. Pour the wet into the dry and mix thoroughly. Pour into an oiled 8" x 8" baking tin. Pre-heat oven to 375°. Bake for 30 minutes or until a toothpick comes out dry and tops begin to crack. Cut into brownies after cooling.

"If we believe absurdities, we shall commit atrocities."

VOLTAIRE (1694-1778)
French philosopher and author

Chocolate or Carob Chip Pecan Squares
yields (1) 9" square pan

3/4 C. Whole Wheat Pastry Flour	1/3 C. Sweetener (dry)
1/2 t. Baking Soda	1 t. Vanilla
1 T. Soy Powder & 2 t. Water, mixed	1/2 C. Pecan Halves
1/3 C. Oil	1/2 C. Carob Chips (non-dairy)

1. Sift flour and baking soda together in a bowl.
2. Blend wet ingredients together, including the sweetener.
3. Combine the wet and dry mixes, stirring in pecans and carob chips.
4. Pour into a lightly oiled 9" square pan. Bake in a pre-heated oven at 350° for 15-20 minutes or until lightly browned. Let cool in pan; then cut into squares.

Zappy Orange and Ginger Squares
Contributed by Wild Ginger Restaurant - Vegan Village, United Kingdom

1/2 C. Vegan Margarine (or oil)	Topping
2 T. Rice Syrup and/or Maple Syrup	1/3 C. or 4 oz. Vegan Margarine
1/2 C. Sucanat™	1 t. Ground Ginger
2 t. Ginger (level) (ground)	1 T. Maple or Rice Syrup
1 Orange (rind & juice)	Orange Rind (saved from earlier)
1 1/8 C. (or 9 oz.) Rolled Oats	1/2 C. Rice Syrup or Fruitsource™

1. Melt the margarine and mix together with syrup, Sucanat™, ginger and orange juice. (Grate orange rind and keep for topping.) When dissolved, add oats and mix well.
2. Spread on to an oiled baking tray and level out. Bake in a pre-heated oven at 375° for 20 minutes or until golden brown. Leave to cool.
3. To make the topping: blend melted margarine, ginger and syrup together. Add orange rind and Rice Syrup or Fruitsource™. Mix well. Make sure there are no lumps.
4. Spread over cooled oat base. Refrigerate. Cut into squares and serve.

"The time will come when men such as I will look upon the murder of animals as they now look upon the murder of men."

LEONARDO DA VINCI (1425-1519)
Italian sculptor, artist and inventor

Sweet-Tarts

yields 17 tarts

4 C. Whole Wheat Pastry Flour
1 t. Baking Soda
3/4 C. Oil
2 Lime or Lemon Peels, grated
1/8 lb. Tofu

2 t. Vanilla
1/4 C. Water
1 C. Maple Syrup and/or Sucanat™
Fruit-Sweetened Jam (to fill tarts with)

1. In a bowl, sift together flour and baking soda.
2. In a blender, blend oil, grated citrus rinds, tofu, vanilla, water and sweetener.
3. Pour wet mixture into the dry. Mix together thoroughly until batter no longer sticks to fingers.
4. Oil one or two muffin tins (enough for 17 tarts).
5. Fill each muffin cup evenly by pressing in the dough, leaving room in middle for jam.
6. Bake in a pre-heated oven at 350° for 10 minutes. Remove and drop 1 t. of jam in each tart's center. Place back in oven for 7-9 minutes. Allow to cool.
7. With a small knife, go around edges of each tart to pop it out.

Maple Pecan Biscotti

yields 2 loaves, sliced

1/2 C. Pecans, finely chopped
(can substitute Almonds or a mix of both)
1/2 C. Tofu (soft)
1/4 C. Maple Syrup
1/4 C. Safflower Oil
2 t. Vanilla

1/4 C. Sweetener (dry)
3 C. Whole Wheat Flour
1 t. Baking Powder
1 t. Baking Soda
1/4 t. Salt

1. In a food processor, chop nuts very finely. Take them out and put aside.
2. In food processor, blend tofu, the remaining wet ingredients and dry sweetener.
3. Add almonds and 1 cup of whole wheat pastry flour to processor; whiz.
4. Take dough out of food processor, place in a bowl and sift in remaining flour, baking soda, baking powder and salt. The dough should be firm but not dry. Add more flour if needed.
5. Place dough on a baking tray and mold into 2 long loaves about 3 inches wide.
6. Bake in pre-heated oven at 375° for 20-25 minutes, until golden brown.
7. Remove from oven and cut (while warm, not hot) into 3/4 inch thick pieces and place back on to the baking tray. In oven, toast each side for 4-5 minutes.

> *"The animals of the world exist for their own reasons. They were not made for humans any more than blacks were made for whites, or women for men."*
>
> ALICE WALKER
> American author
> Author of: The Color Purple

Coffee-Almond Biscotti
yields 16 pieces

2/3 C. Almonds	4 oz. Tofu (soft)
1/2 t. Baking Soda	1/4 C. Water
1/2 t. Baking Powder	1/3 C. Sweetener
1 T. Coffee Substitute	1 t. Vanilla
Pinch of Salt	1 t. Almond Extract
1-1 1/2 C. Whole Wheat Pastry Flour	

1. In a food processor, using the "S"- shaped blade, add almonds and pulse into a meal. Add baking soda and baking powder. Add coffee substitute, salt, tofu, water, sweetener, vanilla and almond extract. Pulse until homogenized.
2. Remove mixture from processor. Place on clean board and fold in flour until dough is dry and not sticky. Divide dough in half and form into 2 long loaves.
3. Place loaves on baking sheet lined with baking paper. Bake in a pre-heated oven at 350° for 25-30 minutes or until set and almost firm. Remove from oven and place on a rack until somewhat cooled. Then transfer to a cutting board.
4. Using a serrated knife, cut loaves into 8 equal slices. Place the slices directly on to the oven rack and bake 4 minutes on each side. Cool and store in an air-tight container.

Easy Biscotti
yields 2 loaves

3 1/2 C. Whole Wheat Pastry Flour	1 t. Vanilla
1 t. each: Baking Powder/Soda	1 t. Almond Extract
1 C. Sweetener (dry)	4 T. Tahini & 5 T. Water, mixed
1/2 C. Oil	1/4 C. Orange Juice

1. Into a medium-sized bowl, sift flour, baking powder and baking soda.
2. In a separate bowl, mix together sweetener and all liquid ingredients. Slowly add the liquid ingredients to the dry, and mix until you get a dough-like texture. Use enough flour so it is not sticking to your fingers. If too dry, add a bit more liquid.
3. Divide dough into 2 sections and form into separate long loaves. Pre-heat oven to 350°. Place on a baking sheet and bake for 25-35 minutes or until golden brown.
4. Take out and slice loaves when warm (not hot) into pieces that are about 1 inch thick.
   - •Optional - For a drier slice, toast in the oven for 4 minutes on each side.
   - •Optional - Add 1/2 cup chopped walnuts and raisins to dough.

> *"You put a baby in a crib with an apple and a rabbit. If it eats the rabbit and plays with the apple, I'll buy you a new car."*
>
> HARVEY DIAMOND
> American author
> Co-author of: Fit for Life

Danish Pastry

yields 2 loaves

2 T. Dry Active Yeast	1 t. Lemon Rind
1 T. + 1/3 C. Date Sugar	1/2 C. Hot Water
1/2 C. Lukewarm Water	4 3/4 C. Whole Wheat Pastry Flour, sifted
1/3 C. (additional) Date Sugar	2 T. Cinnamon
1/2 C. Maple Syrup	1 t. Nutmeg
3/4 C. Soy Milk (thick) or	1/2 C. Raisins, chopped
(6 T. Soy Powder & 1/2 C. Water)	1 C. Nuts, chopped
1 t. Sea Salt	1/3 C. Date Sugar (additional)
1/2 C. Oil	2 + T. Oil

1. In a small bowl, combine the yeast, 1 T. date sugar and the warm water. Let rise until doubled in size, 10-15 minutes.
2. In a large bowl, combine 1/3 cup of date sugar, maple syrup, soy milk, sea salt, oil, lemon rind and the hot water. Mix well. Add the yeast mixture. Gradually add the sifted flour in 4 parts, mixing well each time. Cover and allow to rise for 20 minutes.
3. Turn dough on to a well-floured board and knead for approximately 10 minutes until satiny smooth, adding flour as needed.
4. Place in an oiled bowl and oil the top of the dough. Cover and allow to rise for approximately 1 hour, until doubled in volume. Punch the dough down.
5. Divide the dough in half; roll out one half on a floured board into a 9" x 12" rectangle. Cover with a layer of 2 tablespoons oil. Sprinkle with half of the date sugar, cinnamon, nutmeg, chopped raisins and nuts.
6. Roll up like a jelly roll; pinch ends. Place on an oiled cookie sheet. Repeat for other half of dough. Allow to rise approximately 1 hour, until doubled in size.
7. Bake in a pre-heated oven at 325° for 20-30 minutes, watching carefully to prevent burning.
8. To prepare the Danish Glaze:

3 T. Sweetener (liquid)	1 T. Date Sugar
3 T. Oil	1/4 C. Chopped Nuts

Combine sorghum, oil and date sugar in a saucepan. Bring to a boil over medium heat. When finished, spread the hot glaze over the hot Danish.
9. Sprinkle with chopped nuts. Partially cool and serve.

"There is no escaping the harsh reality that many of the methods employed in the commercial production of honey are cruel and repugnant and provide an overwhelming case for ethical vegans to reject the use of this product and its derivatives."

ARTHUR LING
President/Managing Director of Plamil Foods

Fruit Pastry

yields 3 loaves

1 C. Maple Syrup
1-2 t. Vanilla
1-2 Lemon/Orange Rind, grated
1 C. Oil

1/4 C. Tofu, mashed
4 C. Whole Wheat Pastry Flour
1 t. Baking Soda
12 T. Fruit-Sweetened Jam
   or Apple Sauce, for filling

1. In a blender, blend first 5 ingredients.
2. Sift flour and baking soda together into a bowl.
3. Add wet ingredients to the dry and mix thoroughly. The batter should not stick. If it is sticky, add a small amount of flour and mix.
4. Chill before rolling out. Split batter into three equal balls. Place one ball at a time between two pieces of wax paper. Roll out, using a rolling pin, from the center outward.
5. Place 4 tablespoons of jam, apple sauce (or prune whip) on half the dough and roll up lengthwise into a loaf, tucking ends in.
6. Place each loaf on an oiled baking sheet (3 on the tray).
7. Place on the bottom shelf of pre-heated oven at 350°; then bake 15-20 minutes. Switch to the upper shelf and bake to a golden brown crisp (about 15 more minutes).
8. Cut into slices before the loaves are totally cooled. (When they harden they become more difficult to slice.)

Pumpkin Bread-Cake

yields 1 bread pan

1/3 C. Oil
1/8 C. Soy Milk
1 C. Canned Pumpkin
4 1/2 t. Egg Replacer mixed with 6 T. water
2 1/4 C. Whole Wheat Pastry Flour

1 1/4 C. Sweetener (dry)
1 t. Baking Soda, sifted
2 t. Cinnamon
1/2 t. Sea Salt
1/2 C. Raisins

1. In a blender, blend oil, soy milk, pumpkin and egg replacer/water mixture.
2. Sift flour and combine with remaining dry ingredients (not raisins) into a bowl.
3. Add wet to the dry, mixing lightly, and fold in raisins.
4. Bake in a pre-heated oven at 350°, in a small Pyrex™ baking dish or loaf pan for 45-55 minutes, or when a toothpick comes out dry.

> *"How wonderful it is that nobody need wait a single moment before starting to improve the world."*
>
> ANNE FRANK (1930-1945)
> German-Jewish refugee, holocaust victim
> Author of: <u>The Diary of Anne Frank</u>

Banana Bread
yields 1 loaf

1 C. Sweetener	1 t. Baking Soda
3 Bananas, mashed	1/2 t. Cinnamon
1/2 C. Oil	1/2 C. Walnuts, chopped
1 1/2 C. Whole Wheat Pastry Flour	1/2 C. Raisins

1. Mix sweetener, bananas and oil together. Sift dry ingredients into a bowl.
2. Mix dry and wet batter together. Add walnuts and raisins. Mix again.
3. Pour into an oiled and floured loaf pan. Bake in a pre-heated oven at 350° for about 1 hour, or until a toothpick comes out dry.

Rogolos
yields 15-20

Dough	Filling
2 C. Whole Wheat Pastry Flour	1/2 C. Pecans
2 T. Egg Replacer	1/2 C. Walnuts
1/4 C. Orange Juice	1/4 C. Maple Syrup
1/4 C. Apple Sauce	1/2 C. Raisins
1/4 C. Oil	1 T. Cinnamon
1/2 t. Sweetener	1/2 t. Allspice

Dough
1. Sift flour and egg replacer together in a bowl and mix.
2. Mix the wet dough ingredients in a separate bowl. (For an even healthier treat, substitute more apple sauce for the oil.)
3. Mix the dry into the wet. (You may need to use your hands at the end to mix all the flour in.) Dough should be dry enough so that it does not stick to your fingers.
4. Roll dough out (on wax paper or floured board) into two flattened and thin rectangles.

Filling
1. Chop the nuts into fine pieces. Mix nuts with the rest of the filling ingredients and spread on the rolled out dough. Roll lengthwise, pinch ends together and place on a baking sheet.
2. Bake in a pre-heated oven at 350° for 30-40 minutes until lightly browned on top and bottom.

"To see what is right and not to do it, is want of courage."

CONFUCIUS (551-479 B.C.)
Chinese political and ethical philosopher

Tart Baked Apples - Low Fat

yields 4 baked apples

4 Tart Apples,
  (Granny Smith works well)
1 T. Lemon Juice
1/2 t. Cinnamon

1/4 C. Brown Rice Syrup
1 t. Vanilla
1/3 C. Orange Juice
1/3 C. Golden Raisins

1. Use hard, firm apples. Remove the cores.
2. Place apples in baking dish.
3. Top with lemon juice and sprinkle with cinnamon.
4. Top with sweetener and vanilla, and then orange juice and raisins.
5. Bake (uncovered) in a pre-heated oven at 350° for 30 minutes.

Fruity Bake

yields (1) 9" x 12" casserole

1 C. Fresh Apricots (pitted), chopped
1 C. Dates (pitted), chopped
1 C. Pineapple, diced
1 C. Tofu Yogurt (pg. 21)
1 t. Cinnamon

1 C. Dry Sweetener
1 C. Whole Wheat Pastry Flour
2 C. Rolled Oats
1 T. Vanilla
1 1/2 t. Baking Soda
1 t. Oil

1. Mix together all ingredients in a bowl, except oil. Then, lightly oil a casserole dish and place batter into dish. Bake in a pre-heated oven at 350° for 30 minutes.
2. Serve warm or chilled.

Hot Carob-Espresso-Amaretto Beverage

yields 1/2 blender

1 - 1 1/2 T. Kaffree Roma™
2 T. Carob
1/2 T. Vanilla Powder
(or 1/4 T. Liquid Vanilla)

Almond Flavor, dash
2 T. Tahini
2 T. Maple Syrup
2 C. Boiling Hot Water

In a blender, blend all ingredients. Serve with dessert or after a meal.

"Animals are God's creatures, not human property, nor utilities, nor resources, nor commodities, but precious beings in God's sight."

REV. DR. ANDREW LINZEY
University of Oxford
Animal Theology, 1995

Carob-Mint Beverage

yields 1/2 blender

2 C. Boiling Hot Water
2 T. Carob Powder
3 T. Tahini
2 T. Molasses

1 T. Maple Syrup
1/8 t. Mint Extract (liquid)
1 t. Vanilla

In a blender, blend the above ingredients until smooth, and serve.

Pineapple Heaven Drink

yields 2 1/2 cups

1 C. Frozen Banana, sliced
2 C. Pineapple (fresh), chopped
3/4 C. Orange Juice (fresh)

1/8 t. Almond Extract
Vanilla, dash
3 T. Maple Syrup

In a blender, blend the above ingredients. When drink is creamy, add a handful of ice cubes and whiz again. Serve.

Carob/Peanut Butter Protein Drink

yields 2 cups

1 C. Soy/Rice Milk (Rice Dream®)
1 1/2 T. Carob Powder
2-3 T. Peanut Butter
1 Banana

1-2 T. Sweetener
1 T. Vegan Protein Powder
 (see Vegan Alternatives Section)

In a blender, blend the above ingredients. When drink is creamy, add a handful of ice cubes and whiz again. Serve.

*"Being a vegan is one of the most important roles
I will ever play."*

RIVER PHOENIX (1970-1993)
American actor

Strawberry-Tofu Smoothie
yields 1 cup

1/2 C. Strawberries	2 T. Sweetener
1/2 C. Ice	1/4 lb. Tofu (low-fat, optional)

Place the ingredients in the wet blade container of a Vita-Mix® (or regular blender) in the order listed. Secure lid. Blend on high for 15-30 seconds.

Creamy Chocolate Milk
yields 4 cups

1/2-2/3 C. Cashew Pieces (raw)	1/8 t. Vanilla
1 C. Water	1/2-1 T. Maple Syrup
5 t. Carob (raw)	2 Cups Water (ice cold)
1 T. Sweetener	1/2 t. Tahini

1. In a blender, blend the cashew pieces with 1 cup of water and homogenize to a creamy consistency. Use a rubber spatula to push the small cashew pieces from blender sides into the mixture.
2. Add remaining ingredients. Blend and serve.

Almond-Cashew Drink
yields 2 glasses

1/3 C. Cashew Pieces	1-2 T. Sweetener
1 T. Almond Butter	1 t. Almond Extract
2/3 C. Ice Water	1 C. Ice Water (additional)

1. In a blender, purée the first column of ingredients.
2. Add the second column of ingredients. Blend. Serve.

• Use raw or roasted cashew pieces and almond butter, according to taste.

> *"In order to get meat, we have to kill. And we are certainly not entitled to any other milk except the mother's milk in our infancy."*
>
> MAHATMA GANDHI (1869-1948)
> Hindu pacifist, spiritual leader

The Vegan Paradigm

"Very little of the great cruelty shown by men can really be attributed to cruel instinct. Most of it comes from thoughtlessness or inherited habit. The roots of cruelty, therefore, are not so much strong as widespread. But the time must come when inhumanity protected by custom and thoughtlessness will succumb before humanity championed by thought. Let us work that this time may come."

DR. ALBERT SCHWEITZER (1875-1965)
Alsatian physician, philosopher, theologian

Becoming a Vegan

* Be gentle with yourself. Avoid thinking in terms of forever. Resolve to eliminate all animal products from your diet for two weeks, a month, whatever promise of time you feel you can live up to. Your positive changes will inspire continued commitment.

* Experience a new enjoyment in cooking and dining. Start with the simple (basic) recipes in this book, such as tofu omelettes or easy stir fry. With added confidence, advance to more gourmet dishes. Vegan eating is not a sacrifice, but a fulfilling culinary adventure. If you eat out, support vegan/vegetarian restaurants whenever possible. Be specific about ordering vegan meals in standard restaurants and on airlines. The greater the demand, the higher the quality will become.

* Veganize your home, one room at a time. In the kitchen, replace all animal products with the substitutes listed in the glossary and the Vegan Alternative section. In the bathroom, do the same. Remove all leather, wool, silk and furs from your home.

* We vote for what we believe in with our dollars. Support businesses and products that are humane.

* Find the local vegan/vegetarian groups in your area. If they don't exist, you may create one. A support system is invaluable in helping you to remain strong in your conviction.

* If you are living with loved ones who do not yet understand your new direction, remember the wise words of Albert Schweitzer: "Example is not the main way to influence others, it is the only way."

* If you are a parent, use the recipes in this book to awaken the taste buds of your children. Share with them your reasons for choosing a more compassionate way of eating. Children have a natural kinship with animals.

* A delicious school lunch can easily be prepared that will make your children's schoolmates envious. Include a nondairy milk, vegan burger or VeganRella® burrito or sunny almond paté sandwich and carob cupcake.

* Make your mind your ally. Rather than envisioning the foods that you can no longer eat, replace those visions with the wide variety of foods you now enjoy, and the unlimited treats you have yet to discover.

"The Vegan Paradigm will inspire a heightened spiritual awareness, purify the body, and make possible personal and planetary healing unprecedented in human history."

SUN
Co-founder Gentle World
A Newer Age

Dogs and Cats Can be Vegan

We have experimented for many years with feeding pets and stray animals and have found it quite easy for dogs to enjoy, and thrive on, a vegan diet.

To insure that your dogs get enough protein and calcium, feed them a varied diet of tofu, legumes, grains, potatoes, seitan, tempeh, T.V.P, (see Glossary) and some vegetables. We have determined that approximately 40% of their diet should be derived from a protein source, such as well-cooked legumes (garbanzo beans, lentils, split peas, soy beans, etc.) or tofu, seitan or potatoes. A large portion of their dinner can be well-cooked grains; millet, rice, quinoa, barley, oats, pasta, etc., (a source of carbohydrate and protein). A tablespoon of bran in the dinner aids bowel elimination. Some veterinarians recommend adding pumpkin seed milk and liquid Kyolic® Garlic (available in a plain liquid formula without whey) or 1/2 to 1 clove of diced raw garlic into the dinner bowl to prevent and decrease worms and other intestinal parasites. Grated raw vegetables, such as carrot, beet, cabbage & sprouted lentils should be included in their meal for fiber. Add some sprouts for vitality. The oil requirements are met mostly with avocado (dogs love avocado). Other oil sources include 1-2 tablespoons of tahini or vegetable oil and/or raw wheat germ for a shiny coat. We supplement the meal with Red Star™ Vegetarian Support Formula nutritional yeast, Bragg™ Liquid Aminos, a small amount of (food grade) flax seed oil or soaked flaxseeds and sometimes a sprinkle of spirulina. Calcium requirements are met with tahini or finely chopped raw greens and from the vitamins and minerals found in canned vegetarian dog foods. Dogs seem to enjoy Nori (seaweed) (in bite-sized pieces) added to their meals. Food should be served warm or at least at room temperature. Always serve their meals with a fresh bowl of water. Please note that onions (in large amounts) and chocolate (in small amounts) can be toxic to dogs. There are also several marketed totally vegan dog foods. We mix a bit of canned dog food into the meals, as they find it irresistible! There are several brands of canned vegan formula that are 100% nutritionally complete. (See *Vegan Alternatives.*) Best of all is homemade, fresh food, basically quite similar to what you yourself will be eating. You can feel confident that on the vegan diet, your dog will have a sleek, clean body, clean teeth and a healthy coat.

Cats are more difficult. However, it is possible to feed them vegan meals. They are, by nature, true carnivores, whereas dogs are omnivores. When feeding a cat vegan, to avoid serious consequences, the diet must be supplemented with a Taurine containing product or Veggie-Cat™ , a marketed product made by Harbingers of a New Age. A favorite meal of cats includes mashed tofu with nutritional yeast and kelp, and 'Vegecat' supplementation. Other meal additions include: well-cooked chick peas, seaweeds of all kind, avocado, bread, ground seitan and oatmeal.

Animals become less aggressive, much the same as humans, when eating a vegan diet. Look forward to your pet becoming gentler, healthier, cleaner and even more lovable.

RECOMMENDED READING:

Vegetarian Dogs and Cats, ©Harbingers of a New Age, author, Peden ISBN 0-941319-02-4
Vegetarian Dogs: Towards a World Without Exploitation By Verona re-Bow and Jonathan Dune LiveArt Box 7056 Halcyon, CA. 93421 (805) 481-8581

"A core issue for many guardians is whether cats and dogs can be healthy as vegetarians or vegans. Most veterinarians, including nutritionists, agree that dogs can be healthy eating a vegetarian or vegan diet."

TERI BERNATO
National Director, Association of Veterinarians for Animal Rights.

"There also appeared to be a health advantage to veganism over vegetarianism: 82% of dogs who had been vegan for five years or more were in good to excellent health, while only 77% of dogs who had been vegetarian for five years or more were in good to excellent health."

People For The Ethical Treatment Of Animals' Vegetarian Health Survey Results.
(Participants were solicited through P.E.T.A.'s newsletter;
data on 300 dogs, over a period of 1 year, were received.)

"Our primary goal when we started our research in 1985, was to break the slaughterhouse link for vegetarian pet owners. We had hoped that vegetarian pets would at least be as healthy as those fed slaughterhouse products. Along the way, we had a pleasant surprise: vegetarian pets can be healthier. In retrospect we should have anticipated it. Natural ingredients are so different from those found in commercial diets."

Vegetarian Dogs and Cats
PEDEN, © Harbinger's of a New Age

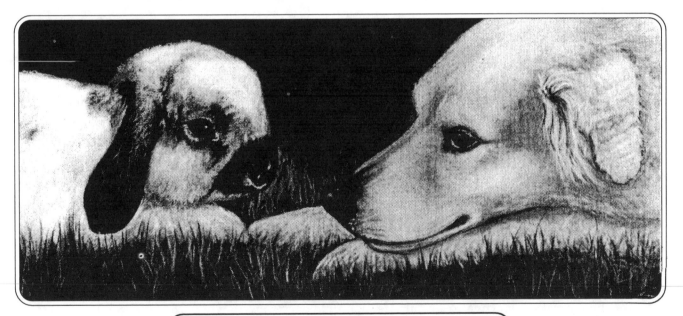

PLEASURE & BEAUTIFUL, Vegan Friends

"The more we come in contact with animals and observe their behavior, the more we love them..."

IMMANUEL KANT (1724-1804)
German philosopher

Healthful Hints

* For those who want to reduce oil usage:
     Sauté with a little water, rather than oil. (or mix with water to stretch)
     When baking, replace a percentage of the oil with an equal amount of apple sauce.
     When baking cookies, replace oil with apple juice.

* When possible, bake rather than fry.

* Steam vegetables lightly; avoid overcooking.

* For easier digestion, soak beans overnight before cooking. Drain, rinse and cook in fresh water.

* Avoid using aluminum-coated cookware; traces of aluminum may taint the food.

* Eat foods in their natural (raw) state as much as possible.

* Avoid chemically sprayed and irradiated foods.

* Eat a variety of colors from the vegetable kingdom to insure a variety of vitamins and minerals.

* Eat fruit alone; don't mix with vegetables. The body produces different enzymes to digest fruits and vegetables. These enzymes work better alone.

* When possible, use cayenne pepper instead of black pepper. Cayenne aids in blood circulation.

* Slippery Elm Bark is an herb from the inner bark of an elm tree that coats the stomach; great for upset stomach. The Soothie Smoothie recipe: 1 C. boiled water, 1 T. slippery elm, 1 t. Sucanat™, 1 t. Tahini, 1/4 banana and 1/2 t. Vanilla whizzed in blender.

* Golden Seal and Myrrh is an herbal combination, used as a mouthwash. It is excellent for gums.

* Peppermint tea aids digestion and relieves flatulence.

* Wheatgrass juice is an excellent source of fresh, alive vitamins, minerals, and chlorophyll. It is a potent mouthwash that draws out toxins from the gums and teeth, and is helpful in relief of toothache pain. 1 oz. of wheatgrass juice is an ample portion with which to begin.

* To relieve hiccups, eat an orange.

* Hot water with lemon or orange juice, along with a dash of cayenne pepper, is great for alleviating cold symptoms.

* Aloe plant leaves are filled with a jellylike substance that soothes and heals the skin, especially when applied to burns and bites.

* Raw garlic is a natural antibiotic that may be included in the diet on a regular basis.

* Ear candles, found in health food stores, help relieve wax buildup in the inner ear. See *Vegan Alternatives* for ear candle companies.

* Wild Yam extracts, in the form of skin creams, found in health food stores, are a source of natural progesterone for menopausal women. They have a molecular structure that is the same as the progesterone found in the female's body, and has no negative side effects. Some creams are not vegan. See *Vegan Alternatives* for companies that market vegan wild yam extracts.

* Echinecea is an herbal antibiotic that strengthens the immune system.

* Periodic fasting is helpful to the body. It gives our ever-working digestive system a break, and allows time for cleansing, detoxifying and healing. High colonics, fasting and fruit-cleansing diets are most beneficial when evolving from an animal-based to a plant-based diet.

* Take a brisk walk in the fresh air and sunshine for your exercise. Spending time with nature, breathing clean air and drinking pure water are essential for vibrant health.

"If you are serious about a vegan diet, start reading labels at the grocery store and look for hidden ingredients. At first you might feel overwhelmed. It seems as though there are animal ingredients -lard, whey, dried milk, egg whites - in everything from bread to margarine and even some veggie burgers. But don't be discouraged - you'll quickly become fimiliar with ingredients that are truly vegan. Eventually you'll have a shopping list of the products you want to eat."

VIRGINIA MESSINA, MPH, RD and MARK MESSINA, Ph.D
<u>Total health for You and Your Family; The Vegetarian Way</u>
Crown Trade Paperbacks, New York

Non-Vegan Products and Ingredients

Meat, Fowl, Fish, Lard - involves the killing of animals.

Dairy - "Sweet gentle Bessie is hardly contented at all. She has been denied the natural life of a cow and the pleasures of foraging, ruminating and caring for her young (who are often taken from her at birth to be made into veal). She has been bred, medicated, implanted with hormones, artificially inseminated and kept perpetually pregnant to provide one thing only - continual milk production... When at last she is unable to keep up the demanded level of milk production, drained and exhausted, Bessie will be packed into a crowded truck for transport to her final destination- the meat processing plant."

JOANNE STEPANIAK
The Uncheese Cookbook

Eggs - "Ninety eight percent of egg-laying hens are housed in battery cages (World Poultry Science Journal, 3/93). Typically, four or five egg-laying hens live in a cage with a wire floor area about the size of a folded newspaper... All free-range, factory farmed and egg-laying animals who don't die from disease are trucked to the slaughterhouse."

VEGAN OUTREACH
"Why Vegan"

Honey - For sweetening purposes, avoid using honey. Honey is a concentrated-sugar obtained by robbing the bees of the fruits of their labor. When bee keepers take the honey, the bees are left with little to eat, or are given an inferior substitute, usually sugar water with antibiotics, as a replacement. From time to time, the hives are smoked out, killing many bees in the process. Honey also carries the risk of botulism, and raw honey is particularly known for breeding bacteria, parasites and viruses. Honey is regurgitated insect food, not intended for human consumption.

Leather and Suede - *"Most of the leather produced and sold in the U.S. is made from skins of cattle and calves. But leather is also made from the hides of horses, sheep, lambs, goats and pigs slaughtered for meat. Myriads of other species around the world are hunted and killed specifically for their skins. Up to one-third of "exotic" leathers come from endangered, illegally poached animals."

* Denotes a quote taken from Save The Animals; 101 Easy Things You Can Do
© 1990, Ingrid Newkirk; National Director: P.E.T.A., Warner Books, ISBN 0-446-39234-0.

> *"As long as humans have lived upon this planet, they have lived in fear of the violence of other humans. Evolution to a vegan consciousness will replace that fear with trust; and trust will lead to love; the only true religion; the source of all healing."*
>
>
>
> SUN
> Co-founder Gentle World
> A Newer Age
>
>

Furs - * "Animals on fur farms live their short lives in wire-mesh cages, victims of stress, fear and self-mutilation. In the interest of profit, animals are dispatched by the cheapest methods possible, which are usually also the most crude and cruel."

"Killing an animal to make a coat is a sin. It wasn't meant to be, and we have no right to do it. A woman gains status when she refuses to see anything killed to be put on her back. Then she's truly beautiful."
DORIS DAY, American actress

"Cruelty is one fashion statement we can all do without." RUE McCLANAHAN, American actress

"No one really needs a mink coat in this world...except minks." GLENDA JACKSON, American actress
From a syndicated newspaper interview

Wool - *"Wool is the sheared coat of sheep. Breeders have created sheep called Merinos who are extremely wrinkly (more wrinkles mean more wool). This unnatural overload of wool causes many sheep to die of heat exhaustion in the summer as well as of exposure to cold and damp after late shearing (a closely shorn sheep is more sensitive to cold than even a naked human, since a sheep's normal body temperature is much higher than ours)."

Gelatin - (protein dissolved from bones, skin, hide trimmings) is an ingredient found in Jello™, marshmallows and photo film. All brands and qualities of films have a fine layer of gelatin. (There is now digital photography that is vegan.) Most capsules are made of gelatin but there are vegetable-based capsules sold at health food stores called "Vegi-Caps".

Silk - A filament of silk is spun by the silkworm to protect itself from enemies during the cycle of growth from caterpillar to chrysalis to moth. The silkworms are either immersed in boiling water or put in ovens to get the filament from cocoons as long strands which can be reeled. To produce 100 grams of silk, approximately 1500 silkworms have to be killed.

Down - insulating stuffing feathers plucked from birds, usually geese and ducks. Used in pillows, quilts, sleeping bags and parkas.

Lanolin - (an extract from sheep's wool fat); found in cosmetics and creams.

Tallow (Hard Animal Fat) - is found in soaps, candles, margarine, crayons & cosmetics.

Stearic Acid - a white, waxy fatty acid from animal fat, found in shampoos, creams and lotions, etc. (There is also vegetable derived stearic acid; call to ascertain its origin.)

Collagen - is usually derived from animal tissue, found in creams, lotions, cosmetics, etc.

Keratin - A protein found in hair, horns and hooves; an ingredient found in shampoos.

Elastin - obtained from the neck ligaments or aorta of cows. Found in cosmetics.

Hydrolyzed Animal Protein - found mostly in shampoos, packaged foods & soya sauce.

Placenta - Derived from the uterus of animals, found in cosmetics and skin creams.

Soaps - usually contain tallow or other animal fats. There are many vegan alternatives.

Candles - Many candles contain animal fat, beeswax and tallow. There are white, kosher candles that don't contain animal by-products. (Paraffin is not animal-based).

Pearls - foreign material is inserted into an oyster to irritate it, causing the oyster to make a pearl. (A pearl is formed around a foreign particle to dull pain.)

Ivory "Ivory comes from elephants & from marine mammals such as whales and walruses, often carved into figurines, curios or jewelry. African elephants live in small herds of closely knit family groups, led by one or two older females. If (and it's a big "if") they survive poaching, they can reach the age of 70. The African Wildlife Foundation has estimated that 80,000 adult African elephants are killed every year for their tusks and that another 10,000 youngsters die as a result...." (P.E.T.A.)

Glues and adhesives - may contain animal by-products. Most are synthetic.

Sable Brushes -from the fur of sables. Used for clothing, cosmetics and artist brushes.

Boar Bristles - hair from hogs. Found in 'natural toothbrushes', bath and shaving brushes.

Catgut - obtained from the intestines of sheep, horses, etc., used for stringing tennis rackets and musical instruments. There are nylon and other synthetic alternatives.

Sperm Oil - from the sperm whale, used in candle making.

Musk Oil - painfully obtained from the genitals of musk deer, beavers and civet cats. The beavers are trapped, the deer shot and cats are whipped about their genitalia to produce scented oils, used mostly in perfumes.

Mink Oil - extracted from minks, used in various cosmetics.

Shark Cartilage - Sharks are killed for this bony material sold in health food stores.

Calcium Carbonate - may come from oyster shells collected from restaurants and is not considered a vegan product. If calcium carbonate is listed on the ingredients of a toothpaste or other product, call the company to verify its source.

Shellac - an insect secretion, used in hair sprays, lip sealer, polishes, painting & glazing.

Many cleaning products, cosmetics and **pharmaceuticals** are cruelly tested on animals. Look for labels that state no animal testing. Every year, many millions of animals are killed testing household cleaners and personal care products.

> *"The most common product tests are the Draize Eye Irritancy Test and the Lethal Dose 50 (%) Test.....Lethal Dose tests involve force-feeding substances, such as toilet bowl cleaner, to animals to observe reactions (including convulsions, emaciation, skin eruptions and diarrhea) until a certain percentage, commonly 50%, of the animals die...Don't be fooled by company claims that animal tests are required or that alternatives don't exist. NO law mandates animal tests for cosmetics and household products—the tests are designed to limit the companies' liability."*

Pharmaceuticals. Most *contraceptive pills* contain animal ingredients; check with your pharmacist. *Premarin*, a female hormone, is '<u>Pregnant</u> <u>Mare</u> <u>Urine</u>'. *Estrogen, Estrone, Estradiol* are hormones from cow ovaries and pregnant mares' urine. *Insulin*, a treatment for diabetics, is traditionally obtained from the pancreas of hogs, sheep and oxen. *Cortisone* is a hormone from cattle liver. There are now synthetic alternatives for all of these.

Fertilizers - bone meal (animal bones), bone ash (ash of burned bones), blood meal, fish meal, feather meal and other slaughterhouse by-products; often used by organic farmers.

Angora and **Cashmere** - Angora is fiber obtained from rabbits or goats. Cashmere is a fine wool used for sweaters and clothing made from domestic or wild goats of Kashmir or Tibet.

Fish Scales are used in shimmery make-ups. Mica and rayon are alternatives.

**The following ingredients are found on labels in food items:</u>

White sugar may be refined through bone char; animal bone ash.
Whey (derived from milk) Used in margarine, baked goods, cleaning products, etc.
Nonfat dry milk, Lactic acid (when from milk), by-products of dairy industry.
Beeswax, bee propolis, honey, royal jelly- all made by bees for the use of bees.
Caramel - A food coloring that now may contain dairy cream or skim milk.
Casein or sodium caseinate, potassium caseinate. The main protein of cow's milk.
   Most marketed soy cheeses contain casein and are therefore not vegan.
Non-dairy creamers often contain dairy or casein.
Lecithin - can be from eggs; more widely used is a soya lecithin substitute.
Cod liver oil and anchovy paste (found in Worcestershire Sauce): from fish.
Beef bouillon and **chicken stock** from cooked meat.
Diglycerides and **Monoglycerides** may be lard (animal fat) unless otherwise noted by
   "vegetable derived" or something to that effect. Glyceride is a chemical name for fat.
Rennet or Rennin - the lining of a calf's stomach, used to coagulate cheese.
Pepsin - from hogs' stomachs is a clotting agent, found in some cheeses and vitamins;
   same uses as rennet. (Plant rennets, are available as an alternative.)
Albumin - protein derived, most often from egg whites, used as a food binder.
Carminic acid, Carmine is a red pigment extracted from crushed cochineal insects. To
   produce 1 lb. of this dye, 70,000 insects are crushed.
Vitamins may have non-vegan sources. Totally vegetarian formulas are available.
   Example: Vitamin D3 is made from fish oil, or sometimes lanolin (wool fat).
Lipase - enzyme from stomachs, etc., of various slaughtered young farm animals. May be
   in some vitamins. Vegetable enzymes are alternatives.

> *"What wisdom can you find that is greater than kindness?"*
>
> JEAN-JACQUES ROUSSEAU (1712-1778)
> Swiss-born French philosopher and author

Non-Vegan Businesses:

*Pet Stores - Puppy Mills - "The Humane Society of The United States estimates that more than one-half million puppies are produced annually to be sold almost exclusively to pet stores." If you want to share your home with a dog or cat, save a life by adopting from a local pound or shelter."

> "The Humane Society of The United States estimates that shelters in the U.S. accept 8-12 million animals each year... of which about 30 - 60% are euthanized."
>
> HUMANE SOCIETY OF THE UNITED STATES

Circuses - "Physical punishment has long been the standard training method for animals in circuses......Some animals are drugged to make them "manageable," and some have their teeth removed."
(People For the Ethical Treatment of Animals, Factsheet #4)

Marine Parks - "Killer whales, or orcas, are members of the dolphin family. They are also the largest animals held in captivity. In the wild, orcas stay with their mothers for life. Family groups, or "pods", consist of a mother, her adult sons and daughters, and the offspring of her daughters. Each member of the pod communicates in a "dialect" specific to that pod. Dolphins swim together in family pods of 3 to 10 individuals or tribes of hundreds. Imagine then, the trauma inflicted on these social animals when they are put in the strange, artificial world of a marine park...In the wild, orcas and dolphins may swim up to 100 miles a day. But captured dolphins are confined to tanks as small as 24' by 24' and only 6' deep. More than half of all dolphins die within the first two years of captivity; the remaining dolphins live an average of only 6 years. One Canadian research team found that captivity shortens an orca's life by as much as 43 years; a dolphin's life by up to 15 years...."
(People For the Ethical Treatment of Animals-Factsheet #8)

> "In the wild, whales and dolphins (cetaceans) spend little time motionless and are under water 90% of the time. Yet in captivity, individuals frequently are observed floating motionless at their pools' surface. It is undoubtedly this unnatural inactivity and lack of below-surface time that cause the gradual and permanent (full or partial) dorsal-fin collapse of all captive male orcas (including Keiko of "Free Willy" fame) and many female orcas and dolphins."
>
> NAOMI A. ROSE, Ph.D
> Marine Mammal Scientist for the U. S. Humane Society

*Rodeos - "In the assorted "events", steers and calves are kicked, prodded, stung with electric "hot shots" and various caustic substances, and jerked to the ground by a neck rope at speeds of up to 27 miles an hour. A flank or "bucking" strap is tightly pinched around their abdomens and causes the otherwise nonviolent animals to buck. Some animals are dragged away from the arena, suffering from torn ligaments, broken bones and other injuries, and then sent on to be slaughtered."

Zoos - "Zoos teach people that it is acceptable to keep animals in captivity, bored, cramped, lonely and far from their natural homes. ...Animals suffer from more than neglect in some zoos. Zoos often sell or kill animals who no longer attract visitors."
(People For The Ethical Treatment of Animals, Factsheet #3)

Animal Acts and Exhibits - "Animals used for entertainment are subjected to rigorous and abusive training methods to force them to perform stressful, confusing, uncomfortable and even painful acts. Training methods can include beatings, the use of electric prods, food deprivation, drugging and surgically removing or impairing teeth and claws...."
(People For the Ethical Treatment of Animals Factsheet #10)

Dog Races - "The cruelty in greyhound racing begins with the dog's training. Each year approximately 100,000 small animals—most of them rabbits—are used as live bait to teach young dogs to chase lures around the track. "Bait animals" may be used repeatedly throughout the day, whether alive or dead. Rabbits' legs are sometimes broken so their cries will excite the dogs; guinea pigs are used because they scream. Less aggressive dogs are sometimes placed in a cage with a rabbit or other animal and not released or fed until they have killed the cage companion."
(People for the Ethical Treatment of Animals, Factsheet #2)

Bullfights - "Perhaps the most notorious tourist attraction is the bullfight, a spectacle so offensive that 90% of those who attend one never return. No fair challenge, it is a fight between bulls who are debilitated and tormented beforehand and "brave" matadors who will face little danger. Vaseline is smeared into the bull's eyes to blur their vision, their horns are filed blunt, irritants are rubbed on their legs to throw them off balance and cotton is stuffed up their nostrils to shorten their breath. In so-called "bloodless bullfights", the only type that is legal in the U.S., the bulls survive the public torment only to be slaughtered immediately afterward."
(People For The Ethical Treatment of Animals Factsheet # 7)

Animals used in traveling shows and menageries are often subjected to severe abuses in order to provide "entertainment" at county fairs, shopping malls and theme parks."
(People For The Ethical Treatment of Animals Factsheet # 7)

Horse racing - "Racehorses have a drug problem. Many have been turned into addicts by their trainers and even by veterinarians, who frequently provide drugs illegally to keep horses on the track even when they shouldn't race. Commonly used drugs, such as 'Lasix' (furosemide) and 'Bute' (phenylbutazone), relieve symptoms like pain and bleeding, but don't treat the underlying disorders. Horses are forced to race with hairline fractures that would, without drugs, be too painful to run on. As a result, injuries and chronic lameness are common...Horse Illustrated Magazine estimates that up to 75% of racehorses wind up at the slaughterhouse...No federal legislation regulates the transport of horses to slaughter."
(P.E.T.A. Factsheet #5)

Hunting Industry - "In the 19th and 20th centuries, hunters have helped wipe out dozens of species, including the passenger pigeon, the great auk and the heath hen. They have brought a long list of others, including the bison and the grizzly bear, to the brink of extinction. With an arsenal of rifles, shotguns, muzzle loaders, handguns and bows and arrows, hunters kill more than 200 million animals yearly. They cripple, orphan and harass millions more."
(MICHAEL MARKARIAN: Director of Campaigns for The Fund For Animals)

Vivisection

"Vivisection is animal experimentation: burning, electric shocking, drugging, starving, irradiating, blinding and outright killing animals. Over 25 million animals in the U.S. suffer and are killed each year in laboratories for product and cosmetic testing, in classrooms and for biomedical experiments."

"The billions of dollars spent yearly on animal studies could be used for population studies, in vitro (test tube) research, clinical studies and for preventive measures that would save human lives."

KARIN ZUPKO, Ph.D.
New England Anti-Vivisection Society

"I believe I am not interested to know whether vivisection produces results that are profitable to the human race or doesn't. To know that the results are profitable to the race would not remove my hostility to it. **The pain which it inflicts upon unconsenting animals** is the basis of my enmity toward it and it is to me sufficient justification of the enmity without looking further."

MARK TWAIN   (1835-1910)
American author and humorist

"There is, however, another subject on which the Queen feels most strongly, and that is this horrible, brutalizing, un-Christian-like vivisection...It must really not be permitted. It is a disgrace to a civilized country."

QUEEN VICTORIA (1819-1901)

"Imagine that you are creating a fabric of human destiny with the object of making men happy in the end, giving them peace and rest at last, but that it was essential and inevitable to torture to death only one tiny creature, and to found that edifice on its unavenged tears. Would you consent to be the architect on those conditions?"

FYODOR DOSTOEVSKY (1821-1881)
Russian novelist

"Vivisection is the blackest of all the black crimes that man is at present committing against God and his animal creations."

"I abhor vivisection with my whole soul. All the scientific discoveries stained with innocent blood I count as of no consequence."

MAHATMA GANDHI (1869-1948)
Hindu nationalist leader

"During my medical education at the University of Basel, I found vivisection horrible, barbarous, and above all, unnecessary."

CARL JUNG (1905-1961)
Swiss psychiatrist

Vegan Alternatives

Non-Dairy Milks

Rice Dream™ - Rice milk. Made by *Imagine Foods,* Palo Alto, CA. at (800) 333-6339.

Vitasoy™ - soy milk. The company is based in San Francisco, CA. at (800) 848-2769.

Edensoy™ - Soy milk. *Eden Foods* is based in Clinton, Michigan at (800) 248-0320.

Naturally Almond™, Naturally Oat™, Soy, Rice & Multi-Grain Milks - found in natural food stores and made by *Pacific Foods of Oregon* - (503) 692-9610.

Westsoy™ - made by *Westbrae,* part of the *Hain Food Group.* Found in health food stores.

Amazaké Rice Drink - refrigerated/frozen drink made from organic brown rice. 13 flavors. Made by *Grainassance* based in Emeryville, CA. at (800) 472-4697.

Solait - economical instant soy beverage produced by *Harvest Direct,* at (800) 838-2727.

Silk™ - refrigerated soymilk in supermarket dairy cases. *White Wave, Inc.* (800) 488-9283.

Non-Dairy Cheese

Red Star Nutritional Yeast ™ - "Vegetarian Support Formula" is a reliable vegan source of Vitamin B-12. *Red Star* can be reached at (800) 558-9892. (See Glossary)

VeganRella™ Cheese alternative - 2 flavors and cream cheese. It is free of soy and dairy. Firm when cold & melts when heated. Reach *Rella Good, Inc.,* at (800) 656-9669.

Soymage™ - Grated Parmesan Cheese alternative, Soymage Soy Singles - 100% dairy-free/Casein-free **American Cheese & Italian slices, Soymage Mozzarella** and **Cheddar chunks** (low fat), **Soymage Cream Cheese** and **Sour Cream** all made by *Soyco Foods,* a division of *Galaxy Foods* based in Orlando, FL. at (800) 808-2325.

Butter Replacements

Willow Run™ Soy Margarine - Produced by *Van Den Bergh Foods* at (800) 872-1252.

Spectrum Natural Spreads™ - a non-hydrogenated oil based margarine. (800) 995-2705

Non-Dairy Ice Cream

Organic Soy Delicious™ - Quart-sized, soy based (non-genetically engineered soybeans). So Incredible!! Produced by *Turtle Mountain, Inc.,* Junction City, OR. Call (541) 998-6778.

Rice Dream™ - Many flavors; pints, quarts, pops & pies. The cones contain honey. Found in the health food stores. Non-soy base. Made by *Imagine Foods.* (800) 333-6339.

It's Soy Delicious!™ - Tasty, fruit juice sweetened and low fat. Pint size assorted flavors. It is made with organic soybeans. *Turtle Mountain, Inc.,* Junction City, OR. (541) 998-6778.

Sweet Nothings™ - A fruit sweetened frozen dessert with no fat. Found in health food stores and produced by *Turtle Mountain, Inc.,* Junction City, OR. (541) 998-6778.

Vegan Mayonnaise

Veganaise™ - refrigerated item. Made by *Follow Your Heart* at (818) 348-3240 or 347-9946.

Nayonaise™ - made by *Nasoya* - (also comes in fat-free) Call (800) 229-TOFU.

Egg Replacement

Ener-G® Foods Egg Replacer - a replacement for eggs in baking & casseroles. It comes in a box, in powdered form, and is made from potato starch, tapioca flour, carbohydrate gum, etc. *Ener-G-Foods* can be reached at (800) 331-5222.
(See **Baking Guide** for other egg replacement ideas.)

Non-Dairy Yogurt

Silk Dairyless - a soy yogurt alternative found in the refrigerated section of health food stores. It is made by *White Wave,Inc.* based in Boulder, CO. (800) 488-9283.

Vegan Burgers

Nature's Burger™ - made by *Fantastic Foods* - (found in health food stores)
GardenBurger® Hamburger Style and the **GardenVegan™.** Based in Portland, OR., *Garden Burger, Inc.* can be reached at (800) 636-0109.
Natural Touch Vegan Burger™ -*Worthington Foods* of Columbus, OH. at (614) 885-9511.
Boca Burger's Vegan™- (only 1 of their four is vegan; check label) *Boca Burger, Inc.* is based in Ft. Lauderdale, FL.
Yves Garden Vegetable Patties -*Yves Fine Foods* (604) 525-1345. All products are vegan.
Lightburgers™ - Made by *Lightlife Foods*, in Turner's Falls, MA. at (800) 274-6001.
Veggie Burgers - Produced by *Mud Pie Frozen Foods* at (612) 870-4888.

Meat Analogs

Yves Veggie Cuisine® - Pepperoni, Canadian Bacon, Hot and Spicy Jumbo Veggie Dogs, Chili Dogs, Bologna and Deli Slices, Burgers and a new product called "Just like Ground!". All products made by this company are vegan (found in health food stores' refrigerator or freezer). *Yves Fine Foods* - Canadian based company - (604) 525-1345.
Tofu Pups® - the classic vegan hot dog marketed by *Lightlife Foods*, in Turner's Falls, MA. at (800) 274-6001 or (413) 774-6001.
Lean Links™ - Sausage flavor, low fat meat analog. *Lightlife Foods* (800) 274-6001.
Smart Deli Slices® - fat-free luncheon meat alternatives; turkey or ham style. All made by *Lightlife Foods,* Turner's Falls, MA. at (800) 274-6001or (877) SOY EASY.
Savory Seitan™ - made by *Lightlife Foods,* Turner's Falls, MA.. (800) 274-6001.
Meatless Gimme Lean! - (instead of ground meat). *Lightlife Foods* (800) 274-6001.
UnTurkey™ - A vegan, fully cooked (just needs reheating) holiday centerpiece turkey alternative. It's made by *Now and Zen™,* a vegan restaurant and bakery in San Francisco, CA. For information call (415) 695-2805.
Slice of Life - meatless pepperoni, meatless salami, chicken, turkey styles and summer sausages. The Vegi-Deli product line is low-fat, zero cholesterol, high protein, completely vegan and kosher certified. Vegi-Deli™ and the line of "Slice of Life" is marketed by *Green Options* , based in San Francisco, at (888) 473-3667.
Veggie Ribs, Chicken Chunks & Protean™- (alternative to ground beef in various flavors: Sausage, Chili, Barbecue, Taco, etc.) - Non frozen or refrigerated. Easy preparation, dry mixes. Produced by *Harvest Direct, Inc.*, based in Knoxville, TN. at (800) 838-2727.
White Wave - Sandwich Slices/Lemon Broil Tempeh, Stir Fry Seitan/ Meat of Wheat Chicken Style/Baked Tofu - refrigerated product line found in health food stores.
Heartline Meatless Meats - A meat analog has the texture of "jerky" or you can reconstitute with water. Made by *Lumen Foods* (800) 256-2253 or (318) 436-6748.
New Menu Vegi Dogs - "Meatless Hot Dogs" - made by *Vitasoy* in Brisbane, CA.

Nut Butters, Nuts, Tahini

Maranatha - full line of nut butters and tahini. *Maranatha Natural Foods* - (800) 299-0048.

Once Again Nut Butters - A worker-owned co-operative in upstate New York that markets assorted nut butters, including cashew butter. Bulk tubs available. Reach the company at (888) 800-8075 or (716) 468-2535.

Chocolate and Carob Products Without Dairy

Tropical Source - 100% dairy-free chocolate bars and chips. Made in Israel in non-dairy machinery. Found in health food stores nationwide. *Cloud Nine, Inc.* is based in Hoboken, NJ. They can be reached at (800) 398-2380. Website at www.cloudninecandy.com

Sunspire Dairy-free Organic Chocolate Chips - found in health food stores. Sunspire products are labeled 99% dairy-free because it is processed in machines that have processed dairy chocolates. Although they are thoroughly cleaned, they may contain traces. To reach *Sunspire* call (510) 569-9731.

Rapunzel Pure Organics dairy-free Chocolate Bars - Semi-sweet Chocolate & Almonds or (hazelnuts), Semi-sweet Rapunzel, and Bittersweet 70% Cocoa Bar. The sweetener used is organic whole cane sugar called 'rapadura'. For more information call *Rapunzel Pure Organics*, based in Volatie, N.Y. at (800) 207-2814.

Rio Bar - found in health food stores. Produced by *Rapunzel Pure Organics*.

Chattfield's - Non-Dairy Carob and Chocolate Chips are made in machinery that dairy chocolate is made in. Trace amounts of dairy may be found in the product.

Breakfast Cereals

Health Valley Brown Rice Flakes, Amaranth Flakes, Fiber 7 Flakes, Oat Bran Flakes and **Breakfast Bars.** *Health Valley* is based in Irwindale, CA. at (800) 662-1991.

Nature's Path Multigrain, Millet-Rice, Mesa Sunrise, Fruit Juice Corn Flakes & hot cereals in a carton. 100% organic. (Some of their cereals contain honey). Found in health food stores. *Nature's Path* is based in Delta, Canada, at (604) 940-0505.

Cinnamon Flakes - organic, fruit juice sweetened cereal with no artificial additives and **Teddy Puffs** - a wheat-free cereal snack for toddlers (or adults). Both are made by *Healthy Times* - El Cajon, CA. (619) 593-2229. Found in health food stores.

Barbara's Shredded Spoonfuls, Puffins, Bite-Size Shredded Oats, Shredded Wheat, Corn Flakes, Breakfast O's, Brown Rice Crisps; these do not contain honey. (Some products do contain honey.) *Barbara's Bakery*, based in Petaluma, CA., at (707) 765-2273.

Flax Plus Multi-Bran Cereal - made by *LifeStream Natural Foods* in Blaine, WA. Lifestream is part of *Nature's Path Foods* (604) 940-0505. e-mail cereal@naturespath.bc.ca

Puffed Kashi, Kashi Breakfast Pilaf®, and brand new **Kashi go®** (cooked organic grains with real fruit) - Natural and delicious cereals made from seven whole grains and sesame. *The Kashi Co.*, based in La Jolla, CA. at (619) 274-8870.

Kamut Whole Grain Cereal - made by *Arrowhead Mills*, *The Hain Food Group*.

Natural Wafflers® - 4 varieties: original, maple, cinnamon and vanilla-nut Found in health food stores. Produced by *U.S. Mills* in Omaha, NE. at (402) 451-4567.

Erewhon - Aztec, Corn Flakes, Kamut Flakes, Fruit 'n Wheat, Wheat Flakes, Raisin Bran, Crispy Brown Rice Cereal, Banana O's, Apple Stroodles, Poppets - are all ready to eat cereals found in health food stores. Call *U.S. Mills* at (781) 444-0440.

Uncle Sam's Cereal - a hot cereal that acts as a natural laxative (made with flaxseed). Produced by *U.S. Mills* who have been producing 100% natural cereals since 1908! Based in Omaha, Nebraska, reach *U.S. Mills* at (402) 451-4567.

New Morning Organic Cereals - *New Morning*, based in Boxboro, MA. at (978)-263-1201.

Salad Dressings
Nasoya - 2 excellent salad dressings: Creamy Dill and Garden Herb. (415) 583-9888.
Simply Delicious, Inc. - line of organic salad dressings & sauces; some contain honey. Based in Cedar Grove, NC. The company can be reached at (919) 732-5294.
Annie's Naturals - 8 vegan products: Check labels for honey in their line. *Annie's Naturals* is based in E. Calais, VT. at (800) 434-1234.

Salt Flavorings or Substitutes
San J Tamari - organic, wheat-free, reduced-sodium, Shoyu, etc. *San-J International*, based in Richmond, VA., can be reached at (804) 226-8333 or (800) 446-5500.
Bragg™ Liquid Aminos - a delicious salty flavored seasoning and source of protein made from soybeans. It is an important staple in a vegan kitchen. *Bragg's* - (800) 446-1990.

Vegan Cookies, Baked Goods, Desserts
The Alternative Baking Co. - a vegan baking company that markets individually wrapped, jumbo-size cookies, in five assorted flavors. The company located in Sacramento, CA., can be reached at (916) 488-9725.
Jacqui's Gourmet Cookies - A variety of wheat-free, fructose sweetened, cookies. The company makes only vegan cookies. They are based in Grass Valley, CA. at (800) 310-0107.
Frankly Natural Bakers - markets the following vegan treats: tahini cookies & squares, rice bars and Vegan Decadence brownies and blondies. Sold at health food stores or directly to the public from their San Diego base. (619) 536-5910. Order line - (800) 727-7229.
Barbara's Bakery Homestyle Cookies - a fruit juice sweetened health food store item.
Now and Zen™ - offers a line of fancy cakes and deep dish cookies made by their vegan restaurant & bakery in California. The wholesale bakery can be reached at (415) 695-2805.
Allison's Cookies™- organic, unrefined sweeteners, wheat-free options. By mail order only. Based in Seattle, WA. reach *Allison's Cookies* at (206) 567-5292. www.allisonscookies.com
Cliff Bars - a quick energy, high carbohydrate, naturally sweet treat made especially for hikers. Made by *Kali's Sport Naturals* of Berkeley, CA. at (800) 884-5254.
Imagine Foods Pudding - 3 flavors of a non-dairy pudding. Found in health food stores.
Mrs. Denson's Cookies - **markets 11 varieties that are vegan** & some varieties are not. Check labels. Try the Chocolate Chip Macaroon, Quinoa Macaroon, Date Walnut or Oatmeal Raisin. Based in Ukiah, CA. at (707) 462-2272 or (800) 219-3199.
Grainassance- Amazake Pudding - refrigerated health food store item - at (800) 472-4697.
Barbara's Bakery Whole Wheat Fig Bars - found in health food stores.
Creme Supreme Cookies - vegan version of an Oreo-like cookie. *Tree of Life* distributor.

Miso Products
Cold Mountain Miso - made from organic soybeans, rice, sea salt & water. This fine miso is marketed by *Miyako Oriental Foods,* Baldwin Park, CA. at (818) 962-9633.
Organic Miso Master Miso - This miso is fresh, unpasteurized, and truly a living food. It is produced by *The American Miso Co.* for *Great Eastern Sun* at (800) 334-5809.
Westbrae Natural Foods - unpasteurized miso found in the refrigerated section of health food stores. Reach the company at (310) 886-8200.

Bouillon Cubes (Instant Broth)
Vegetable Harvest Bouillon Cubes - *Edward & Sons Trading Co.* at (805)-684-8500.

Sugar Alternatives

The Ultimate Sweetener® - 100% pure birch sugar. Safe even for diabetics. No birch trees are ever cut down for the sugar. It is free of sugar, honey, corn syrup, fructose, bone ash, any animal products or anything artificial. Sold directly to the public by calling (800) THE-MEAL (843-6325) or (805) 962-2221 or visit www. ultimatelife.com.

Sucanat™ - organic & non-organic evaporated cane crystals. *Wholesome Foods*, based in Florida, can be reached at (800) 860-1896.

Shady Maple Farms - produced with a vegetable oil (organic and Kosher certified) which is used in the defoaming process. Their product is animal-fat free. (418) 459-6161.

Spring Tree - an amber, 100% pure, animal-fat free, certified organic maple syrup. Made in Canada and distributed by the *Spring Tree Corporation* in Brattelboro, VT. (802) 254-8784.

Maverick Sugarbush Maple Syrup - Located in Sharon, VT. at (802) 763-8680.

Maple Acres Inc., an all natural, deep amber maple syrup made in a traditional fashion. Based in Kewadin, Michigan. You can reach the Luchenbill's at (616) 264-9265.

Maple Grove Farms of Vermont, Inc. - Maple syrup found in grocery stores or through catalog. Based in St. Johnsbury, VT., call (802) 748-5141 or (800) 525-2540 for orders.

Date Sugar - distributed by Health Best at (760) 752-5230. Distributed by *Nature's Cuisine*.

Sweet Dreams ® - brown rice syrup made by *Lundberg Family Farms* at (916) 882-4551.

Malt Barley - syrup made from sprouted barley. Marketed by *Eden Foods* at (313) 973-9400.

Sorghum - a delicious & sweet liquid sweetener. *Arrowhead Mills* produces a line of it.

Fruitsource® - available in liquid (good honey alternative) or dry granular form. Marketed by *Advanced Products* at (888) 238-4647.

Plantation Molasses - A liquid sweetener that is good in making gravies, seitan, etc. Based in Port Reading, N.J., *Allied Old English* can be reached at (800) 225-0122.

Rapadura - whole organic cane sugar. *Rapunzel Pure Organics* - (800) 207-2814

Quick and Easy Meals in a Cup or Carton

Fantastic Foods - *Fantastic Foods* has many convenient vegan soups & cereals in a cup (great for traveling), tofu helpers, frozen burgers, burger mixes, hummus, bean, pasta mixes and Tabouli in a carton. Please note that some products are not vegan, containing cheese, whey, etc. Read labels. *Fantastic Foods* - (800) 832-6345.

Casbah - Timeless Cuisine items such as Rice Pilaf, Cous-Cous Lemon Spinach, Gyros, Perfect Corn Fritter, Teriyaki Burger, Tabouli, Nutted Cous-Cous with Currants & Spices, all made by *Sahara Natural Foods* (510) 352-5111.

Dried Fruits

Made in Nature - an assortment of organic natural dried fruits. (800) 906-7426.

The Date People - market a wide variety of dates, including date/coconut rolls and date/nut rolls. Based in Niland, CA. They can be reached at (760) 359-3211.

Vegan Fruit Spreads

Sorrel Ridge - a jam made without refined white sugar. (Because white sugar is most often refined through bone char, most jellies/jams are not considered vegan.)
This jam is marketed by *Allied Old English* and they can be reached at (800) 225-0122.

Flour

Giusto's - offer a full line of all-natural bakery ingredients, including flours, some of which are organic. To reach the company call (650) 873-6566.

Arrowhead Mills - high quality flours found nationwide in health food stores.

Recommended Oils:

Barlean's Organic Oils - a high quality flaxseed oil and rich source of vegetable Omega-3 fatty acids. Based in Ferndale, WA. They can be reached at (800) 445-3529.

Arrowhead Mills Flaxseed Oil - found in health food stores. (800) 749-0730.

Santa Barbara Olive Co. - produce a cold-pressed extra virgin olive oil. They manufacture 70 items all derived from the olive. Based in Santa Ynez, CA. They can be reached at (800) 624-4896.

The Golden Eagle Olive Products - virgin olive oil. Porterville, CA. at (209) 784-3468.

Spectrum Oils - Oils are all created without solvent extraction. Some organic and unrefined & some are refined. They also market flax oils. Based in Petaluma CA. at (800) 995-2705 or (707) 778-8900.

Loriva Rice Bran Oil - a light and healthy oil. Call them at (800) - 94-LORIVA.

Oils of Aloha - 100% pure cold-pressed oil from Hawaiian macadamia nuts. They are based in Waialua, HI. at (800) 367-6010.

Pasta Products

Ancient Harvest Quinoa Pasta - wheat-free supergrain Elbows, Spaghetti, Shells, etc. *The Quinoa Corporation*, based in Torrance, CA. can be reached at (310) 530-8666.

Vita Spelt - organic whole grain spelt pasta. Call *Purity Foods* at (800) 997-7358.

DeBoles - A subsidiary of *Arrowhead Mills, DeBoles* can be reached at (800) 749-0730.

Tempeh and Tofu (Soy Products)

SuperBuger™ - 8 flavors of tempeh, including the line of Superburgers made from whole grains in Original, Bar-B-Q and Tex Mex flavors. **TOFURKY**- The Delicious Vegetarian Feast available seasonally or year round as **Extra Thin Deli Sliced Tofurky.** Products are 100% vegan. To contact *Turtle Island Products,* based in OR., call (800) 508-8100.

Lightlife Foods - 6 varieties of tempeh. Based in Turner's Falls, MA. at (800) 274-6001.

Lean Green Foods - Soy and sea vegetable tempeh. Based in Chico, CA. and Hilo, HI.

Nasoya Tofu -organic pound packages found in health food/grocery stores. (800) 229-TOFU.

Sea Vegetables

Maine Coast Sea Vegetables - A variety of sea vegetables, sweet treats made with sea vegetables, Sea Seasonings™ in shakers & sea chips. Sea vegetables are high in vitamins & minerals, including vitamin B-12. Based in Franklin, ME., reach them at (207) 565-2907.

Eden Foods - Assorted sea vegetables and Nori found in health food stores.

Emerald Cove Sea Salads - *Great Eastern Sun*, based in NC. at (800) 334-5809.

Breads

Ezekiel 4:9 Bread - a delicious sprouted grain bread made without honey. Marketed by *Food for Life® Baking Company* in Corona, CA. at (909) 279-5090 or (800) 797-5090.

Food for Life Rice Pecan Bread, Rice Almond and **Millet Bread** - (800) 797-5090.

Manna Bread™- Essene bread that is sprouted, unleavened with no added fat, sweetener or salt. Produced by *Nature's Path*, in Canada, at (604) 940-0505.

Garden of Eatin' - offers whole wheat tortillas and chapatis. (800) 333-5244.

Giustos Vita-Grain - Sprouted 9-Grain Bread & Sprouted Whole Wheat Amaranth . Marketed by Guistos at (650) 873-6566.

Non-irradiated Spices

San Francisco Herb and Natural Food - markets spice blends, herbal teas, dehydrated soup mixes, etc. Catalogs available. Based in Fremont, CA. at (800) 227-2830.

Frontier Herbs - quality spices and herbs. Based in Norway, IA. at (319) 227-7996.
Spice Garden - **Spike™ Seasoning** and **Vegit™** produced by *Modern Products*, Milwaukee, WI. Found in health food stores.
Herbamere™- an herb seasoning salt, with fresh organically grown herbs. **Trocomare** - spicy herb seasoning. *Bioforce America*, based in Kinderhook, N.Y. at (800) 645-9135.
The Spice Hunter - 160 varieties (some organic) of assorted spices and blends. Based in San Luis Obispo, CA. at (800) 444-3061 or (805) 544-4466.

Non-Alcoholic Vanilla
Pure Vanilla Powder - Madagascar Bourbon pure vanilla powder; alcohol free and liquid vanilla. *Nielsen-Massey Vanillas, Inc.* can be reached at (800) 525-pure. (7873)
Spicery Shoppe - non-alcoholic, pure vanilla flavor. Call (800) 323-1301.

Teas and Coffee Substitutes
San Francisco Herbs - beautifully packaged assorted herbal teas. (800) 227-2830.
Celestial Seasonings - herbal teas. Company is based in Boulder, CO.
Kaffree Roma - a coffee substitute made by *Worthington Foods* (614) 885-9511.
Raja's Cup™ - Antioxidant coffee alternative; non-irradiated. *Maharishi Ayur-Ved Products* in Colorado Springs, CO. at (800) 255-8332.
Organic Haiku Tea Line - (green tea) made by *Great Eastern Sun* at (800) 334-5809.

Sauces
The Wizard's™ Vegetarian Worcestershire Sauce - a kosher, zesty, full-bodied flavoring marketed by *Edward & Son's Trading Co.*, based in Santa Barbara, CA. at (805) 684-8500.
Muir Glen Organic Tomato Products - a wide variety of tomato sauces, pastes, salsa, etc. Some products have honey. Reach them at (800) 832-6345.
Annie's Naturals - Original & Smoky Maple Bar-B-Q Sauces marketed by *Annies Naturals* at (800) 434-1234.

Special Products
Just Like Ground! - made by *Yves Veggie Cuisine* - for use in Lasagna, Chili, loaves and casseroles instead of ground seitan, tempeh or T.V.P. Found in health food stores.
Bob's Red Mill Steel Cut Oats - cut whole oat groat. Bob's Red Mill is based in Milwaukee, OR. at (503) 654-3215 - markets a full line of grains found in health food stores.
Wild Rice Products - *Grey Owl Foods*, Canada - (800) 527-0172 or (413) 584-3013.
Brown Rice Snaps - Distributed by *Edward & Sons Co* ., based in CA. at (805) 684-8500.
Soy Lavasch Crackers - found in health food stores. *Tofutti Brands* at (908) 272-2400.
Fat-Free Healthy Tarts - (except chocolate). *Health Valley* at (800) 334-3204.
Hain Saltine Crackers & Oyster Crackers - *The Hain Food Group* , based in Compton, CA. at (310) 886-8200 or (800) 434-HAIN.

All Natural Juices (no sugar)
Mountain Sun- Based in southern Colorado, they can be reached at (970) 882-2283.
(The lemon juices may contain honey, but all others are vegan)

Healthy Food Supplements
The Ultimate Meal ®- The highest quality vegan ingredients in a tasty meal you can drink. Found in health food stores nationwide or call (800) THE-MEAL (843-6325) or (805) 962-2221 or visit www.ultimatelife.com.

Spirulina Pacifica - certified organically grown spirulina. Crystal Flakes (spirulina) to sprinkle on food or mix in juices, tablets or powder made by *Nutrex Inc.*, Kailua-Kona, HI. (800) 453-1187.

Earthrise™ Spirulina - A source of all vegetable protein as well as vitamin B12. This spirulina is pesticide and herbicide free. Call Earthrise at (800) 949-RISE.

Peaceful Planet High Protein Energy Shake - instant powder that mixes easily with juice or rice/soy milk. *VegLife™* - *Nutraceutical Corporation*, located in Park City, UT. at (800) VEG-0250.

Kyolic Garlic - Liquid aged garlic. Not all products are vegan; check label for whey or gelatin capsules. *Wakunaga of America* at (714) 458-2764.

NutriBiotic ® - offers a vegan nutritionally balanced drink called Prozone in assorted flavors and a rice protein drink. Based in Lakeport, CA., they can be reached at (800) 225-4345 or (707) 769-2266.

Spirulina - made by *Cyanotech Corp.* (800) 453-1187.

Herbal Supplements and Vitamins

VegLife™ - is committed to providing a complete line of premium quality supplements free of animal by-products. The Tablite™ and supplements in vegicaps are 100% vegetarian. Their supplements consist of herbal extracts, as well as vitamins and minerals. Found in health food stores. For comments call *Nutraceutical Corporation*, located in Park City, UT. at (800) VEG-0250.

St. John's Wart Herbal Tincture - Based in Soquel, CA., *Planetary Formulations* can be reached at (408) 438-1700.

Herb Pharm - is an 85-acre certified organic herb farm & Botanical Education Garden. They offer a line of over 250 quality Certified Organically Grown and Custom Wildcrafted™ herbal extracts and health-care products, including wild yam extract. They can be reached at (541) 846-6262.

SuperNutrition Women's Blend is a woman's comprehensive multi-vitamin/mineral (totally vegan) blend. They also market Perfect Blend, a food-based herbal multivitamin for men. Call *SuperNutrition*, based in San Francisco, CA. for more information at (800) 262-2116.

Wise Women Essentials - Wild Yam extract topical cremes (Liposome Natural Progesterone & Anti-oxidant Creme), for PMS & menopausal comfort, and for controlling hormones naturally. It does not contain beeswax. Call *Wise Essentials, Inc.*, baseed in Hallandale, FL. at (954) 454-9888.

Born Again™ - markets vegan Wild Yam Cream and Gel. They can be reached at (800) 527-8123.

Indian Meadow Herbals - herbal tinctures preserved in organic apple alcohol. The medicinal herbs are grown on a 102 acre farm in Maine. Call (888) 464-3729.

New Chapter - Herbal extracts, vitamins and supplements. All products are vegan, except Ginger Syrup and acidophilus. *New Chapter* is based in Brattleboro, VT. at (800) 543-7279.

Eclectic Institute - market herbal tinctures, including wild yam. The wild yam tincture (as opposed to the chemically manipulated creams) won't make progesterone but can relieve symptoms of menopause and is a muscle relaxant. Based in Sandy, OR., *Eclectic Institute* can be reached at (888) 799-4372.

VegiCaps (non-gelatin based capsules)

Vegicaps is a registered trademark of *GS Technologies, Inc.* - They replace animal-based gelatin capsules. Empty vegan capsules can be purchased in bulk. *GS Technologies (Solgar)* can be reached at (800) 645-2246 or (516) 599-2442.

Healing Salves

Living Seed Products - distribute exotic oils (such as hemp seed oil) and herbal medicinals. The oils are cold-pressed; kept at temperatures below zero. They market **Hemp Zap™ Vegan Analgesic**, as well as **Kind Help™ Vegan Ointment**. *Merry Hempsters* is located in Eugene, OR. at (541) 345-9317. Their toll-free order line is (888) SEED-OIL.

Cruelty-Free Cosmetics

Beauty Without Cruelty -a complete line (20 skin care products) and cosmetics derived from natural sources, all within the vegetarian ethic. All make-up is fragrance free and contains no mineral oil, carmine or animal by-products. To reach *The Cosmetics that Care*™, based in Petaluma, CA., call (707) 769-5120.

Cruelty-Free Hair Care Products

Aubrey Organics has been producing 100% natural hair, skin and body care products for the past 30 years. They offer over 100 completely vegan shampoos, conditioners, cleansers, masks, astringents, moisturizers, baby products, sun care, etc. The products are preserved with citrus seed extract, and Vitamins A, C and E. Never tested on animals. Look for the 'Vegan' label on their products. They do, however, have a small percentage of products that are not vegan. Based in Tampa, FL., *Aubrey Organics* can be reached at (800) 282-7394.

Nature's Gate/Levlad, Inc. - **Herbal Shampoo** and **Hair Conditioner** & **Forest Pure Shampoo** and **Conditioner** - a line of over 100 items selling under the brand names of *Nature' Gate, Petal Fresh, Forest Pure*, etc., many of which are vegan. The company has been in business since 1973, with a continued philosophy to develop effective, cruelty-free products. Their products can be found in health food stores. Reach *Nature's Gate/Levlad, Inc.* at (800) 327-2012.

Beauty Without Cruelty - Shampoo, Conditioner, Natural Hair Spray and Gel, etc. The company uses no animal ingredients. They have a strict 'no testing on animals' policy of all their ingredients. Based in Petaluma, CA., they can be reached at (707) 769-5120.

Kiss My Face - **Kiss & Go Shampoo, Everyday Care Shampoo** and **Conditioner. Olive & Aloe Shampoo & Conditioner.** Call *Kiss My Face* at (800) 262-5477.

Essential Botanicals by **Morganics** - organic shampoo of pure flower & plant essences. Located in Scottsdale, AZ., *Morganics* can be reached at (800) 820-9235.

Emerald Forest Shampoo and **Botanical Conditioner** - found in health food stores. Made by *Natural Nectar* at (888) 4NECTAR or (909) 372-2606.

Head Original Shampoo and Conditioner - *Pure and Basic* is a complete line of hair, skin and personal products and can be reached at (800) 432-3787.

Henna Highlighting Shampoo - made by *Rainbow Research* at (800) 722-9595.

Avalon Organic Botanicals Therapeutic Shampoos and **Conditioners** - made by *Avalon Natural Products*, based in Petaluma, CA. at (707) 769-5120.

Vegetable Based Soaps

Dr. Bronner's Magic Soaps - are all-purpose, pure castile, biodegradable soaps in bars and liquid, as well as several varieties. *Dr. Bronner's* is in Escondido, CA. at (760) 743-2211.

Clearly Natural Soap - vegetable glycerin soaps in assorted scents. The company is in Petaluma, CA. (707) 762-5815 or (800) 274-7627.

Sappo Hill - All vegetable oil, glycerine creme soap. Found in health food stores or call the company in Ashland, OR. (541) 482-4485.

Aura Cacia Bath Soaps - No synthetic fragrances. Found nationwide in health food stores. Based in Weaverville, CA., call them at (800) 437-3301. All products are vegan!

Vermont Soapworks - a variety of old-fashioned vegetable based soaps (except for one that does contain honey). Order directly from Larry Plesent, owner at (802) 388-4302.

Kirk's Castile Soap - found in grocery stores nationwide, as well as some health food stores. *Kirk's Natural Products Corp.* - (800) 82-KIRKS.

Nature's Gate - liquid soap and glycerin bar soaps. (800) 327-2012.

San Francisco Soap Company - natural 100% pure vegetable glycerin soap in assorted fruit and floral scents. (There is one non-vegan bar: Milk & Honey.) Biodegradable ingredients. Based in Glenrock, NJ. They can be reached at (800) 254-8656.

Kiss My Face Olive Oil Bar & liquid soaps. Based in Gardiner, NY at (800) 262-5477.

Wild Body Butter Soap - made by *Ecco Bella Botanicals* (973) 696-7766.

Rainbow Aloe-Oatmeal Bar - Reach the *Rainbow Research Corp.* at (800) 722-9595.

Rainbow Antibacterial Soap - All products contain no animal ingredients or testing. Based in Bohemia, N.Y., *Rainbow Research Corp.* can be reached at (800) 722-9595.

Sonoma Soap Co. -100% pure vegetable glycerin (except honey or milk & honey). Marketed by *Avalon Natural Products*, based in Petaluma, CA. at (707) 769-0868.

100% Coconut Oil Soap (Serena) - made by *The Tropical Soap Co.*, (800) 527-2368.

Cruelty-Free Oral Care Products

Eco-Dent - offers oral care products, almost all of which are vegan. Products include Daily Rinse and Oral Wound Cleanser, a natural Peroxide Baking Soda Whitener, a tartar control product, GentleFloss® with vegan wax and Eco-DenT toothpowder (was called Merfluan). (The pain relief formula contains bee propolis.) *Eco-DenT International*, based in Redwood City, CA. can be reached at (650) 364-6343 or (800) 369-6933.

Tom's of Maine - Baking Soda Toothpaste with Fluoride and floss made of vegetable wax. (Some of their toothpastes contain bee propolis & bee products.) They market mouth-wash, vegetable soaps, shampoo & deodorants, most of which are vegan. (207) 985-2944.

Nature's Gate - Fine Herbal Cream and Gel toothpastes. (800) 327-2012

Auromere- ayurvedic formula toothpaste, (mint-free, herbal & fresh-mint), found in health food stores. *Auromére Ayurvedic Imports*, (from India) based in Lodi, CA. at (800) 735-4691.

Weleda Plant-Gel Toothpaste & Salt Toothpaste with Baking Soda - found in health food stores. Based in Congers, N.Y., reach Weleda at (800) 241-1030 or (800) 289-1969.

Vicco Toothpaste - herbal toothpaste from India found in health food stores. It is distributed by *Lotus Brands* in Silver Lake, WI. at (800) 824-6396.

Herbal-Vedic- herbal toothpaste from India marketed by Auroma- International. It's distributors, *Lotus Brands* based in Silver Lake, WI., can be reached at (800) 824-6396.

Sun Blocks and Sun Care Products

Kiss my Face - After sun aloe soother and sun block.*Kiss My Face Corporation* is based in Gardiner, N.Y. at (800) 262-5477.

Titania - made by *Aubrey Organics* - based in Tampa, FL. at (800) 282-7394.

Earth Science - paba-free sunscreen. Based in Corona, CA. at (800) 222-6720.

Ear Candles

Wally's Natural Products - makes ear candles of paraffin and no beeswax. Based in Auburn CA. They can be reached at (800) 215-1566.

Cruelty-Free Moisturizers and Body Care Products

ShiKai - a variety of vegan moisturizing lotions found in health food stores. They conscientiously support no animal testing. The company is based in Santa Rosa, CA. and can be reached at (800) 448-0298.

Beauty Without Cruelty - Full line of lotions, facial cleansers, etc. (707) 769-5120.

Emerald Forest® Botanical - body lotions, *Siempre Bella Moisturizers* and other skin care products. Available in health food stores nationwide or call (888) 4-Nectar.

San Francisco Soap Co. - pure plant botanical skin care products such as facial mask, facial scrub & toner, oil-free moisturizer and facial moisturizer with alpha hydroxy. They also feature fruit and floral body lotions. The company can be reached at (800) 254-8656.

Nature's Gate - lotions and body care products. (800) 327-2012.

Lily of Colorado - Facial cleansers & herbal moisturizers. (800) 333-LILY.

Kiss My Face - Based in Gardiner, NY at (800) 262-5477.

Aubrey Organics - full line of cleansers, masks, astringents and moisturizers found in health food stores nationwide. Look for their 'Vegan' label.

Aura Cacia - aroma therapy massage oils and mineral baths. *Aura Cacia* - (800) 437-3301.

CamoCare - Chamomile hand and body lotion for dry skin care. Found in natural food stores nationwide. Marketed by *Abkit, Inc.* at (800) 226-6227.

Wild Body Butter Lotion - Made by *Ecco Bella Botanicals* at (201) 696-7766.

Stonybrook Botanicals™ - Aloe and Chamomile, oil free body lotion. Stony Brook Botanicals is a line from *Rainbow Research Inc.* at (800) 722-9595.

Alba Naturals Moisturizer - made by *Alba Naturals* at (800) 347-5211.

Island Essence - Hawaiian Hand and Body Lotions, massage and moisturizing oils. Contact *Island Essence, Inc.* at (808) 878-3800 on Maui, HI.

Kaleidoscope Naturals - Vegan, hemp-based body care products made with pure aroma-therapeutic grade essential oils, live hempseed oil & love. Body cream, massage oil, eye & face cream, soaps, etc. Call (808) 243-0283 or write P.O. Box 520 #228, Paia, HI. 96779.

Woman Wise™ Wild Yam Hand and Body Therapy - No animal products or testing. Marketed by *Jason Natural Cosmetics*, based in Culver City, CA. at (800) JASON-05.

Earth Science- moisturizers and skin cleansers. Based in Corona, CA. at (800) 222-6720.

Pet Care Products

Harbingers of a New Age, market Vegecat™ and Vegedog™ supplements that enable feeding cats a vegan diet as well as dogs. Owner, James Peden, authored <u>Vegetarian Cats and Dogs</u>. Vegecat™ and Vegedog™ are both supplemented with synthesized (non-animal) Taurine. Most mammals biosynthesize taurine from other amino acids. Cats lack that ability making a dietary source necessary. (The only natural source would be animal tissue.) Vegecat™ makes it possible for cats to be vegan. The company is based in Troy, Montana at (800) 884-6262.

Evolution Diet Pet Food - A complete dog food using whole natural protein rather than animal by-products or diseased slaughterhouse animals. No growth hormones or antibiotic residues. The canned food comes in 2 varieties: Vegetarian Stew and Peas & Avocado. Based in St. Paul, MN, Evolution Diet can be reached at (800) 659-0104 or (612) 228-0632.

"Vegetarian Dog Formula" - *Natural Life, Inc.* offers a canned and dry vegan dog food. Based in Frontenac, Kansas, *Natural Life* can be reached at (800) 367-2391.

"Mr. Barkey's"- vegan dog biscuits made of all whole grains. **Vegetarian Feast Formula** (canned dog food). Both are marketed by *Pet Guard* in Orange Park, FL. at (800) 874-3221.

Wow Bow Distributors - offers a line of gourmet vegan dog biscuits. They are located in Deer Park, New York at (800) -326-0230 or (516) 254-6064.

'Vegetarian Canine' - canned dog food marketed by*Nature's Recipe*. Please note their dry formula is not vegan. (The company markets mostly non-vegan dog food, including venison.) Based in Corona, CA., Nature's Recipe can be reached at (800) 843-4008.

Natural Animal/Ecozone - non-toxic animal care products, natural deodorizers, etc., found in health stores. Natural Animal is located in St. Augustine, FL. (800) 274-7387.

Synthetic Artist Brushes

Grumbacher - manufacturer of fine quality artist brushes, market two types of synthetic brushes; Erminette (red handle with white bristles) and Goldedge. (800) 877-3165.

Winsor & Newton - synthetic artist brushes. Yellow handles with white bristles. Economically priced at art supply stores or call *Winsor & Newton* at (732) 562-0770. See their website at www.winsornewton.com

Non-Leather Shoes

Payless Shoes Stores - carry many all-man-made material shoes and their own line of quality man-made material hiking boots called Rugged Outback. Payless- (800) 426-1141.

Aesop, Inc.- Mail order catalog based in North Cambridge, MA. at (617) 628-8030.

Heartland Products - Dakota City, Iowa (515) 332-3087.

Earth Friendly and Cruelty-Free Cleaning Products

(The following products contain no animal ingredients and were not tested on animals.)

Planet - *Planet, Inc.* is based in West Hills, CA. and can be reached at (800) 858-8449.

Earth Friendly Products - laundry, all-purpose cleaner, drain maintenance, dish washing, window cleaning, furniture polish, air fresheners & bathroom care. Call (800) 335 3267.

Life Tree Products (made by Sierra Dawn) - dishwashing liquid, laundry liquid, all-purpose cleaner and liquid soaps. To reach *Sierra Dawn*, call (707) 588-0755.

Bi-O-Kleen - markets a full line of cleaning products. Their all-purpose cleaner contains grapefruit seed extract which they recommend for washing pesticide residue from produce. The company is based in Portland, OR. at (503) 557-0216.

Seventh Generation Cleaning Products - laundry liquid and powder, fabric softener, glass cleaner, all-purpose and toilet bowl cleaners and dish washing liquid. Found nationwide in health food stores. Call the company at (802) 658-3773.

Morganics - dishwashing detergent, odor and stain eliminator, oxygenated bleach, shampoo. Morganics is based in Scottsdale, AZ. and can be reached at (800) 820-9235.

Citra-Solv™ - It is a concentrated cleaner that dissolves grease, oil, adhesives, ink, and more. Citra-Solve is marketed by *Shadow Lake, Inc.* in Ridgefield, CT. Purveyors of naturally-derived household & personal care products. For information call (800) 343-6588.

Earth Rite - this line is found in health food stores or call the company at (203) 618-5200.

Country Save - markets a non-chlorine bleach, automatic dishwashing detergent and laundry detergent. To reach *Country Save* call (425) 258-1171.

Ecover - markets a full line of household cleaners. Their products are found nationwide in health food stores or you can reach them at (800) 449-4925.

"We divert our attention from disease and death as much as we can; the slaughterhouses are huddled out of sight and never mentioned, so that the world we recognize officially in literature and in society is a poetic fiction far handsomer, cleaner and better than the world that really is."

WILLIAM JAMES, M.D., LLD. (1842-1910)
American physiologist, psychologist,
philosopher and teacher

Companies that market only vegan products

The Ultimate Life® - based in Santa Barbara, CA, was founded, is owned and managed by Sam Gerard, a dedicated vegan & environmentalist. It manufactures the following products: The Ultimate Meal® - a potent and complete source of nourishment in powder form. The Ultimate MealBar® - a potent and complete source of nourishment. The Ultimate Acidophilus ® - helps create friendly bacteria for a healthy digestive system. The Ultimate FloraZyme® - helps digest cooked, processed or gas-producing foods. The Ultimate Defense ® - antioxidants to help the body and mind deal with stress. The Ultimate Blue-Green® - combination of organic Hawaiian spirulina and blue-green. The Ultimate Sweetener ® - is 100% birch sugar which tastes like sugar, but safe even for diabetics. Each of the products above are vegan, hypo-allergenic and set an entirely new standard within their own field. They are sold in health food stores or direct by mail. Call (800) THE-MEAL (843-6325) or (805) 962-2221 or visit www.ultimatelife.com

Yves Fine Foods - a Canadian-based company. Makers of Vegan meat analogs, such as Canadian Bacon, Just Like Ground, Pepperoni, Chili Dogs, etc. (604) 525-1345.

Now and Zen™ - a vegan wholefood manufacturer of deep dish cookies and fancy cakes, 'Savory Select' meat substitutes and the 'Unturkey'. Based in San Francisco, California, the company can be reached at (800) 335-1959 or (415) 695-2805.

Vegi-Deli™ - producers of meat analogs such as salami and pepperoni, etc. *Green Options, Inc.*, based in San Francisco, can be reached at (888) 473-3667.

Turtle Island Foods - makers of the SuperBuger™ and Tofurky. All products are 100% vegan and delicious. For more information, contact them at P.O. Box 176, Hood River, OR. 97031 or (800) 508-8100 or email: tofurky@gorge.net.

Jacqui's Gourmet Cookies - based in Grass Valley, CA. at (800) 310-0107. A variety of soft, sweet and healthy cookies, made with organic flour (wheat-free).

Lumen Foods - makers of Heartline Meatless Meats. (800) 256-2253 or (318) 436-6748.

The Alternative Baking Co. - Markets incredibly delicious, individually wrapped, jumbo-sized cookies, in five assorted flavors. Based in Sacramento, CA., call (916) 488-9725.

Beauty Without Cruelty - To reach The Cosmetics that Care™, based in Petaluma, CA., call (707) 769-0868. They offer a complete line (20 skin care products) and cosmetics .

Harbingers of a New Age - based in Troy, Montana at (800) 884-6262. Market food supplements for feeding cats a vegan diet, as well as dogs.

Morganics - is based in Scottsdale, AZ. and can be reached at (800) 820-9235. They produce automatic dishwashing detergent, oxygenated bleach, shampoo, etc.

Dr. Bronner's -based in Escondido, California at (760) 743-2211. They market Dr. Bronner's Balanced Mineral Bouillon and all-purpose, pure castile, biodegradable soaps.

Clearly Natural Soap - based in Petaluma, CA. (707) 762-5815 or (800) 274-7627.

Kirk's Castile Soap - soaps that are found in grocery stores. *Kirk's Natural Products Corp.* can be reached at (800) 82-KIRKS.

Aura Cacia - Based in Weaverville, CA., call them at (800) 437-3301. High quality soaps, massage oils and aroma therapy products.

Sappo Hill - makers of fine soaps. Call the company in Ashland, OR. (541) 482-4485.

Maine Coast Sea Vegetables - A variety of sea vegetables and sea vegetable products. Based in Franklin, ME. They can be reached at (207) 565-2907.

The Date People - market a variety of dates. Based in Niland, CA. at (760) 359-3211.

Turtle Mountain, Inc.,-market Organic Soy Delicious!™- Sweet Nothings™ and Soy Delicious, non-dairy frozen desserts. Based in Junction City, OR. at (541) 998-6778.

Vegan Mail Order Companies

Gentle World, Inc.
P.O. Box 238
Kapa'au, HI 96755 (808) 884-5551
email: gentle@aloha.net   http://www.veganbooks-gentle.com
(Vegan books)

The American Vegan Society
56 Dinshah Lane P.O. Box 369
Malaga, NJ. 08328
(856) 694-2887; Fax: (856) 694-2288
(Vegan books, video and audio tapes)

Amberwood
Route 2, Box 300, Milford Rd.
Leary, GA. 31762   (912) 792-6246
(Toiletries, cosmetics, laundry & household cleaning products)

Pangea
7829 Woodmont Ave. Bethesda, MD 20814
(301) 652-3181   Mail Order Catalog
(A vegan store and mail order business- no silk, leather, wool or bee products)

Aesop, Inc.
P.O. Box 315
North Cambridge, MA. 02140 (617) 628-8030
(Non-leather footwear, belts, wallets, briefcases)

The Vegan Society
Donald Watson House
7 Battle Rd. St. Leonards-on-Sea
East Sussex TN37 7AA U.K.
Telephone (01424) 427393

Veg Essentials
7722 W. Menomonee River Parkway
Wauwatosa, WI. 53213 (877) 881-6477 or (414) 607-1953
(Products for Vegan Living: Toiletries, Cosmetics, Household & Pantry Items)

Heartland Products
Box 218
Dakota City, IA. 50529 (515) 332-3087
(Non-leather footwear, luggage, belts, baseball gloves)

Recommended Reading

Gentle World Publications (see page 2)

Animal Liberation by Peter Singer
At Sunrise Dies the Ogre by Knut Scharnhorst Hesstreadt Ph, D.
Beyond Beef by Jeremy Rifkin
Compassion: The Ultimate Ethic by Victoria Moran
The Compassionate Cook by People for the Ethical Treatment of Animals, Ingrid Newkirk
Diet for A New America by John Robbins
Eat Right, Live Longer by Neal Barnard, M.D.
The Extended Circle by Jon Wynne-Tyson
Food for Life by Neal Barnard, M.D.
Love Yourself Thin by Victoria Moran
Mad Cowboy by Howard Lyman
The Most Noble Diet by George Eisman
The Naked Empress by Hans Ruesch
Out of the Jungle by Jay Dinshah, American Vegan Society
The Peaceful Palate by Jennifer Raymond
The Power of Your Plate by Dr. Neal Barnard
Prisoned Chickens; Poisoned Eggs by Karen Davis
The Really Real Foods Cookbook by Brook Katz
Reclaiming Our Health by John Robbins, HJ Kramer Publisher.
You Can Save the Animals, 251 Simple Ways to Stop Thoughtless Cruelty by Ingrid Newkirk; National Director: P.E.T.A
The Sunfood Diet Success System by David Wolfe
Tofu Cookery by Louise Hagler
The Uncheese Cookbook by Joanne Stepaniak
The Vegan Kitchen by Freya Dinshah, The American Vegan Society
Vegan Nutrition; A Survey of Research by Gill Langley, Ph.D., Vegan Society of England
The Vegan Source Book by Joanne Stepaniak
Vegan: The New Ethics of Eating by Erik Marcus

Videos

A Diet for All Reasons - with Michael Klaper, M.D.
    (dist: Paulette Eisen Nutritional Services) (310) 289-4173.
Diet for A New America - hosted by John Robbins

Recommended Kitchen Appliances

Blenders
Hamilton Beach/Procter-Silex Blender - 16 speed, maximum power blender. Quick clean setting. Procter-Silex is based in Washington, NC., at (804) 273-9777.
Osterizer® Blender - 10 speed. 5 cup scratch-resistant, dishwasher safe, glass jar with plastic lid. Ice crushing power. Sunbeam-Oster Corporation - (800) 882-5842.

Food Processors
Cuisinart® Deluxe 11 - Introduced in 1973, this food processor is one of the most practical and well-designed kitchen appliances--the ideal culinary tool for the home chef. It has an 11 cup capacity bowl. Cuisinart®, based in Stamford, CT., can be reached at (800) 726-0190 or (203) 975-4600.
La Machine® by Regal - a professional quality processor. Sleek/compact style for less counter space. Regal Ware, Inc., based in Kewaskum, WI., can be reached at (414) 626-2121.
Krups Master Pro Deluxe® - Fine quality machine. Krups North America, Inc., based in Closter, N.J., can be reached at (201) 784-5109. Look for their products in finer stores nationwide.
Krups Speedy Pro® - Multi-purpose mini chopper for chopping, mincing and blending. Found in department stores nationwide or call Krups, based in Closter, N.J., at (201) 784-5109.
KitchenAid® - 11 cup Ultra Power and Professional Food Processor. KitchenAid®, based in Greenville, OH., can be reached at (800) 541-6390.
Power Pro® Food Processor - 400 watts of power. Large 6 cup bowl. Economical. To reach Black and Decker call (800) 231-9786 or look for their products nationwide.

Vita-Mix
A powerful total nutrition center that performs amazing food feats at the flip of a switch. Vita-Mix is a powerful blender and a versatile machine that enables you to make whole food juice, smoothies, soups or non-dairy ice cream in about a minute. It cooks sauces without lumping, curdling or scorching. It easily chops salad bar items. It will puree a half a cup of baby food as well as it will 2 quarts. It also makes nut butters. For more information call the Vita-Mix Corporation, based in Cleveland, OH., at (800) 848-2649 or (440 or 216) 235-4840.

Cookware
Cuisinart® Stainless Steel Cookware- 25 years of culinary excellence, markets 'Everyday Stainless Steel Cookware®'. It is 100% aluminum-free with wide hand-grips for easy lifting. It is hand-polished & mirror-finished in top quality 18/10 stainless steel, with copper bottoms for fast, even heating. The tight-fitting covers seal in flavor & nutrients. The cookware is dishwasher and oven safe and comes with a lifetime warranty. Cuisinart™, your kitchen resource, is based in Stamford, CT. and can be reached at (800) 726-0190 or (203) 975-4600.
Farberware® - Farberware® Classic Series Stainless Steel Cookware has been a standard in American kitchens for generations. The cookware has a "full-cap" stainless steel over aluminum base. Farberware Cookware Division is based in Vallejo, CA. For more information call (800) 809-7166.
All-Clad Stainless Steel Cookware - The stainless collection features a magnetic stainless exterior. The cooking surface is hand-polished 18/10 stainless steel that will not react with food. The inner core is pure aluminum, not just at the bottom, but all the way up the sides. All three layers are bonded together for optimum heat conductivity. All styles feature long, stay cool handles. They are dishwasher safe, easy to care for, and come with a lifetime guarantee. Based in New York, N.Y., Patrice Tanaka & Co. can be reached at (212) 229-0523.
LeCreuset® - makers of colorful enamel coated cast iron for use in oven/microwave to table, and freezer to oven. A product of France, this elegant designed stoneware resists chipping and staining. Call Le Creuset of America, based in Early Branch, S.C., at (803) 943-4308.

CorningWear™ - CorningWear products are ideal pieces for preparing, cooking and serving in one beautiful dish. They're also safe for repeated microwave and oven use, are non-staining, non-warping, odor resistant and dishwasher compatible. For more information, call CorningWear's consumer division at (800) 999-3436.

VapoSeal Cookware - 7-ply stainless steel cookware/bakeware designed for nutrient retention. Vapo-Seal Cookware is <u>not</u> found in retail stores. Based in Harrisonburg, VA., reach them at (800) 434-4628.

WearEver® - durable porcelain coated (non-stick) WearEver™. It is lightweight, easy to clean, great for low fat cooking (as less oil is needed), and economical. Based in Manitowoc, WI., The Mirro Company can be reached at (800) 518-6245.

Lodge Cast Iron - Lodge Manufacturing, based in South Pittsburgh, TN., carries a variety of cookware, skillets, and bakeware...great for corn breads. New cast iron cookware needs to be seasoned; an easy process. Call Lodge at (423) 837-7181.

Presto Pride® Pressure Cooker - heavy gauge stainless steel for quick pressure cooking that preserves flavors, colors and nutrients. For information on Presto small appliances call Customer Service at (715) 839-2209.

Bread-Making Machines

Kitchen Pro® - Automatic Breadmaker by Regal. Large capacity - up to a 2 lb. loaf. Great for making whole grain breads. Regal Ware, Inc., based in Kewaskum, WI., at (414) 626-2121.

Juicers

Krups Optifruit Juice Extractor - Easy to assemble, operate, and clean. Krups products are found in stores nationwide or call Krups North America, Inc., based in Closter, N.J. at (201) 784-5109.

Toaster Ovens

Toast-R-Oven - bakes/broils/toasts, browns, defrosts/re-heats. Economical. Black & Decker can be reached at (800) 231-9786.

Steamers

Krups Optisteam® - multi-purpose food steamer. To reach Krups North America, Inc., based in Closter, N.J. call (201) 784-5109.

Good Earth Steam Pot - a Joyce Chen product. Order from: Oriental Pantry at (800) 828-0368. E-Mail: oriental@orientalpantry.com

Equipment

"Saladacco" - handy for making spiral cuttings, fine strips, and thin slices of vegetables, as well as mincing onion. Great for salads and raw food preparation. Based in Camarillo, CA., SCI Cuisine International can be reached at (805) 482-0791.

Presto Professional Salad Shooter® - For information call Customer Service at (715) 839-2209.

Joyce Chen Oriental Cookware Products - "Eastern Cookware for the Western kitchen"...woks, peking pans, stove-top ceramic casseroles and tea kettles, Japanese stoneware mortar and pestle, cutting boards, chopsticks, Japanese cutlery, etc. Oriental Pantry is a retail mail order source for Joyce Chen Products. Based in Acton, MA., they can be reached at (800) 828-0368.

OXO - Good Grip Kitchen Tools - A variety of high quality, stainless steel, kitchen tools, serving utensils, gadgets, and cutlery. Based in New York, N.Y., OXO, a division of General Housewares, can be reached at (800) 545-4411 or (212) 242-3333. E-mail - oxo@ghc.com

Dinnerware

Noritake - Noritake is one of the world's largest manufacturers of quality china, fine china, stoneware and casual dinnerware. Noritake offers styles, patterns and colors to fit every taste and lifestyle, and every budget. You can find Noritake in department stores and specialty shops. Call (800) 562-1991 for more information. Noritake at www.noritake.com

Sango American Stoneware - for table, dishwasher, microwave. Many patterns of dinnerware. Found nationwide. Call Sango America Stoneware at (201) 330-8100.

Wheatgrass Juicers

<u>The Green Power</u> juice extractor, with its powerful Twin Gear Technology, easily makes chlorophyll-high juice from wheatgrass, barley grass, alfalfa and other grasses as well as juice from therapeutic herbs, fibrous plants, pulpy fruits and leafy vegetables. It also has practical accessories that allow you to make mochi, baby food, frozen fruit sorbet, etc. It is made for life with its precision 1/4 horsepower motor. Order from: Green Power International, 12020 Woodruff Ave., Suite C, Downey, CA. 90241 or call: (888) 254-7336 or (562) 940-4241. E-mail: service@greenpower.com

<u>Wheateena Wheatgrass Juicers</u> - Manufactured in the U.S.A., these juicers are sturdy, efficient, and reliable. They come in many models; commercial and compact electric, as well as manual. The machines are especially designed to juice wheat grass, sprouts, herbs and make nut butters. UL & NSF approved. Serving the health food market since 1966, the Sundance Industries, Inc., P.O. Box 1446, Newburgh, N.Y., can be reached at (914) 565-6065.

<u>Miracle Wheatgrass Juicers</u> - These machines are plastic and lightweight. Miracles Exclusives, Inc. market a commercial as well as a smaller electric model and a stainless steel hand juicer. The company has a catalog and a wide selection of juice extractors, stainless steel cookware, grain mills, grinders, pasta makers, dehydrators, sprouters and more. Based in Port Washington, New York, order by phone at (800) 645-6360.

A special thank-you to Casio, Inc.

for donating a digital camera to Gentle World, Inc.,
making it possible for us to have vegan photography.
Casio, Inc., P.O. Box 7000, Dover, N.J., 07801.
(201) 361-5400.

> *"....We treat them as sticks or stones, as trees and other non-sentient things that are not possessed of organs of sense and feeling. We are wrong in this; they are not things, but beings. We forget the wonderful likeness that exists between us and these 'lower' creatures. We neglect the fact that their brains are much like our brains, their muscles like our muscles, their bones like our bones, that they digest as we digest, that they have hearts that beat as ours beat, nerves that thrill as ours thrill, that they possess to a wonderful degree the same faculties, the same appetites and are subject to the same impulses as we. An ox, a sheep, can hear, see, feel, smell, taste and even think, if not as well as man, at least to some degree after the same fashion....A horse or a cow can learn, remember, love, hate, mourn, rejoice and suffer, as human beings do...."*

JOHN HARVEY KELLOGG, M.D., LLD, FACS (1852-1943)
American, Director of Battle Creek Sanitarium,
educator of the medical profession, author of 50 books,
held 30 patents for food products, processes and machines

About the Authors

Gentle World is a non-profit educational organization, incorporated in Florida in 1979, based in Hawaii since 1989. Its purpose is to prevent and alleviate human and animal suffering, by educating the public as to the health, environmental and spiritual benefits of a plant-based diet and lifestyle.

Toward that end, Gentle World has served as a source of vegan information since its inception. Member volunteers have offered free seminars, cooking classes, and meals to thousands of interested people. They have authored: "The Cookbook for People Who Love Animals" and published two books by Michael A. Klaper M.D.: "Vegan Nutrition, Pure and Simple" and "Pregnancy, Children and the Vegan Diet". They created and catered two Celebrity Vegetarian Banquets in Hollywood, California, inspiring those who are an inspiration to others. In Maui, they established "The Vegan Restaurant".

Presently, Gentle World is in the process of organizing two Vegan Paradigm centers: one on the Big Island of Hawaii, and another on the North Island of New Zealand.

For more information e-mail- gentle@aloha.net   or write: PO. Box 238
visit our website at www.veganbooks-gentle.com   Kapa'au HI, 96755

Recipe Index

A

B

❀ = RAWSOME RECIPES — Unfired foods

D

M

MILKS (NON DAIRY)

R

RAWSOME RECIPES — Unfired foods
(See recipes marked ✿ in Index) 179

S

SALADS

SOUPS

V

VEGAN ALTERNATIVES 279

Contents